Silver Coin Pricing Guide, 1800-2000: A Reference for Buying and Selling 19th and 20th Century World Coins on eBay, Websites and at Coin Shows

by

Donald O. Case

Cover Photo by Joseph Dietz

CreateSpace

2012

Foreword

This guide is dedicated to those who buy and sell silver coins—on eBay, on other Internet websites, at coin shows or coin stores, or elsewhere. It is a guide for people who buy coins for their investment value, not their design or their value to collectors. With this book you can easily see the bullion value of any silver coins you own or contemplate buying—no matter what the country or year of their origin. Using an alphabetical look-up of the country and denomination (and sometimes a simple addition), one can determine the base value of any common silver coin from 1800 through to 2000. *This is critical information, because most recent coin guides have not recalculated bullion values, and continue to estimate coin value based on what silver cost in 2009, or even 1999!*

Silver has been a wonderful investment over the last decade. Between 1985 and 2006, silver stayed mostly in the range of $4 to $10 per troy ounce. Then it started to move up. From 2006 to 2010, it bounced around between $10 and $20 per troy ounce. Beginning in 2011 it climbed to $48, a price not seen since the unusual two-year period from 1979 to 1981 when the Hunt brothers tried to corner the market on silver, briefly sending it up to $50/ounce. Thus far in 2012 it has increased from $30 to $35 per ounce. Given global financial difficulties, national debts, trade imbalances, and growing demand for precious metals, silver is unlikely to fall very much, but instead is very likely to continue to gain in value. Most experts agree that silver is undervalued compared to the price of gold.

But whether silver increases or declines, you still need this book! It covers two centuries of what we might call the "golden era" of silver coinage. At least half of the regular issue coins traded today were minted between 1845 and 1970. During that period, coins such as the American and Canadian Dime, British 6 Pence, German 1 Mark and French 5 Francs were each made in the millions in the 19th century, and tens of millions per year in the 20th. Here are a few examples of this impressive mintage history:

Canadian Dime (10 Cents):	1871, 2 million; 1965, 57 million
French 5 Francs:	1873, 27 million; 1934, 52 million
German 1 Mark:	1875, 30 million; 1924, 75 million
Great Britain 6 Pence:	1846, 4 million; 1943, 47 million
United States Dime (10 Cents):	1853, 12 million; 1964, 2.29 *billion*

That is a lot of sliver coins! And nearly all of them are still around.

In the 1960s most countries stopped making silver coins for regular circulation: The United States in 1965, Canada in 1968, and France in 1970, for example. After the 1960s silver coins were issued only as bullion or as "commemoratives"—and in most cases just a few thousand or tens of thousands were made of each type. Most of these commemorative coins were made in a particular design for only a year or two; they are still traded, typically one at a time. In contrast, regular issue, "legal tender" coins minted before 1965 are often sold in large quantities (e.g., "$100 Face Value of U.S. Silver Coins").

How to Use this Guide

First, consult the Internet (www.kitco.com is one useful site) or daily newspaper to learn the current "spot" price for silver; this will be listed in U.S. Dollars and changes daily, although usually not by much. Round that figure, up or down, to the nearest Dollar.

Next, consult the tables in this book to find the coin you have or are interested in. Coins are listed alphabetically, by issuing nation. Within nation coins are listed by denomination (e.g. 10 Cents), starting with the smallest and oldest. If a single denomination changes content over time, the years of production are listed separately, starting with the oldest. Because some nations have often changed the names of their coins, the lists do not always proceed from smallest to largest silver value uniformly.

Once you have located the coin of interest, scan across the table to find the "$ Value" column that best approximates the current value of silver. The columns on the right list silver values from $10/ounce to $50/ounce, by $5 increments. These may be close enough to obtain a fair estimate, especially for the smaller coins (see examples, below). If you want a more accurate price, the middle columns of the table (in italics) list the value of the coin as if silver were priced at $1/ounce, $2, $3 or $4/ounce. Add the appropriate amount to one of the $5-increment columns.

Here are two examples. Let's say that the current value of silver is $31.00 per troy ounce. I want to know the value of a 1964 United States 10 Cent coin. Under the $30/ounce column it says Dimes of that year are worth $2.16 at that value of silver—about $2.20, I might guess. But if I wish to be more accurate, I can add the $0.07 from the $1 value column to arrive at a total value of $2.23. (As you work with these tables you will become adept at estimating the values of small coins without having to add single dollar amounts.)

Now let's say I have a 1964 Canadian silver Dollar. Again, I look across the table to find that is worth $18.00 at $30 per ounce. With such a large coin, though, it is wise to be more precise. Adding $0.60 from the $1/ounce column yields a final value of $18.60.

Don't become too obsessed with precise values unless you are buying multiple coins at once. Keep in mind that tomorrow's spot price for silver might be 2% lower than today's, or 4% higher.

To keep this guide to a reasonable page length the highest price listed in the tables is $50/ounce—about 50% higher than it has been in 2012, and close to its historic high. What if silver goes to $60 or $100? You can always add or multiply the figures in the columns. That is, one can find the $60 value by adding the $10 column to the $50 column, and get to $100 by doubling the $50 value. These tables make it possible to calculate any value of silver from $51 to $1,000 per ounce with no more than one to three arithmetic operations (e.g., multiplying one number, or adding three together).

About Weights of Coins (Grams and Troy Ounces)

When someone says something weighs an ounce, the chances are that they are referring to an *avoirdupois ounce*, which is the seldom-used "official" name for the old English system ounce still used in the United States. Bathroom scales, kitchen scales, produce scales and other "ordinary" scales calibrated in ounces, use these ordinary avoirdupois ounces.

However gold, silver, platinum and gunpowder are measured in troy ounces. The prices of gold, silver and platinum we hear quoted in the commodities markets, e.g., the "spot price," are listed in troy ounces. Not everyone knows the difference; if you are buying precious metals on eBay, you really need to be sure which type of ounce you are getting - because a troy ounce is over 9.7% heavier than an avoirdupois ounce:

An *avoirdupois* ounce is 28.3495 grams - or 437.5 grains

A *troy* ounce is 31.1035 grams - or 480 grains

For troy ounces, 31.1 grams is a close enough approximation.

How to Avoid Being Cheated Buying Coins Online

• First of all, check this book, other coin guides, and the Internet. There are many websites that offer pictures of coins, although few of them provide complete information about the weight and fineness (purity) of coins.

• Second, ask questions! Ask for photos or scans of the coins. If it is a commemorative coin, ask if they have a "certificate of authenticity" that should have come with the coin; the certificate lists the composition. Many commemorative coins were made in brilliant nickel versions as well as silver, and sometimes the buyer honestly cannot tell the difference.

• Finally, make certain that the buyer is referring to troy ounces, and not the ordinary kind, when they list the weight. Check the description for the designation ASW (Actual Silver Weight), which factors in both the weight of the coin and the fineness of the silver it is composed of. If the seller provides the weight in grams, and the purity, you can calculate the ASW with this formula:

(grams divided by 31.1) X fineness = ASW

e.g.,

28.28 grams divided by 31.1 = .9093   AND   .9093 X .925 = .8411 ASW

Cautions and Limitations

Three cautions are in order regarding the coins listed in this book. First is that the values herein do not reflect the numismatic, or "collector's" value of the coins. Most coins, especially from the 20th century, are worth only their bullion value; even if they are worth more to a collector, their valuation starts with the silver content and goes up from that point—and usually by just a modest amount. The most common, modern silver coins, such as American and Canadian Dimes and Quarters from the 1950s and 1960s—are rarely worth more than their bullion value in silver.

Second, this guide does not attempt to describe variants in the *design* of coins—for that you will need to consult another guide or website that has illustrations of the coin's obverse and reverse. Likewise, the tables do not indicate condition or mint marks (for the city in which the coin was struck) because design, condition and mint and mint marks matter only when you are collecting coins for their appearance, subject matter or rarity. When design *might* matter is when you are considering buying or selling some of the low-mintage commemorative coins. The People's Republic of China, for example, minted at least a dozen different versions of silver 10 Yuan coin between 1984 and 2000. In order to determine the value of those coins (all of which are listed in this guide), you simply need to know the weight of the coin in grams, along with its year. If you do not know that, you will need to consult pictures of the coin, which are almost always available on the Internet.

Third, while the weights, purities and values in the guide are deemed to be reliable, some are estimates and there will always be the occasional error. When purchasing silver coins—whether as bullion or collectibles—it is always advisable to check multiple sources. To that end the values listed in this book are *advisory only*, and we take no responsibility for trades or purchases that rely solely on the estimates in this guide. They have been compiled from many sources, not all of which agree.

Please note that some year ranges (e.g., 1939-1955) may contain one or more years in which no such denomination was minted. Ranges across which the entire run of one coin type was minted are listed for the sake of simplicity. Ordinarily this has no implication for purchases of investment coins, but may puzzle some collectors. These will be marked by the letter "S" in the Notes column, for "Skips years."

Counter-marked coins—typically coins from other countries that have been stamped with a mark indicating a second nation—are not normally included in the listings for the appropriating country. Some European countries and many Latin American nations used each others' coins in this way on a temporary basis, especially in the 17th and 18th centuries. For one example, El Salvador used standard coins from Guatemala during a period of shortage in the 1860s.

Key to the Codes Column

A: <u>A</u>nno Hegirae (AH) are Muslim (Islamic) lunar calendar dates. These may be calculated by subtracting three percent of the AH date and adding 622, however this is not always reliable. A translation of AH century dates into Christian Era dates looks like this:

1100 = 1688,   1200 = 1785,   1300 = 1882,   1400 = 1979,   1430=2008

C: <u>C</u>ountermarked. As a general rule, countermarked coins are not included here, except for El Salvador, which used them later in the 19th century than was usual.

E: <u>E</u>thiopian Era dates, appearing mainly between 1893 and 1974 in the Christian Era (CE) calendar. These indicate a date 7 years and 8 months behind that of our own, e.g., EE 1885 is approximately 1893 in the CE calendar, while EE 1974 is 1982.

H: Solar <u>H</u>ejri (SH) are Muslim (Islamic) solar calendar dates. Such dates are found mainly in Afghanistan (from 1929 to 1981), and in Iran (from 1920 through 1976, and 1979 to the present). These may be approximated by subtracting 621 from the Christian Era (CE) date. Examples of SH equivalents:

1309 = 1930, 1329 = 1950, 1349 = 1970, 1359 = 1980, 1369 = 1990, 1389 = 2000

N: <u>N</u>on-silver (usually <u>N</u>ickel but sometimes gold or platinum) varieties exist for this denomination and/or design; sizes may vary. Be particularly cautious about buying coins of years and dominations marked with an "N," even if claimed to be silver, unless you can inspect and weigh them. *Never assume that all coins of a certain nation, year and denomination are silver if they are marked with an "N" in this guide.*

R: <u>R</u>estrike. Some nations repeatedly reminted the same design coin for many years, yet listing the original date. Two examples are Eritrea's 1918 Tallero, and the 1780 Maria Theresa Thaler of Austria, both of which were produced for decades past their nominal date.

S: <u>S</u>kips years. No coins were minted in one or more years in the indicated range. E.g., silver-clad versions of the US Eisenhower Dollar were minted 1971-1974 and again in 1976; this is recorded as "1971-1976" in the tables, but with an "S" in the code column.

V: <u>V</u>aries as to weight, or sometimes fineness. Within the same denomination and year range, other silver varieties exist with slightly differing weights (e.g., 21.16 grams versus 22.23 grams), purities (.9 versus .925); the design often varies as well, but "V" is not used solely to indicate this. In all cases the resulting ASW varies by less than 5%, and usually by less than 2%. In cases of varying weight a value near the mid-point is typically shown in the grams column. Early 20th century Chinese coins are a common example, due to differing practices among the provinces. For example, in one province the 20 Cent coin was 5.2 grams of 0.89 silver (ASW=.1388), while in another province the same denomination was 5.3 grams of 0.82 silver (ASW=.1397)—a difference of less than 1%.

Abbreviations and Notes

Abbreviations Used in the Country & Denomination column:

Am. = American

ASW = Actual Silver Weight

Bav = Bavaria

Brit. = British

Can. = Canada

Cent. = Centimes

Dem. = Democratic

E. = East

Karab. = Karabakh (i.e., Nagorno-Karabakh)

Isl. = Island or Islands

Neth. = Netherlands

N. = North

Port. = Portuguese

Pru = Prussia

Rep. = Republic

S. = South

sa = see also

Sar = Sardinia

Sax = Saxony

Soc. = Socialist

South. = Southern

Tus = Tuscany

U. = United

W. = West

Individual Country Notes

Notes specific to one nation are indicated with an asterisk (*) by the first coin in the series. These abbreviations and notes not only provide additional detail about the listings for each country, they also make it possible to shorten the entries through abbreviations and the use of codes, thus making the individual coin prices easier to scan and read.

Afghanistan: All AH dates have been converted. Previous to 1890 (AH 1308), Rupee and Half Rupee coins were minted of uncertain silver composition. Rupees 1808-1842 are assumed to be 0.500 silver (as were later coins of those denominations), although weights also vary widely. Like many early 19th century coins, their value to collectors is higher than that of their silver content.

Ajman: One of the United Arab Emirates (UAE). All AH dates have been converted. The 7-1/2 Riyals of 1970 has two versions; only the 0.835 version shows the likeness of Nassar.

Alderney: One of the Channel Islands which lie between England and France.

Algeria: Previous to 1837 a number of Budju coins were minted, of uncertain composition; some of them are merely silver coated. These coins were minted in denominations of 1/6, ¼, 1/3, ½, 1 and 2 Budjus.

Austria: The one Thaler Maria Theresa coin has been restruck many times since the (nominal) date of 1780. All such modern "Restrikes" have the date 1780.

Belize: For earlier years, see British Honduras.

British Honduras: for later years, see Belize.

Cape Verde (or Cabo Verde): A collection of a dozen islands off the west coast of Africa, and once a colony of Portugal.

China, People's Republic of: Many coins of varying design and weight were minted in the provinces. Many counterfeits have been documented, especially of late 19th and early 20th century silver dollar-sized coins.

Danish West Indies: The Danish West Indies are now the United States Virgin Islands. St. Croix was purchased by the Danes from the French West Indies Company, which is why two of the silver coins are denominated in Francs: 1 Franc (alternate value 20 Cents) and 2 Francs (value 40 Cents).

Ecuador: Silver Real coins were minted prior to 1841, but their fineness is uncertain.

Egypt: Other Para and Girsh coins were minted prior to 1839, but contained a high percentage of copper and an unknown proportion of silver. They are not listed here.

El Salvador: Coins marked with a "C" are Countermarked Guatemala coins of the same denomination.

Equatorial Guinea: Earlier known as Spanish Guinea, their coins are marked "Rep. de Guinea Equatorial."

Essequibo: Originally the Dutch colony of Demerara-Esequibo, or Essequibo and Demerary (as the coins are marked). In 1831 it united with the colony of British Guiana, now Guyana.

Ethiopia: All years are listed using the Ethiopian calendar, which indicates a date 7 years and 8 months behind that of our own, e.g., the 1982-dated 20 Birr also carries the Ethiopian date 1974. Most of their coins show *only* Ethiopian dates in their symbols.

France: Note that during the period of 1794-1806 some French coins bear Napoleonic dates, e.g., "L'AN 4" for the fourth year of the new republic.

Germany: Prior to 1871, Germany was made up of hundreds of autonomous states. As examples, all of the coins for three of the major pre-1871 German states – Bavaria (Bav), Prussia (Pru) and Saxony (Sax) – are listed here, as many other states shared similar denominations and silver content. Note the overlap: for example, all 3 states issued identical sizes of 1 Thaler and 2 Thaler (aka 3-1/2 Gulden) coins during the same years. After 1873, all of the states used the same silver coinage (Marks). Other states and cities minting several varieties of silver coins (but not included in the table) include Anhalt-Bernburg, Baden, Berg, Bremen, Brunswick, Frankfurt, Hamburg, Hannover, Hesse, Hohenzollern, Mecklenburg, Nassau, Oldenburg, Reuss-Schleiz, Saxe, Saxony, Schaumburg, Schwarzburg, Waldeck, Westphalia and Wurttemberg. Most of the others issued few silver coins, or none at all (e.g., minting only copper coins).

Goa: See Portuguese India.

Haiti: 1827-1880 silver coins exist but composition varies and counterfeits are common.

Honduras: Pre-1871 silver coins (1/2 Real to 8 Reales) were minted of silver composition ranging from 0.1 to 0.33, but actual silver weight varies widely, so they are not listed here.

Hungary: Before 1837 other 20 Krajczar silver coins were also minted, but the composition is unknown so they are not listed here.

India: Pre-1841 silver coins were minted by princely states and independent kingdoms in India, but their composition is uncertain. Coins listed begin with British colony, while the Portuguese colony of Goa is listed separately.

Iran: All AH and SH dates have been converted. Pre-AH1297 (1879) coins are not listed due to uncertainty about their silver composition. Iran switched from the AH (lunar) calendar to the SH (solar) calendar in 1925, and briefly used a third (monarchial) calendar type during 1976-1978, before restoring the SH system.
Iran has multiple names for many of its denominations; here are a few:
2 Shahi =100 Dinars, 4 Kran = 5 Shahis = 1 Robi,
½ Kran = 10 Shahis = 500 Dinars, 1 Kran = 1000 Dinars, 2 Kran = 2000 Dinars

Iraq: 19th century silver Paras and Piastres also exist, of uncertain composition. The Iraq system of currency is: 1 Dinar = 5 Riyal = 20 Dirham = 1000 Fils

Italy: 19th century coins include those of pre-national (before 1861) Italian states.; only unusual weights, purities, denominations or dates of issue are indicated with the name of the province. Two abbreviations are used: Sar=Sardinia, Tus=Tuscany. Other states minting silver coins (but not noted in the table) include Emilia, Genoa, the Kingdom of Napoleon, Lombardy-Venetia, Naples, Parma and Venice, among others more short-lived.

Japan: Prior to 1873 a number of rectangular and oblong hammered silver pieces of uncertain composition or weight were made, some of them blends of silver and gold.

Keeling Cocos: Islands northwest of Australia.

Libya: 19th century silver Paras exist but are of unknown size and purity.

Myanmar (Burma): 19th century dates are converted from the Burmese Era calendar.

Nagorno-Karabakh: Part of Azerbaijan and a former part of the Soviet Union.

Nepal: All Bikram Samvat Era (1888 and after) dates have been converted to the corresponding Christian Era year. Mohar coins minted before 1914 are of uncertain fineness, and so are not listed.

Philippines: Many countermarked Real coins were used prior to 1838.

Portugal: Prior to 1836, large countermarked Latin American silver Reales were used, along with some smaller, locally-produced coins of uncertain composition.

Quaiti Hadhramaut: All AH dates have been converted.

Saint Helena: includes the islands of Ascension and Tristan da Cunha, but Saint Helena is the only island with a bank and authority to issue coins, which are based on the British system of Pound and Pence. After 1984, the coins also include the name of Ascension.

Saint Kitts: Includes the islands of Saint Kitts and Nevis.

São Tomé and **Principe**: Former Portuguese colonies off the coast of West Africa, also known as Saint Thomas and Prince.

Switzerland: The 23 Swiss cantons minted or countermarked very small numbers of silver coins before 1842. Many of these are of low-grade silver, or even silver-coated.

Thailand: Dates have been converted from the BE, CS and RS dating systems. Fuang (1/8 Baht) and Salung (1/4 Baht) silver coins were made 1856-1908, but are not listed as their weight and purity vary widely.

Tibet: The few Tibet coins made of silver are not listed, due to uncertainty about their silver content and wide variation in weight.

Turkey: All AH dates have been converted. Previous to 1839 a variety of 1, 5 and 10 Para coins, and 1, 2 and 5 Kurush coins were minted that are not listed here. These varied widely in weight within each denomination, while fineness ranged between 0.22 and 0.73 silver.

United States: Prior to 1916 50 Cent coins were usually labeled "Half Dollar".

USSR: See new country names, e.g., Russia, Ukraine, Georgia, Azerbaijan, Tajikistan.

Venezuela: The 25 Centimos was also known as the Quarter Bolivar, while the 50 Centimos was the Half Bolivar.

Vietnam: In the last half of the 19th century, Vietnam issued many silver Tien coins of various denominations, however their silver content is uncertain.

Zambia: The 2000 Kwacha coin of 1994 is also marked 100 Guilders.

Country & Denomination	Years Minted	Grams Weight	Fine-ness	Troy (ASW)	Code	$ Value 1	$ Value 2	$ Value 3	$ Value 4	$ Value 10	$ Value 15	$ Value 20	$ Value 25	$ Value 30	$ Value 35	$ Value 40	$ Value 45	$ Value 50
Afghanistan 1 Abbasi*	1895-1918	3.11	0.500	0.050	A, s	0.05	0.10	0.15	0.20	0.50	0.75	1.00	1.25	1.50	1.75	2.00	2.25	2.50
Afghanistan 1 Sanar	1897	1.55	0.500	0.025	A	0.03	0.05	0.08	0.10	0.25	0.38	0.50	0.63	0.75	0.88	1.00	1.13	1.25
Afghanistan 1/6 Rupee	1841	1.80	0.500	0.029	A, v	0.03	0.06	0.09	0.12	0.29	0.44	0.58	0.73	0.87	1.02	1.16	1.31	1.45
Afghanistan 1/6 Rupee	1868	1.50	0.500	0.024	A, v	0.02	0.05	0.07	0.10	0.24	0.36	0.48	0.60	0.72	0.84	0.96	1.08	1.20
Afghanistan 1/4 Rupee	1839	2.30	0.500	0.037	A, v	0.04	0.07	0.11	0.15	0.37	0.56	0.74	0.93	1.11	1.30	1.48	1.67	1.85
Afghanistan 1/2 Rupee	1808-1842	5.40	0.500	0.087	A, v	0.09	0.17	0.26	0.35	0.87	1.31	1.74	2.18	2.61	3.05	3.48	3.92	4.35
Afghanistan 1/2 Rupee	1890-1896	4.65	0.500	0.075	A, s	0.08	0.15	0.23	0.30	0.75	1.13	1.50	1.88	2.25	2.63	3.00	3.38	3.75
Afghanistan 1/2 Rupee	1901-1918	4.75	0.500	0.076	A, v	0.08	0.15	0.23	0.30	0.76	1.14	1.52	1.90	2.28	2.66	3.04	3.42	3.80
Afghanistan 1/2 Rupee	1928, 1929	4.70	0.500	0.076	A, v	0.08	0.15	0.23	0.30	0.76	1.14	1.52	1.90	2.28	2.66	3.04	3.42	3.80
Afghanistan 1 Rupee	1808-1829	10.60	0.500	0.170	A, v	0.17	0.34	0.51	0.68	1.70	2.55	3.40	4.25	5.10	5.95	6.80	7.65	8.50
Afghanistan 1 Rupee	1831-1868	9.10	0.925	0.270	A, v	0.27	0.54	0.81	1.08	2.70	4.05	5.40	6.75	8.10	9.45	10.80	12.15	13.50
Afghanistan 1 Rupee	1879	9.00	0.800	0.232		0.23	0.46	0.70	0.93	2.32	3.48	4.64	5.80	6.96	8.12	9.28	10.44	11.60
Afghanistan 1 Rupee	1890-1897	9.20	0.900	0.266	A	0.27	0.53	0.80	1.06	2.66	3.99	5.32	6.65	7.98	9.31	10.64	11.97	13.30
Afghanistan 1 Rupee	1902-1919	9.20	0.500	0.148	A, v	0.15	0.30	0.44	0.59	1.48	2.22	2.96	3.70	4.44	5.18	5.92	6.66	7.40
Afghanistan 1 Rupee	1920-1924	9.25	0.900	0.267	A	0.27	0.53	0.80	1.07	2.67	4.01	5.34	6.68	8.01	9.35	10.68	12.02	13.35
Afghanistan 1 Rupee	1928	9.10	0.900	0.263	A	0.26	0.53	0.79	1.05	2.63	3.95	5.26	6.58	7.89	9.21	10.52	11.84	13.15
Afghanistan 2-1/2 Rupee	1919-1924	22.92	0.900	0.663	H	0.66	1.33	1.99	2.65	6.63	9.95	13.26	16.58	19.89	23.21	26.52	29.84	33.15
Afghanistan 5 Rupee	1896	45.40	0.900	1.333	A	1.33	2.67	4.00	5.33	13.33	20.00	26.66	33.33	39.99	46.66	53.32	59.99	66.65
Afghanistan 5 Rupee	1898-1919	45.60	0.900	1.319	A	1.32	2.64	3.96	5.28	13.19	19.79	26.38	32.98	39.57	46.17	52.76	59.36	65.95
Afghanistan 1/2 Afghani	1926-1937	5.00	0.500	0.080	H	0.08	0.16	0.24	0.32	0.80	1.20	1.60	2.00	2.40	2.80	3.20	3.60	4.00
Afghanistan 1/2 Afghani	1931-1932	4.75	0.500	0.076	H	0.08	0.15	0.23	0.30	0.76	1.14	1.52	1.90	2.28	2.66	3.04	3.42	3.80
Afghanistan 1 Afghani	1925-1932	10.00	0.900	0.289	A	0.29	0.58	0.87	1.16	2.89	4.34	5.78	7.23	8.67	10.12	11.56	13.01	14.45
Afghanistan 2-1/2 Afghani	1926-1927	25.00	0.900	0.723	H	0.72	1.45	2.17	2.89	7.23	10.85	14.46	18.08	21.69	25.31	28.92	32.54	36.15
Afghanistan 250 Afghani	1978	28.28	0.925	0.841	H	0.84	1.68	2.52	3.36	8.41	12.62	16.82	21.03	25.23	29.44	33.64	37.85	42.05
Afghanistan 250 Afghani	1978	28.57	0.925	0.850	H	0.85	1.70	2.55	3.40	8.50	12.74	16.99	21.24	25.49	29.74	33.98	38.23	42.48
Afghanistan 250 Afghani	1978	28.57	0.925	0.850	H	0.85	1.70	2.55	3.40	8.50	12.74	16.99	21.24	25.49	29.74	33.98	38.23	42.48
Afghanistan 500 Afghani	1978	35.00	0.925	1.041	H	1.04	2.08	3.12	4.16	10.41	15.61	20.82	26.02	31.22	36.43	41.63	46.84	52.04
Afghanistan 500 Afghani	1978	35.30	0.925	1.050	H	1.05	2.10	3.15	4.20	10.50	15.75	21.00	26.25	31.49	36.74	41.99	47.24	52.49
Afghanistan 500 Afghani	1981	9.06	0.900	0.262	H	0.26	0.52	0.79	1.05	2.62	3.93	5.24	6.56	7.87	9.18	10.49	11.80	13.11
Afghanistan 500 Afghani	1986-1991	12.00	0.999	0.386		0.39	0.77	1.16	1.54	3.86	5.78	7.71	9.64	11.57	13.49	15.42	17.35	19.28
Afghanistan 500 Afghani	1989-1995	16.00	0.999	0.515		0.51	1.03	1.54	2.06	5.15	7.72	10.29	12.86	15.44	18.01	20.58	23.15	25.73
Afghanistan 500 Afghani	1992-1999	20.00	0.999	0.643		0.64	1.29	1.93	2.57	6.43	9.65	12.86	16.08	19.29	22.51	25.72	28.94	32.15
Afghanistan 500 Afghani	1996-1997	15.00	0.999	0.482		0.48	0.96	1.45	1.93	4.82	7.23	9.64	12.05	14.46	16.87	19.28	21.69	24.10
Ajman (UAE) 1 Riyal*	1969-1970	3.90	0.640	0.081	A	0.08	0.16	0.24	0.32	0.81	1.22	1.62	2.03	2.43	2.84	3.24	3.65	4.05
Ajman (UAE) 2 Riyals	1969-1970	6.50	0.835	0.173	A	0.17	0.35	0.52	0.69	1.73	2.60	3.46	4.33	5.19	6.06	6.92	7.79	8.65
Ajman (UAE) 5 Riyals	1969-1970	15.00	0.835	0.403	A	0.40	0.81	1.21	1.61	4.03	6.05	8.06	10.08	12.09	14.11	16.12	18.14	20.15
Ajman (UAE) 5 Riyals	1970-1971	15.00	0.925	0.446	A	0.45	0.89	1.34	1.78	4.46	6.69	8.92	11.15	13.38	15.61	17.84	20.07	22.30
Ajman (UAE) 7-1/2 Riyals	1970	23.00	0.925	0.684	A	0.68	1.37	2.05	2.74	6.84	10.26	13.68	17.10	20.52	23.94	27.36	30.78	34.20
Ajman (UAE) 7-1/2 Riyals	1970	23.00	0.835	0.618	A	0.62	1.24	1.85	2.47	6.18	9.27	12.36	15.45	18.54	21.63	24.72	27.81	30.90
Ajman (UAE) 10 Riyals	1970	29.90	0.925	0.892	A	0.89	1.78	2.68	3.57	8.92	13.38	17.84	22.30	26.76	31.22	35.68	40.14	44.60
Albania Franga Ar	1927-1937	5.00	0.835	0.134	s	0.13	0.27	0.40	0.54	1.34	2.01	2.68	3.35	4.02	4.69	5.36	6.03	6.70
Albania 2 Franga Ari	1926-1937	10.00	0.835	0.268	s	0.27	0.54	0.81	1.07	2.68	4.03	5.37	6.71	8.05	9.39	10.74	12.08	13.42
Albania 5 Franga Ari	1926-1927	25.00	0.900	0.723		0.72	1.45	2.17	2.89	7.23	10.85	14.47	18.09	21.70	25.32	28.94	32.55	36.17

Country & Denomination	Years Minted	Grams Weight	Fine-ness	Troy (ASW)	Code	$ Value 1	$ Value 2	$ Value 3	$ Value 4	$ Value 10	$ Value 15	$ Value 20	$ Value 25	$ Value 30	$ Value 35	$ Value 40	$ Value 45	$ Value 50
Albania 5 Leke	1939	5.00	0.835	0.134		0.13	0.27	0.40	0.54	1.34	2.01	2.68	3.36	4.03	4.70	5.37	6.04	6.71
Albania 5 Leke	1968-1970	16.66	0.999	0.517		0.52	1.03	1.55	2.07	5.17	7.76	10.34	12.93	15.51	18.10	20.68	23.27	25.85
Albania 10 Leke	1939	10.00	0.835	0.268		0.27	0.54	0.80	1.07	2.68	4.02	5.36	6.70	8.04	9.38	10.72	12.06	13.40
Albania 10 Leke	1968-1970	33.33	0.999	1.035		1.04	2.07	3.11	4.14	10.35	15.53	20.71	25.89	31.06	36.24	41.42	46.59	51.77
Albania 10 Leke	1991	52.50	0.925	1.560		1.56	3.12	4.68	6.24	15.60	23.40	31.20	39.00	46.80	54.60	62.40	70.20	78.00
Albania 10 Leke	1992	28.46	0.925	0.846		0.85	1.69	2.54	3.38	8.46	12.69	16.92	21.15	25.38	29.61	33.84	38.07	42.30
Albania 25 Leke	1968-1970	83.33	0.999	2.588		2.59	5.18	7.76	10.35	25.88	38.82	51.76	64.70	77.64	90.58	103.52	116.46	129.40
Albania 50 Leke	1987-1988	168.15	0.925	5.001		5.00	10.00	15.00	20.00	50.01	75.02	100.02	125.03	150.04	175.04	200.05	225.05	250.06
Alderney 1 Pound*	1993, 1995	9.50	0.925	0.283	N	0.28	0.57	0.85	1.13	2.83	4.25	5.66	7.08	8.49	9.91	11.32	12.74	14.15
Alderney 2 Pounds	1989-1999	28.28	0.925	0.841	N	0.84	1.68	2.52	3.36	8.41	12.62	16.82	21.03	25.23	29.44	33.64	37.85	42.06
Alderney 5 Pounds	1995-2000	28.28	0.925	0.841	N	0.84	1.68	2.52	3.36	8.41	12.62	16.82	21.03	25.23	29.44	33.64	37.85	42.06
Alderney 5 Pounds	2000	28.03	0.925	0.834	N	0.83	1.67	2.50	3.34	8.34	12.51	16.68	20.85	25.02	29.19	33.36	37.53	41.70
Alderney 25 Pounds	1997	28.28	0.925	0.841	N	0.84	1.68	2.52	3.36	8.41	12.62	16.82	21.03	25.23	29.44	33.64	37.85	42.06
Algeria 5 Dinars*	1972	12.00	0.750	0.290	A	0.29	0.58	0.87	1.16	2.90	4.35	5.80	7.25	8.70	10.15	11.60	13.05	14.50
Algeria 10 Dinars	1979, 1994	14.60	0.835	0.392	A	0.39	0.78	1.18	1.57	3.92	5.88	7.84	9.80	11.76	13.72	15.68	17.64	19.60
American Somoa 5 Dollars	1988	31.10	0.999	1.000		1.00	2.00	3.00	4.00	10.00	15.00	20.00	25.00	30.00	35.00	40.00	45.00	50.00
American Somoa 25 Dollars	1988	155.52	0.999	5.000		5.00	10.00	15.00	20.00	50.00	75.00	100.00	125.00	150.00	175.00	200.00	225.00	250.00
Andorra 1 Diner	1990	10.30	0.999	0.331		0.33	0.66	0.99	1.32	3.31	4.97	6.62	8.28	9.93	11.59	13.24	14.90	16.55
Andorra 5 Diners	1993	15.00	0.925	0.446		0.45	0.89	1.34	1.78	4.46	6.69	8.92	11.15	13.38	15.61	17.84	20.07	22.30
Andorra 5 Diners	1993	10.00	0.500	0.161		0.16	0.32	0.48	0.64	1.61	2.42	3.22	4.03	4.83	5.64	6.44	7.25	8.05
Andorra 10 Diners	1984-1988	8.00	0.925	0.238		0.24	0.48	0.71	0.95	2.38	3.57	4.76	5.95	7.14	8.33	9.52	10.71	11.90
Andorra 10 Diners	1989-1992	12.00	0.925	0.357		0.36	0.71	1.07	1.43	3.57	5.35	7.14	8.92	10.71	12.49	14.28	16.06	17.85
Andorra 10 Diners	1993-1999	31.47	0.925	0.936		0.94	1.87	2.81	3.74	9.36	14.04	18.72	23.40	28.08	32.76	37.44	42.12	46.80
Andorra 20 Diners	1984-1987	16.00	0.900	0.463		0.46	0.93	1.39	1.85	4.63	6.95	9.26	11.58	13.89	16.21	18.52	20.84	23.15
Andorra 20 Diners	1988-1990	16.00	0.925	0.476		0.48	0.95	1.43	1.90	4.76	7.14	9.52	11.90	14.28	16.66	19.04	21.42	23.80
Andorra 20 Diners	1991	21.00	0.925	0.625		0.63	1.25	1.88	2.50	6.25	9.38	12.50	15.63	18.75	21.88	25.00	28.13	31.25
Andorra 20 Diners	1992-1994	26.50	0.925	0.788		0.79	1.58	2.36	3.15	7.88	11.82	15.76	19.70	23.64	27.58	31.52	35.46	39.40
Andorra 20 Diners	1995-2000	25.00	0.925	0.744		0.74	1.49	2.23	2.98	7.44	11.16	14.88	18.60	22.32	26.04	29.76	33.48	37.20
Andorra 25 Diners	1963-1965	14.00	0.900	0.440		0.44	0.88	1.32	1.76	4.40	6.60	8.80	11.00	13.20	15.40	17.60	19.80	22.00
Andorra 25 Diners	1984-1989	20.00	0.900	0.579		0.58	1.16	1.74	2.31	5.79	8.68	11.57	14.47	17.36	20.25	23.15	26.04	28.94
Andorra 25 Diners	1991	28.28	0.925	0.841		0.84	1.68	2.52	3.36	8.41	12.62	16.82	21.03	25.23	29.44	33.64	37.85	42.05
Andorra 25 Diners	1991	25.00	0.925	0.744		0.74	1.49	2.23	2.98	7.44	11.16	14.88	18.60	22.32	26.04	29.76	33.48	37.20
Andorra 50 Diners	1960-1965	28.00	0.900	0.890		0.89	1.78	2.67	3.56	8.90	13.35	17.80	22.25	26.70	31.15	35.60	40.05	44.50
Andorra 50 Diners	1994-1996	155.51	0.925	4.630		4.63	9.26	13.89	18.52	46.30	69.45	92.60	115.75	138.90	162.05	185.20	208.35	231.50
Angola 10 Escudos	1952, 1955	5.00	0.720	0.116		0.12	0.23	0.35	0.46	1.16	1.74	2.31	2.89	3.47	4.05	4.63	5.21	5.79
Angola 20 Escudos	1952, 1955	10.00	0.720	0.232		0.23	0.46	0.69	0.93	2.32	3.47	4.63	5.79	6.95	8.10	9.26	10.42	11.58
Anguilla 1/2 Dollar	1967-1970	3.61	0.999	0.116		0.12	0.23	0.35	0.46	1.16	1.74	2.32	2.90	3.48	4.06	4.64	5.22	5.80
Anguilla 1 Dollars	1967-1970	7.18	0.999	0.231		0.23	0.46	0.69	0.92	2.31	3.46	4.62	5.77	6.92	8.08	9.23	10.39	11.54
Anguilla 2 Dollars	1967-1970	14.14	0.999	0.459		0.46	0.92	1.38	1.84	4.59	6.89	9.18	11.48	13.77	16.07	18.36	20.66	22.95

Country & Denomination	Years Minted	Grams Weight	Fineness	Troy (ASW)	Code	$ Value 1	$ Value 2	$ Value 3	$ Value 4	$ Value 10	$ Value 15	$ Value 20	$ Value 25	$ Value 30	$ Value 35	$ Value 40	$ Value 45	$ Value 50
Anguilla 4 Dollars	1967-1970	28.48	0.999	0.916		0.92	1.83	2.75	3.66	9.16	13.73	18.31	22.89	27.47	32.05	36.62	41.20	45.78
Anguilla 25 Dollars	1968	31.00	0.999	0.996		1.00	1.99	2.99	3.98	9.96	14.94	19.91	24.89	29.87	34.85	39.83	44.81	49.79
Antigua & Barbuda 10 Dollars	1985	28.28	0.925	0.841		0.84	1.68	2.52	3.36	8.41	12.61	16.82	21.02	25.23	29.43	33.64	37.84	42.05
Antigua & Barbuda 30 Dollars	1982	31.10	0.500	0.500		0.50	1.00	1.50	2.00	5.00	7.50	10.00	12.50	15.00	17.50	20.00	22.50	25.00
Antigua & Barbuda 100 Dollars	1988	129.59	0.925	3.850		3.85	7.70	11.55	15.40	38.50	57.75	77.00	96.25	115.50	134.75	154.00	173.25	192.50
Argentina 1/2 Real / 1/2 Sol	1813, 1815	1.69	0.896	0.049		0.05	0.10	0.15	0.20	0.49	0.74	0.98	1.23	1.47	1.72	1.96	2.21	2.45
Argentina 1 Real / 1 Sol	1813-1825	3.38	0.896	0.097	S	0.10	0.19	0.29	0.39	0.97	1.46	1.94	2.43	2.91	3.40	3.88	4.37	4.85
Argentina 2 Reales / 2 Soles	1813-1826	6.77	0.896	0.195	S	0.20	0.39	0.59	0.78	1.95	2.93	3.90	4.88	5.85	6.83	7.80	8.78	9.75
Argentina 4 Reales / 4 Soles	1813-1832	13.53	0.896	0.896	S	0.90	1.79	2.69	3.58	8.96	13.44	17.92	22.40	26.88	31.36	35.84	40.32	44.80
Argentina 8 Reales / 8 Soles	1813-1837	27.06	0.896	0.780	S	0.78	1.56	2.34	3.12	7.80	11.70	15.60	19.50	23.40	27.30	31.20	35.10	39.00
Argentina 10 Centavos	1881-1883	2.50	0.900	0.072		0.07	0.14	0.22	0.29	0.72	1.08	1.44	1.80	2.16	2.52	2.88	3.24	3.60
Argentina 20 Centavos	1881-1883	5.00	0.900	0.145		0.15	0.29	0.44	0.58	1.45	2.18	2.90	3.63	4.35	5.08	5.80	6.53	7.25
Argentina 50 Centavos	1881-1883	12.50	0.900	0.362		0.36	0.72	1.09	1.45	3.62	5.43	7.24	9.05	10.86	12.67	14.48	16.29	18.10
Argentina 1 Peso	1881-1883	25.00	0.900	0.723		0.72	1.45	2.17	2.89	7.23	10.85	14.46	18.08	21.69	25.31	28.92	32.54	36.15
Argentina 1 Peso	1995, 1999	25.00	0.900	0.723	N	0.72	1.45	2.17	2.89	7.23	10.85	14.46	18.08	21.69	25.31	28.92	32.54	36.15
Argentina 2 Pesos	1994	12.48	0.900	0.361	N	0.36	0.72	1.08	1.44	3.61	5.42	7.22	9.03	10.83	12.64	14.44	16.25	18.05
Argentina 5 Pesos	1994	24.80	0.900	0.718	N	0.72	1.44	2.15	2.87	7.18	10.77	14.36	17.95	21.54	25.13	28.72	32.31	35.90
Argentina 25 Pesos	1997, 2000	27.00	0.925	0.800		0.80	1.60	2.40	3.20	8.00	12.00	16.00	20.00	24.00	28.00	32.00	36.00	40.00
Argentina 1000 Pesos	1977-1978	10.00	0.900	0.289		0.29	0.58	0.87	1.16	2.89	4.34	5.79	7.23	8.68	10.13	11.57	13.02	14.47
Argentina 2000 Pesos	1977-1978	15.00	0.900	0.434		0.43	0.87	1.30	1.74	4.34	6.51	8.68	10.85	13.02	15.19	17.36	19.53	21.70
Argentina 3000 Pesos	1977-1978	25.00	0.900	0.723		0.72	1.45	2.17	2.89	7.23	10.85	14.47	18.09	21.70	25.32	28.94	32.55	36.17
Argentina 1000 Australes	1991	27.00	0.925	0.803	>	0.80	1.61	2.41	3.21	8.03	12.05	16.06	20.08	24.09	28.11	32.12	36.14	40.15
Armenia 5 Dram	1998	31.37	0.999	1.008		1.01	2.02	3.02	4.03	10.08	15.12	20.16	25.20	30.24	35.28	40.32	45.36	50.40
Armenia 10 Dram	1998	31.45	0.999	1.013		1.01	2.03	3.04	4.05	10.13	15.20	20.26	25.33	30.39	35.46	40.52	45.59	50.65
Armenia 25 Dram	1994	31.10	0.999	1.000		1.00	2.00	3.00	4.00	10.00	15.00	20.00	25.00	30.00	35.00	40.00	45.00	50.00
Armenia 25 Dram	1994	28.28	0.925	0.841		0.84	1.68	2.52	3.36	8.41	12.62	16.82	21.03	25.23	29.44	33.64	37.85	42.06
Armenia 100 Dram	1996, 1997	31.10	0.999	1.000		1.00	2.00	3.00	4.00	10.00	15.00	20.00	25.00	30.00	35.00	40.00	45.00	50.00
Armenia 100 Dram	1995-1998	28.28	0.925	0.841		0.84	1.68	2.52	3.36	8.41	12.62	16.82	21.03	25.23	29.44	33.64	37.85	42.06
Armenia 200 Dram	1999	31.10	0.999	1.000		1.00	2.00	3.00	4.00	10.00	15.00	20.00	25.00	30.00	35.00	40.00	45.00	50.00
Armenia 500 Dram	1995	155.50	0.925	4.625		4.63	9.25	13.88	18.50	46.25	69.38	92.50	115.63	138.75	161.88	185.00	208.13	231.25
Armenia 1000 Dram	1994	31.10	0.999	1.000		1.00	2.00	3.00	4.00	10.00	15.00	20.00	25.00	30.00	35.00	40.00	45.00	50.00
Armenia 1000 Dram	1998	31.31	0.999	1.006		1.01	2.01	3.02	4.02	10.06	15.09	20.12	25.15	30.18	35.21	40.24	45.27	50.30
Armenia 2000 Dram	2000	28.50	0.925	0.848		0.85	1.70	2.54	3.39	8.48	12.72	16.96	21.20	25.44	29.68	33.92	38.16	42.40
Armenia 5000 Dram	1999	31.10	0.999	1.000		1.00	2.00	3.00	4.00	10.00	15.00	20.00	25.00	30.00	35.00	40.00	45.00	50.00
Aruba 25 Florin	1986-2001	25.00	0.925	0.744		0.74	1.49	2.23	2.97	7.44	11.15	14.87	18.59	22.31	26.02	29.74	33.46	37.18
Aruba 50 Florin	1996	25.00	0.925	0.744		0.74	1.49	2.23	2.97	7.44	11.15	14.87	18.59	22.31	26.02	29.74	33.46	37.18
Ascension Isl. 1 Crown (25 P.)	1978	28.28	0.925	0.841		0.84	1.68	2.52	3.36	8.41	12.62	16.82	21.03	25.23	29.44	33.64	37.85	42.06
Ascension Island 50 Pence	1984-2000	28.28	0.925	0.841		0.84	1.68	2.52	3.36	8.41	12.62	16.82	21.03	25.23	29.44	33.64	37.85	42.06
Australia 3 Pence	1910-1944	1.41	0.925	0.042		0.04	0.08	0.13	0.17	0.42	0.63	0.84	1.05	1.26	1.47	1.68	1.89	2.10

Country & Denomination	Years Minted	Grams Weight	Fineness	Troy (ASW)	Code	$ Value 1	$ Value 2	$ Value 3	$ Value 4	$ Value 10	$ Value 15	$ Value 20	$ Value 25	$ Value 30	$ Value 35	$ Value 40	$ Value 45	$ Value 50
Australia 3 Pence	1947-1964	1.41	0.500	0.023		0.02	0.05	0.07	0.09	0.23	0.35	0.46	0.58	0.69	0.81	0.92	1.04	1.15
Australia 6 Pence	1910-1944	2.82	0.925	0.084		0.08	0.17	0.25	0.34	0.84	1.26	1.68	2.10	2.52	2.94	3.36	3.78	4.20
Australia 6 Pence	1946-1963	2.82	0.500	0.045		0.05	0.09	0.14	0.18	0.45	0.68	0.90	1.13	1.35	1.58	1.80	2.03	2.25
Australia 1 Shilling	1910-1945	5.65	0.925	0.168		0.17	0.34	0.50	0.67	1.68	2.52	3.36	4.20	5.04	5.88	6.72	7.56	8.40
Australia 1 Shilling	1946-1963	5.65	0.500	0.091		0.09	0.18	0.27	0.36	0.91	1.37	1.82	2.28	2.73	3.19	3.64	4.10	4.55
Australia 1 Florin	1910-1944	11.31	0.900	0.336		0.34	0.67	1.01	1.35	3.36	5.04	6.73	8.41	10.09	11.77	13.45	15.13	16.82
Australia 1 Florin	1946-1963	11.31	0.500	0.182		0.18	0.36	0.55	0.73	1.82	2.73	3.64	4.55	5.45	6.36	7.27	8.18	9.09
Australia 1 Crown	1937-1938	28.28	0.925	0.841		0.84	1.68	2.52	3.36	8.41	12.62	16.82	21.03	25.23	29.44	33.64	37.85	42.05
Australia 1 Cent	1991	3.01	0.925	0.090	N	0.09	0.18	0.27	0.36	0.90	1.35	1.80	2.25	2.70	3.15	3.60	4.05	4.50
Australia 2 Cents	1991	6.06	0.925	0.180	N	0.18	0.36	0.54	0.72	1.80	2.70	3.60	4.50	5.40	6.30	7.20	8.10	9.00
Australia 5 Cents	1991	3.27	0.925	0.097	N	0.10	0.19	0.29	0.39	0.97	1.46	1.94	2.43	2.91	3.40	3.88	4.37	4.85
Australia 5 Cents	1999	5.53	0.999	0.178	N	0.18	0.36	0.53	0.71	1.78	2.67	3.56	4.45	5.34	6.23	7.12	8.01	8.90
Australia 10 Cents	1991	6.52	0.925	0.194	N	0.19	0.39	0.58	0.78	1.94	2.91	3.88	4.85	5.82	6.79	7.76	8.73	9.70
Australia 10 Cents	1999	8.36	0.999	0.269	N	0.27	0.54	0.81	1.08	2.69	4.04	5.38	6.73	8.07	9.42	10.76	12.11	13.45
Australia 20 Cents	1991	13.09	0.925	0.389	N	0.39	0.78	1.17	1.56	3.89	5.84	7.78	9.73	11.67	13.62	15.56	17.51	19.45
Australia 20 Cents	1999	13.36	0.999	0.429	N	0.43	0.86	1.29	1.72	4.29	6.44	8.58	10.73	12.87	15.02	17.16	19.31	21.45
Australia 25 Cents (Dump)	1988-1990	7.78	0.999	0.250		0.25	0.50	0.75	1.00	2.50	3.75	5.00	6.25	7.50	8.75	10.00	11.25	12.50
Australia 50 Cents	1966	13.28	0.800	0.342		0.34	0.68	1.03	1.37	3.42	5.13	6.84	8.55	10.26	11.97	13.68	15.39	17.10
Australia 50 Cents	1988-1991	18.00	0.925	0.535	N	0.54	1.07	1.61	2.14	5.35	8.03	10.71	13.38	16.06	18.74	21.41	24.09	26.77
Australia 50 Cents	1998, 2000	36.31	0.999	1.366	N	1.37	2.73	4.10	5.46	13.66	20.49	27.32	34.15	40.98	47.81	54.64	61.47	68.30
Australia 50 Cents	1999	3.24	0.999	0.104	N	0.10	0.21	0.31	0.42	1.04	1.56	2.08	2.60	3.12	3.64	4.16	4.68	5.20
Australia 50 Cents	1999, 2000	16.89	0.999	0.542	N	0.54	1.08	1.63	2.17	5.42	8.13	10.84	13.55	16.26	18.97	21.68	24.39	27.10
Australia 50 Cents	2000	18.24	0.999	0.586	N	0.59	1.17	1.76	2.34	5.86	8.79	11.72	14.65	17.58	20.51	23.44	26.37	29.30
Australia 1 Dollar	1988-1996	11.49	0.925	0.342	N, S	0.34	0.68	1.03	1.37	3.42	5.13	6.83	8.54	10.25	11.96	13.67	15.38	17.09
Australia 1 Dollar (Holey)	1988-1990	31.00	0.999	1.000	N	1.00	2.00	3.00	4.00	10.00	15.00	20.00	25.00	30.00	35.00	40.00	45.00	50.00
Australia 1 Dollar	1994, 1995	14.49	0.925	0.342	N	0.34	0.68	1.03	1.37	3.42	5.13	6.84	8.55	10.26	11.97	13.68	15.39	17.10
Australia 1 Dollar	1996-2000	31.10	0.925	1.000	N	1.00	2.00	3.00	4.00	10.00	15.00	20.00	25.00	30.00	35.00	40.00	45.00	50.00
Australia 1 Dollar	1997-2000	11.66	0.925	0.375	N	0.38	0.75	1.13	1.50	3.75	5.63	7.50	9.38	11.25	13.13	15.00	16.88	18.75
Australia 1 Dollar	1988, 1991	8.43	0.925	0.251		0.25	0.50	0.75	1.00	2.51	3.76	5.01	6.27	7.52	8.77	10.03	11.28	12.54
Australia 2 Dollars	1992-2000	62.21	0.999	2.000	N	2.00	4.00	6.00	8.00	20.00	30.00	40.00	50.00	60.00	70.00	80.00	90.00	100.00
Australia 2 Dollars	1999	13.36	0.999	0.429	N	0.43	0.86	1.29	1.72	4.29	6.44	8.58	10.73	12.87	15.02	17.16	19.31	21.45
Australia 2 Dollars	2000	8.55	0.999	0.275	N	0.28	0.55	0.83	1.10	2.75	4.13	5.50	6.88	8.25	9.63	11.00	12.38	13.75
Australia 5 Dollars	1988-1997	35.79	0.925	1.065		1.06	2.13	3.19	4.26	10.65	15.97	21.29	26.61	31.94	37.26	42.58	47.90	53.23
Australia 5 Dollars	1990, 1991	31.10	0.999	1.000		1.00	2.00	3.00	4.00	10.00	15.00	20.00	25.00	30.00	35.00	40.00	45.00	50.00
Australia 5 Dollars	1994	31.10	0.925	1.087		1.09	2.17	3.26	4.35	10.87	16.31	21.74	27.18	32.61	38.05	43.48	48.92	54.35
Australia 5 Dollars	2000	31.64	0.999	1.016		1.02	2.03	3.05	4.06	10.16	15.24	20.32	25.40	30.48	35.56	40.64	45.72	50.80
Australia 10 Dollars	1982-1996	20.00	0.925	0.595		0.59	1.19	1.78	2.38	5.95	8.92	11.90	14.87	17.85	20.82	23.80	26.77	29.75
Australia 10 Dollars	1991	62.21	0.999	2.000		2.00	4.00	6.00	8.00	20.00	30.00	40.00	50.00	60.00	70.00	80.00	90.00	100.00
Australia 10 Dollars	1992-2000	311.04	0.999	10.000		10.00	20.00	30.00	40.00	100.00	150.00	200.00	250.00	300.00	350.00	400.00	450.00	500.00
Australia 10 Dollars	1994-1999	20.77	0.999	0.667		0.67	1.33	2.00	2.67	6.67	10.01	13.34	16.68	20.01	23.35	26.68	30.02	33.35
Australia 10 Dollars	2000	36.01	0.999	1.157		1.16	2.31	3.47	4.63	11.57	17.36	23.14	28.93	34.71	40.50	46.28	52.07	57.85
Australia 20 Dollars	1993	33.62	0.925	1.000		1.00	2.00	3.00	4.00	10.00	15.00	20.00	25.00	30.00	35.00	40.00	45.00	50.00
Australia 25 Dollars	1992	33.62	0.925	1.000		1.00	2.00	3.00	4.00	10.00	15.00	20.00	25.00	30.00	35.00	40.00	45.00	50.00
Australia 30 Dollars	1992, 1993	1100.10	0.999	35.338		35.34	70.68	106.01	141.35	353.38	530.07	706.76	883.45	1060.14	1236.83	1413.52	1590.21	1766.90
Australia 30 Dollars	1993-2000	1002.50	0.999	32.231	V	32.23	64.46	96.69	128.92	322.31	483.47	644.62	805.78	966.93	1128.09	1289.24	1450.40	1611.55

Country & Denomination	Years Minted	Grams Weight	Fine-ness	Troy (ASW)	Code	$ Value 1	$ Value 2	$ Value 3	$ Value 4	$ Value 10	$ Value 15	$ Value 20	$ Value 25	$ Value 30	$ Value 35	$ Value 40	$ Value 45	$ Value 50
Australia 50 Dollars	1991	311.04	0.999	10.000		10.00	20.00	30.00	40.00	100.00	150.00	200.00	250.00	300.00	350.00	400.00	450.00	500.00
Australia 150 Dollars	1991	1000.10	0.999	32.158		32.16	64.32	96.47	128.63	321.58	482.37	643.16	803.95	964.74	1125.53	1286.32	1447.11	1607.90
Austria 3 Kreuzer	1814-1848	1.70	0.346	0.019		0.02	0.04	0.06	0.08	0.19	0.29	0.38	0.48	0.57	0.67	0.76	0.86	0.95
Austria 5 Kreuzer	1815-1848	2.16	0.438	0.032		0.03	0.06	0.10	0.13	0.32	0.48	0.64	0.80	0.96	1.12	1.28	1.44	1.60
Austria 5 Kreuzer	1858-1867	1.33	0.375	0.016	S	0.02	0.03	0.05	0.06	0.16	0.24	0.32	0.40	0.48	0.56	0.64	0.72	0.80
Austria 6 Kreuzer	1848	2.23	0.428	0.031		0.03	0.06	0.09	0.12	0.31	0.47	0.62	0.78	0.93	1.09	1.24	1.40	1.55
Austria 6 Kreuzer	1849	1.19	0.438	0.027		0.03	0.05	0.08	0.11	0.27	0.41	0.54	0.68	0.81	0.95	1.08	1.22	1.35
Austria 7 Kreuzer	1802	4.68	0.250	0.038		0.04	0.08	0.11	0.15	0.38	0.57	0.76	0.95	1.14	1.33	1.52	1.71	1.90
Austria 10 Kreuzer	1801, 1802	3.89	0.500	0.063		0.06	0.13	0.19	0.25	0.63	0.95	1.26	1.58	1.89	2.21	2.52	2.84	3.15
Austria 10 Kreuzer	1809-1848	2.00	0.500	0.032		0.03	0.06	0.10	0.13	0.32	0.48	0.64	0.80	0.96	1.12	1.28	1.44	1.60
Austria 10 Kreuzer	1852-1855	2.16	0.900	0.063		0.06	0.13	0.19	0.25	0.63	0.95	1.26	1.58	1.89	2.21	2.52	2.84	3.15
Austria 10 Kreuzer	1858-1867	2.00	0.500	0.032	S	0.03	0.06	0.10	0.13	0.32	0.48	0.64	0.80	0.96	1.12	1.28	1.44	1.60
Austria 10 Kreuzer	1868-1872	1.67	0.400	0.021		0.02	0.04	0.06	0.08	0.21	0.32	0.42	0.53	0.63	0.74	0.84	0.95	1.05
Austria 20 Kreuzer	1801-1852	6.68	0.583	0.125	S	0.13	0.25	0.38	0.50	1.25	1.88	2.50	3.13	3.75	4.38	5.00	5.63	6.25
Austria 20 Kreuzer	1852-1856	4.32	0.900	0.125		0.13	0.25	0.38	0.50	1.25	1.88	2.50	3.13	3.75	4.38	5.00	5.63	6.25
Austria 20 Kreuzer	1868-1872	2.67	0.500	0.043		0.04	0.09	0.13	0.17	0.43	0.65	0.86	1.08	1.29	1.51	1.72	1.94	2.15
Austria 1/2 Thaler	1802-1856	14.03	0.833	0.376	S	0.38	0.75	1.13	1.50	3.76	5.64	7.52	9.40	11.28	13.16	15.04	16.92	18.80
Austria 1 Thaler	1780-1852	28.06	0.833	0.752		0.75	1.50	2.26	3.01	7.52	11.28	15.04	18.80	22.56	26.32	30.08	33.84	37.60
Austria 1 Thaler	1852-1856	26.00	0.900	0.752		0.75	1.50	2.26	3.01	7.52	11.28	15.04	18.80	22.56	26.32	30.08	33.84	37.60
Austria 1 Thaler	1857-1868	18.52	0.900	0.536		0.54	1.07	1.61	2.14	5.36	8.04	10.72	13.40	16.08	18.76	21.44	24.12	26.80
Austria 2 Thaler	1857-1867	37.04	0.900	1.072		1.07	2.14	3.22	4.29	10.72	16.08	21.44	26.80	32.16	37.52	42.88	48.24	53.60
Austria 1/4 Florin	1857-1875	5.35	0.520	0.089		0.09	0.18	0.27	0.36	0.89	1.34	1.78	2.23	2.67	3.12	3.56	4.01	4.45
Austria 1 Florin	1857-1892	12.34	0.900	0.357		0.36	0.71	1.07	1.43	3.57	5.36	7.14	8.93	10.71	12.50	14.28	16.07	17.85
Austria 2 Florin	1859-1892	24.69	0.900	0.715		0.72	1.43	2.15	2.86	7.15	10.73	14.30	17.88	21.45	25.03	28.60	32.18	35.75
Austria 1 Corona	1892-1916	5.00	0.835	0.134		0.13	0.27	0.40	0.54	1.34	2.01	2.68	3.35	4.02	4.69	5.36	6.03	6.70
Austria 2 Corona	1912-1913	10.00	0.835	0.268		0.27	0.54	0.80	1.07	2.68	4.02	5.36	6.70	8.04	9.38	10.72	12.06	13.40
Austria 5 Corona	1900-1909	24.00	0.900	0.695	S	0.70	1.39	2.09	2.78	6.95	10.43	13.90	17.38	20.85	24.33	27.80	31.28	34.75
Austria 1/2 Schilling	1925-1926	3.00	0.640	0.062		0.06	0.12	0.19	0.25	0.62	0.93	1.24	1.55	1.86	2.17	2.48	2.79	3.10
Austria 1 Schilling	1924	7.00	0.800	0.180		0.18	0.36	0.54	0.72	1.80	2.70	3.60	4.50	5.40	6.30	7.20	8.10	9.00
Austria 1 Schilling	1925-1926	6.00	0.640	0.124		0.12	0.25	0.37	0.50	1.24	1.86	2.48	3.10	3.72	4.34	4.96	5.58	6.20
Austria 2 Schillings	1928-1937	12.00	0.640	0.247		0.25	0.49	0.74	0.99	2.47	3.71	4.94	6.18	7.41	8.65	9.88	11.12	12.35
Austria 5 Schillings	1934-1936	15.00	0.835	0.403		0.40	0.81	1.21	1.61	4.03	6.05	8.06	10.08	12.09	14.11	16.12	18.14	20.15
Austria 5 Schillings	1960-1968	5.20	0.640	0.107		0.11	0.21	0.32	0.43	1.07	1.61	2.14	2.68	3.21	3.75	4.28	4.82	5.35
Austria 10 Schillings	1957-1973	7.50	0.640	0.154		0.15	0.31	0.46	0.62	1.54	2.31	3.09	3.86	4.63	5.40	6.17	6.94	7.72
Austria 25 Schillings	1957-1973	13.00	0.800	0.334		0.33	0.67	1.00	1.34	3.34	5.02	6.69	8.36	10.03	11.70	13.38	15.05	16.72
Austria 50 Schillings	1959-1973	20.00	0.900	0.579		0.58	1.16	1.74	2.31	5.79	8.68	11.57	14.47	17.36	20.25	23.15	26.04	28.94
Austria 50 Schillings	1974-1978	20.00	0.640	0.412		0.41	0.82	1.23	1.65	4.12	6.17	8.23	10.29	12.35	14.40	16.46	18.52	20.58
Austria 100 Schillings	1974-1979	24.00	0.640	0.492		0.49	0.98	1.48	1.97	4.92	7.39	9.85	12.31	14.77	17.23	19.70	22.16	24.62
Austria 200 Schillings	1995	33.63	0.925	1.000		1.00	2.00	3.00	4.00	10.00	15.00	20.00	25.00	30.00	35.00	40.00	45.00	50.00
Austria 500 Schillings	1980-1982	24.00	0.640	0.492		0.49	0.98	1.48	1.97	4.92	7.39	9.85	12.31	14.77	17.23	19.70	22.16	24.62
Austria 500 Schillings	1983-1997	24.00	0.925	0.713		0.71	1.43	2.14	2.85	7.13	10.69	14.25	17.81	21.38	24.94	28.50	32.06	35.63
Austria 1/2 Thaler	1804-1848	14.03	0.833	0.357		0.36	0.71	1.07	1.43	3.57	5.36	7.14	8.93	10.71	12.50	14.28	16.07	17.85
Austria 1/2 Thaler	1852-1856	12.99	0.900	0.377		0.38	0.75	1.13	1.51	3.77	5.66	7.54	9.43	11.31	13.20	15.08	16.97	18.85
Austria 1 Thaler	1780	28.06	0.833	0.752	R	0.75	1.50	2.26	3.01	7.52	11.28	15.04	18.80	22.56	26.32	30.08	33.84	37.60

Country & Denomination	Years Minted	Grams Weight	Fine-ness	Troy (ASW)	Code	$ Value 1	$ Value 2	$ Value 3	$ Value 4	$ Value 10	$ Value 15	$ Value 20	$ Value 25	$ Value 30	$ Value 35	$ Value 40	$ Value 45	$ Value 50
Austria 1 Thaler	1801-1852	28.06	0.833	0.751		0.75	1.50	2.25	3.00	7.51	11.27	15.02	18.78	22.53	26.29	30.04	33.80	37.55
Austria 1 Thaler	1852-1856	25.99	0.900	0.752		0.75	1.50	2.26	3.01	7.52	11.28	15.04	18.80	22.56	26.32	30.08	33.84	37.60
Austria 1 Thaler	1857-1868	18.52	0.900	0.536		0.54	1.07	1.61	2.14	5.36	8.04	10.72	13.40	16.08	18.76	21.44	24.12	26.80
Austria 2 Thaler	1857-1867	37.04	0.900	1.072		1.07	2.14	3.22	4.29	10.72	16.08	21.44	26.80	32.16	37.52	42.88	48.24	53.60
Azerbaijan 50 Manat	1996	28.28	0.925	0.841		0.84	1.68	2.52	3.36	8.41	12.62	16.82	21.03	25.23	29.44	33.64	37.85	42.05
Azores 25 Escudos	1980	11.00	0.925	0.327	N	0.33	0.65	0.98	1.31	3.27	4.91	6.54	8.18	9.82	11.45	13.09	14.72	16.36
Azores 100 Escudos	1980-1986	16.50	0.925	0.491	N	0.49	0.98	1.47	1.96	4.91	7.36	9.82	12.27	14.72	17.18	19.63	22.09	24.54
Azores 100 Escudos	1991, 1996	18.50	0.925	0.550	N	0.55	1.10	1.65	2.20	5.50	8.25	11.00	13.75	16.50	19.25	22.00	24.75	27.50
B																		
Bahamas 50 Cents	1966-1980	10.37	0.800	0.267	N, S	0.27	0.53	0.80	1.07	2.67	4.00	5.33	6.67	8.00	9.33	10.67	12.00	13.34
Bahamas 1 Dollar	1966-1980	18.10	0.800	0.467	N	0.47	0.93	1.40	1.87	4.67	7.00	9.33	11.67	14.00	16.33	18.66	21.00	23.33
Bahamas 1 Dollar	1996	31.18	0.999	1.002	N	1.00	2.00	3.00	4.01	10.02	15.02	20.03	25.04	30.05	35.05	40.06	45.07	50.08
Bahamas 2 Dollars	1967-1980	29.80	0.925	0.886	N	0.89	1.77	2.66	3.55	8.86	13.29	17.73	22.16	26.59	31.02	35.45	39.88	44.32
Bahamas 2 Dollars	1989-1991	16.85	0.925	0.501	N	0.50	1.00	1.50	2.00	5.01	7.52	10.02	12.53	15.04	17.54	20.05	22.55	25.06
Bahamas 2 Dollars	1994-2000	28.28	0.925	0.841	S	0.84	1.68	2.52	3.36	8.41	12.62	16.82	21.03	25.23	29.44	33.64	37.85	42.05
Bahamas 2 Dollars	1995	31.00	0.999	1.000	V	1.00	2.00	3.00	4.00	10.00	15.00	20.00	25.00	30.00	35.00	40.00	45.00	50.00
Bahamas 2 Dollars	1995-1997	23.33	0.925	0.694		0.69	1.39	2.08	2.78	6.94	10.41	13.88	17.35	20.82	24.29	27.76	31.23	34.70
Bahamas 5 Dollars	1966-1980	42.12	0.925	1.253	N, S	1.25	2.51	3.76	5.01	12.53	18.80	25.06	31.33	37.59	43.86	50.12	56.39	62.65
Bahamas 5 Dollars	1981-1985	42.12	0.500	0.677	N	0.68	1.35	2.03	2.71	6.77	10.16	13.54	16.93	20.31	23.70	27.08	30.47	33.86
Bahamas 5 Dollars	1989-1992	19.44	0.925	0.578		0.58	1.16	1.73	2.31	5.78	8.67	11.56	14.46	17.35	20.24	23.13	26.02	28.91
Bahamas 5 Dollars	1993	23.33	0.925	0.694		0.69	1.39	2.08	2.78	6.94	10.41	13.88	17.35	20.82	24.29	27.76	31.23	34.70
Bahamas 5 Dollars	1994	31.10	0.999	1.000		1.00	2.00	3.00	4.00	10.00	15.00	20.00	25.00	30.00	35.00	40.00	45.00	50.00
Bahamas 5 Dollars	1994	31.47	0.925	0.936		0.94	1.87	2.81	3.74	9.36	14.04	18.72	23.40	28.08	32.76	37.44	42.12	46.80
Bahamas 5 Dollars	1973	49.75	0.925	1.480		1.48	2.96	4.44	5.92	14.80	22.19	29.59	36.99	44.39	51.78	59.18	66.58	73.98
Bahamas 10 Dollars	1974	50.42	0.925	1.499		1.50	3.00	4.50	6.00	14.99	22.49	29.99	37.49	44.98	52.48	59.98	67.47	74.97
Bahamas 10 Dollars	1975-1977	49.10	0.925	1.460		1.46	2.92	4.38	5.84	14.60	21.90	29.20	36.51	43.81	51.11	58.41	65.71	73.01
Bahamas 10 Dollars	1978	45.36	0.500	0.729	N	0.73	1.46	2.19	2.92	7.29	10.94	14.58	18.23	21.87	25.52	29.16	32.81	36.46
Bahamas 10 Dollars	1980	30.28	0.500	0.487	N	0.49	0.97	1.46	1.95	4.87	7.30	9.74	12.17	14.60	17.04	19.47	21.91	24.34
Bahamas 10 Dollars	1981-1995	28.28	0.925	0.841	N	0.84	1.68	2.52	3.36	8.41	12.62	16.82	21.03	25.23	29.44	33.64	37.85	42.05
Bahamas 10 Dollars	1983	30.28	0.500	0.487		0.49	0.97	1.46	1.95	4.87	7.30	9.74	12.17	14.60	17.04	19.47	21.91	24.34
Bahamas 10 Dollars	1983-1984	23.33	0.925	0.694		0.69	1.39	2.08	2.78	6.94	10.41	13.88	17.35	20.82	24.29	27.76	31.23	34.70
Bahamas 10 Dollars	1984	29.17	0.500	0.469		0.47	0.94	1.41	1.88	4.69	7.04	9.38	11.73	14.07	16.42	18.76	21.11	23.45
Bahamas 10 Dollars	1986	28.28	0.500	0.455		0.45	0.91	1.36	1.82	4.55	6.82	9.09	11.37	13.64	15.91	18.18	20.46	22.73
Bahamas 10 Dollars	1998	31.10	0.999	1.000		1.00	2.00	3.00	4.00	10.00	15.00	20.00	25.00	30.00	35.00	40.00	45.00	50.00
Bahamas 25 Dollars	1979	37.38	0.925	1.112		1.11	2.22	3.34	4.45	11.12	16.68	22.24	27.80	33.36	38.92	44.48	50.04	55.60
Bahamas 25 Dollars	1985	120.00	0.925	3.569		3.57	7.14	10.71	14.27	35.69	53.53	71.37	89.22	107.06	124.90	142.75	160.59	178.44
Bahamas 25 Dollars	1985-1987	129.60	0.925	3.855		3.85	7.71	11.56	15.42	38.55	57.82	77.09	96.37	115.64	134.91	154.19	173.46	192.74
Bahamas 25 Dollars	1988-1992	136.00	0.925	4.045	N	4.04	8.09	12.13	16.18	40.45	60.67	80.89	101.12	121.34	141.56	161.78	182.01	202.23
Bahamas 50 Dollars	1996	2000.00	0.999	64.237		64.24	128.47	192.71	256.95	642.37	963.56	1284.74	1605.93	1927.11	2248.30	2569.48	2890.67	3211.85
Bahamas 100 Dollars	1992-1995	1000.00	0.999	32.150		32.15	64.30	96.45	128.60	321.50	482.25	643.00	803.75	964.50	1125.25	1286.00	1446.75	1607.50
Bahrain 5 Fils	1983	2.00	0.925	0.060	A	0.06	0.12	0.18	0.24	0.60	0.89	1.19	1.49	1.79	2.08	2.38	2.68	2.98
Bahrain 10 Fils	1983	4.75	0.925	0.141	A	0.14	0.28	0.42	0.57	1.41	2.12	2.83	3.53	4.24	4.95	5.65	6.36	7.07

Country & Denomination	Years Minted	Grams Weight	Fine-ness	Troy (ASW)	Code	$ Value 1	$ Value 2	$ Value 3	$ Value 4	$ Value 10	$ Value 15	$ Value 20	$ Value 25	$ Value 30	$ Value 35	$ Value 40	$ Value 45	$ Value 50
Bahrain 25 Fils	1983	1.75	0.925	0.052	A	0.05	0.10	0.16	0.21	0.52	0.78	1.04	1.30	1.56	1.82	2.08	2.34	2.61
Bahrain 50 Fils	1983	3.10	0.925	0.092	A	0.09	0.18	0.28	0.37	0.92	1.38	1.84	2.31	2.77	3.23	3.69	4.15	4.61
Bahrain 100 Fils	1983	6.50	0.925	0.193	A	0.19	0.39	0.58	0.77	1.93	2.90	3.87	4.83	5.80	6.77	7.73	8.70	9.67
Bahrain 250 Fils	1983	15.00	0.925	0.446	A	0.45	0.89	1.34	1.78	4.46	6.69	8.92	11.15	13.38	15.61	17.84	20.07	22.31
Bahrain 500 Fils	1965-1968	18.30	0.800	0.471	A	0.47	0.94	1.41	1.88	4.71	7.07	9.42	11.78	14.13	16.49	18.84	21.20	23.55
Bahrain 500 Fils	1983	18.06	0.925	0.537	A	0.54	1.07	1.61	2.15	5.37	8.06	10.74	13.43	16.12	18.80	21.49	24.17	26.86
Bahrain 5 Dinars	1986-1990	19.44	0.925	0.578	A	0.58	1.16	1.73	2.31	5.78	8.67	11.56	14.46	17.35	20.24	23.13	26.02	28.91
Bahrain 5 Dinars	1995	28.23	0.925	0.840	A	0.84	1.68	2.52	3.36	8.40	12.59	16.79	20.99	25.19	29.38	33.58	37.78	41.98
Bahrain 5 Dinars	1998	19.40	0.925	0.577	A	0.58	1.15	1.73	2.31	5.77	8.65	11.54	14.42	17.31	20.19	23.08	25.96	28.85
Bangladesh 1 Taka	1991-1993	31.35	0.925	0.932		0.93	1.86	2.80	3.73	9.32	13.98	18.65	23.31	27.97	32.63	37.29	41.95	46.62
Barbados 1 Dollar	1994	10.00	0.500	0.161		0.16	0.32	0.48	0.64	1.61	2.42	3.22	4.03	4.83	5.64	6.44	7.25	8.05
Barbados 1 Dollar	1995	9.94	0.925	0.296	N	0.30	0.59	0.89	1.18	2.96	4.44	5.92	7.40	8.88	10.36	11.84	13.32	14.80
Barbados 5 Dollars	1973-1984	31.10	0.800	0.800		0.80	1.60	2.40	3.20	8.00	12.00	16.00	20.00	24.00	28.00	32.00	36.00	40.00
Barbados 5 Dollars	1994	31.47	0.925	0.936		0.94	1.87	2.81	3.74	9.36	14.04	18.72	23.40	28.08	32.76	37.44	42.12	46.80
Barbados 5 Dollars	1994, 1995	28.28	0.925	0.841	V	0.84	1.68	2.52	3.36	8.41	12.62	16.82	21.03	25.23	29.44	33.64	37.85	42.05
Barbados 5 Dollars	1999, 2000	28.10	0.925	0.836		0.84	1.67	2.51	3.34	8.36	12.54	16.72	20.90	25.08	29.26	33.44	37.62	41.80
Barbados 10 Dollars	1973-1981	37.90	0.925	1.127		1.13	2.25	3.38	4.51	11.27	16.91	22.54	28.18	33.81	39.45	45.08	50.72	56.35
Barbados 10 Dollars	1982-1984	35.52	0.925	1.056		1.06	2.11	3.17	4.23	10.56	15.85	21.13	26.41	31.69	36.97	42.26	47.54	52.82
Barbados 10 Dollars	1991	28.28	0.925	0.841		0.84	1.68	2.52	3.36	8.41	12.62	16.82	21.03	25.23	29.44	33.64	37.85	42.05
Barbados 20 Dollars	1991, 1992	23.33	0.925	0.694		0.69	1.39	2.08	2.78	6.94	10.41	13.88	17.35	20.81	24.28	27.75	31.22	34.69
Barbados 20 Dollars	1985-1988	23.33	0.925	0.694		0.69	1.39	2.08	2.78	6.94	10.41	13.88	17.35	20.81	24.28	27.75	31.22	34.69
Barbados 25 Dollars	1978	28.28	0.925	0.841		0.84	1.68	2.52	3.36	8.41	12.62	16.82	21.03	25.23	29.44	33.64	37.85	42.05
Barbados 25 Dollars	1980-1983	30.28	0.500	0.487		0.49	0.97	1.46	1.95	4.87	7.30	9.74	12.17	14.60	17.04	19.47	21.91	24.34
Barbados 25 Dollars	1978-1986	28.28	0.925	0.841	S	0.84	1.68	2.52	3.36	8.41	12.62	16.82	21.03	25.23	29.44	33.64	37.85	42.05
Barbados 25 Dollars	1986	28.28	0.500	0.455		0.45	0.91	1.36	1.82	4.55	6.82	9.09	11.37	13.64	15.91	18.18	20.46	22.73
Barbados 50 Dollars	1981	27.35	0.500	0.440		0.44	0.88	1.32	1.76	4.40	6.60	8.79	10.99	13.19	15.39	17.59	19.79	21.99
Barbados 50 Dollars	1984	16.85	0.500	0.271		0.27	0.54	0.81	1.08	2.71	4.06	5.42	6.77	8.13	9.48	10.84	12.19	13.55
Barbados 50 Dollars	1989	33.63	0.925	1.000	V	1.00	2.00	3.00	4.00	10.00	15.00	20.00	25.00	30.00	35.00	40.00	45.00	50.00
Belarus 1 Rouble	1996	28.51	0.925	0.848	N	0.85	1.70	2.54	3.39	8.48	12.72	16.96	21.20	25.44	29.68	33.92	38.16	42.40
Belarus 10 Roubles	1998, 1999	16.96	0.925	0.504		0.50	1.01	1.51	2.02	5.04	7.56	10.08	12.60	15.12	17.64	20.16	22.68	25.20
Belarus 20 Roubles	1996-1999	33.80	0.925	1.000	S, V	1.00	2.00	3.00	4.00	10.00	15.00	20.00	25.00	30.00	35.00	40.00	45.00	50.00
Belarus 20 Roubles	1997	34.70	0.900	1.005		1.01	2.01	3.02	4.02	10.05	15.08	20.10	25.13	30.15	35.18	40.20	45.23	50.25
Belarus 20 Roubles	1997	31.48	0.999	1.011		1.01	2.02	3.03	4.04	10.11	15.17	20.22	25.28	30.33	35.39	40.44	45.50	50.55
Belarus 20 Roubles	1997, 2000	31.10	0.925	0.930		0.93	1.86	2.79	3.72	9.30	13.95	18.60	23.25	27.90	32.55	37.20	41.85	46.50
Belarus 20 Roubles	1998, 1999	33.52	0.925	0.997	V	1.00	1.99	2.99	3.99	9.97	14.96	19.94	24.93	29.91	34.90	39.88	44.87	49.85
Belgian Congo 50 Francs	1944	17.50	0.500	0.281		0.28	0.56	0.84	1.13	2.81	4.22	5.63	7.04	8.44	9.85	11.26	12.66	14.07
Belgium 1/4 Franc	1834-1850	1.25	0.900	0.036	S	0.04	0.07	0.11	0.14	0.36	0.54	0.72	0.90	1.08	1.26	1.44	1.62	1.80
Belgium 1/2 Franc	1833-1850	2.50	0.900	0.072	S	0.07	0.14	0.22	0.29	0.72	1.08	1.44	1.80	2.16	2.52	2.88	3.24	3.60
Belgium 20 Centimes	1852-1858	1.00	0.900	0.029	S	0.03	0.06	0.09	0.12	0.29	0.44	0.58	0.73	0.87	1.02	1.16	1.31	1.45
Belgium 50 Centimes	1866-1914	2.50	0.835	0.067	S	0.07	0.13	0.20	0.27	0.67	1.01	1.34	1.68	2.01	2.35	2.68	3.02	3.35

Country & Denomination	Years Minted	Grams Weight	Fineness	Troy (ASW)	Code	$ Value 1	$ Value 2	$ Value 3	$ Value 4	$ Value 10	$ Value 15	$ Value 20	$ Value 25	$ Value 30	$ Value 35	$ Value 40	$ Value 45	$ Value 50
Belgium 1 Franc	1833-1850	5.00	0.900	0.145	S	0.15	0.29	0.44	0.58	1.45	2.18	2.90	3.63	4.35	5.08	5.80	6.53	7.25
Belgium 1 Franc	1866-1914	5.00	0.835	0.134	S	0.13	0.27	0.40	0.54	1.34	2.01	2.68	3.35	4.02	4.69	5.36	6.03	6.70
Belgium 2 Francs	1834-1865	10.00	0.900	0.289	S	0.29	0.58	0.87	1.16	2.89	4.34	5.78	7.23	8.67	10.12	11.56	13.01	14.45
Belgium 2 Francs	1866-1912	10.00	0.835	0.269	S	0.27	0.54	0.81	1.08	2.69	4.04	5.38	6.73	8.07	9.42	10.76	12.11	13.45
Belgium 2-1/2 Francs	1848-1865	12.50	0.900	0.362	S	0.36	0.72	1.09	1.45	3.62	5.43	7.24	9.05	10.86	12.67	14.48	16.29	18.10
Belgium 5 Francs	1832-1868	25.00	0.900	0.723	S	0.72	1.45	2.17	2.89	7.23	10.85	14.46	18.08	21.69	25.31	28.92	32.54	36.15
Belgium 20 Francs	1933-1935	11.00	0.680	0.241		0.24	0.48	0.72	0.96	2.41	3.62	4.82	6.03	7.23	8.44	9.64	10.85	12.05
Belgium 20 Francs	1949-1955	8.00	0.835	0.215	S	0.22	0.43	0.65	0.86	2.15	3.23	4.30	5.38	6.45	7.53	8.60	9.68	10.75
Belgium 50 Francs	1935	22.00	0.680	0.481		0.48	0.96	1.44	1.92	4.81	7.22	9.62	12.03	14.43	16.84	19.24	21.65	24.05
Belgium 50 Francs	1939-1940	20.00	0.835	0.537		0.54	1.07	1.61	2.15	5.37	8.06	10.74	13.43	16.11	18.80	21.48	24.17	26.85
Belgium 50 Francs	1948-1960	12.50	0.835	0.336	S	0.34	0.67	1.01	1.34	3.36	5.04	6.72	8.40	10.08	11.76	13.44	15.12	16.80
Belgium 100 Francs	1948-1954	18.00	0.835	0.483	S	0.48	0.97	1.45	1.93	4.83	7.25	9.66	12.08	14.49	16.91	19.32	21.74	24.15
Belgium 250 Francs	1976	25.20	0.835	0.671		0.67	1.34	2.01	2.68	6.71	10.07	13.42	16.78	20.13	23.49	26.84	30.20	33.55
Belgium 250 Francs	1994-1999	18.75	0.925	0.557		0.56	1.11	1.67	2.23	5.57	8.36	11.14	13.93	16.71	19.50	22.28	25.07	27.85
Belgium 500 Francs	1980-1999	22.85	0.833	0.612		0.61	1.22	1.84	2.45	6.12	9.18	12.24	15.30	18.36	21.42	24.48	27.54	30.60
Belgium 5 ECU	1987-1991	22.85	0.833	0.612		0.61	1.22	1.84	2.45	6.12	9.18	12.24	15.30	18.36	21.42	24.48	27.54	30.60
Belgium 5 ECU	1993-1998	22.85	0.900	0.680	S	0.68	1.36	2.04	2.72	6.80	10.20	13.60	17.00	20.40	23.80	27.20	30.60	34.00
Belize 1 Cent*	1974-1985	3.02	0.925	0.090		0.09	0.18	0.27	0.36	0.90	1.35	1.80	2.25	2.69	3.14	3.59	4.04	4.49
Belize 5 Cents	1974-1985	4.35	0.925	0.129		0.13	0.26	0.39	0.52	1.29	1.94	2.59	3.23	3.88	4.53	5.17	5.82	6.47
Belize 10 Cents	1974-1985	2.79	0.925	0.083		0.08	0.17	0.25	0.33	0.83	1.24	1.66	2.07	2.49	2.90	3.32	3.73	4.15
Belize 25 Cents	1974-1985	6.60	0.925	0.196		0.20	0.39	0.59	0.78	1.96	2.94	3.92	4.91	5.89	6.87	7.85	8.83	9.81
Belize 50 Cents	1974-1985	9.94	0.925	0.320		0.32	0.64	0.96	1.28	3.20	4.80	6.39	7.99	9.59	11.19	12.79	14.39	15.99
Belize 1 Dollar	1974-1985	19.89	0.925	0.592		0.59	1.18	1.77	2.37	5.92	8.87	11.83	14.79	17.75	20.70	23.66	26.62	29.58
Belize 2 Dollars	1990-1998	28.28	0.925	0.841		0.84	1.68	2.52	3.36	8.41	12.62	16.82	21.03	25.23	29.44	33.64	37.85	42.06
Belize 5 Dollars	1974-1985	26.70	0.925	0.785		0.79	1.57	2.36	3.14	7.85	11.78	15.70	19.63	23.55	27.48	31.40	35.33	39.26
Belize 10 Dollars	1974-1979	29.80	0.925	0.886		0.89	1.77	2.66	3.55	8.86	13.29	17.73	22.16	26.59	31.02	35.45	39.88	44.32
Belize 10 Dollars	1980-1985	25.50	0.925	0.758		0.76	1.52	2.27	3.03	7.58	11.37	15.17	18.96	22.75	26.54	30.33	34.12	37.92
Belize 20 Dollars	1984-1985	23.33	0.925	0.694		0.69	1.39	2.08	2.78	6.94	10.41	13.88	17.35	20.81	24.28	27.75	31.22	34.69
Belize 25 Dollars	1978	27.81	0.925	0.827		0.83	1.65	2.48	3.31	8.27	12.41	16.54	20.68	24.81	28.95	33.08	37.22	41.35
Belize 25 Dollars	1980-1983	30.28	0.500	0.469		0.47	0.94	1.41	1.87	4.69	7.03	9.37	11.72	14.06	16.40	18.74	21.09	23.43
Belize 25 Dollars	1985-1992	28.28	0.925	0.841		0.84	1.68	2.52	3.36	8.41	12.62	16.82	21.03	25.23	29.44	33.64	37.85	42.06
Belize 50 Dollars	1985	129.60	0.925	3.855		3.85	7.71	11.56	15.42	38.55	57.82	77.09	96.37	115.64	134.91	154.19	173.46	192.74
British North Borneo 25 Cents	1929	2.83	0.500	0.045		0.05	0.09	0.14	0.18	0.45	0.68	0.91	1.14	1.36	1.59	1.82	2.04	2.27
Benin 500 Francs	1992	12.00	0.999	0.386		0.39	0.77	1.16	1.54	3.86	5.79	7.72	9.65	11.58	13.51	15.44	17.37	19.30
Benin 500 Francs	1995, 1996	8.25	0.999	0.265		0.27	0.53	0.80	1.06	2.65	3.98	5.30	6.63	7.95	9.28	10.60	11.93	13.25
Benin 1000 Francs	1992-1999	20.00	0.999	0.641	S, V	0.64	1.28	1.92	2.56	6.41	9.62	12.82	16.03	19.23	22.44	25.64	28.85	32.05
Benin 1000 Francs	1994	15.86	0.994	0.510		0.51	1.02	1.53	2.04	5.10	7.65	10.20	12.75	15.30	17.85	20.40	22.95	25.50
Benin 1000 Francs	1996-1999	15.00	0.999	0.481	S, V	0.48	0.96	1.44	1.92	4.81	7.22	9.62	12.03	14.43	16.84	19.24	21.65	24.05
Benin 6000 Francs	1993	20.13	0.999	0.647		0.65	1.29	1.94	2.59	6.47	9.71	12.94	16.18	19.41	22.65	25.88	29.12	32.35
Benin 6000 Francs	1995	28.34	0.925	0.825		0.83	1.65	2.48	3.30	8.25	12.38	16.50	20.63	24.75	28.88	33.00	37.13	41.25
Benin 15,000 Francs	1996, 1997	500.00	0.999	16.060		16.06	32.12	48.18	64.24	160.60	240.90	321.20	401.50	481.80	562.10	642.40	722.70	803.00
Benin 20,000 Francs	1997	806.02	0.999	27.200		27.20	54.40	81.60	108.80	272.00	408.00	544.00	680.00	816.00	952.00	1088.00	1224.00	1360.00

Country & Denomination	Years Minted	Grams Weight	Fine-ness	Troy (ASW)	Code	$ Value 1	$ Value 2	$ Value 3	$ Value 4	$ Value 10	$ Value 15	$ Value 20	$ Value 25	$ Value 30	$ Value 35	$ Value 40	$ Value 45	$ Value 50
Bermuda 1 Crown	1959	28.28	0.925	0.841		0.84	1.68	2.52	3.36	8.41	12.62	16.82	21.03	25.23	29.44	33.64	37.85	42.05
Bermuda 1 Crown	1964	22.62	0.500	0.364		0.36	0.73	1.09	1.46	3.64	5.46	7.28	9.10	10.92	12.74	14.56	16.38	18.20
Bermuda 1 Cent	1995	3.70	0.925	0.110	N	0.11	0.22	0.33	0.44	1.10	1.65	2.20	2.75	3.30	3.85	4.40	4.95	5.50
Bermuda 5 Cents	1995	5.70	0.925	0.170	N	0.17	0.34	0.51	0.68	1.70	2.55	3.40	4.25	5.10	5.95	6.80	7.65	8.50
Bermuda 10 Cents	1995	2.80	0.925	0.083	N	0.08	0.17	0.25	0.33	0.83	1.25	1.66	2.08	2.49	2.91	3.32	3.74	4.15
Bermuda 25 Cents	1984	5.96	0.925	0.177	N	0.18	0.35	0.53	0.71	1.77	2.66	3.55	4.44	5.32	6.21	7.10	7.98	8.87
Bermuda 25 Cents	1995	7.00	0.925	0.210	N	0.21	0.42	0.63	0.84	2.10	3.15	4.20	5.25	6.30	7.35	8.40	9.45	10.50
Bermuda 1 Dollar	1970	28.28	0.800	0.727		0.73	1.45	2.18	2.91	7.27	10.91	14.54	18.18	21.81	25.45	29.08	32.72	36.35
Bermuda 1 Dollar	1972	28.28	0.500	0.456		0.46	0.91	1.37	1.82	4.56	6.84	9.12	11.40	13.68	15.96	18.24	20.52	22.80
Bermuda 1 Dollar	1972	28.28	0.925	0.841		0.84	1.68	2.52	3.36	8.41	12.62	16.82	21.03	25.23	29.44	33.64	37.85	42.05
Bermuda 1 Dollar	1981-1990	28.28	0.925	0.841	N	0.84	1.68	2.52	3.36	8.41	12.62	16.82	21.03	25.23	29.44	33.64	37.85	42.05
Bermuda 1 Dollar	1993	31.47	0.925	0.936		0.94	1.87	2.81	3.74	9.36	14.04	18.72	23.40	28.08	32.76	37.44	42.12	46.80
Bermuda 1 Dollar	1996	28.37	0.925	0.844	N, V	0.84	1.69	2.53	3.38	8.44	12.66	16.88	21.10	25.32	29.54	33.76	37.98	42.20
Bermuda 2 Dollars	1990-2000	28.28	0.925	0.841	S	0.84	1.68	2.52	3.36	8.41	12.62	16.82	21.03	25.23	29.44	33.64	37.85	42.05
Bermuda 5 Dollars	1987-1992	155.52	0.999	5.000	S	5.00	10.00	15.00	20.00	50.00	75.00	100.00	125.00	150.00	175.00	200.00	225.00	250.00
Bermuda 5 Dollars	1995	56.56	0.925	1.680		1.68	3.36	5.04	6.72	16.80	25.20	33.60	42.00	50.40	58.80	67.20	75.60	84.00
Bermuda 9 Dollars	1996-1998	155.52	0.999	5.000		5.00	10.00	15.00	20.00	50.00	75.00	100.00	125.00	150.00	175.00	200.00	225.00	250.00
Bermuda 25 Dollars	1975	48.70	0.925	1.448		1.45	2.90	4.34	5.79	14.48	21.72	28.96	36.20	43.44	50.68	57.92	65.16	72.40
Bermuda 25 Dollars	1977	54.75	0.925	1.628		1.63	3.26	4.88	6.51	16.28	24.42	32.56	40.70	48.84	56.98	65.12	73.26	81.40
Bhutan 3 Rupees	1966	28.28	0.925	0.841		0.84	1.68	2.52	3.36	8.41	12.62	16.82	21.03	25.23	29.44	33.64	37.85	42.05
Bhutan 15 Ngultrums	1974	22.50	0.500	0.358		0.36	0.72	1.07	1.43	3.58	5.37	7.16	8.95	10.74	12.53	14.32	16.11	17.90
Bhutan 30 Ngultrums	1975	25.00	0.500	0.402		0.40	0.80	1.21	1.61	4.02	6.03	8.04	10.05	12.06	14.07	16.08	18.09	20.10
Bhutan 50 Ngultrums	1981	28.28	0.925	0.841		0.84	1.68	2.52	3.36	8.41	12.62	16.82	21.03	25.23	29.44	33.64	37.85	42.06
Bhutan 100 Ngultrums	1984	23.33	0.925	0.694		0.69	1.39	2.08	2.78	6.94	10.41	13.88	17.35	20.81	24.28	27.75	31.22	34.69
Bhutan 100 Ngultrums	1998	20.00	0.925	0.595		0.60	1.19	1.79	2.38	5.95	8.93	11.90	14.88	17.85	20.83	23.80	26.78	29.75
Bhutan 200 Ngultrums	1981-1982	28.28	0.925	0.841		0.84	1.68	2.52	3.36	8.41	12.62	16.82	21.03	25.23	29.44	33.64	37.85	42.06
Bhutan 200 Ngultrums	1996	10.00	0.500	0.161		0.16	0.32	0.48	0.64	1.61	2.42	3.22	4.03	4.83	5.64	6.44	7.25	8.05
Bhutan 300 Ngultrums	1990-1995	28.28	0.925	0.841	S	0.84	1.68	2.52	3.36	8.41	12.62	16.82	21.03	25.23	29.44	33.64	37.85	42.06
Bhutan 300 Ngultrums	1992-1993	31.47	0.925	0.936	V	0.94	1.87	2.81	3.74	9.36	14.04	18.72	23.40	28.08	32.76	37.44	42.12	46.80
Bhutan 300 Ngultrums	1994-1996	31.50	0.925	0.937	V	0.94	1.87	2.81	3.75	9.37	14.06	18.74	23.43	28.11	32.80	37.48	42.17	46.85
Biafra 1 Pound	1969	19.76	0.750	0.477		0.48	0.95	1.43	1.91	4.77	7.15	9.53	11.91	14.30	16.68	19.06	21.44	23.83
Bolivia 1/4 Real	1800-1809	0.85	0.896	0.024		0.02	0.05	0.07	0.10	0.24	0.37	0.49	0.61	0.73	0.85	0.98	1.10	1.22
Bolivia 1/2 Real	1800-1825	1.69	0.896	0.049	S	0.05	0.10	0.15	0.20	0.49	0.74	0.98	1.23	1.47	1.72	1.96	2.21	2.45
Bolivia 1 Real	1800-1825	3.38	0.896	0.098	S	0.10	0.20	0.29	0.39	0.98	1.47	1.96	2.45	2.94	3.43	3.92	4.41	4.90
Bolivia 2 Reals	1800-1825	6.77	0.896	0.195		0.19	0.39	0.58	0.78	1.95	2.92	3.90	4.87	5.85	6.82	7.80	8.77	9.75
Bolivia 4 Reals	1800-1825	13.53	0.896	0.390	S	0.39	0.78	1.17	1.56	3.90	5.85	7.80	9.75	11.70	13.65	15.60	17.55	19.50
Bolivia 8 Reals	1800-1825	27.07	0.896	0.780	S	0.78	1.56	2.34	3.12	7.80	11.70	15.60	19.50	23.40	27.30	31.20	35.10	39.00
Bolivia 1/4 Sole	1852-1853	0.85	0.667	0.018		0.02	0.04	0.05	0.07	0.18	0.27	0.36	0.45	0.54	0.63	0.72	0.81	0.90
Bolivia 1/2 Sole	1827-1829	1.50	0.903	0.044		0.04	0.09	0.13	0.18	0.44	0.66	0.88	1.10	1.32	1.54	1.76	1.98	2.20
Bolivia 1/2 Sole	1830-1858	1.50	0.667	0.032	S	0.03	0.06	0.10	0.13	0.32	0.48	0.64	0.80	0.96	1.12	1.28	1.44	1.60
Bolivia 1/2 Sole	1859	1.30	0.667	0.028		0.03	0.06	0.08	0.11	0.28	0.42	0.56	0.70	0.84	0.98	1.12	1.26	1.40

Country & Denomination	Years Minted	Grams Weight	Fine-ness	Troy (ASW)	Code	$ Value 1	$ Value 2	$ Value 3	$ Value 4	$ Value 10	$ Value 15	$ Value 20	$ Value 25	$ Value 30	$ Value 35	$ Value 40	$ Value 45	$ Value 50
Bolivia 1/2 Sole	1859-1863	1.30	0.903	0.038		0.04	0.08	0.11	0.15	0.38	0.57	0.76	0.95	1.14	1.33	1.52	1.71	1.90
Bolivia 1 Sole	1827-1829	3.00	0.903	0.087		0.09	0.17	0.26	0.35	0.87	1.31	1.74	2.18	2.61	3.05	3.48	3.92	4.35
Bolivia 1 Sole	1830-1859	3.00	0.667	0.064	s	0.06	0.13	0.19	0.26	0.64	0.96	1.28	1.60	1.92	2.24	2.56	2.88	3.20
Bolivia 1 Sole	1859-1863	2.50	0.903	0.073		0.07	0.15	0.22	0.29	0.73	1.10	1.46	1.83	2.19	2.56	2.92	3.29	3.65
Bolivia 2 Soles	1827-1829	6.20	0.903	0.180		0.18	0.36	0.54	0.72	1.80	2.70	3.60	4.50	5.40	6.30	7.20	8.10	9.00
Bolivia 2 Soles	1830-1859	6.20	0.667	0.132	s	0.13	0.26	0.40	0.53	1.32	1.98	2.64	3.30	3.96	4.62	5.28	5.94	6.60
Bolivia 2 Soles	1860-1863	4.50	0.903	0.131		0.13	0.26	0.39	0.52	1.31	1.97	2.62	3.28	3.93	4.59	5.24	5.90	6.55
Bolivia 4 Soles	1827-1829	13.50	0.903	0.392		0.39	0.78	1.18	1.57	3.92	5.88	7.84	9.80	11.76	13.72	15.68	17.64	19.60
Bolivia 4 Soles	1830-1859	13.50	0.667	0.290		0.29	0.58	0.87	1.16	2.90	4.35	5.80	7.25	8.70	10.15	11.60	13.05	14.50
Bolivia 4 Soles	1860	13.50	0.903	0.392		0.39	0.78	1.18	1.57	3.92	5.88	7.84	9.80	11.76	13.72	15.68	17.64	19.60
Bolivia 8 Soles	1827-1859	27.00	0.903	0.784	s	0.78	1.57	2.35	3.14	7.84	11.76	15.68	19.60	23.52	27.44	31.36	35.28	39.20
Bolivia 8 Soles	1859-1863	20.00	0.903	0.581		0.58	1.16	1.74	2.32	5.81	8.72	11.62	14.53	17.43	20.34	23.24	26.15	29.05
Bolivia 1/4 Melgarejo	1865	5.00	0.666	0.107		0.11	0.21	0.32	0.43	1.07	1.61	2.14	2.68	3.21	3.75	4.28	4.82	5.35
Bolivia 1/2 Melgarejo	1865-1868	10.00	0.666	0.214	s	0.21	0.43	0.64	0.86	2.14	3.21	4.28	5.35	6.42	7.49	8.56	9.63	10.70
Bolivia 1 Melgarejo	1865	20.00	0.666	0.428		0.43	0.86	1.28	1.71	4.28	6.42	8.56	10.70	12.84	14.98	17.12	19.26	21.40
Bolivia 1/20 Boliviano	1864-1865	1.25	0.900	0.036		0.04	0.07	0.11	0.14	0.36	0.54	0.72	0.90	1.08	1.26	1.44	1.62	1.80
Bolivia 1/10 Boliviano	1864-1867	2.50	0.900	0.072		0.07	0.14	0.22	0.29	0.72	1.08	1.44	1.80	2.16	2.52	2.88	3.24	3.60
Bolivia 1/5 Boliviano	1864-1866	5.00	0.900	0.145		0.15	0.29	0.44	0.58	1.45	2.18	2.90	3.63	4.35	5.08	5.80	6.53	7.25
Bolivia 1 Boliviano	1864-1893	25.00	0.900	0.723	s	0.72	1.45	2.17	2.89	7.23	10.85	14.46	18.08	21.69	25.31	28.92	32.54	36.15
Bolivia 1 Boliviano	1998	27.00	0.925	0.803		0.80	1.61	2.41	3.21	8.03	12.05	16.06	20.08	24.09	28.11	32.12	36.14	40.15
Bolivia 10 Bolivianos	1991, 1997	27.10	0.925	0.805	v	0.81	1.61	2.42	3.22	8.05	12.08	16.10	20.13	24.15	28.18	32.20	36.23	40.25
Bolivia 50 Bolivianos	1998	27.00	0.925	0.803		0.80	1.61	2.41	3.21	8.03	12.05	16.06	20.08	24.09	28.11	32.12	36.14	40.15
Bolivia 5 Centavos	1872-1900	1.15	0.900	0.033		0.03	0.07	0.10	0.13	0.33	0.50	0.66	0.83	0.99	1.16	1.32	1.49	1.65
Bolivia 10 Centavos	1872-1900	2.30	0.900	0.067		0.07	0.13	0.20	0.27	0.67	1.01	1.34	1.68	2.01	2.35	2.68	3.02	3.35
Bolivia 20 Centavos	1872-1907	4.60	0.900	0.133	s	0.13	0.27	0.40	0.53	1.33	2.00	2.66	3.33	3.99	4.66	5.32	5.99	6.65
Bolivia 20 Centavos	1909	4.00	0.833	0.107		0.11	0.21	0.32	0.43	1.07	1.61	2.14	2.68	3.21	3.75	4.28	4.82	5.35
Bolivia 50 Centavos	1873-1882	12.50	0.900	0.362	s	0.36	0.72	1.09	1.45	3.62	5.43	7.24	9.05	10.86	12.67	14.48	16.29	18.10
Bolivia 50 Centavos	1884-1908	11.50	0.900	0.333		0.33	0.67	1.00	1.33	3.33	5.00	6.66	8.33	9.99	11.66	13.32	14.99	16.65
Bolivia 50 Centavos	1909	10.00	0.833	0.268		0.27	0.54	0.80	1.07	2.68	4.02	5.36	6.70	8.04	9.38	10.72	12.06	13.40
Bolivia 100 Pesos	1975	10.00	0.933	0.300		0.30	0.60	0.90	1.20	3.00	4.50	6.00	7.50	9.00	10.50	12.00	13.50	15.00
Bolivia 200 Pesos	1979	23.33	0.925	0.694		0.69	1.39	2.08	2.78	6.94	10.41	13.88	17.35	20.81	24.28	27.75	31.22	34.69
Bolivia 250 Pesos	1975	15.00	0.933	0.450		0.45	0.90	1.35	1.80	4.50	6.75	9.00	11.25	13.50	15.75	18.00	20.25	22.50
Bolivia 500 Pesos	1975	22.00	0.933	0.660	s	0.66	1.32	1.98	2.64	6.60	9.90	13.20	16.50	19.80	23.10	26.40	29.70	33.00
Bosnia 750 Dinara	1993-1997	28.28	0.925	0.841		0.84	1.68	2.52	3.36	8.41	12.62	16.82	21.03	25.23	29.44	33.64	37.85	42.05
Bosnia 10 Marka	1998	28.28	0.925	0.841		0.84	1.68	2.52	3.36	8.41	12.62	16.82	21.03	25.23	29.44	33.64	37.85	42.05
Bosnia 1 Suverena	1994-1998	31.10	0.999	1.000		1.00	2.00	3.00	4.00	10.00	15.00	20.00	25.00	30.00	35.00	40.00	45.00	50.00
Bosnia 14 ECUs	1993-1995	10.00	0.925	0.297	v	0.30	0.59	0.89	1.19	2.97	4.46	5.94	7.43	8.91	10.40	11.88	13.37	14.85
Bosnia 14 + 2 ECUs	1993	9.97	0.999	0.321		0.32	0.64	0.96	1.28	3.21	4.82	6.42	8.03	9.63	11.24	12.84	14.45	16.05
Bosnia 21 + 3 ECUs	1993	15.56	0.999	0.500		0.50	1.00	1.50	2.00	5.00	7.50	10.00	12.50	15.00	17.50	20.00	22.50	25.00
Bosnia 14 Euros	1996-1999	10.00	0.925	0.297	s	0.30	0.59	0.89	1.19	2.97	4.46	5.94	7.43	8.91	10.40	11.88	13.37	14.85
Botswana 50 Cents	1966	10.00	0.800	0.257		0.26	0.51	0.77	1.03	2.57	3.86	5.14	6.43	7.71	9.00	10.28	11.57	12.85
Botswana 2 Pula	1986	28.28	0.500	0.455		0.46	0.91	1.37	1.82	4.55	6.83	9.10	11.38	13.65	15.93	18.20	20.48	22.75
Botswana 2 Pula	1986-1989	28.28	0.925	0.841		0.84	1.68	2.52	3.36	8.41	12.62	16.82	21.03	25.23	29.44	33.64	37.85	42.06

Country & Denomination	Years Minted	Grams Weight	Fineness	Troy (ASW)	Code	$ Value 1	$ Value 2	$ Value 3	$ Value 4	$ Value 10	$ Value 15	$ Value 20	$ Value 25	$ Value 30	$ Value 35	$ Value 40	$ Value 45	$ Value 50
Botswana 5 Pula	1976-1978	28.28	0.500	0.455		0.46	0.91	1.37	1.82	4.55	6.83	9.10	11.38	13.65	15.93	18.20	20.48	22.75
Botswana 5 Pula	1976-1988	28.50	0.925	0.848	N	0.85	1.70	2.54	3.39	8.48	12.72	16.96	21.20	25.44	29.68	33.92	38.16	42.40
Botswana 10 Pula	1978	35.00	0.500	0.563		0.56	1.13	1.69	2.25	5.63	8.45	11.26	14.08	16.89	19.71	22.52	25.34	28.15
Botswana 10 Pula	1978	35.00	0.925	1.041		1.04	2.08	3.12	4.16	10.41	15.62	20.82	26.03	31.23	36.44	41.64	46.85	52.05
Brazil 80 Reis	1810-1833	2.24	0.917	0.066	S	0.07	0.13	0.20	0.26	0.66	0.99	1.32	1.65	1.98	2.31	2.64	2.97	3.30
Brazil 160 Reis	1809	4.52	0.917	0.133		0.13	0.27	0.40	0.53	1.33	2.00	2.66	3.33	3.99	4.66	5.32	5.99	6.65
Brazil 160 Reis	1810-1833	4.48	0.917	0.131	S	0.13	0.26	0.39	0.52	1.31	1.97	2.62	3.28	3.93	4.59	5.24	5.90	6.55
Brazil 200 Reis	1835-1848	4.48	0.917	0.131	S	0.13	0.26	0.39	0.52	1.31	1.97	2.62	3.28	3.93	4.59	5.24	5.90	6.55
Brazil 200 Reis	1854-1867	2.55	0.917	0.075	S	0.08	0.15	0.23	0.30	0.75	1.13	1.50	1.88	2.25	2.63	3.00	3.38	3.75
Brazil 200 Reis	1867-1869	2.55	0.835	0.067		0.07	0.13	0.20	0.27	0.67	1.01	1.34	1.68	2.01	2.35	2.68	3.02	3.35
Brazil 320 Reis	1809	9.05	0.917	0.267		0.27	0.53	0.80	1.07	2.67	4.01	5.34	6.68	8.01	9.35	10.68	12.02	13.35
Brazil 320 Reis	1800-1833	8.96	0.917	0.264	S	0.26	0.53	0.79	1.06	2.64	3.96	5.28	6.60	7.92	9.24	10.56	11.88	13.20
Brazil 400 Reis	1834-1848	8.96	0.917	0.264	S	0.26	0.53	0.79	1.06	2.64	3.96	5.28	6.60	7.92	9.24	10.56	11.88	13.20
Brazil 400 Reis	1900	5.10	0.917	0.150		0.15	0.30	0.45	0.60	1.50	2.25	3.00	3.75	4.50	5.25	6.00	6.75	7.50
Brazil 500 Reis	1848-1867	6.38	0.917	0.188		0.19	0.38	0.56	0.75	1.88	2.82	3.76	4.70	5.64	6.58	7.52	8.46	9.40
Brazil 500 Reis	1867, 1868	6.25	0.835	0.168		0.17	0.34	0.50	0.67	1.68	2.52	3.36	4.20	5.04	5.88	6.72	7.56	8.40
Brazil 500 Reis	1876-1889	6.38	0.917	0.188	S	0.19	0.38	0.56	0.75	1.88	2.82	3.76	4.70	5.64	6.58	7.52	8.46	9.40
Brazil 500 Reis	1906-1913	5.00	0.900	0.145		0.15	0.29	0.44	0.58	1.45	2.18	2.90	3.63	4.35	5.08	5.80	6.53	7.25
Brazil 640 Reis	1801-1805	17.76	0.917	0.523		0.52	1.05	1.57	2.09	5.23	7.85	10.46	13.08	15.69	18.31	20.92	23.54	26.15
Brazil 640 Reis	1806-1833	17.92	0.917	0.528		0.53	1.06	1.58	2.11	5.28	7.92	10.56	13.20	15.84	18.48	21.12	23.76	26.40
Brazil 640 Reis	1809	18.11	0.917	0.534		0.53	1.07	1.60	2.14	5.34	8.01	10.68	13.35	16.02	18.69	21.36	24.03	26.70
Brazil 640 Reis	1810-1821	19.32	0.917	0.569	S	0.57	1.14	1.71	2.28	5.69	8.54	11.38	14.23	17.07	19.92	22.76	25.61	28.45
Brazil 800 Reis	1835-1846	17.93	0.917	0.528	S	0.53	1.06	1.58	2.11	5.28	7.92	10.56	13.20	15.84	18.48	21.12	23.76	26.40
Brazil 960 Reis	1810-1834	26.89	0.896	0.775	S	0.78	1.55	2.33	3.10	7.75	11.63	15.50	19.38	23.25	27.13	31.00	34.88	38.75
Brazil 960 Reis	1816-1822	27.07	0.903	0.786		0.79	1.57	2.36	3.14	7.86	11.79	15.72	19.65	23.58	27.51	31.44	35.37	39.30
Brazil 1000 Reis	1849-1900	12.75	0.917	0.376	S	0.38	0.75	1.13	1.50	3.76	5.64	7.52	9.40	11.28	13.16	15.04	16.92	18.80
Brazil 1000 Reis	1906-1913	10.00	0.900	0.289		0.29	0.58	0.87	1.16	2.89	4.34	5.78	7.23	8.67	10.12	11.56	13.01	14.45
Brazil 1200 Reis	1834-1847	26.89	0.917	0.792	S	0.79	1.58	2.38	3.17	7.92	11.88	15.84	19.80	23.76	27.72	31.68	35.64	39.60
Brazil 2000 Reis	1851-1900	25.50	0.917	0.752	S	0.75	1.50	2.26	3.01	7.52	11.28	15.04	18.80	22.56	26.32	30.08	33.84	37.60
Brazil 2000 Reis	1906-1913	20.00	0.900	0.579		0.58	1.16	1.74	2.32	5.79	8.69	11.58	14.48	17.37	20.27	23.16	26.06	28.95
Brazil 2000 Reis	1922	7.90	0.900	0.229		0.23	0.46	0.69	0.92	2.29	3.44	4.58	5.73	6.87	8.02	9.16	10.31	11.45
Brazil 2000 Reis	1924-1935	7.90	0.500	0.127		0.13	0.25	0.38	0.51	1.27	1.91	2.54	3.18	3.81	4.45	5.08	5.72	6.35
Brazil 4000 Reis	1900	51.00	0.917	1.500		1.50	3.00	4.50	6.00	15.00	22.50	30.00	37.50	45.00	52.50	60.00	67.50	75.00
Brazil 5000 Reis	1936-1938	10.00	0.600	0.193		0.19	0.39	0.58	0.77	1.93	2.90	3.86	4.83	5.79	6.76	7.72	8.69	9.65
Brazil 10 Cruzeiros	1975	11.30	0.800	0.291		0.29	0.58	0.87	1.16	2.91	4.37	5.82	7.28	8.73	10.19	11.64	13.10	14.55
Brazil 20 Cruzeiros	1972	18.00	0.900	0.521		0.52	1.04	1.56	2.08	5.21	7.82	10.42	13.03	15.63	18.24	20.84	23.45	26.05
Brazil 200 Novos Cruzados	1989	13.47	0.999	0.433		0.43	0.87	1.30	1.73	4.33	6.50	8.66	10.83	12.99	15.16	17.32	19.49	21.65
Brazil 500 Cruzados	1991	27.00	0.925	0.803		0.80	1.61	2.41	3.21	8.03	12.05	16.06	20.08	24.09	28.11	32.12	36.14	40.15
Brazil 2000 Cruzeiros	1992	27.00	0.925	0.803		0.80	1.61	2.41	3.21	8.03	12.05	16.06	20.08	24.09	28.11	32.12	36.14	40.15
Brazil 2 Reais	1994-1995	27.00	0.925	0.803		0.80	1.61	2.41	3.21	8.03	12.05	16.06	20.08	24.09	28.11	32.12	36.14	40.15
Brazil 3 Reais	1997	11.50	0.925	0.342		0.34	0.68	1.03	1.37	3.42	5.13	6.84	8.55	10.26	11.97	13.68	15.39	17.10
Brazil 4 Reais	1994	27.00	0.925	0.803		0.80	1.61	2.41	3.21	8.03	12.05	16.06	20.08	24.09	28.11	32.12	36.14	40.15
Brazil 4 Reais	2000	28.00	0.999	0.899		0.90	1.80	2.70	3.60	8.99	13.49	17.98	22.48	26.97	31.47	35.96	40.46	44.95

Country & Denomination	Years Minted	Grams Weight	Fine-ness	Troy (ASW)	Code	$ Value 1	$ Value 2	$ Value 3	$ Value 4	$ Value 10	$ Value 15	$ Value 20	$ Value 25	$ Value 30	$ Value 35	$ Value 40	$ Value 45	$ Value 50
British Guiana---see Guyana																		
British Honduras 10 Cents*	1894-1946	2.32	0.925	0.069		0.07	0.14	0.21	0.28	0.69	1.04	1.38	1.73	2.07	2.42	2.76	3.11	3.46
British Honduras 25 Cents	1894-1919	5.81	0.925	0.173		0.17	0.35	0.52	0.69	1.73	2.59	3.46	4.32	5.18	6.05	6.91	7.78	8.64
British Honduras 50 Cents	1894-1919	11.62	0.925	0.346		0.35	0.69	1.04	1.38	3.46	5.18	6.91	8.64	10.37	12.10	13.82	15.55	17.28
British North Borneo 25 Cents	1929	2.83	0.500	0.045		0.05	0.09	0.14	0.18	0.45	0.68	0.90	1.13	1.35	1.58	1.80	2.03	2.25
British Virgin Isl. 1 Cent	1977-1985	1.50	0.925	0.050	N	0.05	0.10	0.15	0.20	0.50	0.75	1.00	1.25	1.50	1.75	2.00	2.25	2.50
British Virgin Isl. 5 Cents	1977-1985	3.00	0.925	0.106	N	0.11	0.21	0.32	0.42	1.06	1.59	2.12	2.65	3.18	3.71	4.24	4.77	5.30
British Virgin Isl. 10 Cents	1977-1985	6.50	0.925	0.190	N	0.19	0.38	0.57	0.76	1.90	2.85	3.80	4.75	5.70	6.65	7.60	8.55	9.50
British Virgin Isl. 25 Cents	1977-1985	7.50	0.925	0.262	N	0.26	0.52	0.79	1.05	2.62	3.93	5.24	6.55	7.86	9.17	10.48	11.79	13.10
British Virgin Isl. 50 Cents	1977-1985	15.50	0.925	0.497	N	0.50	0.99	1.49	1.99	4.97	7.46	9.94	12.43	14.91	17.40	19.88	22.37	24.85
British Virgin Isl. 1 Dollar	1973-1984	25.70	0.925	0.764	N	0.76	1.53	2.29	3.06	7.64	11.46	15.28	19.10	22.92	26.74	30.56	34.38	38.20
British Virgin Isl. 1 Dollar	1985	24.74	0.925	0.736	N	0.74	1.47	2.21	2.94	7.36	11.04	14.72	18.40	22.08	25.76	29.44	33.12	36.80
British Virgin Isl. 5 Dollars	1979-1984	40.50	0.925	1.200	N	1.20	2.40	3.60	4.80	12.00	18.00	24.00	30.00	36.00	42.00	48.00	54.00	60.00
British Virgin Isl. 10 Dollars	1983	30.28	0.500	0.487		0.49	0.97	1.46	1.95	4.87	7.31	9.74	12.18	14.61	17.05	19.48	21.92	24.35
British Virgin Isl. 10 Dollars	2000	28.28	0.925	0.841		0.84	1.68	2.52	3.36	8.41	12.62	16.82	21.03	25.23	29.44	33.64	37.85	42.05
British Virgin Isl. 20 Dollars	1985	19.09	0.925	0.568		0.57	1.14	1.70	2.27	5.68	8.52	11.36	14.20	17.04	19.88	22.72	25.56	28.40
British Virgin Isl. 20 Dollars	2000	19.10	0.925	0.570	V	0.57	1.14	1.71	2.28	5.70	8.55	11.40	14.25	17.10	19.95	22.80	25.65	28.50
British Virgin Isl. 25 Dollars	1978	28.10	0.925	0.836		0.84	1.67	2.51	3.34	8.36	12.54	16.72	20.90	25.08	29.26	33.44	37.62	41.80
British Virgin Isl. 25 Dollars	1988	20.09	0.925	0.598		0.60	1.20	1.79	2.39	5.98	8.97	11.96	14.95	17.94	20.93	23.92	26.91	29.90
British Virgin Isl. 25 Dollars	1992-1997	21.54	0.925	0.641	S, V	0.64	1.28	1.92	2.56	6.41	9.62	12.82	16.03	19.23	22.44	25.64	28.85	32.05
British Virgin Isl. 25 Dollars	1993	20.09	0.925	0.598		0.60	1.20	1.79	2.39	5.98	8.97	11.96	14.95	17.94	20.93	23.92	26.91	29.90
British Virgin Isl. 25 Dollars	1993	21.35	0.925	0.635		0.64	1.27	1.91	2.54	6.35	9.53	12.70	15.88	19.05	22.23	25.40	28.58	31.75
British West Africa 3 Pence	1913-1919	1.14	0.925	0.042		0.04	0.08	0.13	0.17	0.42	0.63	0.84	1.05	1.26	1.47	1.68	1.89	2.10
British West Africa 3 Pence	1920	1.14	0.500	0.023		0.02	0.05	0.07	0.09	0.23	0.35	0.46	0.58	0.69	0.81	0.92	1.04	1.15
British West Africa 6 Pence	1913-1919	2.83	0.925	0.084		0.08	0.17	0.25	0.34	0.84	1.26	1.68	2.10	2.52	2.94	3.36	3.78	4.20
British West Africa 6 Pence	1920	2.83	0.500	0.045		0.05	0.09	0.14	0.18	0.45	0.68	0.90	1.13	1.35	1.58	1.80	2.03	2.25
British West Africa 1 Shilling	1913-1936	5.66	0.925	0.168		0.17	0.34	0.50	0.67	1.68	2.52	3.36	4.20	5.04	5.88	6.72	7.56	8.40
British West Africa 2 Shillings	1913-1920	11.31	0.925	0.336		0.34	0.67	1.01	1.34	3.36	5.04	6.72	8.40	10.08	11.76	13.44	15.12	16.80
British West Africa 2 Shillings	1920	11.31	0.500	0.182		0.18	0.36	0.55	0.73	1.82	2.73	3.64	4.55	5.46	6.37	7.28	8.19	9.10
British West Indies 1/16 Dollar	1820-1822	1.64	0.892	0.048		0.05	0.10	0.14	0.19	0.48	0.72	0.96	1.20	1.44	1.68	1.92	2.16	2.40
British West Indies 1/8 Dollar	1820-1822	3.28	0.892	0.096		0.10	0.19	0.29	0.38	0.96	1.44	1.92	2.40	2.88	3.36	3.84	4.32	4.80
British West Indies 1/4 Dollar	1820-1822	6.65	0.892	0.192		0.19	0.38	0.58	0.77	1.92	2.88	3.84	4.80	5.76	6.72	7.68	8.64	9.60
British West Indies 1/2 Dollar	1821, 1822	13.41	0.892	0.384		0.38	0.77	1.15	1.54	3.84	5.76	7.68	9.60	11.52	13.44	15.36	17.28	19.20
Brunei 1 Sen	1987-1993	2.92	0.925	0.087		0.09	0.17	0.26	0.35	0.87	1.31	1.74	2.18	2.61	3.05	3.48	3.92	4.35
Brunei 5 Sen	1987-1993	1.65	0.925	0.049		0.05	0.10	0.15	0.20	0.49	0.74	0.98	1.23	1.47	1.72	1.96	2.21	2.45
Brunei 10 Sen	1987-1993	3.35	0.925	0.100		0.10	0.20	0.30	0.40	1.00	1.50	2.00	2.50	3.00	3.50	4.00	4.50	5.00
Brunei 20 Sen	1987-1993	6.51	0.925	0.194		0.19	0.39	0.58	0.78	1.94	2.91	3.88	4.85	5.82	6.79	7.76	8.73	9.70
Brunei 50 Sen	1987-1993	10.82	0.925	0.322		0.32	0.64	0.97	1.29	3.22	4.83	6.44	8.05	9.66	11.27	12.88	14.49	16.10
Brunei 1 Dollar	1987-1993	18.05	0.925	0.537	N	0.54	1.07	1.61	2.15	5.37	8.06	10.74	13.43	16.11	18.80	21.48	24.17	26.85

Country & Denomination	Years Minted	Grams Weight	Fine-ness	Troy (ASW)	Code	$ Value 1	$ Value 2	$ Value 3	$ Value 4	$ Value 10	$ Value 15	$ Value 20	$ Value 25	$ Value 30	$ Value 35	$ Value 40	$ Value 45	$ Value 50
Brunei 1 Dollar	1992-1994	18.20	0.925	0.539	N	0.54	1.08	1.62	2.16	5.39	8.09	10.78	13.48	16.17	18.87	21.56	24.26	26.95
Brunei 5 Dollars	1994	28.28	0.925	0.841	N	0.84	1.68	2.52	3.36	8.41	12.62	16.82	21.03	25.23	29.44	33.64	37.85	42.05
Brunei 10 Dollars	1977-1978	28.28	0.925	0.841		0.84	1.68	2.52	3.36	8.41	12.62	16.82	21.03	25.23	29.44	33.64	37.85	42.05
Brunei 10 Dollars	1994	30.70	0.925	0.913		0.91	1.83	2.74	3.65	9.13	13.70	18.26	22.83	27.39	31.96	36.52	41.09	45.65
Brunei 20 Dollars	1987-1988	28.28	0.925	0.841		0.84	1.68	2.52	3.36	8.41	12.62	16.82	21.03	25.23	29.44	33.64	37.85	42.05
Brunei 20 Dollars	1999	62.20	0.999	2.000		2.00	4.00	6.00	8.00	20.00	30.00	40.00	50.00	60.00	70.00	80.00	90.00	100.00
Brunei 25 Dollars	1992	31.10	0.925	0.925		0.93	1.85	2.78	3.70	9.25	13.88	18.50	23.13	27.75	32.38	37.00	41.63	46.25
Brunei 30 Dollars	1997	62.20	0.999	2.000		2.00	4.00	6.00	8.00	20.00	30.00	40.00	50.00	60.00	70.00	80.00	90.00	100.00
Brunei 50 Dollars	1980	28.28	0.925	0.841		0.84	1.68	2.52	3.36	8.41	12.62	16.82	21.03	25.23	29.44	33.64	37.85	42.05
Brunei 50 Dollars	1992	30.70	0.925	0.913		0.91	1.83	2.74	3.65	9.13	13.70	18.26	22.83	27.39	31.96	36.52	41.09	45.65
Brunei 50 Dollars	1996	62.20	0.999	2.000		2.00	4.00	6.00	8.00	20.00	30.00	40.00	50.00	60.00	70.00	80.00	90.00	100.00
Brunei 100 Dollars	1984	28.28	0.925	0.841		0.84	1.68	2.52	3.36	8.41	12.62	16.82	21.03	25.23	29.44	33.64	37.85	42.05
Brunei 100 Dollars	1988	31.10	0.925	0.925		0.93	1.85	2.78	3.70	9.25	13.88	18.50	23.13	27.75	32.38	37.00	41.63	46.25
Bulgaria 50 Stotinki	1883, 1891	2.50	0.835	0.067		0.07	0.13	0.20	0.27	0.67	1.01	1.34	1.68	2.01	2.35	2.68	3.02	3.35
Bulgaria 1 Lev	1882-1916	5.00	0.835	0.134	S	0.13	0.27	0.40	0.54	1.34	2.01	2.68	3.35	4.02	4.69	5.36	6.03	6.70
Bulgaria 2 Leva	1882-1916	10.00	0.835	0.269	S	0.27	0.54	0.81	1.08	2.69	4.04	5.38	6.73	8.07	9.42	10.76	12.11	13.45
Bulgaria 2 Leva	1963-1964	8.88	0.900	0.257		0.26	0.51	0.77	1.03	2.57	3.86	5.14	6.43	7.71	9.00	10.28	11.57	12.85
Bulgaria 5 Leva	1884-1894	25.00	0.900	0.723	S	0.72	1.45	2.17	2.89	7.23	10.85	14.46	18.08	21.69	25.31	28.92	32.54	36.15
Bulgaria 5 Leva	1963-1964	16.67	0.900	0.482		0.48	0.96	1.45	1.93	4.82	7.23	9.64	12.05	14.46	16.87	19.28	21.69	24.10
Bulgaria 5 Leva	1970-1976	20.50	0.900	0.593		0.59	1.19	1.78	2.37	5.93	8.90	11.86	14.83	17.79	20.76	23.72	26.69	29.65
Bulgaria 5 Leva	1976-1979	20.50	0.500	0.330		0.33	0.66	0.99	1.32	3.30	4.95	6.60	8.25	9.90	11.55	13.20	14.85	16.50
Bulgaria 10 Leva	1975	29.95	0.900	0.867		0.87	1.73	2.60	3.47	8.67	13.01	17.34	21.68	26.01	30.35	34.68	39.02	43.35
Bulgaria 10 Leva	1978	29.85	0.500	0.490		0.49	0.98	1.47	1.96	4.90	7.35	9.80	12.25	14.70	17.15	19.60	22.05	24.50
Bulgaria 10 Leva	1979	23.33	0.925	0.694		0.69	1.39	2.08	2.78	6.94	10.41	13.88	17.35	20.82	24.29	27.76	31.23	34.70
Bulgaria 10 Leva	1979	14.00	0.500	0.225		0.23	0.45	0.68	0.90	2.25	3.38	4.50	5.63	6.75	7.88	9.00	10.13	11.25
Bulgaria 10 Leva	1979, 1984	23.32	0.925	0.694		0.69	1.39	2.08	2.78	6.94	10.41	13.88	17.35	20.82	24.29	27.76	31.23	34.70
Bulgaria 10 Leva	1979	23.85	0.900	0.690		0.69	1.38	2.07	2.76	6.90	10.35	13.80	17.25	20.70	24.15	27.60	31.05	34.50
Bulgaria 10 Leva	1982	18.88	0.500	0.304		0.30	0.61	0.91	1.22	3.04	4.56	6.08	7.60	9.12	10.64	12.16	13.68	15.20
Bulgaria 10 Leva	1985-1988	18.75	0.640	0.386		0.39	0.77	1.16	1.54	3.86	5.79	7.72	9.65	11.58	13.51	15.44	17.37	19.30
Bulgaria 10 Leva	1999, 2000	23.30	0.925	0.694		0.69	1.39	2.08	2.78	6.94	10.41	13.88	17.35	20.82	24.29	27.76	31.23	34.70
Bulgaria 20 Leva	1930	4.00	0.500	0.064		0.06	0.13	0.19	0.26	0.64	0.96	1.28	1.60	1.92	2.24	2.56	2.88	3.20
Bulgaria 20 Leva	1979	21.80	0.500	0.351		0.35	0.70	1.05	1.40	3.51	5.27	7.02	8.78	10.53	12.29	14.04	15.80	17.55
Bulgaria 20 Leva	1979	32.00	0.900	0.926		0.93	1.85	2.78	3.70	9.26	13.89	18.52	23.15	27.78	32.41	37.04	41.67	46.30
Bulgaria 20 Leva	1982	14.00	0.500	0.225		0.23	0.45	0.68	0.90	2.25	3.38	4.50	5.63	6.75	7.88	9.00	10.13	11.25
Bulgaria 20 Leva	1987-1988	11.20	0.500	0.180	V	0.18	0.36	0.54	0.72	1.80	2.70	3.60	4.50	5.40	6.30	7.20	8.10	9.00
Bulgaria 20 Leva	1989	12.13	0.500	0.214		0.21	0.43	0.64	0.86	2.14	3.21	4.28	5.35	6.42	7.49	8.56	9.63	10.70
Bulgaria 25 Leva	1982-1984	14.00	0.500	0.225		0.23	0.45	0.68	0.90	2.25	3.38	4.50	5.63	6.75	7.88	9.00	10.13	11.25
Bulgaria 25 Leva	1986-1990	23.33	0.925	0.694		0.69	1.39	2.08	2.78	6.94	10.41	13.88	17.35	20.82	24.29	27.76	31.23	34.70
Bulgaria 50 Leva	1930-1934	10.00	0.500	0.161		0.16	0.32	0.48	0.64	1.61	2.42	3.22	4.03	4.83	5.64	6.44	7.25	8.05
Bulgaria 50 Leva	1981	20.50	0.900	0.593		0.59	1.19	1.78	2.37	5.93	8.90	11.86	14.83	17.79	20.76	23.72	26.69	29.65
Bulgaria 100 Leva	1930-1937	20.00	0.500	0.322		0.32	0.64	0.97	1.29	3.22	4.83	6.44	8.05	9.66	11.27	12.88	14.49	16.10
Bulgaria 100 Leva	1992-1993	23.33	0.925	0.694		0.69	1.39	2.08	2.78	6.94	10.41	13.88	17.35	20.82	24.29	27.76	31.23	34.70
Bulgaria 500 Leva	1993	33.63	0.925	1.000		1.00	2.00	3.00	4.00	10.00	15.00	20.00	25.00	30.00	35.00	40.00	45.00	50.00
Bulgaria 500 Leva	1994	23.00	0.925	0.684		0.68	1.37	2.05	2.74	6.84	10.26	13.68	17.10	20.52	23.94	27.36	30.78	34.20

Country & Denomination	Years Minted	Grams Weight	Fine-ness	Troy (ASW)	Code	$ Value 1	$ Value 2	$ Value 3	$ Value 4	$ Value 10	$ Value 15	$ Value 20	$ Value 25	$ Value 30	$ Value 35	$ Value 40	$ Value 45	$ Value 50
Bulgaria 500 Leva	1996	10.00	0.925	0.297		0.30	0.59	0.89	1.19	2.97	4.46	5.94	7.43	8.91	10.40	11.88	13.37	14.85
Bulgaria 1000 Leva	1995-1997	23.33	0.925	0.694		0.69	1.39	2.08	2.78	6.94	10.41	13.88	17.35	20.82	24.29	27.76	31.23	34.70
Bulgaria 1000 Leva	1996	33.63	0.925	1.000		1.00	2.00	3.00	4.00	10.00	15.00	20.00	25.00	30.00	35.00	40.00	45.00	50.00
Bulgaria 5000 Leva	1998	10.00	0.925	0.297		0.30	0.59	0.89	1.19	2.97	4.46	5.94	7.43	8.91	10.40	11.88	13.37	14.85
Burma--see Myanmar																		
C																		
Burundi 5 Francs	1962	24.11	0.900	0.698		0.70	1.40	2.09	2.79	6.98	10.47	13.96	17.45	20.94	24.43	27.92	31.41	34.90
Cambodia 25 Centimes	1860	1.25	0.900	0.036		0.04	0.07	0.11	0.14	0.36	0.54	0.72	0.90	1.08	1.26	1.44	1.62	1.80
Cambodia 50 Centimes	1860	2.50	0.900	0.072		0.07	0.14	0.22	0.29	0.72	1.08	1.44	1.80	2.16	2.52	2.88	3.24	3.60
Cambodia 1 Franc	1860	5.00	0.900	0.145	>	0.15	0.29	0.44	0.58	1.45	2.18	2.90	3.63	4.35	5.08	5.80	6.53	7.25
Cambodia 1 Franc	1860	10.00	0.900	0.289	>	0.29	0.58	0.87	1.16	2.89	4.34	5.78	7.23	8.67	10.12	11.56	13.01	14.45
Cambodia 4 Francs	1860	20.00	0.900	0.579	>	0.58	1.16	1.74	2.32	5.79	8.69	11.58	14.48	17.37	20.27	23.16	26.06	28.95
Cambodia 1 Piastre	1860	27.00	0.900	0.781		0.78	1.56	2.34	3.12	7.81	11.72	15.62	19.53	23.43	27.34	31.24	35.15	39.05
Cambodia (Kampuchea) 20 Riels	1988-1989	16.00	0.999	0.515		0.52	1.03	1.55	2.06	5.15	7.73	10.30	12.88	15.45	18.03	20.60	23.18	25.75
Cambodia (Kampuchea) 20 Riels	1988-1989	12.00	0.999	0.386		0.39	0.77	1.16	1.54	3.86	5.79	7.72	9.65	11.58	13.51	15.44	17.37	19.30
Cambodia 20 Riels	1991-1992	11.96	0.999	0.386		0.39	0.77	1.16	1.54	3.86	5.79	7.72	9.65	11.58	13.51	15.44	17.37	19.30
Cambodia 20 Riels	1993	19.95	0.999	0.641		0.64	1.28	1.92	2.56	6.41	9.62	12.82	16.03	19.23	22.44	25.64	28.85	32.05
Cambodia 20 Riels	1993-1995	16.06	0.999	0.515	>	0.52	1.03	1.55	2.06	5.15	7.73	10.30	12.88	15.45	18.03	20.60	23.18	25.75
Cambodia 5000 Riels	1974	19.01	0.925	0.565		0.57	1.13	1.70	2.26	5.65	8.48	11.30	14.13	16.95	19.78	22.60	25.43	28.25
Cambodia 10,000 Riels	1974	38.03	0.925	1.130		1.13	2.26	3.39	4.52	11.30	16.95	22.60	28.25	33.90	39.55	45.20	50.85	56.50
Canada 5 Cents	1858-1917	1.16	0.925	0.035		0.04	0.07	0.11	0.14	0.35	0.53	0.70	0.88	1.05	1.23	1.40	1.58	1.75
Canada 5 Cents	1920-1921	1.16	0.800	0.030		0.03	0.06	0.09	0.12	0.30	0.45	0.60	0.75	0.90	1.05	1.20	1.35	1.50
Canada 5 Cents	1998	1.16	0.925	0.035	N	0.04	0.07	0.11	0.14	0.35	0.53	0.70	0.88	1.05	1.23	1.40	1.58	1.75
Canada 5 Cents	2000	5.35	0.925	0.159	N	0.16	0.32	0.48	0.64	1.59	2.39	3.18	3.98	4.77	5.57	6.36	7.16	7.95
Canada 10 Cents	1858-1917	2.33	0.925	0.069		0.07	0.14	0.21	0.28	0.69	1.04	1.38	1.73	2.07	2.42	2.76	3.11	3.45
Canada 10 Cents	1920-1967	2.33	0.800	0.060		0.06	0.12	0.18	0.24	0.60	0.90	1.20	1.50	1.80	2.10	2.40	2.70	3.00
Canada 10 Cents	1967-1968	2.33	0.500	0.037		0.04	0.07	0.11	0.15	0.37	0.56	0.74	0.93	1.11	1.30	1.48	1.67	1.85
Canada 10 Cents	1997, 2000	2.40	0.925	0.071	N	0.07	0.14	0.21	0.28	0.71	1.07	1.42	1.78	2.13	2.49	2.84	3.20	3.55
Canada 10 Cents	1998	2.33	0.925	0.069	N	0.07	0.14	0.21	0.28	0.69	1.04	1.38	1.73	2.07	2.42	2.76	3.11	3.45
Canada 20 Cents	1858	4.65	0.925	0.138		0.14	0.28	0.41	0.55	1.38	2.07	2.76	3.45	4.14	4.83	5.52	6.21	6.90
Canada 25 Cents	1870-1919	5.83	0.925	0.173		0.17	0.35	0.52	0.69	1.73	2.60	3.46	4.33	5.19	6.06	6.92	7.79	8.65
Canada 25 Cents	1920-1967	5.83	0.800	0.150		0.15	0.30	0.45	0.60	1.50	2.25	3.00	3.75	4.50	5.25	6.00	6.75	7.50
Canada 25 Cents	1968	5.83	0.500	0.094	N	0.09	0.19	0.28	0.38	0.94	1.41	1.88	2.35	2.82	3.29	3.76	4.23	4.70
Canada 25 Cents	1992-2000	5.83	0.925	0.173		0.17	0.35	0.52	0.69	1.73	2.60	3.46	4.33	5.19	6.06	6.92	7.79	8.65
Canada 50 Cents	1870-1910	11.62	0.925	0.345		0.35	0.69	1.04	1.38	3.45	5.18	6.90	8.63	10.35	12.08	13.80	15.53	17.25
Canada 50 Cents	1910-1919	11.66	0.925	0.346		0.35	0.69	1.04	1.38	3.46	5.19	6.92	8.65	10.38	12.11	13.84	15.57	17.30
Canada 50 Cents	1920-1967	11.66	0.800	0.300		0.30	0.60	0.90	1.20	3.00	4.50	6.00	7.50	9.00	10.50	12.00	13.50	15.00
Canada 50 Cents	1995-2000	11.66	0.925	0.346	N	0.35	0.69	1.04	1.38	3.46	5.19	6.92	8.65	10.38	12.11	13.84	15.57	17.30
Canada 1 Dollar	1935-1967	23.33	0.800	0.600		0.60	1.20	1.80	2.40	6.00	9.00	12.00	15.00	18.00	21.00	24.00	27.00	30.00
Canada 1 Dollar	1971-1991	23.33	0.500	0.375	N	0.38	0.75	1.13	1.50	3.75	5.63	7.50	9.38	11.25	13.13	15.00	16.88	18.75
Canada 1 Dollar	1992-2000	25.18	0.925	0.749	N	0.75	1.50	2.25	3.00	7.49	11.24	14.98	18.73	22.47	26.22	29.96	33.71	37.45
Canada 5 Dollars Olympic	1973-1976	24.30	0.925	0.723		0.72	1.45	2.17	2.89	7.23	10.85	14.46	18.08	21.69	25.31	28.92	32.54	36.15

Country & Denomination	Years Minted	Grams Weight	Fine-ness	Troy (ASW)	Code	$ Value 1	$ Value 2	$ Value 3	$ Value 4	$ Value 10	$ Value 15	$ Value 20	$ Value 25	$ Value 30	$ Value 35	$ Value 40	$ Value 45	$ Value 50
Canada 5 Dollars Mapleleaf	1988-2000	31.10	0.999	1.000		1.00	2.00	3.00	4.00	10.00	15.00	20.00	25.00	30.00	35.00	40.00	45.00	50.00
Canada 10 Dollars Olympic	1973-1976	48.60	0.925	1.450		1.45	2.90	4.35	5.80	14.50	21.75	29.00	36.25	43.50	50.75	58.00	65.25	72.50
Canada 20 Dollars Olympic	1985-1987	34.10	0.925	1.000		1.00	2.00	3.00	4.00	10.00	15.00	20.00	25.00	30.00	35.00	40.00	45.00	50.00
Canada 20 Dollars	1990-2000	31.10	0.925	0.974		0.97	1.95	2.92	3.90	9.74	14.61	19.48	24.35	29.22	34.09	38.96	43.83	48.70
Canada 50 Dollars Mapleleaf	1998	311.04	0.999	10.000		10.00	20.00	30.00	40.00	100.00	150.00	200.00	250.00	300.00	350.00	400.00	450.00	500.00
Cape Verde 1 Escudo*	1985	4.00	0.925	0.119		0.12	0.24	0.36	0.48	1.19	1.79	2.38	2.98	3.57	4.17	4.76	5.36	5.95
Cape Verde 10 Escudos	1953	5.00	0.720	0.116		0.12	0.23	0.35	0.46	1.16	1.74	2.32	2.90	3.48	4.06	4.64	5.22	5.80
Cape Verde 50 Escudos	1984	27.00	0.925	0.796		0.80	1.59	2.39	3.18	7.96	11.94	15.92	19.90	23.88	27.86	31.84	35.82	39.80
Cape Verde 250 Escudos	1976	16.40	0.900	0.475		0.48	0.95	1.43	1.90	4.75	7.13	9.50	11.88	14.25	16.63	19.00	21.38	23.75
Cape Verde 1,000 Escudos	1994	28.11	0.925	0.836		0.84	1.67	2.51	3.34	8.36	12.54	16.72	20.90	25.08	29.26	33.44	37.62	41.80
Cayman Islands 50 Cents	1972-1978	10.30	0.925	0.306		0.31	0.61	0.92	1.22	3.06	4.59	6.12	7.65	9.18	10.71	12.24	13.77	15.30
Cayman Islands 1 Dollar	1972-1988	18.00	0.925	0.535		0.54	1.07	1.61	2.14	5.35	8.03	10.70	13.38	16.05	18.73	21.40	24.08	26.75
Cayman Islands 1 Dollar	1990-1994	18.14	0.925	0.540		0.54	1.08	1.62	2.16	5.40	8.10	10.80	13.50	16.20	18.90	21.60	24.30	27.00
Cayman Islands 2 Dollars	1972-1988	29.45	0.925	0.876		0.88	1.75	2.63	3.50	8.76	13.14	17.52	21.90	26.28	30.66	35.04	39.42	43.80
Cayman Islands 5 Dollars	1972-1983	35.50	0.925	1.056		1.06	2.11	3.17	4.22	10.56	15.84	21.12	26.40	31.68	36.96	42.24	47.52	52.80
Cayman Islands 5 Dollars	1985-1996	28.28	0.925	0.841		0.84	1.68	2.52	3.36	8.41	12.62	16.82	21.03	25.23	29.44	33.64	37.85	42.06
Cayman Islands 5 Dollars	1986	28.28	0.500	0.455		0.46	0.91	1.37	1.82	4.55	6.83	9.10	11.38	13.65	15.93	18.20	20.48	22.75
Cayman Islands 5 Dollars	1988	35.64	0.925	1.060		1.06	2.12	3.18	4.24	10.60	15.90	21.20	26.50	31.80	37.10	42.40	47.70	53.00
Cayman Islands 10 Dollars	1981	28.28	0.925	0.841		0.84	1.68	2.52	3.36	8.41	12.62	16.82	21.03	25.23	29.44	33.64	37.85	42.06
Cayman Islands 10 Dollars	1982	27.89	0.925	0.830		0.83	1.66	2.49	3.32	8.30	12.45	16.60	20.75	24.90	29.05	33.20	37.35	41.50
Cayman Islands 10 Dollars	1983	23.45	0.925	0.698		0.70	1.40	2.09	2.79	6.98	10.47	13.96	17.45	20.94	24.43	27.92	31.41	34.90
Cayman Islands 25 Dollars	1972-1978	51.35	0.925	1.527		1.53	3.05	4.58	6.11	15.27	22.91	30.54	38.18	45.81	53.45	61.08	68.72	76.35
Cayman Islands 25 Dollars	1980	35.64	0.500	0.573		0.57	1.15	1.72	2.29	5.73	8.60	11.46	14.33	17.19	20.06	22.92	25.79	28.65
Cayman Islands 25 Dollars	1983	64.80	0.925	1.927		1.93	3.85	5.78	7.71	19.27	28.91	38.54	48.18	57.81	67.45	77.08	86.72	96.35
Cayman Islands 50 Dollars	1975-1978	64.94	0.925	1.931		1.93	3.86	5.79	7.72	19.31	28.97	38.62	48.28	57.93	67.59	77.24	86.90	96.55
Cayman Islands 50 Dollars	1985	129.60	0.925	3.850		3.85	7.70	11.55	15.40	38.50	57.75	77.00	96.25	115.50	134.75	154.00	173.25	192.50
Central Am. Rep. 1/4 Real	1824-1845	0.85	0.903	0.025	s	0.02	0.05	0.07	0.10	0.25	0.37	0.49	0.62	0.74	0.86	0.98	1.11	1.23
Central Am. Rep. 1/2 Real	1824-1849	1.69	0.903	0.049	s	0.05	0.10	0.15	0.20	0.49	0.74	0.98	1.23	1.47	1.72	1.96	2.21	2.45
Central Am. Rep. 1 Real	1824-1849	3.38	0.903	0.178	s	0.18	0.36	0.53	0.71	1.78	2.67	3.56	4.45	5.34	6.23	7.12	8.01	8.90
Central Am. Rep. 2 Reales	1831-1849	6.77	0.903	0.157	s	0.16	0.31	0.47	0.63	1.57	2.35	3.13	3.92	4.70	5.48	6.27	7.05	7.84
Central Am. Rep. 8 Reales	1824-1831	27.07	0.903	0.786		0.79	1.57	2.36	3.14	7.86	11.79	15.72	19.65	23.58	27.51	31.44	35.37	39.30
Ceylon 10 Cents	1892-1917	1.17	0.800	0.030	s	0.03	0.06	0.09	0.12	0.30	0.45	0.60	0.75	0.90	1.05	1.20	1.35	1.50
Ceylon 10 Cents	1919-1928	1.17	0.550	0.021		0.02	0.04	0.06	0.08	0.21	0.32	0.42	0.53	0.63	0.74	0.84	0.95	1.05
Ceylon 10 Cents	1941	1.17	0.800	0.030		0.03	0.06	0.09	0.12	0.30	0.45	0.60	0.75	0.90	1.05	1.20	1.35	1.50
Ceylon 25 Cents	1892-1917	2.92	0.800	0.075	s	0.08	0.15	0.23	0.30	0.75	1.13	1.50	1.88	2.25	2.63	3.00	3.38	3.75
Ceylon 25 Cents	1919-1926	2.92	0.550	0.052		0.05	0.10	0.16	0.21	0.52	0.78	1.04	1.30	1.56	1.82	2.08	2.34	2.60
Ceylon 50 Cents	1892-1917	5.83	0.800	0.150	s	0.15	0.30	0.45	0.60	1.50	2.25	3.00	3.75	4.50	5.25	6.00	6.75	7.50
Ceylon 50 Cents	1919-1929	5.83	0.550	0.103		0.10	0.21	0.31	0.41	1.03	1.55	2.06	2.58	3.09	3.61	4.12	4.64	5.15
Ceylon 50 Cents	1942	5.83	0.800	0.150		0.15	0.30	0.45	0.60	1.50	2.25	3.00	3.75	4.50	5.25	6.00	6.75	7.50
Ceylon 5 Rupees	1957	28.28	0.925	0.841		0.84	1.68	2.52	3.36	8.41	12.62	16.82	21.03	25.23	29.44	33.64	37.85	42.05

Country & Denomination	Years Minted	Grams Weight	Fineness	Troy (ASW)	Code	$ Value 1	$ Value 2	$ Value 3	$ Value 4	$ Value 10	$ Value 15	$ Value 20	$ Value 25	$ Value 30	$ Value 35	$ Value 40	$ Value 45	$ Value 50
Chad 100 Francs	1970	5.00	0.925	0.096		0.10	0.19	0.29	0.38	0.96	1.44	1.92	2.40	2.88	3.36	3.84	4.32	4.80
Chad 200 Francs	1970	15.00	0.925	0.446		0.45	0.89	1.34	1.78	4.46	6.69	8.92	11.15	13.38	15.61	17.84	20.07	22.30
Chad 300 Francs	1970	25.00	0.925	0.892		0.89	1.78	2.68	3.57	8.92	13.38	17.84	22.30	26.76	31.22	35.68	40.14	44.60
Chad 1000 Francs	1999	14.97	0.985	0.474		0.47	0.95	1.42	1.90	4.74	7.11	9.48	11.85	14.22	16.59	18.96	21.33	23.70
Chile 1/4 Real	1800-1818	0.85	0.896	0.024		0.02	0.05	0.07	0.10	0.24	0.36	0.48	0.60	0.72	0.84	0.96	1.08	1.20
Chile 1/2 Real	1800-1817	1.69	0.896	0.049		0.05	0.10	0.15	0.20	0.49	0.74	0.98	1.23	1.47	1.72	1.96	2.21	2.45
Chile 1/2 Real	1833-1851	1.60	0.902	0.045	S, V	0.05	0.09	0.14	0.18	0.45	0.68	0.90	1.13	1.35	1.58	1.80	2.03	2.25
Chile 1 Real	1800-1817	3.38	0.896	0.098		0.10	0.20	0.29	0.39	0.98	1.47	1.96	2.45	2.94	3.43	3.92	4.41	4.90
Chile 1 Real	1834-1842	3.35	0.902	0.098	S, V	0.10	0.20	0.29	0.39	0.98	1.47	1.96	2.45	2.94	3.43	3.92	4.41	4.90
Chile 1 Real	1843-1850	3.00	0.902	0.087		0.09	0.17	0.26	0.35	0.87	1.31	1.74	2.18	2.61	3.05	3.48	3.92	4.35
Chile 2 Reales	1800-1817	6.77	0.896	0.195		0.20	0.39	0.59	0.78	1.95	2.93	3.90	4.88	5.85	6.83	7.80	8.78	9.75
Chile 2 Reales	1834-1853	5.70	0.902	0.165	>	0.17	0.33	0.50	0.66	1.65	2.48	3.30	4.13	4.95	5.78	6.60	7.43	8.25
Chile 4 Reales	1800-1815	13.54	0.896	0.390		0.39	0.78	1.17	1.56	3.90	5.85	7.80	9.75	11.70	13.65	15.60	17.55	19.50
Chile 8 Reales	1800-1817	27.07	0.896	0.780		0.78	1.56	2.34	3.12	7.80	11.70	15.60	19.50	23.40	27.30	31.20	35.10	39.00
Chile 8 Reales	1837-1849	26.70	0.902	0.771	S	0.77	1.54	2.31	3.08	7.71	11.57	15.42	19.28	23.13	26.99	30.84	34.70	38.55
Chile 1/2 Decimo	1851-1859	1.25	0.900	0.036		0.04	0.07	0.11	0.14	0.36	0.54	0.72	0.90	1.08	1.26	1.44	1.62	1.80
Chile 1/2 Decimo	1860-1866	1.15	0.900	0.033		0.03	0.07	0.10	0.13	0.33	0.50	0.66	0.83	0.99	1.16	1.32	1.49	1.65
Chile 1/2 Decimo	1867-1881	1.25	0.835	0.034	S	0.03	0.07	0.10	0.14	0.34	0.51	0.68	0.85	1.02	1.19	1.36	1.53	1.70
Chile 1/2 Decimo	1879-1894	1.25	0.500	0.020	S	0.02	0.04	0.06	0.08	0.20	0.30	0.40	0.50	0.60	0.70	0.80	0.90	1.00
Chile 5 Centavos	1896	1.00	0.835	0.027		0.03	0.05	0.08	0.11	0.27	0.41	0.54	0.68	0.81	0.95	1.08	1.22	1.35
Chile 5 Centavos	1899-1907	1.00	0.500	0.016	S	0.02	0.03	0.05	0.06	0.16	0.24	0.32	0.40	0.48	0.56	0.64	0.72	0.80
Chile 5 Centavos	1908-1919	1.00	0.400	0.013		0.01	0.03	0.04	0.05	0.13	0.20	0.26	0.33	0.39	0.46	0.52	0.59	0.65
Chile 1 Decimo	1851-1859	2.50	0.900	0.072		0.07	0.14	0.22	0.29	0.72	1.08	1.44	1.80	2.16	2.52	2.88	3.24	3.60
Chile 1 Decimo	1860-1866	2.30	0.900	0.067		0.07	0.13	0.20	0.27	0.67	1.01	1.34	1.68	2.01	2.35	2.68	3.02	3.35
Chile 1 Decimo	1867-1880	2.50	0.835	0.067		0.07	0.13	0.20	0.27	0.67	1.01	1.34	1.68	2.01	2.35	2.68	3.02	3.35
Chile 1 Decimo	1879-1894	2.50	0.500	0.040		0.04	0.08	0.12	0.16	0.40	0.60	0.80	1.00	1.20	1.40	1.60	1.80	2.00
Chile 1 Decimo	1891	2.00	0.500	0.032		0.03	0.06	0.10	0.13	0.32	0.48	0.64	0.80	0.96	1.12	1.28	1.44	1.60
Chile 10 Centavos (Decimo)	1896	2.50	0.835	0.067		0.07	0.13	0.20	0.27	0.67	1.01	1.34	1.68	2.01	2.35	2.68	3.02	3.35
Chile 10 Centavos	1899-1907	2.00	0.500	0.032		0.03	0.06	0.10	0.13	0.32	0.48	0.64	0.80	0.96	1.12	1.28	1.44	1.60
Chile 10 Centavos	1908-1920	1.50	0.400	0.019		0.02	0.04	0.06	0.08	0.19	0.29	0.38	0.48	0.57	0.67	0.76	0.86	0.95
Chile 20 Centavos	1852-1859	5.00	0.900	0.145		0.14	0.29	0.43	0.58	1.45	2.17	2.89	3.62	4.34	5.06	5.78	6.51	7.23
Chile 20 Centavos	1860-1866	4.60	0.900	0.133		0.13	0.27	0.40	0.53	1.33	2.00	2.66	3.33	3.99	4.66	5.32	5.99	6.65
Chile 20 Centavos	1867-1879	5.00	0.835	0.134		0.13	0.27	0.40	0.54	1.34	2.01	2.69	3.36	4.03	4.70	5.37	6.04	6.72
Chile 20 Centavos	1879-1893	5.00	0.500	0.080		0.08	0.16	0.24	0.32	0.80	1.20	1.60	2.00	2.40	2.80	3.20	3.60	4.00
Chile 20 Centavos	1890-1891	4.00	0.500	0.064		0.06	0.13	0.19	0.26	0.64	0.96	1.29	1.61	1.93	2.25	2.57	2.89	3.22
Chile 20 Centavos	1891-1893	5.00	0.500	0.080		0.08	0.16	0.24	0.32	0.80	1.20	1.60	2.00	2.40	2.80	3.20	3.60	4.00
Chile 20 Centavos	1891	4.60	0.200	0.030		0.03	0.06	0.09	0.12	0.30	0.45	0.60	0.75	0.90	1.05	1.20	1.35	1.50
Chile 20 Centavos	1895	4.00	0.835	0.107		0.11	0.21	0.32	0.43	1.07	1.61	2.14	2.68	3.21	3.75	4.28	4.82	5.35
Chile 20 Centavos	1899-1907	4.00	0.500	0.064		0.06	0.13	0.19	0.26	0.64	0.96	1.29	1.61	1.93	2.25	2.57	2.89	3.22
Chile 20 Centavos	1916	3.00	0.450	0.043		0.04	0.09	0.13	0.17	0.43	0.65	0.86	1.08	1.29	1.51	1.72	1.94	2.15
Chile 20 Centavos	1907-1920	3.00	0.400	0.039		0.04	0.08	0.12	0.16	0.39	0.59	0.78	0.98	1.17	1.37	1.56	1.76	1.95
Chile 40 Centavos	1907-1908	6.00	0.400	0.077		0.08	0.15	0.23	0.31	0.77	1.16	1.54	1.93	2.31	2.70	3.08	3.47	3.85
Chile 50 Centavos	1853-1872	12.50	0.900	0.362		0.36	0.72	1.09	1.45	3.62	5.43	7.24	9.05	10.86	12.67	14.48	16.29	18.10
Chile 50 Centavos	1902-1905	10.00	0.700	0.225		0.23	0.45	0.68	0.90	2.25	3.38	4.50	5.63	6.75	7.88	9.00	10.13	11.25

Country & Denomination	Years Minted	Grams Weight	Fineness	Troy (ASW)	Code	$ Value 1	$ Value 2	$ Value 3	$ Value 4	$ Value 10	$ Value 15	$ Value 20	$ Value 25	$ Value 30	$ Value 35	$ Value 40	$ Value 45	$ Value 50
Chile 1 Peso	1817-1828	27.00	0.902	0.786		0.79	1.57	2.36	3.14	7.86	11.79	15.72	19.65	23.58	27.51	31.44	35.37	39.30
Chile 1 Peso	1853-1891	25.00	0.900	0.723	S	0.72	1.45	2.17	2.89	7.23	10.85	14.46	18.08	21.69	25.31	28.92	32.54	36.15
Chile 1 Peso	1895-1897	20.00	0.835	0.537		0.54	1.07	1.61	2.15	5.37	8.06	10.74	13.43	16.11	18.80	21.48	24.17	26.85
Chile 1 Peso	1902-1905	20.00	0.700	0.450		0.45	0.90	1.35	1.80	4.50	6.75	9.00	11.25	13.50	15.75	18.00	20.25	22.50
Chile 1 Peso	1910	12.00	0.900	0.347		0.35	0.69	1.04	1.39	3.47	5.21	6.94	8.68	10.42	12.15	13.89	15.62	17.36
Chile 1 Peso	1915-1917	9.00	0.720	0.208		0.21	0.42	0.62	0.83	2.08	3.12	4.16	5.20	6.24	7.28	8.32	9.36	10.40
Chile 1 Peso	1921-1927	9.00	0.500	0.145	S	0.15	0.29	0.44	0.58	1.45	2.18	2.90	3.63	4.35	5.08	5.80	6.53	7.25
Chile 1 Peso	1932	6.00	0.400	0.077		0.08	0.15	0.23	0.31	0.77	1.16	1.54	1.93	2.31	2.70	3.08	3.47	3.85
Chile 2 Pesos	1927	18.00	0.500	0.289		0.29	0.58	0.87	1.16	2.89	4.34	5.78	7.23	8.67	10.12	11.56	13.01	14.45
Chile 5 Pesos	1927	25.00	0.900	0.723		0.72	1.45	2.17	2.89	7.23	10.85	14.46	18.08	21.69	25.31	28.92	32.54	36.15
Chile 5 Pesos	1968	22.50	0.999	0.723		0.72	1.45	2.17	2.89	7.23	10.85	14.46	18.08	21.69	25.31	28.92	32.54	36.15
Chile 10 Pesos	1968	44.50	0.999	1.446		1.45	2.89	4.34	5.78	14.46	21.69	28.92	36.15	43.38	50.61	57.84	65.07	72.30
Chile 10 Pesos	1976	44.80	0.999	1.439		1.44	2.88	4.32	5.76	14.39	21.59	28.78	35.98	43.17	50.37	57.56	64.76	71.95
Chile 2000 Pesos	1993	8.20	0.500	0.132		0.13	0.26	0.40	0.53	1.32	1.98	2.64	3.30	3.96	4.62	5.28	5.94	6.60
China 5 Cents	1889-1908	1.35	0.820	0.034	s, v	0.03	0.07	0.10	0.14	0.34	0.51	0.68	0.85	1.02	1.19	1.36	1.53	1.70
China 10 Cents	1889-1908	2.70	0.820	0.071	>	0.07	0.14	0.21	0.28	0.71	1.07	1.42	1.78	2.13	2.49	2.84	3.20	3.55
China 10 Cents	1910	3.20	0.650	0.067	>	0.07	0.13	0.20	0.27	0.67	1.01	1.34	1.68	2.01	2.35	2.68	3.02	3.35
China 10 Cents	1913-1932	2.60	0.820	0.071		0.07	0.14	0.21	0.28	0.71	1.07	1.42	1.78	2.13	2.49	2.84	3.20	3.55
China 20 Cents	1889-1911	5.40	0.820	0.140	>	0.14	0.28	0.42	0.56	1.40	2.10	2.80	3.50	4.20	4.90	5.60	6.30	7.00
China 20 Cents	1907-1912	5.20	0.890	0.139	>	0.14	0.28	0.42	0.56	1.39	2.09	2.78	3.48	4.17	4.87	5.56	6.26	6.95
China 20 Cents	1913-1927	5.20	0.700	0.117	>	0.12	0.23	0.35	0.47	1.17	1.76	2.34	2.93	3.51	4.10	4.68	5.27	5.85
China 25 Cents	1910	6.70	0.800	0.172		0.17	0.34	0.52	0.69	1.72	2.59	3.45	4.31	5.17	6.03	6.90	7.76	8.62
China 50 Cents	1889-1911	13.50	0.860	0.370	>	0.37	0.74	1.11	1.48	3.70	5.55	7.40	9.25	11.10	12.95	14.80	16.65	18.50
China 50 Cents	1908-1911	13.20	0.800	0.340	>	0.34	0.68	1.02	1.36	3.40	5.10	6.80	8.50	10.20	11.90	13.60	15.30	17.00
China 50 Cents	1914	13.60	0.700	0.306		0.31	0.61	0.92	1.22	3.06	4.59	6.12	7.65	9.18	10.71	12.24	13.77	15.30
China 1 Dollar	1889-1908	27.40	0.900	0.790	>	0.79	1.58	2.37	3.16	7.90	11.85	15.80	19.75	23.70	27.65	31.60	35.55	39.50
China 1 Dollar	1907	26.40	0.890	0.756	>	0.76	1.51	2.27	3.02	7.56	11.34	15.12	18.90	22.68	26.46	30.24	34.02	37.80
China 1 Dollar	1901-1911	26.80	0.900	0.776	>	0.78	1.55	2.33	3.10	7.76	11.64	15.52	19.40	23.28	27.16	31.04	34.92	38.80
China 1 Dollar	1914, 1928	26.60	0.900	0.747	>	0.75	1.49	2.24	2.99	7.47	11.21	14.94	18.68	22.41	26.15	29.88	33.62	37.35
China 1 Tael	1904	37.70	0.877	1.063		1.06	2.13	3.19	4.25	10.63	15.95	21.26	26.58	31.89	37.21	42.52	47.84	53.15
China, Rep. (Taiwan) 10 Cents	1912-1927	2.30	0.700	0.061	s, v	0.06	0.12	0.18	0.24	0.61	0.92	1.22	1.53	1.83	2.14	2.44	2.75	3.05
China, Rep. (Taiwan) 20 Cents	1912-1927	5.40	0.700	0.122	s, v	0.12	0.24	0.37	0.49	1.22	1.83	2.44	3.05	3.66	4.27	4.88	5.49	6.10
China, Rep. (Taiwan) 50 Cents	1914	13.60	0.700	0.306		0.31	0.61	0.92	1.22	3.06	4.59	6.12	7.65	9.18	10.71	12.24	13.77	15.30
China, Rep. (Taiwan) 1 Yuan	1912, 1923	26.90	0.900	0.779	>	0.78	1.56	2.34	3.12	7.79	11.69	15.58	19.48	23.37	27.27	31.16	35.06	38.95
China, Rep. (Taiwan) 1 Yuan	1912-1927	26.50	0.900	0.756	>	0.76	1.51	2.27	3.02	7.56	11.34	15.12	18.90	22.68	26.46	30.24	34.02	37.80
China, Rep. (Taiwan) 1 Yuan	1927-1934	27.00	0.880	0.770	>	0.77	1.54	2.31	3.08	7.70	11.55	15.40	19.25	23.10	26.95	30.80	34.65	38.50
China, Rep. (Taiwan) 50 Yuan	1965	17.10	0.750	0.412		0.41	0.82	1.24	1.65	4.12	6.18	8.24	10.30	12.36	14.42	16.48	18.54	20.60
China, Rep. (Taiwan) 50 Yuan	1998, 2000	15.57	0.999	0.500		0.50	1.00	1.50	2.00	5.00	7.50	10.00	12.50	15.00	17.50	20.00	22.50	25.00
China, Rep. (Taiwan) 50 Yuan	1999	15.55	0.925	0.462		0.46	0.92	1.39	1.85	4.62	6.93	9.24	11.55	13.86	16.17	18.48	20.79	23.10
China, Rep. (Taiwan) 100 Yuan	1965	22.20	0.750	0.534		0.53	1.07	1.60	2.14	5.34	8.01	10.68	13.35	16.02	18.69	21.36	24.03	26.70
China, Rep. (Taiwan) 100 Yuan	1997	15.57	0.999	0.500		0.50	1.00	1.50	2.00	5.00	7.50	10.00	12.50	15.00	17.50	20.00	22.50	25.00
China, Rep. (Taiwan) 200 Yuan	1996, 2000	31.14	0.999	1.000		1.00	2.00	3.00	4.00	10.00	15.00	20.00	25.00	30.00	35.00	40.00	45.00	50.00

Country & Denomination	Years Minted	Grams Weight	Fineness	Troy (ASW)	Code	$ Value 1	$ Value 2	$ Value 3	$ Value 4	$ Value 10	$ Value 15	$ Value 20	$ Value 25	$ Value 30	$ Value 35	$ Value 40	$ Value 45	$ Value 50
China, People's Rep. 5 Jiao	1983	2.20	0.900	0.064		0.06	0.13	0.19	0.26	0.64	0.96	1.28	1.60	1.92	2.24	2.56	2.88	3.20
China, People's Rep. 5 Jiao	1990	2.00	0.999	0.064		0.06	0.13	0.19	0.26	0.64	0.96	1.28	1.60	1.92	2.24	2.56	2.88	3.20
China, People's Rep. 3 Yuan	1992-1997	15.00	0.900	0.434	s	0.43	0.87	1.30	1.74	4.34	6.51	8.68	10.85	13.02	15.19	17.36	19.53	21.70
China, People's Rep. 5 Yuan	1983-1997	22.22	0.900	0.643	v	0.64	1.29	1.93	2.57	6.43	9.65	12.86	16.08	19.29	22.51	25.72	28.94	32.15
China, People's Rep. 5 Yuan	1984	8.45	0.800	0.217		0.22	0.43	0.65	0.87	2.17	3.26	4.34	5.43	6.51	7.60	8.68	9.77	10.85
China, People's Rep. 5 Yuan	1986	17.06	0.800	0.439		0.44	0.88	1.32	1.76	4.39	6.59	8.78	10.98	13.17	15.37	17.56	19.76	21.95
China, People's Rep. 5 Yuan	1986	18.61	0.925	0.554		0.55	1.11	1.66	2.22	5.54	8.31	11.08	13.85	16.62	19.39	22.16	24.93	27.70
China, People's Rep. 5 Yuan	1987, 1988	31.47	0.900	0.911		0.91	1.82	2.73	3.64	9.11	13.67	18.22	22.78	27.33	31.89	36.44	41.00	45.55
China, People's Rep. 5 Yuan	1992, 1993	15.00	0.900	0.434		0.43	0.87	1.30	1.74	4.34	6.51	8.68	10.85	13.02	15.19	17.36	19.53	21.70
China, People's Rep. 5 Yuan	1994-1998	15.55	0.999	0.500	v	0.50	1.00	1.50	2.00	5.00	7.50	10.00	12.50	15.00	17.50	20.00	22.50	25.00
China, People's Rep. 10 Yuan	1984	17.06	0.800	0.439		0.44	0.88	1.32	1.76	4.39	6.58	8.78	10.97	13.16	15.36	17.55	19.75	21.94
China, People's Rep. 10 Yuan	1984	16.81	0.925	0.500		0.50	1.00	1.50	2.00	5.00	7.50	10.00	12.50	15.00	17.50	20.00	22.50	25.00
China, People's Rep. 10 Yuan	1983-1993	27.00	0.900	0.780	s, v	0.78	1.56	2.34	3.12	7.80	11.70	15.60	19.50	23.40	27.30	31.20	35.10	39.00
China, People's Rep. 10 Yuan	1985	34.56	0.900	1.000		1.00	2.00	3.00	4.00	10.00	15.00	20.00	25.00	30.00	35.00	40.00	45.00	50.00
China, People's Rep. 10 Yuan	1986	29.10	0.925	0.868		0.87	1.74	2.60	3.47	8.68	13.02	17.36	21.70	26.04	30.38	34.72	39.06	43.40
China, People's Rep. 10 Yuan	1988-1997	27.00	0.925	0.803	s, v	0.80	1.61	2.41	3.21	8.03	12.05	16.06	20.08	24.09	28.11	32.12	36.14	40.15
China, People's Rep. 10 Yuan	1989	15.00	0.850	0.410		0.41	0.82	1.23	1.64	4.10	6.15	8.20	10.25	12.30	14.35	16.40	18.45	20.50
China, People's Rep. 10 Yuan	1990-1993	30.00	0.900	0.868	s	0.87	1.74	2.60	3.47	8.68	13.02	17.36	21.70	26.04	30.38	34.72	39.06	43.40
China, People's Rep. 10 Yuan	1987-2000	31.10	0.999	1.000	s, v	1.00	2.00	3.00	4.00	10.00	15.00	20.00	25.00	30.00	35.00	40.00	45.00	50.00
China, People's Rep. 10 Yuan	1993	24.26	0.900	0.780		0.78	1.56	2.34	3.12	7.80	11.70	15.60	19.50	23.40	27.30	31.20	35.10	39.00
China, People's Rep. 10 Yuan	1994	20.74	0.900	0.601		0.60	1.20	1.80	2.40	6.01	9.02	12.02	15.03	18.03	21.04	24.04	27.05	30.05
China, People's Rep. 10 Yuan	2000	23.04	0.900	0.666		0.67	1.33	2.00	2.66	6.66	9.99	13.32	16.65	19.98	23.31	26.64	29.97	33.30
China, People's Rep. 20 Yuan	1980	10.35	0.850	0.283		0.28	0.57	0.85	1.13	2.83	4.25	5.66	7.08	8.49	9.91	11.32	12.74	14.15
China, People's Rep. 20 Yuan	1990-1996	62.21	1.000	2.000		2.00	4.00	6.00	8.00	20.00	30.00	40.00	50.00	60.00	70.00	80.00	90.00	100.00
China, People's Rep. 25 Yuan	1982	19.44	0.800	0.500		0.50	1.00	1.50	2.00	5.00	7.50	10.00	12.50	15.00	17.50	20.00	22.50	25.00
China, People's Rep. 30 Yuan	1980	15.00	0.850	0.410		0.41	0.82	1.23	1.64	4.10	6.15	8.20	10.25	12.30	14.35	16.40	18.45	20.50
China, People's Rep. 35 Yuan	1979	19.44	0.800	0.500		0.50	1.00	1.50	2.00	5.00	7.50	10.00	12.50	15.00	17.50	20.00	22.50	25.00
China, People's Rep. 35 Yuan	1981	33.58	0.800	0.868		0.87	1.74	2.60	3.47	8.68	13.02	17.36	21.70	26.04	30.38	34.72	39.06	43.40
China, People's Rep. 50 Yuan	1986-2000	155.50	0.999	5.000	s	5.00	10.00	15.00	20.00	50.00	75.00	100.00	125.00	150.00	175.00	200.00	225.00	250.00
China, People's Rep. 100 Yuan	1987-1998	373.24	0.999	12.000	s	12.00	24.00	36.00	48.00	120.00	180.00	240.00	300.00	360.00	420.00	480.00	540.00	600.00
China, People's Rep. 150 Yuan	1990-1996	622.04	0.999	20.000	s	20.00	40.00	60.00	80.00	200.00	300.00	400.00	500.00	600.00	700.00	800.00	900.00	1000.00
China, People's Rep. 200 Yuan	1992-1999	1000.00	0.999	32.160	s, v	32.16	64.32	96.48	128.64	321.60	482.40	643.20	804.00	964.80	1125.60	1286.40	1447.20	1608.00
Columbia 1/4 Real	1800-1816	0.85	0.896	0.024	s	0.02	0.05	0.07	0.10	0.24	0.37	0.49	0.61	0.73	0.85	0.98	1.10	1.22
Columbia 1/4 Real (Provincial)	1814-1815	0.70	0.583	0.013		0.01	0.03	0.04	0.05	0.13	0.20	0.26	0.33	0.39	0.46	0.52	0.59	0.66
Columbia 1/4 Real	1820-1846	0.68	0.666	0.015	s	0.02	0.03	0.05	0.06	0.15	0.23	0.30	0.38	0.45	0.53	0.60	0.68	0.75
Columbia 1/4 Real	1849-1858	0.90	0.900	0.026	s	0.03	0.05	0.08	0.10	0.26	0.39	0.52	0.65	0.78	0.91	1.04	1.17	1.30
Columbia 1/2 Real	1801-1818	1.69	0.896	0.049	s	0.05	0.10	0.15	0.19	0.49	0.73	0.97	1.22	1.46	1.70	1.95	2.19	2.44
Columbia 1/2 Real (Provincial)	1814, 1821	1.30	0.666	0.028	s	0.03	0.06	0.08	0.11	0.28	0.42	0.56	0.70	0.84	0.98	1.12	1.26	1.40
Columbia 1/2 Real	1833-1836	1.55	0.666	0.033		0.03	0.07	0.10	0.13	0.33	0.50	0.66	0.83	0.99	1.16	1.32	1.49	1.65
Columbia 1/2 Real	1838-1848	1.26	0.666	0.027	s	0.03	0.05	0.08	0.11	0.27	0.40	0.54	0.67	0.81	0.94	1.08	1.21	1.35
Columbia 1/2 Real	1850-1853	1.40	0.900	0.041		0.04	0.08	0.12	0.16	0.41	0.62	0.82	1.03	1.23	1.44	1.64	1.85	2.05
Columbia 1 Real	1800-1819	3.38	0.896	0.097	s	0.10	0.19	0.29	0.39	0.97	1.46	1.94	2.43	2.91	3.40	3.88	4.37	4.85
Columbia 1 Real (Provincial)	1813-1816	2.50	0.583	0.047		0.05	0.09	0.14	0.19	0.47	0.71	0.94	1.18	1.41	1.65	1.88	2.12	2.35
Columbia 1 Real (Provisional)	1819	3.15	0.666	0.067		0.07	0.13	0.20	0.27	0.67	1.01	1.34	1.68	2.01	2.35	2.68	3.02	3.35

Country & Denomination	Years Minted	Grams Weight	Fineness	Troy (ASW)	Code	$ Value 1	$ Value 2	$ Value 3	$ Value 4	$ Value 10	$ Value 15	$ Value 20	$ Value 25	$ Value 30	$ Value 35	$ Value 40	$ Value 45	$ Value 50
Columbia 1 Real	1821	2.78	0.666	0.060		0.06	0.12	0.18	0.24	0.60	0.90	1.20	1.50	1.80	2.10	2.40	2.70	3.00
Columbia 1 Real	1827-1836	3.10	0.666	0.066		0.07	0.13	0.20	0.26	0.66	0.99	1.32	1.65	1.98	2.31	2.64	2.97	3.30
Columbia 1 Real	1837-1846	2.70	0.666	0.058	s	0.06	0.12	0.17	0.23	0.58	0.87	1.16	1.45	1.74	2.03	2.32	2.61	2.90
Columbia 1 Real	1847-1853	2.50	0.900	0.072	s	0.07	0.14	0.22	0.29	0.72	1.08	1.44	1.80	2.16	2.52	2.88	3.24	3.60
Columbia 2 Reales	1800-1822	6.77	0.896	0.195	s	0.20	0.39	0.59	0.78	1.95	2.93	3.90	4.88	5.85	6.83	7.80	8.78	9.75
Columbia 2 Reales (Provincial)	1815, 1816	4.90	0.583	0.092		0.09	0.18	0.28	0.37	0.92	1.38	1.84	2.30	2.76	3.22	3.68	4.14	4.60
Columbia 2 Reales (Provincial)	1820-1823	4.98	0.666	0.107	s	0.11	0.21	0.32	0.43	1.07	1.61	2.14	2.68	3.21	3.75	4.28	4.82	5.35
Columbia 2 Reales	1819, 1820	5.90	0.666	0.126		0.13	0.25	0.38	0.50	1.26	1.89	2.52	3.15	3.78	4.41	5.04	5.67	6.30
Columbia 2 Reales	1840-1849	5.50	0.666	0.118	s	0.12	0.24	0.35	0.47	1.18	1.77	2.36	2.95	3.54	4.13	4.72	5.31	5.90
Columbia 2 Reales	1849-1853	5.00	0.900	0.145		0.15	0.29	0.44	0.58	1.45	2.18	2.90	3.63	4.35	5.08	5.80	6.53	7.25
Columbia 2 Reales	1880	5.00	0.835	0.134		0.13	0.27	0.40	0.54	1.34	2.01	2.68	3.35	4.02	4.69	5.36	6.03	6.70
Columbia 8 Reales	1810-1820	27.07	0.917	0.780	s	0.78	1.56	2.34	3.12	7.80	11.70	15.60	19.50	23.40	27.30	31.20	35.10	39.00
Columbia 8 Reales (Provincial)	1819-1821	23.00	0.666	0.492		0.49	0.98	1.48	1.97	4.92	7.38	9.84	12.30	14.76	17.22	19.68	22.14	24.60
Columbia 8 Reales	1834-1836	27.02	0.835	0.725		0.73	1.45	2.18	2.90	7.25	10.88	14.50	18.13	21.75	25.38	29.00	32.63	36.25
Columbia 8 Reales	1847	20.00	0.900	0.579		0.58	1.16	1.74	2.32	5.79	8.69	11.58	14.48	17.37	20.27	23.16	26.06	28.95
Columbia 10 Reales	1847-1851	25.00	0.900	0.723		0.72	1.45	2.17	2.89	7.23	10.85	14.46	18.08	21.69	25.31	28.92	32.54	36.15
Columbia 1/4 Decimo	1863-1867	0.85	0.900	0.025		0.03	0.05	0.08	0.10	0.25	0.38	0.50	0.63	0.75	0.88	1.00	1.13	1.25
Columbia 1/4 Decimo	1868-1881	0.85	0.666	0.018		0.02	0.04	0.05	0.07	0.18	0.27	0.36	0.45	0.54	0.63	0.72	0.81	0.90
Columbia 1/2 Decimo	1853-1858	1.50	0.900	0.043		0.04	0.09	0.13	0.17	0.43	0.65	0.86	1.08	1.29	1.51	1.72	1.94	2.15
Columbia 1/2 Decimo	1863-1865	1.25	0.900	0.036		0.04	0.07	0.11	0.14	0.36	0.54	0.72	0.90	1.08	1.26	1.44	1.62	1.80
Columbia 1/2 Decimo	1867-1878	1.25	0.666	0.027		0.03	0.05	0.08	0.11	0.27	0.41	0.54	0.68	0.81	0.95	1.08	1.22	1.35
Columbia 1/2 Decimo	1870-1874	1.25	0.835	0.034		0.03	0.07	0.10	0.14	0.34	0.51	0.68	0.85	1.02	1.19	1.36	1.53	1.70
Columbia 1 Decimo	1853-1866	2.50	0.900	0.072	s	0.07	0.14	0.22	0.29	0.72	1.08	1.44	1.80	2.16	2.52	2.88	3.24	3.60
Columbia 1 Decimo	1866-1874	2.50	0.835	0.067	s	0.07	0.13	0.20	0.27	0.67	1.01	1.34	1.68	2.01	2.35	2.68	3.02	3.35
Columbia 2 Decimos	1854-1865	5.00	0.900	0.145	s	0.15	0.29	0.44	0.58	1.45	2.18	2.90	3.63	4.35	5.08	5.80	6.53	7.25
Columbia 2 Decimos	1866-1874	5.00	0.835	0.134	s	0.13	0.27	0.40	0.54	1.34	2.01	2.68	3.35	4.02	4.69	5.36	6.03	6.70
Columbia 5 Decimos	1866-1883	12.50	0.835	0.336		0.34	0.67	1.01	1.34	3.36	5.04	6.72	8.40	10.08	11.76	13.44	15.12	16.80
Columbia 5 Decimos	1886-1889	12.50	0.500	0.200		0.20	0.40	0.60	0.80	2.00	3.00	4.00	5.00	6.00	7.00	8.00	9.00	10.00
Columbia 5 Centavos	1872-1885	1.25	0.666	0.027	s	0.03	0.05	0.08	0.11	0.27	0.41	0.54	0.68	0.81	0.95	1.08	1.22	1.35
Columbia 5 Centavos	1874	1.25	0.835	0.033		0.03	0.07	0.10	0.13	0.33	0.50	0.66	0.83	0.99	1.16	1.32	1.49	1.65
Columbia 5 Centavos	1902	1.25	0.666	0.027		0.03	0.05	0.08	0.11	0.27	0.41	0.54	0.68	0.81	0.95	1.08	1.22	1.35
Columbia 10 Centavos	1872-1885	2.50	0.835	0.067	s	0.07	0.13	0.20	0.27	0.67	1.01	1.34	1.68	2.01	2.35	2.68	3.02	3.35
Columbia 10 Centavos	1885-1886	2.50	0.500	0.040		0.04	0.08	0.12	0.16	0.40	0.60	0.80	1.00	1.20	1.40	1.60	1.80	2.00
Columbia 10 Centavos	1897	2.50	0.666	0.054		0.05	0.11	0.16	0.22	0.54	0.81	1.08	1.35	1.62	1.89	2.16	2.43	2.70
Columbia 10 Centavos	1911-1942	2.50	0.900	0.072	s	0.07	0.14	0.22	0.29	0.72	1.08	1.44	1.80	2.16	2.52	2.88	3.24	3.60
Columbia 10 Centavos	1945-1952	2.50	0.500	0.040		0.04	0.08	0.12	0.16	0.40	0.60	0.80	1.00	1.20	1.40	1.60	1.80	2.00
Columbia 20 Centavos	1874-1886	5.00	0.835	0.134		0.13	0.27	0.40	0.54	1.34	2.01	2.68	3.35	4.02	4.69	5.36	6.03	6.70
Columbia 20 Centavos	1886	5.00	0.500	0.080		0.08	0.16	0.24	0.32	0.80	1.20	1.60	2.00	2.40	2.80	3.20	3.60	4.00
Columbia 20 Centavos	1897	5.00	0.666	0.107		0.11	0.21	0.32	0.43	1.07	1.61	2.14	2.68	3.21	3.75	4.28	4.82	5.35
Columbia 20 Centavos	1911-1942	5.00	0.900	0.145	s	0.15	0.29	0.44	0.58	1.45	2.18	2.90	3.63	4.35	5.08	5.80	6.53	7.25
Columbia 20 Centavos	1945-1952	5.00	0.500	0.080		0.08	0.16	0.24	0.32	0.80	1.20	1.60	2.00	2.40	2.80	3.20	3.60	4.00
Columbia 20 Centavos	1953	5.00	0.300	0.048		0.05	0.10	0.14	0.19	0.48	0.72	0.96	1.20	1.44	1.68	1.92	2.16	2.40
Columbia 50 Centavos	1872-1908	12.50	0.835	0.336	s	0.34	0.67	1.01	1.34	3.36	5.04	6.72	8.40	10.08	11.76	13.44	15.12	16.80
Columbia 50 Centavos	1885-1889	12.50	0.500	0.201		0.20	0.40	0.60	0.80	2.01	3.02	4.02	5.03	6.03	7.04	8.04	9.05	10.05
Columbia 50 Centavos	1912-1934	12.50	0.900	0.362	s	0.36	0.72	1.09	1.45	3.62	5.43	7.24	9.05	10.86	12.67	14.48	16.29	18.10

Country & Denomination	Years Minted	Grams Weight	Fineness	Troy (ASW)	Code	$ Value 1	$ Value 2	$ Value 3	$ Value 4	$ Value 10	$ Value 15	$ Value 20	$ Value 25	$ Value 30	$ Value 35	$ Value 40	$ Value 45	$ Value 50
Columbia 50 Centavos	1947-1948	12.50	0.500	0.201		0.20	0.40	0.60	0.80	2.01	3.02	4.02	5.03	6.03	7.04	8.04	9.05	10.05
Columbia 1/2 Peso	1868	12.50	0.835	0.336		0.34	0.67	1.01	1.34	3.36	5.04	6.72	8.40	10.08	11.76	13.44	15.12	16.80
Columbia 1 Peso	1855-1871	25.00	0.900	0.723	S	0.72	1.45	2.17	2.89	7.23	10.85	14.46	18.08	21.69	25.31	28.92	32.54	36.15
Columbia 1 Peso	1956	25.00	0.900	0.723		0.72	1.45	2.17	2.89	7.23	10.85	14.46	18.08	21.69	25.31	28.92	32.54	36.15
Columbia 500 Pesos	1978-1979	28.28	0.925	0.841		0.84	1.68	2.52	3.36	8.41	12.62	16.82	21.03	25.23	29.44	33.64	37.85	42.06
Columbia 750 Pesos	1978-1979	35.00	0.925	1.041		1.04	2.08	3.12	4.16	10.41	15.62	20.82	26.03	31.23	36.44	41.64	46.85	52.05
Columbia 10000 Pesos	1991	27.00	0.925	0.803		0.80	1.61	2.41	3.21	8.03	12.05	16.06	20.08	24.09	28.11	32.12	36.14	40.15
Comoros 5000 Francs	1976	44.83	0.925	0.373		0.37	0.75	1.12	1.49	3.73	5.60	7.46	9.33	11.19	13.06	14.92	16.79	18.65
Congo Free State 50 Centimes	1887-1896	2.50	0.835	0.067	S	0.07	0.13	0.20	0.27	0.67	1.01	1.34	1.68	2.01	2.35	2.68	3.02	3.35
Congo Free State 1 Franc	1887-1896	5.00	0.835	0.134	S	0.13	0.27	0.40	0.54	1.34	2.01	2.68	3.35	4.02	4.69	5.36	6.03	6.70
Congo Free State 2 Francs	1887-1896	10.00	0.835	0.269	S	0.27	0.54	0.81	1.08	2.69	4.04	5.38	6.73	8.07	9.42	10.76	12.11	13.45
Congo Free State 5 Francs	1887-1896	25.00	0.900	0.723	S	0.72	1.45	2.17	2.89	7.23	10.85	14.46	18.08	21.69	25.31	28.92	32.54	36.15
Congo Free State 5 Francs	1887	25.00	0.900	0.723		0.72	1.45	2.17	2.89	7.23	10.85	14.46	18.08	21.69	25.31	28.92	32.54	36.15
Congo Republic 500 Francs	1991	16.00	0.999	0.514		0.51	1.03	1.54	2.06	5.14	7.71	10.28	12.85	15.42	17.99	20.56	23.13	25.70
Congo Republic 500 Francs	1991	12.00	0.999	0.386		0.39	0.77	1.16	1.54	3.86	5.79	7.72	9.65	11.58	13.51	15.44	17.37	19.30
Congo Republic 500 Francs	1991	16.07	0.999	0.517		0.52	1.03	1.55	2.07	5.17	7.76	10.34	12.93	15.51	18.10	20.68	23.27	25.85
Congo Republic 500 Francs	1991-1992	20.00	0.999	0.643		0.64	1.29	1.93	2.57	6.43	9.65	12.86	16.08	19.29	22.51	25.72	28.94	32.15
Congo Republic 500 Francs	1992	19.95	0.999	0.642		0.64	1.28	1.93	2.57	6.42	9.63	12.84	16.05	19.26	22.47	25.68	28.89	32.10
Congo Republic 500 Francs	1996	13.81	0.999	0.444		0.44	0.89	1.33	1.78	4.44	6.66	8.88	11.10	13.32	15.54	17.76	19.98	22.20
Congo Republic 1000 Francs	1993-1997	20.00	0.999	0.643		0.64	1.29	1.93	2.57	6.43	9.65	12.86	16.08	19.29	22.51	25.72	28.94	32.15
Congo Republic 1000 Francs	1993	15.90	0.999	0.511		0.51	1.02	1.53	2.04	5.11	7.67	10.22	12.78	15.33	17.89	20.44	23.00	25.55
Congo Republic 1000 Francs	1993	20.10	0.999	0.646		0.65	1.29	1.94	2.58	6.46	9.69	12.92	16.15	19.38	22.61	25.84	29.07	32.30
Congo Republic 1000 Francs	1994	15.88	0.999	0.511		0.51	1.02	1.53	2.04	5.11	7.67	10.22	12.78	15.33	17.89	20.44	23.00	25.55
Congo Republic 1000 Francs	1997	15.00	0.999	0.482		0.48	0.96	1.45	1.93	4.82	7.23	9.64	12.05	14.46	16.87	19.28	21.69	24.10
Congo Dem. Rep. 10 Francs	1999, 2000	20.00	0.925	0.594	V	0.59	1.19	1.78	2.38	5.94	8.91	11.88	14.85	17.82	20.79	23.76	26.73	29.70
Congo Dem. Rep. 10 Francs	1999, 2000	25.31	0.925	0.752	V	0.75	1.50	2.26	3.01	7.52	11.28	15.04	18.80	22.56	26.32	30.08	33.84	37.60
Congo Dem. Rep. 10 Francs	2000	31.55	0.925	0.938		0.94	1.88	2.81	3.75	9.38	14.07	18.76	23.45	28.14	32.83	37.52	42.21	46.90
Congo Dem. Rep. 10 Francs	2000	30.87	0.999	0.992		0.99	1.98	2.98	3.97	9.92	14.88	19.84	24.80	29.76	34.72	39.68	44.64	49.60
Congo Dem. Rep. 10 Francs	2000	31.26	0.999	1.000		1.00	2.00	3.00	4.00	10.00	15.00	20.00	25.00	30.00	35.00	40.00	45.00	50.00
Congo Dem. Rep. 20 Francs	2000	62.20	0.999	2.000		2.00	4.00	6.00	8.00	20.00	30.00	40.00	50.00	60.00	70.00	80.00	90.00	100.00
Cook Islands 1 Dollar	1985-1986	27.22	0.925	0.810	N	0.81	1.62	2.43	3.24	8.10	12.15	16.20	20.25	24.30	28.35	32.40	36.45	40.50
Cook Islands 1 Dollar	1996	10.00	0.500	0.161		0.16	0.32	0.48	0.64	1.61	2.42	3.22	4.03	4.83	5.64	6.44	7.25	8.05
Cook Islands 1 Dollar	1996	31.10	0.999	1.000	N, V	1.00	2.00	3.00	4.00	10.00	15.00	20.00	25.00	30.00	35.00	40.00	45.00	50.00
Cook Islands 1 Dollar	1997-1999	31.64	0.999	1.020		1.02	2.04	3.06	4.08	10.20	15.30	20.40	25.50	30.60	35.70	40.80	45.90	51.00
Cook Islands 1 Dollar	2000	28.28	0.925	0.841		0.84	1.68	2.52	3.36	8.41	12.62	16.82	21.03	25.23	29.44	33.64	37.85	42.05
Cook Islands 2 Dollars	1973	25.70	0.925	0.765		0.77	1.53	2.30	3.06	7.65	11.48	15.30	19.13	22.95	26.78	30.60	34.43	38.25
Cook Islands 2 Dollars	1996-1998	10.00	0.500	0.161		0.16	0.32	0.48	0.64	1.61	2.42	3.22	4.03	4.83	5.64	6.44	7.25	8.05
Cook Islands 2 Dollars	1997	15.84	0.999	0.509		0.51	1.02	1.53	2.04	5.09	7.64	10.18	12.73	15.27	17.82	20.36	22.91	25.45
Cook Islands 2 Dollars	1999	31.10	0.999	1.000		1.00	2.00	3.00	4.00	10.00	15.00	20.00	25.00	30.00	35.00	40.00	45.00	50.00
Cook Islands 2-1/2 Dollars	1973-1974	27.35	0.925	0.813		0.81	1.63	2.44	3.25	8.13	12.20	16.26	20.33	24.39	28.46	32.52	36.59	40.65

Country & Denomination	Years Minted	Grams Weight	Fineness	Troy (ASW)	Code	$ Value 1	$ Value 2	$ Value 3	$ Value 4	$ Value 10	$ Value 15	$ Value 20	$ Value 25	$ Value 30	$ Value 35	$ Value 40	$ Value 45	$ Value 50
Cook Islands 5 Dollars	1976-1979	27.30	0.500	0.439		0.44	0.88	1.32	1.76	4.39	6.59	8.78	10.98	13.17	15.37	17.56	19.76	21.95
Cook Islands 5 Dollars	1991-1995	10.00	0.500	0.161	S	0.16	0.32	0.48	0.64	1.61	2.42	3.22	4.03	4.83	5.64	6.44	7.25	8.05
Cook Islands 5 Dollars	1996	28.00	0.925	0.833	V	0.83	1.67	2.50	3.33	8.33	12.50	16.66	20.83	24.99	29.16	33.32	37.49	41.65
Cook Islands 5 Dollars	1996-2000	31.50	0.925	0.936	N, S, V	0.94	1.87	2.81	3.74	9.36	14.04	18.72	23.40	28.08	32.76	37.44	42.12	46.80
Cook Islands 5 Dollars	1996, 1997	15.52	0.999	0.499	N	0.50	1.00	1.50	2.00	4.99	7.49	9.98	12.48	14.97	17.47	19.96	22.46	24.95
Cook Islands 7-1/2 Dollars	1973-1974	33.80	0.925	1.000		1.00	2.00	3.00	4.00	10.00	15.00	20.00	25.00	30.00	35.00	40.00	45.00	50.00
Cook Islands 10 Dollars	1978	27.30	0.925	0.830		0.83	1.66	2.49	3.32	8.30	12.45	16.60	20.75	24.90	29.05	33.20	37.35	41.50
Cook Islands 10 Dollars	1990	10.00	0.925	0.297		0.30	0.59	0.89	1.19	2.97	4.46	5.94	7.43	8.91	10.40	11.88	13.37	14.85
Cook Islands 10 Dollars	1990	28.00	0.925	0.833		0.83	1.67	2.50	3.33	8.33	12.50	16.66	20.83	24.99	29.16	33.32	37.49	41.65
Cook Islands 10 Dollars	1992	31.47	0.925	0.936		0.94	1.87	2.81	3.74	9.36	14.04	18.72	23.40	28.08	32.76	37.44	42.12	46.80
Cook Islands 10 Dollars	1994	14.80	0.925	0.440		0.44	0.88	1.32	1.76	4.40	6.60	8.80	11.00	13.20	15.40	17.60	19.80	22.00
Cook Islands 10 Dollars	1996-1998	28.00	0.925	0.833	N	0.83	1.67	2.50	3.33	8.33	12.50	16.66	20.83	24.99	29.16	33.32	37.49	41.65
Cook Islands 20 Dollars	1983	28.28	0.925	0.841		0.84	1.68	2.52	3.36	8.41	12.62	16.82	21.03	25.23	29.44	33.64	37.85	42.05
Cook Islands 20 Dollars	1993-1997	31.50	0.925	0.936	V	0.94	1.87	2.81	3.74	9.36	14.04	18.72	23.40	28.08	32.76	37.44	42.12	46.80
Cook Islands 20 Dollars	1996	155.52	0.999	5.000	N	5.00	10.00	15.00	20.00	50.00	75.00	100.00	125.00	150.00	175.00	200.00	225.00	250.00
Cook Islands 25 Dollars	1977	48.85	0.925	0.145		0.15	0.29	0.44	0.58	1.45	2.18	2.90	3.63	4.35	5.08	5.80	6.53	7.25
Cook Islands 25 Dollars	1988	37.00	0.925	1.100		1.10	2.20	3.30	4.40	11.00	16.50	22.00	27.50	33.00	38.50	44.00	49.50	55.00
Cook Islands 25 Dollars	1996	155.52	0.999	5.000	N	5.00	10.00	15.00	20.00	50.00	75.00	100.00	125.00	150.00	175.00	200.00	225.00	250.00
Cook Islands 30 Dollars	1997	1000.00	0.999	32.120		32.12	64.24	96.36	128.48	321.20	481.80	642.40	803.00	963.60	1124.20	1284.80	1445.40	1606.00
Cook Islands 50 Dollars	1974	97.20	0.925	2.891		2.89	5.78	8.67	11.56	28.91	43.37	57.82	72.28	86.73	101.19	115.64	130.10	144.55
Cook Islands 50 Dollars	1987-1989	28.28	0.925	0.841		0.84	1.68	2.52	3.36	8.41	12.62	16.82	21.03	25.23	29.44	33.64	37.85	42.05
Cook Islands 50 Dollars	1988	20.94	0.925	0.623		0.62	1.25	1.87	2.49	6.23	9.35	12.46	15.58	18.69	21.81	24.92	28.04	31.15
Cook Islands 50 Dollars	1989	29.90	0.925	0.889		0.89	1.78	2.67	3.56	8.89	13.34	17.78	22.23	26.67	31.12	35.56	40.01	44.45
Cook Islands 50 Dollars	1989-1992	19.40	0.925	0.577	N, V	0.58	1.15	1.73	2.31	5.77	8.66	11.54	14.43	17.31	20.20	23.08	25.97	28.85
Cook Islands 50 Dollars	1989-1997	31.10	0.925	0.925	N, S	0.93	1.85	2.78	3.70	9.25	13.88	18.50	23.13	27.75	32.38	37.00	41.63	46.25
Cook Islands 50 Dollars	1990-1997	31.30	0.925	0.932	N, S, V	0.93	1.86	2.80	3.73	9.32	13.98	18.64	23.30	27.96	32.62	37.28	41.94	46.60
Cook Islands 50 Dollars	1990	19.80	0.925	0.589		0.59	1.18	1.77	2.36	5.89	8.83	11.78	14.72	17.66	20.61	23.55	26.50	29.44
Cook Islands 50 Dollars	1991	19.20	0.925	0.577	N	0.58	1.15	1.73	2.31	5.77	8.66	11.54	14.43	17.31	20.20	23.08	25.97	28.85
Cook Islands 50 Dollars	1997	32.22	0.925	0.958	N	0.96	1.92	2.87	3.83	9.58	14.37	19.16	23.95	28.74	33.53	38.32	43.11	47.90
Cook Islands 100 Dollars	1990-1993	172.11	0.925	5.100	N	5.10	10.20	15.30	20.40	51.00	76.50	102.00	127.50	153.00	178.50	204.00	229.50	255.00
Costa Rica 1/2 Real	1842	1.50	0.903	0.084		0.08	0.17	0.25	0.34	0.84	1.26	1.68	2.10	2.52	2.94	3.36	3.78	4.20
Costa Rica 1 Real	1849, 1850	2.90	0.750	0.070		0.07	0.14	0.21	0.28	0.70	1.05	1.40	1.75	2.10	2.45	2.80	3.15	3.50
Costa Rica 1/16 Peso	1850-1862	1.46	0.903	0.042	S	0.04	0.08	0.13	0.17	0.42	0.63	0.84	1.05	1.26	1.47	1.68	1.89	2.10
Costa Rica 1/8 Peso	1850-1855	2.95	0.903	0.086	S	0.09	0.17	0.26	0.34	0.86	1.29	1.72	2.15	2.58	3.01	3.44	3.87	4.30
Costa Rica 1/4 Peso	1850-1855	6.40	0.903	0.186	S	0.19	0.37	0.56	0.74	1.86	2.79	3.72	4.65	5.58	6.51	7.44	8.37	9.30
Costa Rica 5 Centavos	1865-1887	1.27	0.750	0.031	S	0.03	0.06	0.09	0.12	0.31	0.47	0.62	0.78	0.93	1.09	1.24	1.40	1.55
Costa Rica 5 Centavos	1889-1892	1.20	0.750	0.029	S	0.03	0.06	0.09	0.12	0.29	0.44	0.58	0.73	0.87	1.02	1.16	1.31	1.45
Costa Rica 10 Centavos	1865-1875	2.54	0.750	0.061	S	0.06	0.12	0.18	0.24	0.61	0.92	1.22	1.53	1.83	2.14	2.44	2.75	3.05
Costa Rica 10 Centavos	1886-1892	2.50	0.750	0.060	S	0.06	0.12	0.18	0.24	0.60	0.90	1.20	1.50	1.80	2.10	2.40	2.70	3.00
Costa Rica 25 Centavos	1864-1887	6.25	0.750	0.151	S	0.15	0.30	0.45	0.60	1.51	2.27	3.02	3.78	4.53	5.29	6.04	6.80	7.55
Costa Rica 25 Centavos	1889-1893	6.30	0.750	0.152	S	0.15	0.30	0.46	0.61	1.52	2.28	3.04	3.80	4.56	5.32	6.08	6.84	7.60
Costa Rica 50 Centavos	1865-1890	12.50	0.750	0.301	S	0.30	0.60	0.90	1.20	3.01	4.52	6.02	7.53	9.03	10.54	12.04	13.55	15.05
Costa Rica 50 Centavos	1889	12.50	0.835	0.336		0.34	0.67	1.01	1.34	3.36	5.04	6.72	8.40	10.08	11.76	13.44	15.12	16.80
Costa Rica 5 Centimos	1905-1914	1.00	0.900	0.029		0.03	0.06	0.09	0.12	0.29	0.43	0.58	0.72	0.87	1.01	1.16	1.30	1.45

Country & Denomination	Years Minted	Grams Weight	Fineness	Troy (ASW)	Code	$ Value 1	$ Value 2	$ Value 3	$ Value 4	$ Value 10	$ Value 15	$ Value 20	$ Value 25	$ Value 30	$ Value 35	$ Value 40	$ Value 45	$ Value 50
Costa Rica 10 Centimos	1905-1914	2.00	0.900	0.058	s	0.06	0.12	0.17	0.23	0.58	0.87	1.16	1.45	1.74	2.03	2.32	2.61	2.90
Costa Rica 10 Centimos	1917	2.00	0.500	0.032		0.03	0.06	0.10	0.13	0.32	0.48	0.64	0.80	0.96	1.12	1.28	1.44	1.60
Costa Rica 10 Centimos	1924	3.45	0.650	0.072		0.07	0.14	0.22	0.29	0.72	1.08	1.44	1.80	2.16	2.52	2.88	3.24	3.60
Costa Rica 25 Centimos	1902-1914	10.00	0.900	0.289	s	0.29	0.58	0.87	1.16	2.89	4.34	5.78	7.23	8.67	10.12	11.56	13.01	14.45
Costa Rica 50 Centimos	1917-1918	10.00	0.500	0.161		0.16	0.32	0.48	0.64	1.61	2.42	3.22	4.03	4.83	5.64	6.44	7.25	8.05
Costa Rica 50 Centimos	1923	6.25	0.750	0.151		0.15	0.30	0.45	0.60	1.51	2.27	3.02	3.78	4.53	5.29	6.04	6.80	7.55
Costa Rica 1 Colon (1914)	1923	10.00	0.900	0.289		0.29	0.58	0.87	1.16	2.89	4.34	5.78	7.23	8.67	10.12	11.56	13.01	14.45
Costa Rica 2 Colones	1970	4.30	0.999	0.138		0.14	0.28	0.41	0.55	1.38	2.07	2.76	3.45	4.14	4.83	5.52	6.21	6.90
Costa Rica 5 Colones	1970	10.78	0.999	0.346		0.35	0.69	1.04	1.38	3.46	5.19	6.92	8.65	10.38	12.11	13.84	15.57	17.30
Costa Rica 10 Colones	1970	21.70	0.999	0.698		0.70	1.40	2.09	2.79	6.98	10.46	13.95	17.44	20.93	24.42	27.90	31.39	34.88
Costa Rica 20 Colones	1970	43.70	0.999	1.405		1.41	2.81	4.22	5.62	14.05	21.08	28.10	35.13	42.15	49.18	56.20	63.23	70.25
Costa Rica 20 Colones	1970	53.90	0.999	1.731		1.73	3.46	5.19	6.92	17.31	25.97	34.62	43.28	51.93	60.59	69.24	77.90	86.55
Costa Rica 50 Colones	1974	25.55	0.500	0.411		0.41	0.82	1.23	1.64	4.11	6.16	8.21	10.27	12.32	14.37	16.43	18.48	20.54
Costa Rica 50 Colones	1974	28.28	0.925	0.841		0.84	1.68	2.52	3.36	8.41	12.62	16.82	21.03	25.23	29.44	33.64	37.85	42.06
Costa Rica 100 Colones	1974	32.10	0.500	0.516		0.52	1.03	1.55	2.06	5.16	7.74	10.32	12.90	15.48	18.06	20.64	23.22	25.80
Costa Rica 100 Colones	1974, 1979	35.00	0.925	1.041		1.04	2.08	3.12	4.16	10.41	15.62	20.82	26.03	31.23	36.44	41.64	46.85	52.05
Costa Rica 250 Colones	1982-1983	30.33	0.925	0.902		0.90	1.80	2.71	3.61	9.02	13.53	18.04	22.55	27.06	31.57	36.08	40.59	45.10
Costa Rica 300 Colones	1981	10.97	0.925	0.326		0.33	0.65	0.98	1.30	3.26	4.89	6.52	8.16	9.79	11.42	13.05	14.68	16.31
Costa Rica 1000 Colones	1987	10.97	0.925	0.327		0.33	0.65	0.98	1.31	3.27	4.91	6.54	8.18	9.82	11.45	13.09	14.72	16.36
Costa Rica 3000 Colones	1994	25.36	0.925	0.754		0.75	1.51	2.26	3.02	7.54	11.31	15.08	18.86	22.63	26.40	30.17	33.94	37.71
Costa Rica 5000 Colones	1997	25.06	0.925	0.745		0.75	1.49	2.24	2.98	7.45	11.18	14.90	18.63	22.35	26.08	29.80	33.53	37.25
Costa Rica 5000 Colones	2000	31.10	0.925	0.943		0.94	1.89	2.83	3.77	9.43	14.15	18.86	23.58	28.29	33.01	37.72	42.44	47.15
Crete 50 Lepta	1901	2.50	0.835	0.067		0.07	0.13	0.20	0.27	0.67	1.01	1.34	1.68	2.01	2.35	2.68	3.02	3.36
Crete 1 Drachma	1901	5.00	0.835	0.134		0.13	0.27	0.40	0.54	1.34	2.01	2.68	3.36	4.03	4.70	5.37	6.04	6.71
Crete 2 Drachmai	1901	10.00	0.835	0.269		0.27	0.54	0.81	1.07	2.69	4.03	5.37	6.71	8.06	9.40	10.74	12.08	13.43
Crete 5 Drachmai	1901	25.00	0.900	0.723		0.72	1.45	2.17	2.89	7.23	10.85	14.46	18.08	21.69	25.31	28.92	32.54	36.15
Croatia 100 Kuna	1994-1996	20.00	0.925	0.594		0.59	1.19	1.78	2.38	5.94	8.91	11.88	14.85	17.82	20.79	23.76	26.73	29.70
Croatia 150 Kuna	1995-1998	24.00	0.925	0.714		0.71	1.43	2.14	2.86	7.14	10.71	14.28	17.85	21.42	24.99	28.56	32.13	35.70
Croatia 200 Kuna	1994-1998	33.63	0.925	1.000		1.00	2.00	3.00	4.00	10.00	15.00	20.00	25.00	30.00	35.00	40.00	45.00	50.00
Cuba 10 Centavos	1915-1952	2.50	0.900	0.072		0.07	0.14	0.22	0.29	0.72	1.08	1.44	1.80	2.16	2.52	2.88	3.24	3.60
Cuba 20 Centavos	1915-1952	5.00	0.900	0.145		0.15	0.29	0.44	0.58	1.45	2.18	2.90	3.63	4.35	5.08	5.80	6.53	7.25
Cuba 25 Centavos	1953	6.25	0.900	0.181		0.18	0.36	0.54	0.72	1.81	2.72	3.62	4.53	5.43	6.34	7.24	8.15	9.05
Cuba 40 Centavos	1915-1952	10.00	0.900	0.289		0.29	0.58	0.87	1.16	2.89	4.34	5.78	7.23	8.67	10.12	11.56	13.01	14.45
Cuba 50 Centavos	1953	12.50	0.900	0.362		0.36	0.72	1.09	1.45	3.62	5.43	7.23	9.04	10.85	12.66	14.47	16.28	18.09
Cuba 1 Peso	1898	22.55	0.900	0.653		0.65	1.31	1.96	2.61	6.53	9.80	13.06	16.33	19.59	22.86	26.12	29.39	32.65
Cuba 1 Peso	1915-1953	26.73	0.900	0.774		0.77	1.55	2.32	3.10	7.74	11.61	15.48	19.35	23.22	27.09	30.96	34.83	38.70
Cuba 5 Pesos	1975	13.30	0.900	0.386		0.39	0.77	1.16	1.54	3.86	5.79	7.71	9.64	11.57	13.50	15.43	17.36	19.29
Cuba 5 Pesos	1980-1988	12.00	0.999	0.386		0.39	0.77	1.16	1.54	3.86	5.78	7.71	9.64	11.57	13.49	15.42	17.35	19.28
Cuba 5 Pesos	1988	6.00	0.999	0.193		0.19	0.39	0.58	0.77	1.93	2.89	3.85	4.82	5.78	6.74	7.71	8.67	9.64
Cuba 5 Pesos	1988-1990	16.00	0.999	0.512		0.51	1.02	1.54	2.05	5.12	7.68	10.24	12.80	15.36	17.92	20.48	23.04	25.60
Cuba 10 Pesos	1975	28.66	0.900	0.772		0.77	1.54	2.31	3.09	7.72	11.57	15.43	19.29	23.15	27.00	30.86	34.72	38.58
Cuba 10 Pesos	1980	18.00	0.999	0.578		0.58	1.16	1.73	2.31	5.78	8.67	11.56	14.46	17.35	20.24	23.13	26.02	28.91

Country & Denomination	Years Minted	Grams Weight	Fineness	Troy (ASW)	Code	$ Value 1	$ Value 2	$ Value 3	$ Value 4	$ Value 10	$ Value 15	$ Value 20	$ Value 25	$ Value 30	$ Value 35	$ Value 40	$ Value 45	$ Value 50
Cuba 10 Pesos	1987-1993	31.10	0.999	1.000		1.00	2.00	3.00	4.00	10.00	15.00	20.00	25.00	30.00	35.00	40.00	45.00	50.00
Cuba 20 Pesos	1977-1979	26.00	0.925	0.773		0.77	1.55	2.32	3.09	7.73	11.60	15.46	19.33	23.19	27.06	30.92	34.79	38.65
Cuba 20 Pesos	1987-1995	62.20	0.999	2.000		2.00	4.00	6.00	8.00	20.00	30.00	40.00	50.00	60.00	70.00	80.00	90.00	100.00
Cuba 30 Pesos	1991-1992	93.25	0.999	3.000		3.00	6.00	9.00	12.00	30.00	45.00	60.00	75.00	90.00	105.00	120.00	135.00	150.00
Cuba 50 Pesos	1990-1995	155.52	0.999	5.000	N	5.00	10.00	15.00	20.00	50.00	75.00	100.00	125.00	150.00	175.00	200.00	225.00	250.00
Cuba 150 Pesos	1996	411.43	0.999	13.228		13.23	26.46	39.68	52.91	132.28	198.42	264.56	330.70	396.84	462.98	529.12	595.26	661.40
Cuba 300 Pesos	1996	822.85	0.999	27.566		27.57	55.13	82.70	110.26	275.66	413.49	551.32	689.15	826.98	964.81	1102.64	1240.47	1378.30
Curacao 1/10 Gulden	1901	1.40	0.640	0.029		0.03	0.06	0.09	0.12	0.29	0.43	0.58	0.72	0.86	1.01	1.15	1.30	1.44
Curacao 10 Cents	1941, 1943	1.40	0.640	0.029		0.03	0.06	0.09	0.12	0.29	0.43	0.58	0.72	0.86	1.01	1.15	1.30	1.44
Curacao 1/10 Gulden	1944-1948	1.40	0.640	0.029		0.03	0.06	0.09	0.12	0.29	0.43	0.58	0.72	0.86	1.01	1.15	1.30	1.44
Curacao 25 Cents	1941, 1943	3.58	0.640	0.074		0.07	0.15	0.22	0.29	0.74	1.10	1.47	1.84	2.21	2.58	2.94	3.31	3.68
Curacao 1/4 Gulden	1900	3.58	0.640	0.074		0.07	0.15	0.22	0.30	0.74	1.11	1.48	1.85	2.22	2.59	2.96	3.33	3.70
Curacao 1/4 Gulden	1944-1947	3.58	0.640	0.074		0.07	0.15	0.22	0.30	0.74	1.11	1.48	1.85	2.22	2.59	2.96	3.33	3.70
Curacao Gulden	1944	10.00	0.720	0.232		0.23	0.46	0.69	0.93	2.32	3.47	4.63	5.79	6.95	8.10	9.26	10.42	11.58
Curacao 2-1/2 Gulden	1944	25.00	0.720	0.579		0.58	1.16	1.74	2.31	5.79	8.68	11.57	14.47	17.36	20.25	23.15	26.04	28.94
Cyprus 3 Piastres	1901	1.90	0.925	0.056		0.06	0.11	0.17	0.22	0.56	0.84	1.12	1.40	1.68	1.96	2.24	2.52	2.80
Cyprus 4-1/2 Piastres	1921, 1938	2.80	0.925	0.084		0.08	0.17	0.25	0.34	0.84	1.26	1.68	2.10	2.52	2.94	3.36	3.78	4.20
Cyprus 9 Piastres	1901-1940	5.70	0.925	0.168		0.17	0.34	0.50	0.67	1.68	2.52	3.36	4.20	5.04	5.88	6.72	7.56	8.40
Cyprus 18 Piastres	1901-1940	11.30	0.925	0.336		0.34	0.67	1.01	1.34	3.36	5.04	6.72	8.40	10.08	11.76	13.44	15.12	16.80
Cyprus 45 Piastres	1928	28.28	0.925	0.841		0.84	1.68	2.52	3.36	8.41	12.62	16.82	21.03	25.23	29.44	33.64	37.85	42.05
Cyprus 500 Mils	1970	22.62	0.800	0.582	N	0.58	1.16	1.75	2.33	5.82	8.73	11.64	14.55	17.46	20.37	23.28	26.19	29.10
Cyprus 500 Mils	1975	14.14	0.800	0.364	N	0.36	0.73	1.09	1.46	3.64	5.46	7.28	9.10	10.92	12.74	14.56	16.38	18.20
Cyprus 500 Mils	1976	14.14	0.925	0.421	N	0.42	0.84	1.26	1.68	4.21	6.32	8.42	10.53	12.63	14.74	16.84	18.95	21.05
Cyprus 50 Cents	1985, 1988	14.14	0.925	0.421	N	0.42	0.84	1.26	1.68	4.21	6.32	8.42	10.53	12.63	14.74	16.84	18.95	21.05
Cyprus 1 Pound	1976	28.28	0.925	0.841	N	0.84	1.68	2.52	3.36	8.41	12.62	16.82	21.03	25.23	29.44	33.64	37.85	42.05
Cyprus 1 Pound	1986-1997	28.28	0.925	0.841	N	0.84	1.68	2.52	3.36	8.41	12.62	16.82	21.03	25.23	29.44	33.64	37.85	42.06
Cyprus 2 Pounds	2000	15.00	0.925	0.446	N	0.45	0.89	1.34	1.78	4.46	6.69	8.92	11.15	13.38	15.61	17.84	20.07	22.30
Czech Republic 200 Korun	1993-2000	13.00	0.900	0.376		0.38	0.75	1.13	1.50	3.76	5.64	7.52	9.40	11.28	13.16	15.04	16.92	18.80
Czechoslovakia 5 Korun	1928-1932	7.00	0.500	0.125		0.13	0.25	0.38	0.50	1.25	1.88	2.50	3.13	3.75	4.38	5.00	5.63	6.25
Czechoslovakia 10 Korun	1928-1932	10.00	0.700	0.225		0.23	0.45	0.68	0.90	2.25	3.38	4.50	5.63	6.75	7.88	9.00	10.13	11.25
Czechoslovakia 10 Korun	1955-1957	12.00	0.500	0.193		0.19	0.39	0.58	0.77	1.93	2.90	3.86	4.83	5.79	6.76	7.72	8.69	9.65
Czechoslovakia 10 Korun	1964-1968	12.00	0.500	0.193		0.19	0.39	0.58	0.77	1.93	2.90	3.86	4.83	5.79	6.76	7.72	8.69	9.65
Czechoslovakia 20 Korun	1933-1937	12.00	0.700	0.270		0.27	0.54	0.81	1.08	2.70	4.05	5.40	6.75	8.10	9.45	10.80	12.15	13.50
Czechoslovakia 20 Korun	1972	9.00	0.500	0.145		0.15	0.29	0.44	0.58	1.45	2.18	2.90	3.63	4.35	5.08	5.80	6.53	7.25
Czechoslovakia 25 Korun	1954-1955	12.00	0.500	0.193		0.19	0.39	0.58	0.77	1.93	2.90	3.86	4.83	5.79	6.76	7.72	8.69	9.65
Czechoslovakia 25 Korun	1965-1970	16.00	0.500	0.257	S	0.26	0.51	0.77	1.03	2.57	3.86	5.14	6.43	7.71	9.00	10.28	11.57	12.85
Czechoslovakia 50 Korun	1947-1949	10.00	0.500	0.161		0.16	0.32	0.48	0.64	1.61	2.42	3.22	4.03	4.83	5.64	6.44	7.25	8.05
Czechoslovakia 50 Korun	1955, 1968	20.00	0.900	0.579		0.58	1.16	1.74	2.32	5.79	8.69	11.58	14.48	17.37	20.27	23.16	26.06	28.95
Czechoslovakia 50 Korun	1970-1979	13.00	0.700	0.293		0.29	0.59	0.88	1.17	2.93	4.40	5.86	7.33	8.79	10.26	11.72	13.19	14.65
Czechoslovakia 50 Korun	1986-1991	7.00	0.500	0.113	N	0.11	0.23	0.34	0.45	1.13	1.70	2.26	2.83	3.39	3.96	4.52	5.09	5.65
Czechoslovakia 50 Korun	1991	7.00	0.700	0.158		0.16	0.32	0.47	0.63	1.58	2.37	3.16	3.95	4.74	5.53	6.32	7.11	7.90

Country & Denomination	Years Minted	Grams Weight	Fineness	Troy (ASW)	Code	$ Value 1	$ Value 2	$ Value 3	$ Value 4	$ Value 10	$ Value 15	$ Value 20	$ Value 25	$ Value 30	$ Value 35	$ Value 40	$ Value 45	$ Value 50
Czechoslovakia 100 Korun	1948-1951	14.00	0.500	0.225		0.23	0.45	0.68	0.90	2.25	3.38	4.50	5.63	6.75	7.88	9.00	10.13	11.25
Czechoslovakia 100 Korun	1955	24.00	0.900	0.695		0.70	1.39	2.09	2.78	6.95	10.43	13.90	17.38	20.85	24.33	27.80	31.28	34.75
Czechoslovakia 100 Korun	1971-1980	15.00	0.700	0.338	S	0.34	0.68	1.01	1.35	3.38	5.07	6.76	8.45	10.14	11.83	13.52	15.21	16.90
Czechoslovakia 100 Korun	1980-1985	9.00	0.500	0.145		0.15	0.29	0.44	0.58	1.45	2.18	2.90	3.63	4.35	5.08	5.80	6.53	7.25
Czechoslovakia 100 Korun	1986-1993	13.00	0.500	0.209		0.21	0.42	0.63	0.84	2.09	3.14	4.18	5.23	6.27	7.32	8.36	9.41	10.45
Czechoslovakia 100 Korun	1991	13.00	0.700	0.293		0.29	0.59	0.88	1.17	2.93	4.40	5.86	7.33	8.79	10.26	11.72	13.19	14.65
Czechoslovakia 100 Korun	1993	13.00	0.750	0.314		0.31	0.63	0.94	1.26	3.14	4.71	6.28	7.85	9.42	10.99	12.56	14.13	15.70
Czechoslovakia 500 Korun	1981-1993	24.00	0.900	0.694	S	0.69	1.39	2.08	2.78	6.94	10.41	13.88	17.35	20.82	24.29	27.76	31.23	34.70
D																		
Dahomey (Benin) 100 Francs	1971	5.10	0.999	0.164		0.16	0.33	0.49	0.66	1.64	2.46	3.28	4.10	4.91	5.73	6.55	7.37	8.19
Dahomey (Benin) 200 Francs	1971	10.25	0.999	0.329		0.33	0.66	0.99	1.32	3.29	4.94	6.58	8.23	9.88	11.52	13.17	14.81	16.46
Dahomey (Benin) 500 Francs	1971	25.20	0.999	0.809		0.81	1.62	2.43	3.24	8.09	12.14	16.19	20.24	24.28	28.33	32.38	36.42	40.47
Dahomey (Benin) 1000 Francs	1971	51.50	0.999	1.654	S	1.65	3.31	4.96	6.62	16.54	24.81	33.08	41.36	49.63	57.90	66.17	74.44	82.71
Danish West Indies 2 Skilling*	1816-1848	1.22	0.250	0.010	S	0.01	0.02	0.03	0.04	0.10	0.15	0.20	0.25	0.30	0.35	0.40	0.45	0.50
Danish West Indies 10 Skilling	1816-1848	2.44	0.625	0.049	S	0.05	0.10	0.15	0.20	0.49	0.74	0.98	1.23	1.47	1.72	1.96	2.21	2.45
Danish West Indies 20 Skilling	1816-1848	4.87	0.625	0.098	S	0.10	0.20	0.29	0.39	0.98	1.47	1.96	2.45	2.94	3.43	3.92	4.41	4.90
Danish West Indies 3 Cents	1859	1.04	0.625	0.021		0.02	0.04	0.06	0.08	0.21	0.32	0.42	0.53	0.63	0.74	0.84	0.95	1.05
Danish West Indies 5 Cents	1859-1879	1.74	0.625	0.035	S	0.04	0.07	0.11	0.14	0.35	0.53	0.70	0.88	1.05	1.23	1.40	1.58	1.75
Danish West Indies 10 Cents	1859-1879	3.49	0.625	0.070	S	0.07	0.14	0.21	0.28	0.70	1.05	1.40	1.75	2.10	2.45	2.80	3.15	3.50
Dan. W. Indies 50 Bit / 10 Cents	1905	2.50	0.800	0.064		0.06	0.13	0.19	0.26	0.64	0.96	1.28	1.60	1.92	2.24	2.56	2.88	3.20
Danish West Indies 20 Cents	1859-1879	6.96	0.625	0.140	S	0.14	0.28	0.42	0.56	1.40	2.10	2.80	3.50	4.20	4.90	5.60	6.30	7.00
Dan. W. Indies 20 Cents / 1 Franc	1905, 1907	5.00	0.800	0.129		0.13	0.26	0.39	0.52	1.29	1.94	2.58	3.23	3.87	4.52	5.16	5.81	6.45
Danish West Indies 40 Cents	1905, 1907	10.00	0.800	0.257		0.26	0.51	0.77	1.03	2.57	3.86	5.14	6.43	7.71	9.00	10.28	11.57	12.85
Dan. W. Indies 40 Cents/ 2 Francs	1905, 1907	10.00	0.800	0.257		0.26	0.51	0.77	1.03	2.57	3.86	5.14	6.43	7.71	9.00	10.28	11.57	12.85
Danzig 1/2 Gulden	1923, 1927	2.50	0.750	0.060	S	0.06	0.12	0.18	0.24	0.60	0.90	1.20	1.50	1.80	2.10	2.40	2.70	3.00
Danzig 1 Gulden	1923	5.00	0.750	0.121	S	0.12	0.24	0.36	0.48	1.21	1.82	2.42	3.03	3.63	4.24	4.84	5.45	6.05
Danzig 2 Gulden	1923	10.00	0.750	0.241		0.24	0.48	0.72	0.96	2.41	3.62	4.82	6.03	7.23	8.44	9.64	10.85	12.05
Danzig 2 Gulden	1932	10.00	0.500	0.161		0.16	0.32	0.48	0.64	1.61	2.42	3.22	4.03	4.83	5.64	6.44	7.25	8.05
Danzig 5 Gulden	1923, 1927	25.00	0.750	0.603	S	0.60	1.21	1.81	2.41	6.03	9.05	12.06	15.08	18.09	21.11	24.12	27.14	30.15
Danzig 5 Gulden	1932	14.82	0.500	0.238		0.24	0.48	0.71	0.95	2.38	3.57	4.76	5.95	7.14	8.33	9.52	10.71	11.90
Denmark 1 Skilling	1808-1819	0.92	0.138	0.004	S	0.00	0.01	0.01	0.02	0.04	0.06	0.08	0.10	0.12	0.14	0.16	0.18	0.20
Denmark 2 Skilling	1801-1805	1.50	0.250	0.012	S	0.01	0.02	0.04	0.05	0.12	0.18	0.24	0.30	0.36	0.42	0.48	0.54	0.60
Denmark 4 Skilling	1807	2.60	0.250	0.021		0.02	0.04	0.06	0.08	0.21	0.32	0.42	0.53	0.63	0.74	0.84	0.95	1.05
Denmark 1/6 Rigsdaler	1808	5.05	0.406	0.066		0.07	0.13	0.20	0.26	0.66	0.99	1.32	1.65	1.98	2.31	2.64	2.97	3.30
Denmark 1 Speciedaler	1801	28.89	0.875	0.813		0.81	1.63	2.44	3.25	8.13	12.20	16.26	20.33	24.39	28.46	32.52	36.59	40.65
Denmark 1 Speciedaler	1819-1853	28.89	0.875	0.813	S	0.81	1.63	2.44	3.25	8.13	12.20	16.26	20.33	24.39	28.46	32.52	36.59	40.65
Denmark 2 RigsbankSkilling	1836	1.11	0.208	0.007		0.01	0.01	0.02	0.03	0.07	0.11	0.14	0.18	0.21	0.25	0.28	0.32	0.35
Denmark 3 RigsbankSkilling	1836-1842	1.52	0.229	0.011	S	0.01	0.02	0.03	0.04	0.11	0.17	0.22	0.28	0.33	0.39	0.44	0.50	0.55
Denmark 4 RigsbankSkilling	1836-1842	1.86	0.250	0.015	S	0.02	0.03	0.05	0.06	0.15	0.23	0.30	0.38	0.45	0.53	0.60	0.68	0.75
Denmark 8 RigsbankSkilling	1843	2.81	0.375	0.034		0.03	0.07	0.10	0.14	0.34	0.51	0.68	0.85	1.02	1.19	1.36	1.53	1.70
Denmark 16 RigsbankSkilling	1842, 1844	4.21	0.500	0.068		0.07	0.14	0.20	0.27	0.68	1.02	1.36	1.70	2.04	2.38	2.72	3.06	3.40
Denmark 32 RigsbankSkilling	1818-1843	6.13	0.687	0.135	S	0.14	0.27	0.41	0.54	1.35	2.03	2.70	3.38	4.05	4.73	5.40	6.08	6.75

Country & Denomination	Years Minted	Grams Weight	Fineness	Troy (ASW)	Code	$ Value 1	$ Value 2	$ Value 3	$ Value 4	$ Value 10	$ Value 15	$ Value 20	$ Value 25	$ Value 30	$ Value 35	$ Value 40	$ Value 45	$ Value 50
Denmark 1 Rigsbankdaler	1813-1851	14.45	0.875	0.406	S	0.41	0.81	1.22	1.62	4.06	6.09	8.12	10.15	12.18	14.21	16.24	18.27	20.30
Denmark 4 Skilling Rigsmont	1854-1874	1.86	0.250	0.015	S	0.02	0.03	0.05	0.06	0.15	0.23	0.30	0.38	0.45	0.53	0.60	0.68	0.75
Denmark 16 Skilling Rigsmont	1856-1858	3.90	0.500	0.063		0.06	0.13	0.19	0.25	0.63	0.95	1.26	1.58	1.89	2.21	2.52	2.84	3.15
Denmark 1/2 Rigsdaler	1854, 1855	7.22	0.875	0.203		0.20	0.41	0.61	0.81	2.03	3.05	4.06	5.08	6.09	7.11	8.12	9.14	10.15
Denmark 1 Rigsdaler	1854, 1855	14.45	0.875	0.406	S	0.41	0.81	1.22	1.62	4.06	6.09	8.12	10.15	12.18	14.21	16.24	18.27	20.30
Denmark 2 Rigsdaler	1854-1872	28.89	0.875	0.813	S	0.81	1.63	2.44	3.25	8.13	12.20	16.26	20.33	24.39	28.46	32.52	36.59	40.65
Denmark 10 Ore	1894-1919	1.45	0.400	0.019	S	0.02	0.04	0.06	0.08	0.19	0.29	0.38	0.48	0.57	0.67	0.76	0.86	0.95
Denmark 25 Ore	1874-1919	2.42	0.600	0.047	S	0.05	0.09	0.14	0.19	0.47	0.71	0.94	1.18	1.41	1.65	1.88	2.12	2.35
Denmark 1 Krone	1875-1916	7.50	0.800	0.193	S	0.19	0.39	0.58	0.77	1.93	2.90	3.86	4.83	5.79	6.76	7.72	8.69	9.65
Denmark 2 Kroner	1875-1958	15.00	0.800	0.386	S	0.39	0.77	1.16	1.54	3.86	5.79	7.72	9.65	11.58	13.51	15.44	17.37	19.30
Denmark 5 Kroner	1960, 1964	17.00	0.800	0.437		0.44	0.87	1.31	1.75	4.37	6.56	8.74	10.93	13.11	15.30	17.48	19.67	21.85
Denmark 10 Kroner	1967-1972	20.40	0.800	0.525		0.53	1.05	1.58	2.10	5.25	7.88	10.50	13.13	15.75	18.38	21.00	23.63	26.25
Denmark 200 Kroner	1990	31.10	0.800	0.800		0.80	1.60	2.40	3.20	8.00	12.00	16.00	20.00	24.00	28.00	32.00	36.00	40.00
Denmark 200 Kroner	1992-2000	31.10	0.999	1.000	S	1.00	2.00	3.00	4.00	10.00	15.00	20.00	25.00	30.00	35.00	40.00	45.00	50.00
Djibouti 100 Francs	1994, 1996	31.47	0.925	0.936		0.94	1.87	2.81	3.74	9.36	14.04	18.72	23.40	28.08	32.76	37.44	42.12	46.80
Djibouti 1500 Francs	1991	24.30	0.999	0.771		0.77	1.54	2.31	3.08	7.71	11.57	15.42	19.28	23.13	26.99	30.84	34.70	38.55
Dominica 10 Dollars	1978-1979	20.50	0.925	0.610		0.61	1.22	1.83	2.44	6.10	9.15	12.20	15.25	18.30	21.35	24.40	27.45	30.50
Dominica 10 Dollars	1985	28.28	0.925	0.841	N	0.84	1.68	2.52	3.36	8.41	12.62	16.82	21.03	25.23	29.44	33.64	37.85	42.05
Dominica 20 Dollars	1978-1979	40.91	0.925	1.217		1.22	2.43	3.65	4.87	12.17	18.26	24.34	30.43	36.51	42.60	48.68	54.77	60.85
Dominica 100 Dollars	1988	129.59	0.925	3.854		3.85	7.71	11.56	15.42	38.54	57.81	77.08	96.35	115.62	134.89	154.16	173.43	192.70
Dominican Rep. 50 Centesimos	1891	2.50	0.835	0.067		0.07	0.13	0.20	0.27	0.67	1.01	1.34	1.68	2.01	2.35	2.68	3.02	3.35
Dominican Rep. 1 Franco	1891	5.00	0.835	0.134		0.13	0.27	0.40	0.54	1.34	2.01	2.68	3.35	4.02	4.69	5.36	6.03	6.70
Dominican Rep. 5 Francos	1891	25.00	0.900	0.723		0.72	1.45	2.17	2.89	7.23	10.85	14.46	18.08	21.69	25.31	28.92	32.54	36.15
Dominican Rep. 5 Centavos	1944	5.00	0.350	0.056		0.06	0.11	0.17	0.22	0.56	0.84	1.12	1.40	1.68	1.96	2.24	2.52	2.80
Dominican Rep. 10 Centavos	1897	2.50	0.350	0.028		0.03	0.06	0.08	0.11	0.28	0.42	0.56	0.70	0.84	0.98	1.12	1.26	1.40
Dominican Rep. 10 Centavos	1937-1961	2.50	0.900	0.072		0.07	0.14	0.22	0.29	0.72	1.08	1.44	1.80	2.16	2.52	2.88	3.24	3.60
Dominican Rep. 10 Centavos	1989	2.90	0.925	0.086	N	0.09	0.17	0.26	0.34	0.86	1.29	1.72	2.15	2.58	3.01	3.44	3.87	4.30
Dominican Rep. 20 Centavos	1897	5.00	0.350	0.056		0.06	0.11	0.17	0.22	0.56	0.84	1.12	1.40	1.68	1.96	2.24	2.52	2.80
Dominican Rep. 25 Centavos	1937-1961	6.25	0.900	0.181		0.18	0.36	0.54	0.72	1.81	2.72	3.62	4.53	5.43	6.34	7.24	8.15	9.05
Dominican Rep. 25 Centavos	1963	6.25	0.650	0.131		0.13	0.26	0.39	0.52	1.31	1.97	2.62	3.28	3.93	4.59	5.24	5.90	6.55
Dominican Rep. 25 Centavos	1983-1986	6.25	0.900	0.181	N, S	0.18	0.36	0.54	0.72	1.81	2.72	3.62	4.53	5.43	6.34	7.24	8.15	9.05
Dominican Rep. 25 Centavos	1989	6.74	0.925	0.201	N	0.20	0.40	0.60	0.80	2.01	3.02	4.02	5.03	6.03	7.04	8.04	9.05	10.05
Dominican Republic 1/2 Peso	1897	12.50	0.350	0.141		0.14	0.28	0.42	0.56	1.41	2.12	2.82	3.53	4.23	4.94	5.64	6.35	7.05
Dominican Republic 1/2 Peso	1937-1961	12.50	0.900	0.362	S	0.36	0.72	1.09	1.45	3.62	5.43	7.24	9.05	10.86	12.67	14.48	16.29	18.10
Dominican Republic 1/2 Peso	1963	12.50	0.650	0.261		0.26	0.52	0.78	1.04	2.61	3.92	5.22	6.53	7.83	9.14	10.44	11.75	13.05
Dominican Republic 1/2 Peso	1983-1986	12.50	0.900	0.362	S	0.36	0.72	1.09	1.45	3.62	5.43	7.24	9.05	10.86	12.67	14.48	16.29	18.10
Dominican Republic 1/2 Peso	1989	14.65	0.925	0.436	N	0.44	0.87	1.31	1.74	4.36	6.54	8.72	10.90	13.08	15.26	17.44	19.62	21.80
Dominican Republic 1 Peso	1897	25.00	0.350	0.281		0.28	0.56	0.84	1.12	2.81	4.22	5.62	7.03	8.43	9.84	11.24	12.65	14.05
Dominican Republic 1 Peso	1939-1955	26.70	0.900	0.773	S	0.77	1.55	2.32	3.09	7.73	11.60	15.46	19.33	23.19	27.06	30.92	34.79	38.65
Dominican Republic 1 Peso	1963	26.70	0.650	0.558		0.56	1.12	1.67	2.23	5.58	8.37	11.16	13.95	16.74	19.53	22.32	25.11	27.90
Dominican Republic 1 Peso	1988-1992	21.10	0.999	1.000	N	1.00	2.00	3.00	4.00	10.00	15.00	20.00	25.00	30.00	35.00	40.00	45.00	50.00
Dominican Republic 1 Peso	1995	28.44	0.925	0.846		0.85	1.69	2.54	3.38	8.46	12.69	16.92	21.15	25.38	29.61	33.84	38.07	42.30

Country & Denomination	Years Minted	Grams Weight	Fineness	Troy ness (ASW)	Code	$ Value 1	$ Value 2	$ Value 3	$ Value 4	$ Value 10	$ Value 15	$ Value 20	$ Value 25	$ Value 30	$ Value 35	$ Value 40	$ Value 45	$ Value 50
Dominican Republic 1 Peso	1988	21.10	0.999	1.000	N	1.00	2.00	3.00	4.00	10.00	15.00	20.00	25.00	30.00	35.00	40.00	45.00	50.00
Dominican Rep. 10 Pesos	1975	28.00	0.900	0.810		0.81	1.62	2.43	3.24	8.10	12.15	16.20	20.25	24.30	28.35	32.40	36.45	40.50
Dominican Rep. 10 Pesos	1982	23.33	0.925	0.694		0.69	1.39	2.08	2.78	6.94	10.41	13.88	17.35	20.82	24.29	27.76	31.23	34.70
Dominican Rep. 10 Pesos	2000	2.45	0.999	0.079		0.08	0.16	0.24	0.32	0.79	1.19	1.58	1.98	2.37	2.77	3.16	3.56	3.95
Dominican Rep. 25 Pesos	1977	65.00	0.925	0.933		0.93	1.87	2.80	3.73	9.33	14.00	18.66	23.33	27.99	32.66	37.32	41.99	46.65
Dominican Rep. 30 Pesos	1977	78.00	0.925	2.320		2.32	4.64	6.96	9.28	23.20	34.80	46.40	58.00	69.60	81.20	92.80	104.40	116.00
Dominican Rep. 100 Pesos	1988-1992	155.50	0.999	5.000		5.00	10.00	15.00	20.00	50.00	75.00	100.00	125.00	150.00	175.00	200.00	225.00	250.00
E																		
East Africa 25 Cents	1906-1918	2.92	0.800	0.075	S	0.08	0.15	0.23	0.30	0.75	1.13	1.50	1.88	2.25	2.63	3.00	3.38	3.75
East Africa 25 Cents	1920	2.92	0.500	0.047		0.05	0.09	0.14	0.19	0.47	0.71	0.94	1.18	1.41	1.65	1.88	2.12	2.35
East Africa 50 Cents	1906-1919	5.83	0.800	0.150	S	0.15	0.30	0.45	0.60	1.50	2.25	3.00	3.75	4.50	5.25	6.00	6.75	7.50
East Africa 50 Cents	1920	5.83	0.500	0.094		0.09	0.19	0.28	0.38	0.94	1.41	1.88	2.35	2.82	3.29	3.76	4.23	4.70
East Africa 50 Cents	1921-1944	3.89	0.250	0.031	S	0.03	0.06	0.09	0.12	0.31	0.47	0.62	0.78	0.93	1.09	1.24	1.40	1.55
East Africa 1 Shilling	1921-1946	7.78	0.250	0.063	S	0.06	0.13	0.19	0.25	0.63	0.95	1.26	1.58	1.89	2.21	2.52	2.84	3.15
East Africa 1 Florin	1920-1921	11.66	0.500	0.188		0.19	0.38	0.56	0.75	1.88	2.82	3.76	4.70	5.64	6.58	7.52	8.46	9.40
E. Caribbean States 10 Dollars	1981	28.28	0.500	0.455		0.46	0.91	1.37	1.82	4.55	6.83	9.10	11.38	13.65	15.93	18.20	20.48	22.75
E. Caribbean States 10 Dollars	1990, 1993	28.28	0.925	0.841		0.84	1.68	2.52	3.36	8.41	12.62	16.82	21.03	25.23	29.44	33.64	37.85	42.05
E. Caribbean States 10 Dollars	1994	31.47	0.925	0.936		0.94	1.87	2.81	3.74	9.36	14.04	18.72	23.40	28.08	32.76	37.44	42.12	46.80
E. Caribbean States 10 Dollars	1996-1999	28.50	0.925	0.848	S	0.85	1.70	2.54	3.39	8.48	12.72	16.96	21.20	25.44	29.68	33.92	38.16	42.40
E. Caribbean States 50 Dollars	1981, 1983	28.28	0.925	0.841		0.84	1.68	2.52	3.36	8.41	12.62	16.82	21.03	25.23	29.44	33.64	37.85	42.05
Ecuador 1/4 Real*	1842-1843	0.76	0.333	0.008	V	0.01	0.02	0.02	0.03	0.08	0.12	0.16	0.20	0.24	0.28	0.32	0.36	0.40
Ecuador 1/4 Real	1849-1862	0.70	0.667	0.015	V	0.02	0.03	0.05	0.06	0.15	0.23	0.30	0.38	0.45	0.53	0.60	0.68	0.75
Ecuador 1/2 Real	1833-1840	1.30	0.667	0.028	V	0.03	0.06	0.08	0.11	0.28	0.42	0.56	0.70	0.84	0.98	1.12	1.26	1.40
Ecuador 1/2 Real	1848, 1849	1.70	0.667	0.036	V	0.04	0.07	0.11	0.14	0.36	0.54	0.72	0.90	1.08	1.26	1.44	1.62	1.80
Ecuador 1 Real	1833-1835	3.20	0.667	0.070	V	0.07	0.14	0.21	0.28	0.70	1.05	1.40	1.75	2.10	2.45	2.80	3.15	3.50
Ecuador 1 Real	1836-1841	3.70	0.667	0.080	V	0.08	0.16	0.24	0.32	0.80	1.20	1.60	2.00	2.40	2.80	3.20	3.60	4.00
Ecuador 2 Reales	1833-1836	5.40	0.667	0.116	S, V	0.12	0.23	0.35	0.46	1.16	1.74	2.32	2.90	3.48	4.06	4.64	5.22	5.80
Ecuador 2 Reales	1837-1862	5.80	0.667	0.125	V	0.13	0.25	0.38	0.50	1.25	1.88	2.50	3.13	3.75	4.38	5.00	5.63	6.25
Ecuador 2 Reales	1862	6.76	0.667	0.145		0.15	0.29	0.44	0.58	1.45	2.18	2.90	3.63	4.35	5.08	5.80	6.53	7.25
Ecuador 4 Reales	1841-1843	12.50	0.667	0.269	V	0.27	0.54	0.81	1.08	2.69	4.04	5.38	6.73	8.07	9.42	10.76	12.11	13.45
Ecuador 4 Reales	1841	15.34	0.892	0.419		0.42	0.84	1.26	1.68	4.19	6.29	8.38	10.48	12.57	14.67	16.76	18.86	20.95
Ecuador 4 Reales	1844, 1845	12.00	0.667	0.260	V	0.26	0.52	0.78	1.04	2.60	3.90	5.20	6.50	7.80	9.10	10.40	11.70	13.00
Ecuador 4 Reales	1855-1862	13.40	0.667	0.288	S, V	0.29	0.58	0.86	1.15	2.88	4.32	5.76	7.20	8.64	10.08	11.52	12.96	14.40
Ecuador 8 Reales	1846	25.00	0.900	0.723		0.72	1.45	2.17	2.89	7.23	10.85	14.46	18.08	21.69	25.31	28.92	32.54	36.15
Ecuador 5 Francos	1858	25.00	0.900	0.723		0.72	1.45	2.17	2.89	7.23	10.85	14.46	18.08	21.69	25.31	28.92	32.54	36.15
Ecuador 1/2 Decimo	1893-1915	1.25	0.900	0.036	S	0.04	0.07	0.11	0.14	0.36	0.54	0.72	0.90	1.08	1.26	1.44	1.62	1.80
Ecuador 1 Decimo	1884-1916	2.50	0.900	0.072	S	0.07	0.14	0.22	0.29	0.72	1.08	1.44	1.80	2.16	2.52	2.88	3.24	3.60
Ecuador 2 Decimos	1884-1916	5.00	0.900	0.145	S	0.15	0.29	0.44	0.58	1.45	2.18	2.90	3.63	4.35	5.08	5.80	6.53	7.25
Ecuador 50 Centavos	1928, 1930	2.50	0.720	0.058		0.06	0.12	0.17	0.23	0.58	0.87	1.16	1.45	1.74	2.03	2.32	2.61	2.90
Ecuador 1/2 Sucre	1884	12.50	0.900	0.362		0.36	0.72	1.09	1.45	3.62	5.43	7.24	9.05	10.86	12.67	14.48	16.29	18.10
Ecuador 1/2 Sucre	1884-1897	25.00	0.900	0.723		0.72	1.45	2.17	2.89	7.23	10.85	14.46	18.08	21.69	25.31	28.92	32.54	36.15
Ecuador 1 Sucre	1928-1934	5.00	0.720	0.116	S	0.12	0.23	0.35	0.46	1.16	1.74	2.32	2.90	3.48	4.06	4.64	5.22	5.80
Ecuador 2 Sucres	1928-1944	10.00	0.720	0.232	S	0.23	0.46	0.70	0.93	2.32	3.48	4.64	5.80	6.96	8.12	9.28	10.44	11.60

Country & Denomination	Years Minted	Grams Weight	Fineness	Troy (ASW)	Code	$ Value 1	$ Value 2	$ Value 3	$ Value 4	$ Value 10	$ Value 15	$ Value 20	$ Value 25	$ Value 30	$ Value 35	$ Value 40	$ Value 45	$ Value 50
Ecuador 5 Sucres	1943-1944	25.00	0.720	0.579		0.58	1.16	1.74	2.32	5.79	8.69	11.58	14.48	17.37	20.27	23.16	26.06	28.95
Ecuador 1000 Sucres	1986	23.33	0.925	0.694		0.69	1.39	2.08	2.78	6.94	10.41	13.88	17.35	20.82	24.29	27.76	31.23	34.70
Ecuador 5000 Sucres	1991-1999	27.10	0.925	0.806	S	0.81	1.61	2.42	3.22	8.06	12.09	16.12	20.15	24.18	28.21	32.24	36.27	40.30
Egypt 10 Para*	1839-1860	0.37	0.833	0.009	A	0.01	0.02	0.03	0.04	0.09	0.14	0.18	0.23	0.27	0.32	0.36	0.41	0.45
Egypt 10 Para	1861-1878	0.31	0.833	0.008	A, N	0.01	0.02	0.02	0.03	0.08	0.12	0.16	0.20	0.24	0.28	0.32	0.36	0.40
Egypt 20 Para	1839-1861	0.68	0.833	0.018	A	0.02	0.04	0.05	0.07	0.18	0.27	0.36	0.45	0.54	0.63	0.72	0.81	0.90
Egypt 20 Para	1876-1879	0.55	0.833	0.015	A	0.02	0.03	0.05	0.06	0.15	0.23	0.30	0.38	0.45	0.53	0.60	0.68	0.75
Egypt Qirsh	1839-1861	1.42	0.833	0.038	A	0.04	0.08	0.11	0.15	0.38	0.57	0.76	0.95	1.14	1.33	1.52	1.71	1.90
Egypt Qirsh	1861-1868	1.22	0.833	0.035	A, V	0.04	0.07	0.11	0.14	0.35	0.53	0.70	0.88	1.05	1.23	1.40	1.58	1.75
Egypt Qirsh	1869-1876	1.22	0.900	0.038	A, V	0.04	0.08	0.11	0.15	0.38	0.57	0.76	0.95	1.14	1.33	1.52	1.71	1.90
Egypt Qirsh	1884-1909	1.40	0.833	0.038	A, S	0.04	0.08	0.11	0.15	0.38	0.57	0.76	0.95	1.14	1.33	1.52	1.71	1.90
Egypt 2 Qirsh	1884-1909	2.80	0.833	0.075	A, S	0.08	0.15	0.23	0.30	0.75	1.13	1.50	1.88	2.25	2.63	3.00	3.38	3.75
Egypt 2-1/2 Qirsh	1863	3.15	0.833	0.084	A	0.08	0.17	0.25	0.34	0.84	1.26	1.68	2.10	2.52	2.94	3.36	3.78	4.20
Egypt 2-1/2 Qirsh	1867, 1868	3.50	0.833	0.094	A	0.09	0.19	0.28	0.38	0.94	1.41	1.88	2.35	2.82	3.29	3.76	4.23	4.70
Egypt 2-1/2 Qirsh	1869-1874	3.60	0.900	0.101	A	0.10	0.20	0.30	0.40	1.01	1.52	2.02	2.53	3.03	3.54	4.04	4.55	5.05
Egypt 5 Qirsh	1839-1861	7.00	0.833	0.188	A, V	0.19	0.38	0.56	0.75	1.88	2.82	3.76	4.70	5.64	6.58	7.52	8.46	9.40
Egypt 5 Qirsh	1861-1874	6.20	0.833	0.166	A	0.17	0.33	0.50	0.66	1.66	2.49	3.32	4.15	4.98	5.81	6.64	7.47	8.30
Egypt 5 Qirsh	1884-1914	7.00	0.833	0.188	A, S	0.19	0.38	0.56	0.75	1.88	2.82	3.76	4.70	5.64	6.58	7.52	8.46	9.40
Egypt 10 Qirsh	1839-1854	13.80	0.833	0.370	A, S, V	0.37	0.74	1.11	1.48	3.70	5.55	7.40	9.25	11.10	12.95	14.80	16.65	18.50
Egypt 10 Qirsh	1861-1870	14.00	0.900	0.405	A, S	0.41	0.81	1.22	1.62	4.05	6.08	8.10	10.13	12.15	14.18	16.20	18.23	20.25
Egypt 10 Qirsh	1863	12.50	0.833	0.362	A	0.36	0.72	1.09	1.45	3.62	5.43	7.24	9.05	10.86	12.67	14.48	16.29	18.10
Egypt 10 Qirsh	1884-1914	14.00	0.833	0.375	A, S	0.38	0.75	1.13	1.50	3.75	5.63	7.50	9.38	11.25	13.13	15.00	16.88	18.75
Egypt 20 Qirsh	1839-1843	28.00	0.833	0.750	A	0.75	1.50	2.25	3.00	7.50	11.25	15.00	18.75	22.50	26.25	30.00	33.75	37.50
Egypt 20 Qirsh	1861	28.00	0.833	0.750	A, S	0.75	1.50	2.25	3.00	7.50	11.25	15.00	18.75	22.50	26.25	30.00	33.75	37.50
Egypt 20 Qirsh	1870	28.00	0.900	0.810	A	0.81	1.62	2.43	3.24	8.10	12.15	16.20	20.25	24.30	28.35	32.40	36.45	40.50
Egypt 20 Qirsh	1876-1880	27.57	0.833	0.739	A	0.74	1.48	2.22	2.96	7.39	11.09	14.78	18.48	22.17	25.87	29.56	33.26	36.95
Egypt 20 Qirsh	1884-1914	28.00	0.833	0.750	A	0.75	1.50	2.25	3.00	7.50	11.25	15.00	18.75	22.50	26.25	30.00	33.75	37.50
Egypt 2 Piastres	1916-1942	2.80	0.833	0.075	A	0.07	0.15	0.22	0.30	0.75	1.12	1.50	1.87	2.25	2.62	3.00	3.37	3.75
Egypt 2 Piastres	1944	2.80	0.500	0.045	A	0.05	0.09	0.14	0.18	0.45	0.68	0.90	1.13	1.35	1.58	1.80	2.03	2.25
Egypt 5 Piastres	1916-1939	7.00	0.833	0.187	A	0.19	0.37	0.56	0.75	1.87	2.81	3.74	4.68	5.61	6.55	7.48	8.42	9.35
Egypt 5 Piastres	1956-1966	3.50	0.720	0.081	A, S	0.08	0.16	0.24	0.32	0.81	1.22	1.62	2.03	2.43	2.84	3.24	3.65	4.05
Egypt 5 Piastres	1964	2.50	0.720	0.058	A	0.06	0.12	0.17	0.23	0.58	0.87	1.16	1.45	1.74	2.03	2.32	2.61	2.90
Egypt 10 Piastres	1916-1939	14.00	0.833	0.375	A	0.38	0.75	1.13	1.50	3.75	5.63	7.50	9.38	11.25	13.13	15.00	16.88	18.75
Egypt 10 Piastres	1955	7.00	0.625	0.141	A	0.14	0.28	0.42	0.56	1.41	2.12	2.82	3.53	4.23	4.94	5.64	6.35	7.05
Egypt 10 Piastres	1956-1966	7.00	0.720	0.162	A, S	0.16	0.32	0.49	0.65	1.62	2.43	3.24	4.05	4.86	5.67	6.48	7.29	8.10
Egypt 10 Piastres	1964	5.00	0.720	0.116	A	0.12	0.23	0.35	0.46	1.16	1.74	2.32	2.90	3.48	4.06	4.64	5.22	5.80
Egypt 20 Piastres	1916-1939	28.00	0.833	0.749	A	0.75	1.50	2.25	3.00	7.49	11.24	14.98	18.73	22.47	26.22	29.96	33.71	37.45
Egypt 20 Piastres	1956-1966	14.00	0.720	0.324	A	0.32	0.65	0.97	1.30	3.24	4.86	6.48	8.10	9.72	11.34	12.96	14.58	16.20
Egypt 25 Piastres	1956-1960	17.50	0.720	0.405	A	0.41	0.81	1.22	1.62	4.05	6.08	8.10	10.13	12.15	14.18	16.20	18.23	20.25
Egypt 25 Piastres	1964	10.00	0.720	0.232	A	0.23	0.46	0.70	0.93	2.32	3.48	4.64	5.80	6.96	8.12	9.28	10.44	11.60
Egypt 25 Piastres	1970, 1973	6.00	0.720	0.139	A	0.14	0.28	0.42	0.56	1.39	2.09	2.78	3.48	4.17	4.87	5.56	6.26	6.95
Egypt 50 Piastres	1956	28.00	0.900	0.810	A	0.81	1.62	2.43	3.24	8.10	12.15	16.20	20.25	24.30	28.35	32.40	36.45	40.50
Egypt 50 Piastres	1964	20.00	0.720	0.463	A	0.46	0.93	1.39	1.85	4.63	6.95	9.26	11.58	13.89	16.21	18.52	20.84	23.15
Egypt 50 Piastres	1970	12.50	0.720	0.289	A	0.29	0.58	0.87	1.16	2.89	4.34	5.78	7.23	8.67	10.12	11.56	13.01	14.45

Country & Denomination	Years Minted	Grams Weight	Fine-ness	Troy (ASW)	Code	$ Value 1	$ Value 2	$ Value 3	$ Value 4	$ Value 10	$ Value 15	$ Value 20	$ Value 25	$ Value 30	$ Value 35	$ Value 40	$ Value 45	$ Value 50
Egypt 1 Pound	1968-1973	25.00	0.720	0.579	A, S	0.58	1.16	1.74	2.32	5.79	8.69	11.58	14.48	17.37	20.27	23.16	26.06	28.95
Egypt 1 Pound	1974-2000	15.00	0.720	0.347	A, S	0.35	0.69	1.04	1.39	3.47	5.21	6.94	8.68	10.41	12.15	13.88	15.62	17.35
Egypt 5 Pounds	1981-1982	24.00	0.925	0.714	A	0.71	1.43	2.14	2.86	7.14	10.71	14.28	17.85	21.42	24.99	28.56	32.13	35.70
Egypt 5 Pounds	1983-1992	17.50	0.720	0.405	A, N	0.41	0.81	1.22	1.62	4.05	6.08	8.10	10.13	12.15	14.18	16.20	18.23	20.25
Egypt 5 Pounds	1993-1994	22.50	0.999	0.723	A, N	0.72	1.45	2.17	2.89	7.23	10.85	14.46	18.08	21.69	25.31	28.92	32.54	36.15
Egypt 5 Pounds	1995	17.50	0.720	0.405	A	0.41	0.81	1.22	1.62	4.05	6.08	8.10	10.13	12.15	14.18	16.20	18.23	20.25
Egypt 5 Pounds	1996-1999	17.50	0.900	0.508	A	0.51	1.02	1.52	2.03	5.08	7.62	10.16	12.70	15.24	17.78	20.32	22.86	25.40
Egypt 5 Pounds	1999	17.33	0.975	0.543	A	0.54	1.09	1.63	2.17	5.43	8.15	10.86	13.58	16.29	19.01	21.72	24.44	27.15
Egypt 5 Pounds	2000	17.50	0.725	0.408	A	0.41	0.82	1.22	1.63	4.08	6.12	8.16	10.20	12.24	14.28	16.32	18.36	20.40
El Salvador 1/2 Real*	1833	1.50	0.633	0.031		0.03	0.06	0.09	0.12	0.31	0.47	0.62	0.78	0.93	1.09	1.24	1.40	1.55
El Salvador 1/2 Real	1835	1.20	0.700	0.027		0.03	0.05	0.08	0.11	0.27	0.41	0.54	0.68	0.81	0.95	1.08	1.22	1.35
El Salvador 1 Real	1833, 1834	2.70	0.633	0.055		0.06	0.11	0.17	0.22	0.55	0.83	1.10	1.38	1.65	1.93	2.20	2.48	2.75
El Salvador 1 Real	1833	3.40	0.633	0.070		0.07	0.14	0.21	0.28	0.70	1.05	1.40	1.75	2.10	2.45	2.80	3.15	3.50
El Salvador 1 Real	1835	2.40	0.700	0.054		0.05	0.11	0.16	0.22	0.54	0.81	1.08	1.35	1.62	1.89	2.16	2.43	2.70
El Salvador 1 Real	1859-1863	3.00	0.903	0.087	C	0.09	0.17	0.26	0.35	0.87	1.31	1.74	2.18	2.61	3.05	3.48	3.92	4.35
El Salvador 2 Reales	1828, 1829	4.70	0.903	0.137		0.14	0.27	0.41	0.55	1.37	2.06	2.74	3.43	4.11	4.80	5.48	6.17	6.85
El Salvador 2 Reales	1832	5.00	0.750	0.110	V	0.11	0.22	0.33	0.44	1.10	1.65	2.20	2.75	3.30	3.85	4.40	4.95	5.50
El Salvador 2 Reales	1833, 1834	5.40	0.633	0.110		0.11	0.22	0.33	0.44	1.10	1.65	2.20	2.75	3.30	3.85	4.40	4.95	5.50
El Salvador 2 Reales	1828, 1829	4.70	0.903	0.137		0.14	0.27	0.41	0.55	1.37	2.06	2.74	3.43	4.11	4.80	5.48	6.17	6.85
El Salvador 2 Reales	1862, 1863	6.30	0.903	0.183	C	0.18	0.37	0.55	0.73	1.83	2.74	3.66	4.57	5.49	6.40	7.32	8.23	9.15
El Salvador 4 Reales	1828	9.40	0.903	0.273		0.27	0.55	0.82	1.09	2.73	4.10	5.46	6.83	8.19	9.56	10.92	12.29	13.65
El Salvador 4 Reales	1860, 1861	12.50	0.903	0.363	C	0.36	0.73	1.09	1.45	3.63	5.45	7.26	9.08	10.89	12.71	14.52	16.34	18.15
El Salvador 4 Reales	1859	25.00	0.903	0.726	C	0.73	1.45	2.18	2.90	7.26	10.89	14.52	18.15	21.78	25.41	29.04	32.67	36.30
El Salvador 5 Centavos	1892-1914	1.25	0.835	0.034	S	0.03	0.07	0.10	0.13	0.34	0.50	0.67	0.84	1.01	1.18	1.34	1.51	1.68
El Salvador 10 Centavos	1892-1914	2.50	0.835	0.067	S	0.07	0.13	0.20	0.27	0.67	1.01	1.34	1.68	2.01	2.35	2.68	3.02	3.35
El Salvador 20 Centavos	1892	5.00	0.835	0.134		0.13	0.27	0.40	0.54	1.34	2.01	2.68	3.35	4.02	4.69	5.36	6.03	6.70
El Salvador 25 Centavos	1911, 1914	6.25	0.835	0.168		0.17	0.34	0.50	0.67	1.68	2.52	3.36	4.20	5.04	5.88	6.72	7.56	8.40
El Salvador 25 Centavos	1943-1944	7.50	0.900	0.217		0.22	0.43	0.65	0.87	2.17	3.26	4.34	5.43	6.51	7.60	8.68	9.77	10.85
El Salvador 25 Centavos	1953	2.50	0.900	0.072		0.07	0.14	0.22	0.29	0.72	1.08	1.44	1.80	2.16	2.52	2.88	3.24	3.60
El Salvador 50 Centavos	1892-1894	12.50	0.900	0.362		0.36	0.72	1.09	1.45	3.62	5.43	7.24	9.05	10.86	12.67	14.48	16.29	18.10
El Salvador 1 Peso (Colon)	1892-1925	25.00	0.900	0.723	S	0.72	1.45	2.17	2.89	7.23	10.85	14.46	18.08	21.69	25.31	28.92	32.54	36.15
El Salvador 1 Peso (Colon)	1971	2.30	0.999	0.074		0.07	0.15	0.22	0.30	0.74	1.11	1.48	1.85	2.22	2.59	2.96	3.33	3.70
El Salvador 5 Colones	1971	11.50	0.999	0.369		0.37	0.74	1.11	1.48	3.69	5.54	7.38	9.23	11.07	12.92	14.76	16.61	18.45
El Salvador 25 Colones	1977	25.00	0.900	0.723		0.72	1.45	2.17	2.89	7.23	10.85	14.46	18.08	21.69	25.31	28.92	32.54	36.15
El Salvador 150 Colones	1992	25.00	0.900	0.723		0.72	1.45	2.17	2.89	7.23	10.85	14.46	18.08	21.69	25.31	28.92	32.54	36.15
Equatorial Guinea 25 Pesetas*	1970	5.00	0.999	0.161		0.16	0.32	0.48	0.64	1.61	2.42	3.22	4.03	4.83	5.64	6.44	7.25	8.05
Equatorial Guinea 50 Pesetas	1970	10.00	0.999	0.321		0.32	0.64	0.96	1.28	3.21	4.82	6.42	8.03	9.63	11.24	12.84	14.45	16.05
Equatorial Guinea 75 Pesetas	1970	15.00	0.999	0.482		0.48	0.96	1.45	1.93	4.82	7.23	9.64	12.05	14.46	16.87	19.28	21.69	24.10
Equatorial Guinea 100 Pesetas	1970	20.00	0.999	0.643		0.64	1.29	1.93	2.57	6.43	9.65	12.86	16.08	19.29	22.51	25.72	28.94	32.15
Equatorial Guinea 150 Pesetas	1970	30.00	0.999	0.964		0.96	1.93	2.89	3.86	9.64	14.46	19.28	24.10	28.92	33.74	38.56	43.38	48.20
Equatorial Guinea 200 Pesetas	1970	40.00	0.999	1.285		1.29	2.57	3.86	5.14	12.85	19.28	25.70	32.13	38.55	44.98	51.40	57.83	64.25
Equatorial Guinea 1000 Ekueles	1978	21.43	0.925	0.637		0.64	1.27	1.91	2.55	6.37	9.56	12.74	15.93	19.11	22.30	25.48	28.67	31.85
Equatorial Guinea 2000 Ekueles	1978-1979	42.87	0.925	1.275		1.28	2.55	3.83	5.10	12.75	19.13	25.50	31.88	38.25	44.63	51.00	57.38	63.75

Country & Denomination	Years Minted	Grams Weight	Fine-ness	Troy (ASW)	Code	$ Value 1	$ Value 2	$ Value 3	$ Value 4	$ Value 10	$ Value 15	$ Value 20	$ Value 25	$ Value 30	$ Value 35	$ Value 40	$ Value 45	$ Value 50
Equatorial Guinea 2000 Ekueles	1979-1980	31.00	0.927	0.927		0.93	1.85	2.78	3.71	9.27	13.91	18.54	23.18	27.81	32.45	37.08	41.72	46.35
Equatorial Guinea 7000 Francos	1991	26.30	0.999	0.846		0.85	1.69	2.54	3.38	8.46	12.68	16.91	21.14	25.37	29.59	33.82	38.05	42.28
Equatorial Guinea 7000 Francos	1991	25.70	0.999	0.826		0.83	1.65	2.48	3.31	8.26	12.39	16.53	20.66	24.79	28.92	33.05	37.18	41.32
Equatorial Guinea 7000 Francos	1991	20.00	0.999	0.643		0.64	1.29	1.93	2.57	6.43	9.65	12.86	16.08	19.29	22.51	25.72	28.94	32.15
Equatorial Guinea 7000 Francos	1992	510.30	0.999	16.406		16.41	32.81	49.22	65.62	164.06	246.09	328.12	410.16	492.19	574.22	656.25	738.28	820.31
Equatorial Guinea 7000 Francos	1992	10.48	0.999	0.337		0.34	0.67	1.01	1.35	3.37	5.06	6.74	8.43	10.11	11.80	13.48	15.17	16.85
Equatorial Guinea 7000 Francos	1993	10.51	0.999	0.338		0.34	0.68	1.01	1.35	3.38	5.07	6.76	8.45	10.14	11.83	13.52	15.21	16.90
Equatorial Guinea 7000 Francos	1993	10.27	0.999	0.330		0.33	0.66	0.99	1.32	3.30	4.95	6.60	8.25	9.90	11.55	13.20	14.85	16.50
Equatorial Guinea 7000 Francos	1993	19.30	0.999	0.634		0.63	1.27	1.90	2.54	6.34	9.51	12.68	15.85	19.02	22.19	25.36	28.53	31.70
Equatorial Guinea 7000 Francos	1993	20.00	0.999	0.643		0.64	1.29	1.93	2.57	6.43	9.65	12.86	16.08	19.29	22.51	25.72	28.94	32.15
Equatorial Guinea 7000 Francos	1993	20.17	0.999	0.648		0.65	1.30	1.94	2.59	6.48	9.72	12.96	16.20	19.44	22.68	25.92	29.16	32.40
Equatorial Guinea 7000 Francos	1993	9.93	0.740	0.236		0.24	0.47	0.71	0.94	2.36	3.54	4.72	5.90	7.08	8.26	9.44	10.62	11.80
Equatorial Guinea 7000 Francos	1994	20.17	0.999	0.665		0.67	1.33	2.00	2.66	6.65	9.98	13.30	16.63	19.95	23.28	26.60	29.93	33.25
Equatorial Guinea 7000 Francos	1995	21.00	0.999	0.675		0.68	1.35	2.03	2.70	6.75	10.13	13.50	16.88	20.25	23.63	27.00	30.38	33.75
Equatorial Guinea 7000 Francos	1995	20.35	0.999	0.654		0.65	1.31	1.96	2.62	6.54	9.81	13.08	16.35	19.62	22.89	26.16	29.43	32.70
Equatorial Guinea 7000 Francos	1995	157.55	0.999	5.060		5.06	10.12	15.18	20.24	50.60	75.90	101.20	126.50	151.80	177.10	202.40	227.70	253.00
Equatorial Guinea 7000 Francos	1997	19.60	0.999	0.630		0.63	1.26	1.89	2.52	6.30	9.45	12.60	15.75	18.90	22.05	25.20	28.35	31.50
Equator. Guinea 15,000 Francos	1992	20.33	0.999	0.635		0.64	1.27	1.91	2.54	6.35	9.53	12.70	15.88	19.05	22.23	25.40	28.58	31.75
Equator. Guinea 15,000 Francos	1992	855.34	0.999	27.490		27.49	54.98	82.47	109.96	274.90	412.35	549.80	687.25	824.70	962.15	1099.60	1237.05	1374.50
Eritrea 50 Centesimi	1890	2.50	0.835	0.067		0.07	0.13	0.20	0.27	0.67	1.01	1.34	1.68	2.01	2.35	2.68	3.02	3.35
Eritrea 1 Lira	1890-1896	5.00	0.835	0.134	S	0.13	0.27	0.40	0.54	1.34	2.01	2.68	3.35	4.02	4.69	5.36	6.03	6.70
Eritrea 2 Lire	1890, 1896	10.00	0.835	0.269		0.27	0.54	0.81	1.08	2.69	4.04	5.38	6.73	8.07	9.42	10.76	12.11	13.45
Eritrea 5 Lire/Tallero	1891, 1896	28.13	0.800	0.724		0.72	1.45	2.17	2.90	7.24	10.86	14.48	18.10	21.72	25.34	28.96	32.58	36.20
Eritrea 1 Tallero	1918	28.07	0.835	0.754	R	0.75	1.51	2.26	3.02	7.54	11.31	15.08	18.85	22.62	26.39	30.16	33.93	37.70
Eritrea 10 Dollars	1993	31.10	0.999	1.000		1.00	2.00	3.00	4.00	10.00	15.00	20.00	25.00	30.00	35.00	40.00	45.00	50.00
Eritrea 10 Dollars	1993-1997	28.28	0.925	0.841		0.84	1.68	2.52	3.36	8.41	12.62	16.82	21.03	25.23	29.44	33.64	37.85	42.05
Essequibo 1/8 Guilder*	1832, 1835	0.97	0.816	0.026		0.03	0.05	0.08	0.10	0.26	0.39	0.52	0.65	0.78	0.91	1.04	1.17	1.30
Essequibo 1/4 Guilder	1809-1835	1.94	0.816	0.051	S	0.05	0.10	0.15	0.20	0.51	0.77	1.02	1.28	1.53	1.79	2.04	2.30	2.55
Essequibo 1/2 Guilder	1809-1835	3.88	0.816	0.102	S	0.10	0.20	0.31	0.41	1.02	1.53	2.04	2.55	3.06	3.57	4.08	4.59	5.10
Essequibo 1 Guilder	1809-1835	7.77	0.816	0.204	S	0.20	0.41	0.61	0.82	2.04	3.06	4.08	5.10	6.12	7.14	8.16	9.18	10.20
Essequibo 2 Guilder	1809-1832	15.50	0.816	0.408	S	0.41	0.82	1.22	1.63	4.08	6.12	8.16	10.20	12.24	14.28	16.32	18.36	20.40
Essequibo 3 Guilder	1809-1832	23.32	0.816	0.612	S	0.61	1.22	1.84	2.45	6.12	9.18	12.24	15.30	18.36	21.42	24.48	27.54	30.60
Estonia 1 Kroon	1933	6.00	0.500	0.965		0.97	1.93	2.90	3.86	9.65	14.48	19.30	24.13	28.95	33.78	38.60	43.43	48.25
Estonia 2 Krooni	1930-1932	12.00	0.500	0.193		0.19	0.39	0.58	0.77	1.93	2.89	3.86	4.82	5.79	6.75	7.72	8.68	9.65
Estonia 10 Krooni	1992	28.28	0.925	0.841		0.84	1.68	2.52	3.36	8.41	12.62	16.82	21.03	25.23	29.44	33.64	37.85	42.05
Estonia 10 Krooni	1998	16.00	0.925	0.476		0.48	0.95	1.43	1.90	4.76	7.14	9.52	11.90	14.28	16.66	19.04	21.42	23.80
Estonia 100 Krooni	1992	24.00	0.925	0.714		0.71	1.43	2.14	2.86	7.14	10.71	14.28	17.85	21.42	24.99	28.56	32.13	35.70
Estonia 100 Krooni	1996	28.28	0.925	0.841		0.84	1.68	2.52	3.36	8.41	12.62	16.82	21.03	25.23	29.44	33.64	37.85	42.05
Estonia 100 Krooni	1998	27.00	0.925	0.803		0.80	1.61	2.41	3.21	8.03	12.05	16.06	20.08	24.09	28.11	32.12	36.14	40.15
Ethiopia 1 Gersh / 1 Mahaleki*	1885	1.40	0.835	0.038	E	0.04	0.08	0.11	0.15	0.38	0.57	0.76	0.95	1.14	1.33	1.52	1.71	1.90
Ethiopia 1 Gersh	1889, 1891	1.40	0.835	0.038	E	0.04	0.08	0.11	0.15	0.38	0.57	0.76	0.95	1.14	1.33	1.52	1.71	1.90

Country & Denomination	Years Minted	Grams Weight	Fine-ness	Troy (ASW)	Code	$ Value 1	$ Value 2	$ Value 3	$ Value 4	$ Value 10	$ Value 15	$ Value 20	$ Value 25	$ Value 30	$ Value 35	$ Value 40	$ Value 45	$ Value 50
Ethiopia 1/8 Birr	1887, 1888	3.51	0.835	0.094	E	0.09	0.19	0.28	0.38	0.94	1.41	1.88	2.35	2.82	3.29	3.76	4.23	4.70
Ethiopia 1/4 Birr	1887-1889	7.11	0.835	0.188	E	0.19	0.38	0.56	0.75	1.88	2.82	3.76	4.70	5.64	6.58	7.52	8.46	9.40
Ethiopia 1/2 Birr	1887-1889	14.04	0.835	0.377	E	0.38	0.75	1.13	1.51	3.77	5.66	7.54	9.43	11.31	13.20	15.08	16.97	18.85
Ethiopia 1 Birr	1887-1892	28.08	0.835	0.754	E	0.75	1.51	2.26	3.02	7.54	11.31	15.08	18.85	22.62	26.39	30.16	33.93	37.70
Ethiopia 50 Cents	1936	7.03	0.800	0.181	E	0.18	0.36	0.54	0.72	1.81	2.72	3.62	4.53	5.43	6.34	7.24	8.15	9.05
Ethiopia 50 Cents	1936	7.03	0.700	0.158	E	0.16	0.32	0.47	0.63	1.58	2.37	3.16	3.95	4.74	5.53	6.32	7.11	7.90
Ethiopia 5 Dollar	1964	20.00	0.925	0.595	E	0.60	1.19	1.79	2.38	5.95	8.93	11.90	14.88	17.85	20.83	23.80	26.78	29.75
Ethiopia 5 Birr	1972	25.00	0.999	0.803	E	0.80	1.61	2.41	3.21	8.03	12.05	16.06	20.08	24.09	28.11	32.12	36.14	40.15
Ethiopia 10 Dollar	1964	40.00	0.925	1.189	E	1.19	2.38	3.57	4.76	11.89	17.84	23.78	29.73	35.67	41.62	47.56	53.51	59.45
Ethiopia 10 Birr	1970	25.31	0.925	0.753	E	0.75	1.51	2.26	3.01	7.53	11.30	15.06	18.83	22.59	26.36	30.12	33.89	37.65
Ethiopia 20 Birr	1972-1998	23.33	0.925	0.694	E, S	0.69	1.39	2.08	2.78	6.94	10.41	13.88	17.35	20.82	24.29	27.76	31.23	34.70
Ethiopia 25 Birr	1970	31.65	0.925	0.941	E	0.94	1.88	2.82	3.76	9.41	14.12	18.82	23.53	28.23	32.94	37.64	42.35	47.05
Ethiopia 50 Birr	1974	28.28	0.925	0.841	E	0.84	1.68	2.52	3.36	8.41	12.62	16.82	21.03	25.23	29.44	33.64	37.85	42.05
F																		
Falkland Islands 50 Pence	1977-1999	28.28	0.925	0.841	N, S	0.84	1.68	2.52	3.36	8.41	12.62	16.82	21.03	25.23	29.44	33.64	37.85	42.05
Falkland Islands 1 Pound	1987	9.50	0.925	0.283		0.28	0.57	0.85	1.13	2.83	4.25	5.66	7.08	8.49	9.91	11.32	12.74	14.15
Falkland Islands 2 Pounds	1986	28.28	0.500	0.455		0.46	0.91	1.37	1.82	4.55	6.83	9.10	11.38	13.65	15.93	18.20	20.48	22.75
Falkland Islands 2 Pounds	1986-2000	28.28	0.925	0.841	N, S	0.84	1.68	2.52	3.36	8.41	12.62	16.82	21.03	25.23	29.44	33.64	37.85	42.05
Falkland Islands 5 Pounds	1979-1992	28.28	0.925	0.841	N, S	0.84	1.68	2.52	3.36	8.41	12.62	16.82	21.03	25.23	29.44	33.64	37.85	42.05
Falkland Islands 10 Pounds	1979	35.00	0.925	1.041		1.04	2.08	3.12	4.16	10.41	15.62	20.82	26.03	31.23	36.44	41.64	46.85	52.05
Falkland Islands 25 Pounds	1985-1986	150.00	0.925	4.461		4.46	8.92	13.38	17.84	44.61	66.92	89.22	111.53	133.83	156.14	178.44	200.75	223.05
Falkland Islands 25 Pounds	1992	155.58	0.999	4.997		5.00	9.99	14.99	19.99	49.97	74.96	99.94	124.93	149.91	174.90	199.88	224.87	249.85
Fiji Islands 6 Pence	1934-1941	2.83	0.500	0.046		0.05	0.09	0.14	0.18	0.46	0.69	0.92	1.15	1.38	1.61	1.84	2.07	2.30
Fiji Islands 6 Pence	1942-1943	2.83	0.900	0.082		0.08	0.16	0.25	0.33	0.82	1.23	1.64	2.05	2.46	2.87	3.28	3.69	4.10
Fiji Islands 1 Shilling	1934-1941	5.66	0.500	0.091		0.09	0.18	0.27	0.36	0.91	1.37	1.82	2.28	2.73	3.19	3.64	4.10	4.55
Fiji Islands 1 Shilling	1942-1943	5.66	0.900	0.167		0.17	0.33	0.50	0.67	1.67	2.51	3.34	4.18	5.01	5.85	6.68	7.52	8.35
Fiji Islands 1 Florin	1934-1945	11.31	0.500	0.180	S	0.18	0.36	0.54	0.72	1.80	2.70	3.60	4.50	5.40	6.30	7.20	8.10	9.00
Fiji Islands 1 Florin	1942-1943	11.31	0.900	0.327		0.33	0.65	0.98	1.31	3.27	4.91	6.54	8.18	9.81	11.45	13.08	14.72	16.35
Fiji 2 Cents	1976	4.53	0.925	0.135	N	0.14	0.27	0.41	0.54	1.35	2.03	2.70	3.38	4.05	4.73	5.40	6.08	6.75
Fiji 5 Cents	1976	3.28	0.925	0.098	N	0.10	0.20	0.29	0.39	0.98	1.47	1.96	2.45	2.94	3.43	3.92	4.41	4.90
Fiji 10 Cents	1976	6.55	0.925	0.195	N	0.20	0.39	0.59	0.78	1.95	2.93	3.90	4.88	5.85	6.83	7.80	8.78	9.75
Fiji 20 Cents	1976	13.09	0.925	0.389	N	0.39	0.78	1.17	1.56	3.89	5.84	7.78	9.73	11.67	13.62	15.56	17.51	19.45
Fiji 50 Cents	1976	18.00	0.925	0.535	N	0.54	1.07	1.61	2.14	5.35	8.03	10.70	13.38	16.05	18.73	21.40	24.08	26.75
Fiji Islands 1 Dollar	1970, 1976	28.28	0.925	0.841		0.84	1.68	2.52	3.36	8.41	12.62	16.82	21.03	25.23	29.44	33.64	37.85	42.05
Fiji Islands 2 Dollars	1998	42.41	0.925	1.364		1.36	2.73	4.09	5.46	13.64	20.46	27.28	34.10	40.92	47.74	54.56	61.38	68.20
Fiji Islands 10 Dollars	1977-2000	28.28	0.925	0.841	S	0.84	1.68	2.52	3.36	8.41	12.62	16.82	21.03	25.23	29.44	33.64	37.85	42.05
Fiji Islands 10 Dollars	1978, 1980	28.28	0.500	0.455		0.46	0.91	1.37	1.82	4.55	6.83	9.10	11.38	13.65	15.93	18.20	20.48	22.75
Fiji Islands 10 Dollars	1977-2000	31.00	0.925	0.910	V	0.91	1.82	2.73	3.64	9.10	13.65	18.20	22.75	27.30	31.85	36.40	40.95	45.50
Fiji Islands 20 Dollars	1978	35.00	0.925	1.040		1.04	2.08	3.12	4.16	10.40	15.60	20.80	26.00	31.20	36.40	41.60	46.80	52.00
Fiji Islands 20 Dollars	1978	35.00	0.500	0.563		0.56	1.13	1.69	2.25	5.63	8.45	11.26	14.08	16.89	19.71	22.52	25.34	28.15
Fiji Islands 25 Dollars	1974, 1975	48.60	0.925	1.450		1.45	2.90	4.35	5.80	14.50	21.75	29.00	36.25	43.50	50.75	58.00	65.25	72.50
Fiji Islands 50 Dollars	1996	1000.00	0.999	32.119		32.12	64.24	96.36	128.48	321.19	481.79	642.38	802.98	963.57	1124.17	1284.76	1445.36	1605.95
Finland 25 Pennia	1865-1917	1.27	0.750	0.031	S	0.03	0.06	0.09	0.12	0.31	0.47	0.62	0.78	0.93	1.09	1.24	1.40	1.55

Country & Denomination	Years Minted	Grams Weight	Fineness	Troy (ASW)	Code	$ Value 1	$ Value 2	$ Value 3	$ Value 4	$ Value 10	$ Value 15	$ Value 20	$ Value 25	$ Value 30	$ Value 35	$ Value 40	$ Value 45	$ Value 50
Finland 50 Pennia	1864-1917	2.55	0.750	0.062	S	0.06	0.12	0.19	0.25	0.62	0.93	1.24	1.55	1.86	2.17	2.48	2.79	3.10
Finland 1 Markkaa	1864-1915	5.18	0.868	0.145	S	0.15	0.29	0.44	0.58	1.45	2.18	2.90	3.63	4.35	5.08	5.80	6.53	7.25
Finland 1 Markkaa	1964-1968	6.40	0.350	0.072		0.07	0.14	0.22	0.29	0.72	1.08	1.44	1.80	2.16	2.52	2.88	3.24	3.60
Finland 2 Markkaa	1865-1908	10.37	0.868	0.289		0.29	0.58	0.87	1.16	2.89	4.34	5.78	7.23	8.67	10.12	11.56	13.01	14.45
Finland 10 Markkaa	1967	23.75	0.900	0.687		0.69	1.37	2.06	2.75	6.87	10.31	13.74	17.18	20.61	24.05	27.48	30.92	34.35
Finland 10 Markkaa	1970	22.75	0.500	0.366		0.37	0.73	1.10	1.46	3.66	5.49	7.32	9.15	10.98	12.81	14.64	16.47	18.30
Finland 10 Markkaa	1971	24.20	0.500	0.389		0.39	0.78	1.17	1.56	3.89	5.84	7.78	9.73	11.67	13.62	15.56	17.51	19.45
Finland 10 Markkaa	1975	23.50	0.500	0.378		0.38	0.76	1.13	1.51	3.78	5.67	7.56	9.45	11.34	13.23	15.12	17.01	18.90
Finland 10 Markkaa	1977	21.78	0.500	0.350		0.35	0.70	1.05	1.40	3.50	5.25	7.00	8.75	10.50	12.25	14.00	15.75	17.50
Finland 25 Markkaa	1978-1979	26.30	0.500	0.423		0.42	0.85	1.27	1.69	4.23	6.35	8.46	10.58	12.69	14.81	16.92	19.04	21.15
Finland 50 Markkaa	1981	20.00	0.500	0.322		0.32	0.64	0.97	1.29	3.22	4.83	6.44	8.05	9.66	11.27	12.88	14.49	16.10
Finland 50 Markkaa	1982	23.10	0.500	0.369		0.37	0.74	1.11	1.48	3.69	5.54	7.38	9.23	11.07	12.92	14.76	16.61	18.45
Finland 50 Markkaa	1983	21.80	0.500	0.354		0.35	0.71	1.06	1.42	3.54	5.31	7.08	8.85	10.62	12.39	14.16	15.93	17.70
Finland 50 Markkaa	1985	19.90	0.500	0.321		0.32	0.64	0.96	1.28	3.21	4.82	6.42	8.03	9.63	11.24	12.84	14.45	16.05
Finland 100 Markkaa	1956-1960	5.20	0.500	0.084		0.08	0.17	0.25	0.34	0.84	1.26	1.68	2.10	2.52	2.94	3.36	3.78	4.20
Finland 100 Markkaa	1989-1991	24.00	0.830	0.641		0.64	1.28	1.92	2.56	6.41	9.62	12.82	16.03	19.23	22.44	25.64	28.85	32.05
Finland 100 Markkaa	1991-1996	24.00	0.925	0.714		0.71	1.43	2.14	2.86	7.14	10.71	14.28	17.85	21.42	24.99	28.56	32.13	35.70
Finland 100 Markkaa	1997-2000	22.00	0.925	0.654		0.65	1.31	1.96	2.62	6.54	9.81	13.08	16.35	19.62	22.89	26.16	29.43	32.70
Finland 200 Markkaa	1956-1959	8.30	0.500	0.133		0.13	0.27	0.40	0.53	1.33	2.00	2.67	3.33	4.00	4.67	5.33	6.00	6.67
Finland 500 Markkaa	1951-1952	12.00	0.500	0.193		0.19	0.39	0.58	0.77	1.93	2.90	3.86	4.83	5.79	6.76	7.72	8.69	9.65
Finland 1000 Markkaa	1960	14.00	0.875	0.394		0.39	0.79	1.18	1.58	3.94	5.91	7.88	9.85	11.82	13.79	15.76	17.73	19.70
France 20 Centimes*	1849-1863	1.00	0.900	0.029		0.03	0.06	0.09	0.12	0.29	0.44	0.58	0.73	0.87	1.02	1.16	1.31	1.45
France 20 Centimes	1864-1869	1.00	0.835	0.027		0.03	0.05	0.08	0.11	0.27	0.41	0.54	0.68	0.81	0.95	1.08	1.22	1.35
France 20 Centimes	1878, 1889	1.00	0.900	0.029		0.03	0.06	0.09	0.12	0.29	0.44	0.58	0.73	0.87	1.02	1.16	1.31	1.45
France 1/4 Franc	1801-1845	1.25	0.900	0.036		0.04	0.07	0.11	0.14	0.36	0.54	0.72	0.90	1.08	1.26	1.44	1.62	1.80
France 25 Centimes	1845-1848	1.25	0.900	0.036		0.04	0.07	0.11	0.14	0.36	0.54	0.72	0.90	1.08	1.26	1.44	1.62	1.80
France 1/2 Franc	1801-1845	2.50	0.900	0.072		0.07	0.14	0.22	0.29	0.72	1.08	1.44	1.80	2.16	2.52	2.88	3.24	3.60
France 50 Centimes	1845-1863	2.50	0.900	0.072		0.07	0.14	0.22	0.29	0.72	1.08	1.44	1.80	2.16	2.52	2.88	3.24	3.60
France 50 Centimes	1864-1920	2.50	0.835	0.067		0.07	0.13	0.20	0.27	0.67	1.01	1.34	1.68	2.01	2.35	2.68	3.02	3.35
France 1 Franc	1801-1846	5.00	0.900	0.145		0.15	0.29	0.44	0.58	1.45	2.18	2.90	3.63	4.35	5.08	5.80	6.53	7.25
France 1 Franc	1849-1863	5.00	0.900	0.145		0.15	0.29	0.44	0.58	1.45	2.18	2.90	3.63	4.35	5.08	5.80	6.53	7.25
France 1 Franc	1866-1920	5.00	0.835	0.134		0.13	0.27	0.40	0.54	1.34	2.01	2.68	3.35	4.02	4.69	5.36	6.03	6.70
France 1 Franc	1988, 1993	22.20	0.900	0.642	N	0.64	1.28	1.93	2.57	6.42	9.63	12.84	16.05	19.26	22.47	25.68	28.89	32.10
France 1 Franc	1992	15.55	0.900	0.450	N	0.45	0.90	1.35	1.80	4.50	6.75	9.00	11.25	13.50	15.75	18.00	20.25	22.50
France 1 Franc	1998, 1999	12.00	0.900	0.346	N	0.35	0.69	1.04	1.38	3.46	5.19	6.92	8.65	10.38	12.11	13.84	15.57	17.30
France 1 Franc	1999, 2000	13.00	0.900	0.376	N	0.38	0.75	1.13	1.50	3.76	5.64	7.52	9.40	11.28	13.16	15.04	16.92	18.80
France 2 Francs	1801-1846	10.00	0.900	0.289		0.29	0.58	0.87	1.16	2.89	4.34	5.78	7.23	8.67	10.12	11.56	13.01	14.45
France 2 Francs	1849-1871	10.00	0.900	0.289		0.29	0.58	0.87	1.16	2.89	4.34	5.78	7.23	8.67	10.12	11.56	13.01	14.45
France 2 Francs	1870-1920	10.00	0.835	0.268		0.27	0.54	0.80	1.07	2.68	4.02	5.36	6.70	8.04	9.38	10.72	12.06	13.40
France 5 Francs	1801-1846	25.00	0.900	0.723		0.72	1.45	2.17	2.89	7.23	10.85	14.46	18.08	21.69	25.31	28.92	32.54	36.15
France 5 Francs	1848-1889	25.00	0.900	0.723		0.72	1.45	2.17	2.89	7.23	10.85	14.46	18.08	21.69	25.31	28.92	32.54	36.15
France 5 Francs	1960-1969	12.00	0.835	0.322	S	0.32	0.64	0.97	1.29	3.22	4.83	6.44	8.05	9.66	11.27	12.88	14.49	16.10
France 5 Francs	1989-2000	12.00	0.900	0.347		0.35	0.69	1.04	1.39	3.47	5.21	6.94	8.68	10.41	12.15	13.88	15.62	17.35
France 10 Francs	1929-1939	10.00	0.680	0.219		0.22	0.44	0.66	0.88	2.19	3.29	4.38	5.48	6.57	7.67	8.76	9.86	10.95

Country & Denomination	Years Minted	Grams Weight	Fine-ness	Troy (ASW)	Code	$ Value 1	$ Value 2	Value 3	Value 4	$ Value 10	$ Value 15	$ Value 20	$ Value 25	$ Value 30	$ Value 35	$ Value 40	$ Value 45	$ Value 50
France 10 Francs	1965-1973	25.00	0.900	0.723		0.72	1.45	2.17	2.89	7.23	10.85	14.46	18.08	21.69	25.31	28.92	32.54	36.15
France 10 Francs	1985	12.00	0.999	0.385		0.39	0.77	1.16	1.54	3.85	5.78	7.70	9.63	11.55	13.48	15.40	17.33	19.25
France 10 Francs	1986	7.00	0.950	0.214		0.21	0.43	0.64	0.86	2.14	3.21	4.28	5.35	6.42	7.49	8.56	9.63	10.70
France 10 Francs	1987-1988	12.00	0.900	0.347	>	0.35	0.69	1.04	1.39	3.47	5.21	6.94	8.68	10.41	12.15	13.88	15.62	17.35
France 10 Francs	1996-2000	21.20	0.900	0.642	>	0.64	1.28	1.93	2.57	6.42	9.63	12.84	16.05	19.26	22.47	25.68	28.89	32.10
France 20 Francs	1929-1939	20.00	0.680	0.437	s	0.44	0.87	1.31	1.75	4.37	6.56	8.74	10.93	13.11	15.30	17.48	19.67	21.85
France 50 Francs	1974-1980	30.00	0.900	0.868		0.87	1.74	2.60	3.47	8.68	13.02	17.36	21.70	26.04	30.38	34.72	39.06	43.40
France 100 Francs	1982-2000	15.00	0.900	0.434	N	0.43	0.87	1.30	1.74	4.34	6.51	8.68	10.85	13.02	15.19	17.36	19.53	21.70
France 100 Francs	1985-1989	15.00	0.950	0.458	N	0.46	0.92	1.37	1.83	4.58	6.87	9.16	11.45	13.74	16.03	18.32	20.61	22.90
France 100 Francs / 15 ECU	1989-1995	22.20	0.900	0.642		0.64	1.28	1.93	2.57	6.42	9.63	12.84	16.05	19.26	22.47	25.68	28.89	32.10
France 100 Francs / 15 Euro	1996, 1997	22.20	0.900	0.642	N	0.64	1.28	1.93	2.57	6.42	9.63	12.84	16.05	19.26	22.47	25.68	28.89	32.10
French Cochin China 10 Cent.	1879-1885	2.72	0.900	0.079	s	0.08	0.16	0.24	0.32	0.79	1.19	1.58	1.98	2.37	2.77	3.16	3.56	3.95
French Cochin China 20 Cent.	1879-1885	5.44	0.900	0.158	s	0.16	0.32	0.47	0.63	1.58	2.37	3.16	3.95	4.74	5.53	6.32	7.11	7.90
French Cochin China 50 Cent.	1879-1885	13.61	0.900	0.394	s	0.39	0.79	1.18	1.58	3.94	5.91	7.88	9.85	11.82	13.79	15.76	17.73	19.70
French Cochin China 1 Piastre	1885	27.22	0.900	0.788	s	0.79	1.58	2.36	3.15	7.88	11.82	15.76	19.70	23.64	27.58	31.52	35.46	39.40
French Indo-China 10 Centimes	1885-1895	2.72	0.900	0.079	s	0.08	0.16	0.24	0.32	0.79	1.19	1.58	1.98	2.37	2.77	3.16	3.56	3.95
French Indo-China 10 Centimes	1895-1897	2.70	0.900	0.078		0.08	0.16	0.23	0.31	0.78	1.17	1.56	1.95	2.34	2.73	3.12	3.51	3.90
French Indo-China 10 Centimes	1898-1919	2.70	0.835	0.073		0.07	0.15	0.22	0.29	0.73	1.10	1.46	1.83	2.19	2.56	2.92	3.29	3.65
French Indo-China 10 Centimes	1920	3.00	0.400	0.039		0.04	0.08	0.12	0.16	0.39	0.59	0.78	0.98	1.17	1.37	1.56	1.76	1.95
French Indo-China 10 Centimes	1921-1937	2.70	0.680	0.059		0.06	0.12	0.18	0.24	0.59	0.89	1.18	1.48	1.77	2.07	2.36	2.66	2.95
French Indo-China 20 Centimes	1885-1895	5.44	0.900	0.158	s	0.16	0.32	0.47	0.63	1.58	2.37	3.16	3.95	4.74	5.53	6.32	7.11	7.90
French Indo-China 20 Centimes	1895-1897	5.40	0.900	0.156	s	0.16	0.31	0.47	0.62	1.56	2.34	3.12	3.90	4.68	5.46	6.24	7.02	7.80
French Indo-China 20 Centimes	1898-1916	5.40	0.835	0.145		0.15	0.29	0.44	0.58	1.45	2.18	2.90	3.63	4.35	5.08	5.80	6.53	7.25
French Indo-China 20 Centimes	1921-1937	5.40	0.680	0.118	s	0.12	0.24	0.35	0.47	1.18	1.77	2.36	2.95	3.54	4.13	4.72	5.31	5.90
French Indo-China 50 Centimes	1885-1895	13.61	0.900	0.394	s	0.39	0.79	1.18	1.58	3.94	5.91	7.88	9.85	11.82	13.79	15.76	17.73	19.70
French Indo-China 50 Centimes	1896-1936	13.50	0.900	0.391	s	0.39	0.78	1.17	1.56	3.91	5.87	7.82	9.78	11.73	13.69	15.64	17.60	19.55
French Indo-China 1 Piastre	1885-1895	27.22	0.900	0.788	s	0.79	1.58	2.36	3.15	7.88	11.82	15.76	19.70	23.64	27.58	31.52	35.46	39.40
French Indo-China 1 Piastre	1895-1922	27.00	0.900	0.781	s	0.78	1.56	2.34	3.12	7.81	11.72	15.62	19.53	23.43	27.34	31.24	35.15	39.05
French Indo-China 1 Piastre	1931	20.00	0.900	0.579		0.58	1.16	1.74	2.32	5.79	8.69	11.58	14.48	17.37	20.27	23.16	26.06	28.95
Fujairah 1 Riyal	1969-1970	3.00	1.000	0.096		0.10	0.19	0.29	0.38	0.96	1.44	1.92	2.40	2.88	3.36	3.84	4.32	4.80
Fujairah 2 Riyals	1969-1970	6.00	1.000	0.193		0.19	0.39	0.58	0.77	1.93	2.90	3.86	4.83	5.79	6.76	7.72	8.69	9.65
Fujairah 5 Riyals	1969-1970	15.00	1.000	0.482	N, S	0.48	0.96	1.45	1.93	4.82	7.23	9.64	12.05	14.46	16.87	19.28	21.69	24.10
Fujairah 10 Riyals	1969	30.00	1.000	0.965		0.97	1.93	2.90	3.86	9.65	14.48	19.30	24.13	28.95	33.78	38.60	43.43	48.25
G																		
Gambia 8 Shillings	1970	32.40	0.925	0.964	N	0.96	1.93	2.89	3.86	9.64	14.46	19.28	24.10	28.92	33.74	38.56	43.38	48.20
Gambia 2 Dalasi	1996	9.92	0.500	0.159	N	0.16	0.32	0.48	0.64	1.59	2.39	3.18	3.98	4.77	5.57	6.36	7.16	7.95
Gambia 10 Dalasis	1975-1996	28.28	0.500	0.455	N, S	0.46	0.91	1.37	1.82	4.55	6.83	9.10	11.38	13.65	15.93	18.20	20.48	22.75
Gambia 10 Dalasis	1975, 1986	28.28	0.925	0.841		0.84	1.68	2.52	3.36	8.41	12.62	16.82	21.03	25.23	29.44	33.64	37.85	42.05
Gambia 20 Dalasis	1977-1989	28.28	0.925	0.841	s	0.84	1.68	2.52	3.36	8.41	12.62	16.82	21.03	25.23	29.44	33.64	37.85	42.05
Gambia 20 Dalasis	1993	31.26	0.925	0.930		0.93	1.86	2.79	3.72	9.30	13.95	18.60	23.25	27.90	32.55	37.20	41.85	46.50
Gambia 20 Dalasis	1993-1996	31.47	0.925	0.936		0.94	1.87	2.81	3.74	9.36	14.04	18.72	23.40	28.08	32.76	37.44	42.12	46.80
Gambia 20 Dalasis	1996	31.36	0.925	0.933		0.93	1.87	2.80	3.73	9.33	14.00	18.66	23.33	27.99	32.66	37.32	41.99	46.65

Country & Denomination	Years Minted	Grams Weight	Fine- ness	Troy (ASW)	Code	$ Value 1	$ Value 2	$ Value 3	$ Value 4	$ Value 10	$ Value 15	$ Value 20	$ Value 25	$ Value 30	$ Value 35	$ Value 40	$ Value 45	$ Value 50
Gambia 40 Dalasis	1977	35.29	0.925	1.050		1.05	2.10	3.15	4.20	10.50	15.75	21.00	26.25	31.50	36.75	42.00	47.25	52.50
Gambia 40 Dalasis	1977	35.00	0.925	1.041		1.04	2.08	3.12	4.16	10.41	15.62	20.82	26.03	31.23	36.44	41.64	46.85	52.05
Gambia 100 Dalasis	1977	1000.00	0.999	32.120		32.12	64.24	96.36	128.48	321.20	481.80	642.40	803.00	963.60	1124.20	1284.80	1445.40	1606.00
Gambia 50 Bututs	1997	24.97	0.980	0.787		0.79	1.57	2.36	3.15	7.87	11.81	15.74	19.68	23.61	27.55	31.48	35.42	39.35
Georgia 1/2 Abazi (10 Kopeks)	1804-1833	1.58	0.917	0.047	S	0.05	0.09	0.14	0.19	0.47	0.71	0.94	1.18	1.41	1.65	1.88	2.12	2.35
Georgia 1 Abazi (20 Kopeks)	1804-1831	3.15	0.917	0.093	S	0.09	0.19	0.28	0.37	0.93	1.40	1.86	2.33	2.79	3.26	3.72	4.19	4.65
Georgia 2 Abazi (40 Kopeks)	1804-1833	6.31	0.917	0.186	S	0.19	0.37	0.56	0.74	1.86	2.79	3.72	4.65	5.58	6.51	7.44	8.37	9.30
Georgia 10 Lari	2000	28.28	0.925	0.841	N	0.84	1.68	2.52	3.36	8.41	12.62	16.82	21.03	25.23	29.44	33.64	37.85	42.05
German East Africa 1/4 Rupie	1891-1914	2.92	0.917	0.086	S	0.09	0.17	0.26	0.34	0.86	1.29	1.72	2.15	2.58	3.01	3.44	3.87	4.30
German East Africa 1/2 Rupie	1891-1914	5.83	0.917	0.172	S	0.17	0.34	0.52	0.69	1.72	2.58	3.44	4.30	5.16	6.02	6.88	7.74	8.60
German East Africa Rupie	1890-1914	11.66	0.917	0.344	S	0.34	0.69	1.03	1.38	3.44	5.16	6.88	8.60	10.32	12.04	13.76	15.48	17.20
German East Africa 2 Rupien	1893, 1894	23.32	0.917	0.687		0.69	1.37	2.06	2.75	6.87	10.31	13.74	17.18	20.61	24.05	27.48	30.92	34.35
German New Guinea 1/2 Mark	1894	2.78	0.900	0.080		0.08	0.16	0.24	0.32	0.80	1.20	1.60	2.00	2.40	2.80	3.20	3.60	4.00
German New Guinea 1 Mark	1894	5.56	0.900	0.161		0.16	0.32	0.48	0.64	1.61	2.42	3.22	4.03	4.83	5.64	6.44	7.25	8.05
German New Guinea 2 Marks	1894	11.11	0.900	0.322		0.32	0.64	0.97	1.29	3.22	4.83	6.44	8.05	9.66	11.27	12.88	14.49	16.10
German New Guinea 5 Marks	1894	27.78	0.900	0.804		0.80	1.61	2.41	3.22	8.04	12.06	16.08	20.10	24.12	28.14	32.16	36.18	40.20
Germany 1 Kreuzer (Bavaria)*	1801-1836	0.77	0.187	0.005		0.01	0.01	0.02	0.02	0.05	0.08	0.10	0.13	0.15	0.18	0.20	0.23	0.25
Germany 1 Kreuzer (Bavaria)	1839-1871	0.84	0.166	0.004		0.00	0.01	0.01	0.02	0.04	0.06	0.08	0.10	0.12	0.14	0.16	0.18	0.20
Germany 3 Kreuzer (Bavaria)	1800-1825	1.35	0.333	0.014		0.01	0.03	0.04	0.06	0.14	0.21	0.28	0.35	0.42	0.49	0.56	0.63	0.70
Germany 3 Kreuzer (Bavaria)	1827-1856	1.30	0.333	0.014		0.01	0.03	0.04	0.06	0.14	0.21	0.28	0.35	0.42	0.49	0.56	0.63	0.70
Germany 3 Kreuzer (Bavaria)	1865-1868	1.23	0.350	0.014		0.01	0.03	0.04	0.06	0.14	0.21	0.28	0.35	0.42	0.49	0.56	0.63	0.70
Germany 6 Kreuzer (Bavaria)	1800-1825	2.70	0.333	0.029		0.03	0.06	0.09	0.12	0.29	0.44	0.58	0.73	0.87	1.02	1.16	1.31	1.45
Germany 6 Kreuzer (Bavaria)	1827-1856	2.60	0.333	0.028		0.03	0.06	0.08	0.11	0.28	0.42	0.56	0.70	0.84	0.98	1.12	1.26	1.40
Germany 6 Kreuzer (Bavaria)	1866, 1867	2.46	0.350	0.028		0.03	0.06	0.08	0.11	0.28	0.42	0.56	0.70	0.84	0.98	1.12	1.26	1.40
Germany 10 Kreuzer (Bavaria)	1800	3.90	0.500	0.063		0.06	0.13	0.19	0.25	0.63	0.95	1.26	1.58	1.89	2.21	2.52	2.84	3.15
Germany 20 Kreuzer (Bavaria)	1800-1825	6.68	0.583	0.125		0.13	0.25	0.38	0.50	1.25	1.88	2.50	3.13	3.75	4.38	5.00	5.63	6.25
Germany 1/2 Groschen (Saxony)	1802-1815	0.97	0.250	0.008	S	0.01	0.02	0.02	0.03	0.08	0.12	0.16	0.20	0.24	0.28	0.32	0.36	0.40
Germany 1/2 Groschen (Prussia)	1821-1873	1.09	0.222	0.008		0.01	0.02	0.02	0.03	0.08	0.12	0.16	0.20	0.24	0.28	0.32	0.36	0.40
Germany 1 Groschen (Prussia)	1821-1873	2.19	0.222	0.016		0.02	0.03	0.05	0.06	0.16	0.24	0.32	0.40	0.48	0.56	0.64	0.72	0.80
Germany 1 Groschen (Saxony)	1800-1828	1.98	0.368	0.023	S, V	0.02	0.05	0.07	0.09	0.23	0.35	0.46	0.58	0.69	0.81	0.92	1.04	1.15
Germany Doppelgroschen (Sax)	1800-1836	3.34	0.437	0.047	S	0.05	0.09	0.14	0.19	0.47	0.71	0.94	1.18	1.41	1.65	1.88	2.12	2.35
Germany 2-1/2 Groschen (Pru)	1842-1873	3.24	0.375	0.039	S	0.04	0.08	0.12	0.16	0.39	0.59	0.78	0.98	1.17	1.37	1.56	1.76	1.95
Germany 4 Groschen (Prussia)	1801-1818	5.35	0.521	0.090		0.09	0.18	0.27	0.36	0.90	1.35	1.80	2.25	2.70	3.15	3.60	4.05	4.50
Germany 1/6 Thaler (Prussia)	1809-1868	5.35	0.521	0.090		0.09	0.18	0.27	0.36	0.90	1.35	1.80	2.25	2.70	3.15	3.60	4.05	4.50
Germany 1/6 Thaler (Saxony)	1803-1871	5.39	0.541	0.094		0.09	0.19	0.28	0.38	0.94	1.41	1.88	2.35	2.82	3.29	3.76	4.23	4.70
Germany 1/3 Thaler (Prussia)	1800-1809	8.35	0.666	0.179		0.18	0.36	0.54	0.72	1.79	2.69	3.58	4.48	5.37	6.27	7.16	8.06	8.95
Germany 1/3 Thaler (Saxony)	1801-1821	7.02	0.833	0.188		0.19	0.38	0.56	0.75	1.88	2.82	3.76	4.70	5.64	6.58	7.52	8.46	9.40
Germany 1/3 Thaler (Saxony)	1827-1860	8.30	0.667	0.179	S, V	0.18	0.36	0.54	0.72	1.79	2.69	3.58	4.48	5.37	6.27	7.16	8.06	8.95
Germany 1/2 Thaler (Bavaria)	1800-1837	14.03	0.833	0.376	S	0.38	0.75	1.13	1.50	3.76	5.64	7.52	9.40	11.28	13.16	15.04	16.92	18.80
Germany 1/2 Thaler (Saxony)	1800-1829	14.03	0.833	0.376	S	0.38	0.75	1.13	1.50	3.76	5.64	7.52	9.40	11.28	13.16	15.04	16.92	18.80
Germany 2/3 Thaler (Prussia)	1801, 1810	17.32	0.750	0.418		0.42	0.84	1.25	1.67	4.18	6.27	8.36	10.45	12.54	14.63	16.72	18.81	20.90

Country & Denomination	Years Minted	Grams Weight	Fine-ness	Troy (ASW)	Code	$ Value 1	$ Value 2	$ Value 3	$ Value 4	$ Value 10	$ Value 15	$ Value 20	$ Value 25	$ Value 30	$ Value 35	$ Value 40	$ Value 45	$ Value 50
Germany 1 Thaler (Bav, Sax)	1800-1838	28.00	0.833	0.750	S, V	0.75	1.50	2.25	3.00	7.50	11.25	15.00	18.75	22.50	26.25	30.00	33.75	37.50
Germany 1 Thaler (Saxony)	1839-1856	22.27	0.750	0.537		0.54	1.07	1.61	2.15	5.37	8.06	10.74	13.43	16.11	18.80	21.48	24.17	26.85
Germany 1 Thaler (Prussia)	1800-1856	22.27	0.750	0.537		0.54	1.07	1.61	2.15	5.37	8.06	10.74	13.43	16.11	18.80	21.48	24.17	26.85
Germany 1 Thaler/Krone (Bav)	1809-1825	29.34	0.868	0.819		0.82	1.64	2.46	3.28	8.19	12.29	16.38	20.48	24.57	28.67	32.76	36.86	40.95
Germany 1 Thaler/Krone (Bav)	1825-1837	29.54	0.871	0.827		0.83	1.65	2.48	3.31	8.27	12.41	16.54	20.68	24.81	28.95	33.08	37.22	41.35
Germany 1 Thaler (Bav Pru Sax)	1857-1871	18.52	0.900	0.536		0.54	1.07	1.61	2.14	5.36	8.04	10.72	13.40	16.08	18.76	21.44	24.12	26.80
Germany 1/2 Gulden (Bavaria)	1838-1871	5.30	0.900	0.153		0.15	0.31	0.46	0.61	1.53	2.30	3.06	3.83	4.59	5.36	6.12	6.89	7.65
Germany 1 Gulden (Bavaria)	1837-1871	10.60	0.900	0.307		0.31	0.61	0.92	1.23	3.07	4.61	6.14	7.68	9.21	10.75	12.28	13.82	15.35
Germany 2 Gulden (Bavaria)	1845-1856	21.21	0.900	0.614		0.61	1.23	1.84	2.46	6.14	9.21	12.28	15.35	18.42	21.49	24.56	27.63	30.70
Germany 2 Thaler (Bav Pru Sax)	1837-1856	37.12	0.900	1.074		1.07	2.15	3.22	4.30	10.74	16.11	21.48	26.85	32.22	37.59	42.96	48.33	53.70
Germany 2 Thaler (Bavaria)	1859-1869	37.04	0.900	1.072		1.07	2.14	3.22	4.29	10.72	16.08	21.44	26.80	32.16	37.52	42.88	48.24	53.60
Germany 3 Pfennig (Prussia)	1801-1806	0.70	0.250	0.006		0.01	0.01	0.02	0.02	0.06	0.09	0.12	0.15	0.18	0.21	0.24	0.27	0.30
Germany 5 Pfennig (Saxony)	1841-1856	1.06	0.229	0.008	S	0.01	0.02	0.02	0.03	0.08	0.12	0.16	0.20	0.24	0.28	0.32	0.36	0.40
Germany 8 Pfennig (Saxony)	1808, 1809	1.29	0.250	0.010		0.01	0.02	0.03	0.04	0.10	0.15	0.20	0.25	0.30	0.35	0.40	0.45	0.50
Germany 10 Pfennig (Saxony)	1841-1873	2.12	0.229	0.016	S	0.02	0.03	0.05	0.06	0.16	0.24	0.32	0.40	0.48	0.56	0.64	0.72	0.80
Germany 20 Pfennig (Saxony)	1841-1873	3.11	0.312	0.031	S	0.03	0.06	0.09	0.12	0.31	0.47	0.62	0.78	0.93	1.09	1.24	1.40	1.55
Germany 20 Pfennig	1873-1877	1.11	0.900	0.032		0.03	0.06	0.10	0.13	0.32	0.48	0.64	0.80	0.96	1.12	1.28	1.44	1.60
Germany 50 Pfennig	1875-1903	2.78	0.900	0.080	S	0.08	0.16	0.24	0.32	0.80	1.20	1.60	2.00	2.40	2.80	3.20	3.60	4.00
Germany 1/2 Mark	1905-1919	2.78	0.900	0.080	S	0.08	0.16	0.24	0.32	0.80	1.20	1.60	2.00	2.40	2.80	3.20	3.60	4.00
Germany 1 Mark	1873-1916	5.55	0.900	0.161		0.16	0.32	0.48	0.64	1.61	2.42	3.22	4.03	4.83	5.64	6.44	7.25	8.05
Germany 1 Mark	1924-1925	5.00	0.500	0.080		0.08	0.16	0.24	0.32	0.80	1.20	1.60	2.00	2.40	2.80	3.20	3.60	4.00
Germany 2 Marks	1876-1914	11.11	0.900	0.322	S	0.32	0.64	0.97	1.29	3.22	4.83	6.44	8.05	9.66	11.27	12.88	14.49	16.10
Germany 2 Reichsmarks	1925-1931	10.00	0.500	0.161		0.16	0.32	0.48	0.64	1.61	2.42	3.22	4.03	4.83	5.64	6.44	7.25	8.05
Germany 2 Reichsmarks	1933-1936	8.00	0.625	0.161		0.16	0.32	0.48	0.64	1.61	2.42	3.22	4.03	4.83	5.64	6.44	7.25	8.05
Germany 3 Marks	1908-1915	16.67	0.900	0.482		0.48	0.96	1.45	1.93	4.82	7.23	9.64	12.05	14.46	16.87	19.28	21.69	24.10
Germany 3 Reichsmarks	1924-1933	15.00	0.500	0.241		0.24	0.48	0.72	0.96	2.41	3.62	4.82	6.03	7.23	8.44	9.64	10.85	12.05
Germany 5 Marks	1874-1914	27.77	0.900	0.804	N, S	0.80	1.61	2.41	3.22	8.04	12.06	16.08	20.10	24.12	28.14	32.16	36.18	40.20
Germany 5 Reichsmarks	1925-1932	25.00	0.500	0.402		0.40	0.80	1.21	1.61	4.02	6.03	8.04	10.05	12.06	14.07	16.08	18.09	20.10
Germany 5 Reichsmarks	1933-1939	13.88	0.900	0.402		0.40	0.80	1.21	1.61	4.02	6.03	8.04	10.05	12.06	14.07	16.08	18.09	20.10
Germany, West 5 Marks	1951-1979	11.20	0.625	0.225	N	0.23	0.45	0.68	0.90	2.25	3.38	4.50	5.63	6.75	7.88	9.00	10.13	11.25
Germany, West 10 Marks	1972-2000	15.50	0.625	0.312	N	0.31	0.62	0.94	1.25	3.12	4.68	6.24	7.80	9.36	10.92	12.48	14.04	15.60
Germany, East 10 Marks	1966-1967	17.00	0.800	0.437		0.44	0.87	1.32	1.76	4.37	6.60	8.80	10.93	13.11	15.30	17.48	19.67	21.85
Germany, East 10 Marks	1968-1975	17.00	0.625	0.342	N	0.44	0.68	1.32	1.76	3.42	6.60	8.80	8.55	10.26	11.97	13.68	15.39	17.10
Germany, East 10 Marks	1975-1990	17.00	0.500	0.273	N	0.44	0.55	1.32	1.76	2.73	6.60	8.80	6.83	8.19	9.56	10.92	12.29	13.65
Germany, East 20 Marks	1966-1968	20.90	0.800	0.538		0.44	1.08	1.32	1.76	5.38	6.60	8.80	13.45	16.14	18.83	21.52	24.21	26.90
Germany, East 20 Marks	1969-1990	20.90	0.625	0.420	N	0.44	0.84	1.32	1.76	4.20	6.60	8.80	10.50	12.60	14.70	16.80	18.90	21.00
Germany, East 20 Marks	1977-1985	20.90	0.500	0.336		0.44	0.67	1.32	1.76	3.36	6.60	8.80	8.40	10.08	11.76	13.44	15.12	16.80
Ghana 10 Shillings	1958	28.28	0.925	0.841		0.84	1.68	2.52	3.36	8.41	12.60	16.80	21.03	25.23	29.44	33.64	37.85	42.05
Ghana 50 Cedis	1981-1984	28.28	0.925	0.841	N	0.84	1.68	2.52	3.36	8.41	12.60	16.80	21.03	25.23	29.44	33.64	37.85	42.05
Ghana 100 Cedis	1986	28.28	0.925	0.841		0.84	1.68	2.52	3.36	8.41	12.60	16.80	21.03	25.23	29.44	33.64	37.85	42.05
Gibraltar 5 New Pence	1990	3.25	0.925	0.097	N	0.10	0.19	0.29	0.39	0.97	1.46	1.94	2.43	2.91	3.40	3.88	4.37	4.85

Country & Denomination	Years Minted	Grams Weight	Fine-ness	Troy (ASW)	Code	$ Value 1	$ Value 2	$ Value 3	$ Value 4	$ Value 10	$ Value 15	$ Value 20	$ Value 25	$ Value 30	$ Value 35	$ Value 40	$ Value 45	$ Value 50
Gibraltar 10 New Pence	1992	6.50	0.925	0.193	N	0.19	0.39	0.58	0.77	1.93	2.90	3.86	4.83	5.79	6.76	7.72	8.69	9.65
Gibraltar 25 Pence	1971	28.28	0.500	0.455	N	0.46	0.91	1.37	1.82	4.55	6.83	9.10	11.38	13.65	15.93	18.20	20.48	22.75
Gibraltar 25 New Pence	1972, 1977	28.28	0.925	0.841	N	0.46	1.68			8.41			21.03	25.23	29.44	33.64	37.85	42.05
Gibraltar 50 New Pence	1988-1996	15.50	0.925	0.461	N	0.46	0.92	1.38	1.84	4.61	6.92	9.22	11.53	13.83	16.14	18.44	20.75	23.05
Gibraltar 1/2 Crown	1993-1999	15.78	0.999	0.507	N	0.46	1.01	1.38	1.84	5.07	6.90	9.20	12.68	15.21	17.75	20.28	22.82	25.35
Gibraltar 1 Crown	1967	28.28	0.500	0.455	N	0.46	0.91	1.38	1.84	4.55	6.90	9.20	11.38	13.65	15.93	18.20	20.48	22.75
Gibraltar 1 Crown	1980-2000	28.28	0.925	0.841	N	0.46	1.68	1.38	1.84	8.41	6.90	9.20	21.03	25.23	29.44	33.64	37.85	42.05
Gibraltar 2 Crown	1993	62.21	0.999	2.000	N	0.46	4.00	1.38	1.84	20.00	6.90	9.20	50.00	60.00	70.00	80.00	90.00	100.00
Gibraltar 5 Crown	1991, 1993	155.92	0.999	5.000	N	0.46	10.00	1.38	1.84	50.00	6.90	9.20	125.00	150.00	175.00	200.00	225.00	250.00
Gibraltar 10 Crown	1991, 1993	311.85	0.999	10.000	N	0.46	20.00	1.38	1.84	100.00	6.90	9.20	250.00	300.00	350.00	400.00	450.00	500.00
Gibraltar 1 Pound	1988-1995	9.50	0.925	0.283	N	0.46	0.57	1.38	1.84	2.83	6.90	9.20	7.08	8.49	9.91	11.32	12.74	14.15
Gibraltar 2 Pounds	1992	9.30	0.925	0.277	N	0.46	0.55	1.38	1.84	2.77	6.90	9.20	6.93	8.31	9.70	11.08	12.47	13.85
Gibraltar 2 Pounds	1994-2000	23.50	0.925	0.699	N	0.46	1.40	1.38	1.84	6.99	6.90	9.20	17.48	20.97	24.47	27.96	31.46	34.95
Gibraltar 10 Pounds / 14 ECUs	1991-1996	10.00	0.925	0.297	N	0.46	0.59	1.38	1.84	2.97	6.90	9.20	7.43	8.91	10.40	11.88	13.37	14.85
Gibraltar 25 Pounds / 35 ECUs	1991-1993	28.28	0.925	0.841	N	0.46	1.68	1.38	1.84	8.41	6.90	9.20	21.03	25.23	29.44	33.64	37.85	42.05
Gibraltar 21 ECUs	1993-1995	19.20	0.925	0.571		0.46	1.14	1.38	1.84	5.71	6.90	9.20	14.28	17.13	19.99	22.84	25.70	28.55
Gibraltar 70 ECUs	1993-1996	155.52	0.925	5.008	N	0.46	10.02	1.38	1.84	50.08	6.90	9.20	125.20	150.24	175.28	200.32	225.36	250.40
Goa--see Portuguese India																		
Gold Coast 1/2 Ackey	1818	7.09	0.925	0.211		0.21	0.42	0.63	0.84	2.11	3.17	4.22	5.28	6.33	7.39	8.44	9.50	10.55
Gold Coast 1 Ackey	1818	14.13	0.925	0.420		0.42	0.84	1.26	1.68	4.20	6.30	8.40	10.50	12.60	14.70	16.80	18.90	21.00
Great Britain Penny	1817-1920	0.47	0.925	0.014	N	0.01	0.03	0.04	0.06	0.14	0.21	0.28	0.35	0.42	0.49	0.56	0.63	0.70
Great Britain Penny	1937-1946	0.47	0.500	0.008	N	0.01	0.02	0.02	0.03	0.08	0.12	0.16	0.20	0.24	0.28	0.32	0.36	0.40
Great Britain Penny	1947-2000	0.47	0.925	0.014	N	0.01	0.03	0.04	0.06	0.14	0.21	0.28	0.35	0.42	0.49	0.56	0.63	0.70
Great Britain 1-1/2 Pence	1834-1870	0.71	0.925	0.021	S	0.02	0.04	0.06	0.08	0.21	0.32	0.42	0.53	0.63	0.74	0.84	0.95	1.05
Great Britain 2 Pence	1817-1920	0.94	0.925	0.028	N	0.03	0.06	0.08	0.11	0.28	0.42	0.56	0.70	0.84	0.98	1.12	1.26	1.40
Great Britain 2 Pence	1921-1946	0.94	0.500	0.014	N	0.01	0.03	0.04	0.06	0.14	0.21	0.28	0.35	0.42	0.49	0.56	0.63	0.70
Great Britain 2 Pence	1947-2000	0.94	0.925	0.028	N	0.03	0.06	0.08	0.11	0.28	0.42	0.56	0.70	0.84	0.98	1.12	1.26	1.40
Great Britain 3 Pence	1817-1920	1.41	0.925	0.042	N	0.04	0.08	0.13	0.17	0.42	0.63	0.84	1.05	1.26	1.47	1.68	1.89	2.10
Great Britain 3 Pence	1920-1946	1.41	0.500	0.023	N	0.02	0.05	0.07	0.09	0.23	0.35	0.46	0.58	0.69	0.81	0.92	1.04	1.15
Great Britain 3 Pence	1947-2000	1.41	0.925	0.042	N	0.04	0.08	0.13	0.17	0.42	0.63	0.84	1.05	1.26	1.47	1.68	1.89	2.10
Great Britain 4 Pence	1817-1920	1.89	0.925	0.056	N	0.06	0.11	0.17	0.22	0.56	0.84	1.12	1.40	1.68	1.96	2.24	2.52	2.80
Great Britain 4 Pence	1921-1946	1.89	0.500	0.030	N	0.03	0.06	0.09	0.12	0.30	0.45	0.60	0.75	0.90	1.05	1.20	1.35	1.50
Great Britain 4 Pence	1947-2000	1.89	0.925	0.056	N	0.06	0.11	0.17	0.22	0.56	0.84	1.12	1.40	1.68	1.96	2.24	2.52	2.80
Great Britain 5 Pence	1990	5.60	0.925	0.168	N	0.17	0.34	0.50	0.67	1.68	2.52	3.36	4.20	5.04	5.88	6.72	7.56	8.40
Great Britain 5 Pence	1990	6.50	0.925	0.193	N	0.19	0.39	0.58	0.77	1.93	2.90	3.86	4.83	5.79	6.76	7.72	8.69	9.65
Great Britain 5 Pence	1990-2000	3.25	0.925	0.097	N,S	0.10	0.19	0.29	0.39	0.97	1.46	1.94	2.43	2.91	3.40	3.88	4.37	4.85
Great Britain 6 Pence	1816-1837	2.83	0.925	0.084		0.08	0.17	0.25	0.34	0.84	1.26	1.68	2.10	2.52	2.94	3.36	3.78	4.20
Great Britain 6 Pence	1838-1920	3.01	0.925	0.089		0.09	0.18	0.27	0.36	0.89	1.34	1.78	2.23	2.67	3.12	3.56	4.01	4.45
Great Britain 6 Pence	1920-1946	2.83	0.500	0.046		0.05	0.09	0.14	0.18	0.46	0.69	0.92	1.15	1.38	1.61	1.84	2.07	2.30
Great Britain 10 Pence	1992	11.31	0.925	0.336	N,S	0.34	0.67	1.01	1.34	3.36	5.04	6.72	8.40	10.08	11.76	13.44	15.12	16.80
Great Britain 10 Pence	1992-2000	6.50	0.925	0.193	N,S	0.19	0.39	0.58	0.77	1.93	2.90	3.86	4.83	5.79	6.76	7.72	8.69	9.65
Great Britain 20 Pence	1996-2000	5.00	0.925	0.149	N,S	0.15	0.30	0.45	0.60	1.49	2.24	2.98	3.73	4.47	5.22	5.96	6.71	7.45

Country & Denomination	Years Minted	Grams Weight	Fine-ness	Troy (ASW)	Code	$ Value 1	$ Value 2	$ Value 3	$ Value 4	$ Value 10	$ Value 15	$ Value 20	$ Value 25	$ Value 30	$ Value 35	$ Value 40	$ Value 45	$ Value 50
Great Britain 25 New Pence	1972-1981	28.28	0.925	0.841	N,S	0.84	1.68	2.52	3.36	8.41	12.62	16.82	21.03	25.23	29.44	33.64	37.85	42.05
Great Britain 50 New Pence	1992-1994	13.50	0.925	0.401	N,S	0.40	0.80	1.20	1.60	4.01	6.02	8.02	10.03	12.03	14.04	16.04	18.05	20.05
Great Britain 50 New Pence	1997-2000	8.00	0.925	0.240	N,S,V	0.24	0.48	0.72	0.96	2.40	3.60	4.80	6.00	7.20	8.40	9.60	10.80	12.00
Great Britain Shilling	1816-1919	5.66	0.925	0.168	S	0.17	0.34	0.50	0.67	1.68	2.52	3.36	4.20	5.04	5.88	6.72	7.56	8.40
Great Britain Shilling	1920-1946	5.66	0.500	0.092		0.09	0.18	0.28	0.37	0.92	1.38	1.84	2.30	2.76	3.22	3.68	4.14	4.60
Great Britain 1 Florin / 2 Shillings	1848-1919	11.31	0.925	0.336	S	0.34	0.67	1.01	1.34	3.36	5.04	6.72	8.40	10.08	11.76	13.44	15.12	16.80
Great Britain 1 Florin / 2 Shillings	1920-1946	11.31	0.500	0.182		0.18	0.36	0.55	0.73	1.82	2.73	3.64	4.55	5.46	6.37	7.28	8.19	9.10
Great Britain 1/2 Crown	1816-1919	14.14	0.925	0.421		0.42	0.84	1.26	1.68	4.21	6.32	8.42	10.53	12.63	14.74	16.84	18.95	21.05
Great Britain 1/2 Crown	1920-1946	14.14	0.500	0.227		0.23	0.45	0.68	0.91	2.27	3.41	4.54	5.68	6.81	7.95	9.08	10.22	11.35
Great Britain Double Florin	1887-1890	22.62	0.925	0.673		0.67	1.35	2.02	2.69	6.73	10.10	13.46	16.83	20.19	23.56	26.92	30.29	33.65
Great Britain 1 Crown	1818-1902	28.28	0.925	0.841	S	0.84	1.68	2.52	3.36	8.41	12.62	16.82	21.03	25.23	29.44	33.64	37.85	42.05
Great Britain 1 Crown	1927-1937	28.80	0.500	0.455		0.46	0.91	1.37	1.82	4.55	6.83	9.10	11.38	13.65	15.93	18.20	20.48	22.75
Great Britain 1 Pound	1983-2000	9.50	0.925	0.283	N,S	0.28	0.57	0.85	1.13	2.83	4.25	5.66	7.08	8.49	9.91	11.32	12.74	14.15
Great Britain 1 Pound	1997	16.22	0.958	0.500	N,S	0.50	1.00	1.50	2.00	5.00	7.50	10.00	12.50	15.00	17.50	20.00	22.50	25.00
Great Britain 2 Pounds	1986	15.98	0.500	0.257	N,S	0.26	0.51	0.77	1.03	2.57	3.86	5.14	6.43	7.71	9.00	10.28	11.57	12.85
Great Britain 2 Pounds	1986-2000	15.98	0.925	0.475	N,S	0.48	0.95	1.43	1.90	4.75	7.13	9.50	11.88	14.25	16.63	19.00	21.38	23.75
Great Britain 2 Pounds	1997-2000	12.00	0.925	0.357	N,S	0.36	0.71	1.07	1.43	3.57	5.36	7.14	8.93	10.71	12.50	14.28	16.07	17.85
Great Britain 2 Pounds	1997-2000	43.54	0.958	1.000	N,S	1.00	2.00	3.00	4.00	10.00	15.00	20.00	25.00	30.00	35.00	40.00	45.00	50.00
Great Britain 2 Pounds	1999	24.00	0.925	0.714	N,S	0.71	1.43	2.14	2.86	7.14	10.71	14.28	17.85	21.42	24.99	28.56	32.13	35.70
Great Britain 5 Pounds	1990-2000	28.28	0.925	0.841	N,S	0.84	1.68	2.52	3.36	8.41	12.62	16.82	21.03	25.23	29.44	33.64	37.85	42.05
Great Britain 1 Trade Dollar	1895-1934	26.96	0.900	0.780	N,S	0.77	1.56	2.31	3.08	7.80	11.55	15.40	19.50	23.40	27.30	31.20	35.10	39.00
Greece 1 Phoenix	1828	3.87	0.943	0.117		0.12	0.23	0.35	0.47	1.17	1.76	2.34	2.93	3.51	4.10	4.68	5.27	5.85
Greece 1/4 Drachma	1833-1855	1.12	0.900	0.032	S	0.03	0.06	0.10	0.13	0.32	0.48	0.64	0.80	0.96	1.12	1.28	1.44	1.60
Greece 1/2 Drachma	1833-1855	2.24	0.900	0.065	S	0.07	0.13	0.20	0.26	0.65	0.98	1.30	1.63	1.95	2.28	2.60	2.93	3.25
Greece 20 Lepta	1874, 1883	1.00	0.835	0.027		0.03	0.05	0.08	0.11	0.27	0.41	0.54	0.68	0.81	0.95	1.08	1.22	1.35
Greece 50 Lepta	1868-1883	2.50	0.835	0.067	S	0.07	0.13	0.20	0.27	0.67	1.01	1.34	1.68	2.01	2.35	2.68	3.02	3.35
Greece 1 Drachma	1832-1851	4.03	0.900	0.130	S	0.13	0.26	0.39	0.52	1.30	1.95	2.60	3.25	3.90	4.55	5.20	5.85	6.50
Greece 1 Drachma	1868-1911	5.00	0.835	0.134	S	0.13	0.27	0.40	0.54	1.34	2.01	2.68	3.36	4.03	4.70	5.37	6.04	6.71
Greece 2 Drachmai	1868-1911	10.00	0.835	0.268		0.27	0.54	0.80	1.07	2.68	4.02	5.36	6.70	8.04	9.38	10.72	12.06	13.40
Greece 5 Drachmai	1833-1851	22.50	0.900	0.651	S	0.65	1.30	1.95	2.60	6.51	9.77	13.02	16.28	19.53	22.79	26.04	29.30	32.55
Greece 5 Drachmai	1875, 1876	25.00	0.900	0.723		0.72	1.45	2.17	2.89	7.23	10.85	14.46	18.08	21.69	25.31	28.92	32.54	36.15
Greece 10 Drachmai	1930	7.00	0.500	0.113		0.11	0.23	0.34	0.45	1.13	1.70	2.26	2.83	3.39	3.96	4.52	5.09	5.65
Greece 20 Drachmai	1930	11.31	0.500	0.182		0.18	0.36	0.55	0.73	1.82	2.73	3.64	4.55	5.46	6.37	7.28	8.19	9.10
Greece 20 Drachmai	1960, 1965	7.50	0.835	0.201		0.20	0.40	0.60	0.80	2.01	3.02	4.02	5.03	6.03	7.04	8.04	9.05	10.05
Greece 30 Drachmai	1963	18.00	0.835	0.483		0.48	0.97	1.45	1.93	4.83	7.25	9.66	12.08	14.49	16.91	19.32	21.74	24.15
Greece 30 Drachmai	1964	12.00	0.835	0.322		0.32	0.64	0.97	1.29	3.22	4.83	6.44	8.05	9.66	11.27	12.88	14.49	16.10
Greece 50 Drachmai	1967	12.50	0.835	0.336		0.34	0.67	1.01	1.34	3.36	5.04	6.72	8.40	10.08	11.76	13.44	15.12	16.80
Greece 100 Drachmai	1940	25.00	0.900	0.724		0.72	1.45	2.17	2.90	7.24	10.86	14.48	18.10	21.72	25.34	28.96	32.58	36.20
Greece 100 Drachmai	1970	25.00	0.835	0.671		0.67	1.34	2.01	2.68	6.71	10.07	13.42	16.78	20.13	23.49	26.84	30.20	33.55
Greece 100 Drachmai	1978	13.00	0.650	0.272		0.27	0.54	0.82	1.09	2.72	4.08	5.44	6.80	8.16	9.52	10.88	12.24	13.60
Greece 100 Drachmai	1981, 1982	5.78	0.900	0.167		0.17	0.33	0.50	0.67	1.67	2.51	3.34	4.18	5.01	5.85	6.68	7.52	8.35
Greece 250 Drachmai	1981, 1982	14.44	0.900	0.418		0.42	0.84	1.25	1.67	4.18	6.27	8.36	10.45	12.54	14.63	16.72	18.81	20.90
Greece 500 Drachmai	1981, 1982	28.88	0.900	0.836		0.84	1.67	2.51	3.34	8.36	12.54	16.72	20.90	25.08	29.26	33.44	37.62	41.80
Greece 500 Drachmes	1979	13.00	0.900	0.376		0.38	0.75	1.13	1.50	3.76	5.64	7.52	9.40	11.28	13.16	15.04	16.92	18.80

Country & Denomination	Years Minted	Grams Weight	Fineness	Troy (ASW)	Code	$ Value 1	$ Value 2	$ Value 3	$ Value 4	$ Value 10	$ Value 15	$ Value 20	$ Value 25	$ Value 30	$ Value 35	$ Value 40	$ Value 45	$ Value 50
Greece 500 Drachmes	1984, 1991	18.00	0.900	0.521		0.52	1.04	1.56	2.08	5.21	7.82	10.42	13.03	15.63	18.24	20.84	23.45	26.05
Greece 500 Drachmes	1988	18.11	0.900	0.524		0.52	1.05	1.57	2.10	5.24	7.86	10.48	13.10	15.72	18.34	20.96	23.58	26.20
Greece 500 Drachmes	1979	13.00	0.900	0.376		0.38	0.75	1.13	1.50	3.76	5.64	7.52	9.40	11.28	13.16	15.04	16.92	18.80
Greece 500 Drachmes	1993, 1994	17.00	0.925	0.506		0.51	1.01	1.52	2.02	5.06	7.59	10.12	12.65	15.18	17.71	20.24	22.77	25.30
Greece 1000 Drachmes	1990	18.00	0.900	0.521		0.52	1.04	1.56	2.08	5.21	7.82	10.42	13.03	15.63	18.24	20.84	23.45	26.05
Greece 1000 Drachmes	1996	33.63	0.925	1.000		1.00	2.00	3.00	4.00	10.00	15.00	20.00	25.00	30.00	35.00	40.00	45.00	50.00
Grenada 10 Dollars	1985	28.28	0.925	0.841	N	0.84	1.68	2.52	3.36	8.41	12.62	16.82	21.03	25.23	29.44	33.64	37.85	42.05
Grenada 100 Dollars	1988	129.59	0.925	3.854		3.85	7.71	11.56	15.42	38.54	57.81	77.08	96.35	115.62	134.89	154.16	173.43	192.70
Guatemala 1/4 Real	1800-1822	0.85	0.896	0.024		0.02	0.05	0.07	0.10	0.24	0.37	0.49	0.61	0.73	0.85	0.98	1.10	1.22
Guatemala 1/4 Real	1859-1869	0.76	0.903	0.022		0.02	0.04	0.07	0.09	0.22	0.33	0.44	0.55	0.66	0.77	0.88	0.99	1.10
Guatemala 1/4 Real	1872-1878	0.77	0.900	0.022		0.02	0.04	0.07	0.09	0.22	0.33	0.44	0.55	0.66	0.77	0.88	0.99	1.10
Guatemala 1/4 Real	1878-1899	0.77	0.835	0.021		0.02	0.04	0.06	0.08	0.21	0.32	0.42	0.53	0.63	0.74	0.84	0.95	1.05
Guatemala 1/2 Real	1800-1821	1.69	0.896	0.049		0.05	0.10	0.15	0.19	0.49	0.73	0.97	1.22	1.46	1.70	1.95	2.19	2.44
Guatemala 1/2 Real	1859-1869	1.55	0.903	0.045		0.05	0.09	0.14	0.18	0.45	0.68	0.90	1.13	1.35	1.58	1.80	2.03	2.25
Guatemala 1/2 Real	1878-1897	1.50	0.835	0.040	S	0.04	0.08	0.12	0.16	0.40	0.60	0.80	1.00	1.20	1.40	1.60	1.80	2.00
Guatemala 1/2 Real	1872, 1873	1.50	0.900	0.044		0.04	0.09	0.13	0.18	0.44	0.66	0.88	1.10	1.32	1.54	1.76	1.98	2.20
Guatemala 1/2 Real	1899	1.55	0.600	0.030		0.03	0.06	0.09	0.12	0.30	0.45	0.60	0.75	0.90	1.05	1.20	1.35	1.50
Guatemala 1 Real	1800-1821	3.38	0.896	0.098		0.10	0.20	0.29	0.39	0.98	1.46	1.95	2.44	2.93	3.41	3.90	4.39	4.88
Guatemala 1 Real	1859-1869	3.00	0.903	0.087		0.09	0.17	0.26	0.35	0.87	1.31	1.74	2.18	2.61	3.05	3.48	3.92	4.35
Guatemala 1 Real	1872-1879	3.15	0.900	0.091	S	0.09	0.18	0.27	0.36	0.91	1.37	1.82	2.28	2.73	3.19	3.64	4.10	4.55
Guatemala 1 Real	1883-1898	3.25	0.835	0.087	S	0.09	0.17	0.26	0.35	0.87	1.31	1.74	2.18	2.61	3.05	3.48	3.92	4.35
Guatemala 1 Real	1899	3.15	0.750	0.076		0.08	0.15	0.23	0.30	0.76	1.14	1.52	1.90	2.28	2.66	3.04	3.42	3.80
Guatemala 1 Real	1899	3.10	0.600	0.060		0.06	0.12	0.18	0.24	0.60	0.90	1.20	1.50	1.80	2.10	2.40	2.70	3.00
Guatemala 1 Real	1899, 1900	3.15	0.500	0.051		0.05	0.10	0.15	0.20	0.51	0.77	1.02	1.28	1.53	1.79	2.04	2.30	2.55
Guatemala 2 Reales	1800-1821	6.77	0.896	0.195		0.20	0.39	0.59	0.78	1.95	2.93	3.90	4.88	5.85	6.83	7.80	8.78	9.75
Guatemala 2 Reales	1859-1869	6.10	0.903	0.177		0.18	0.35	0.53	0.71	1.77	2.66	3.54	4.43	5.31	6.20	7.08	7.97	8.85
Guatemala 2 Reales	1872-1879	6.10	0.900	0.177	S	0.18	0.35	0.53	0.71	1.77	2.66	3.54	4.43	5.31	6.20	7.08	7.97	8.85
Guatemala 2 Reales	1881-1899	6.20	0.835	0.166	S	0.17	0.33	0.50	0.66	1.66	2.49	3.32	4.15	4.98	5.81	6.64	7.47	8.30
Guatemala 4 Reales	1800-1821	13.53	0.896	0.390		0.39	0.78	1.17	1.56	3.90	5.85	7.80	9.75	11.70	13.65	15.60	17.55	19.50
Guatemala 4 Reales	1860-1869	12.50	0.903	0.363	S	0.36	0.73	1.09	1.45	3.63	5.45	7.26	9.08	10.89	12.71	14.52	16.34	18.15
Guatemala 4 Reales	1873-1894	12.50	0.900	0.362	S	0.36	0.72	1.09	1.45	3.62	5.43	7.24	9.05	10.86	12.67	14.48	16.29	18.10
Guatemala 4 Reales	1892	12.50	0.835	0.336		0.34	0.67	1.01	1.34	3.36	5.04	6.72	8.40	10.08	11.76	13.44	15.12	16.80
Guatemala 8 Reales	1800-1821	27.07	0.896	0.780		0.78	1.56	2.34	3.12	7.80	11.70	15.60	19.50	23.40	27.30	31.20	35.10	39.00
Guatemala 5 Centavos	1881	1.25	0.835	0.034		0.03	0.07	0.10	0.14	0.34	0.51	0.68	0.85	1.02	1.19	1.36	1.53	1.70
Guatemala 5 Centavos	1925-1964	1.67	0.720	0.039	N, S	0.04	0.08	0.12	0.16	0.39	0.59	0.78	0.98	1.17	1.37	1.56	1.76	1.95
Guatemala 10 Centavos	1881	2.50	0.835	0.067		0.07	0.13	0.20	0.27	0.67	1.01	1.34	1.68	2.01	2.35	2.68	3.02	3.35
Guatemala 10 Centavos	1925-1964	3.33	0.720	0.077	N, S	0.08	0.15	0.23	0.31	0.77	1.16	1.54	1.93	2.31	2.70	3.08	3.47	3.85
Guatemala 25 Centavos	1869, 1870	6.25	0.900	0.181		0.18	0.36	0.54	0.72	1.81	2.72	3.62	4.53	5.43	6.34	7.24	8.15	9.05
Guatemala 25 Centavos	1881-1892	6.25	0.835	0.168	S	0.17	0.34	0.50	0.67	1.68	2.52	3.36	4.20	5.04	5.88	6.72	7.56	8.40
Guatemala 1/4 Quetzal	1925-1964	8.33	0.720	0.193	S	0.19	0.39	0.58	0.77	1.93	2.90	3.86	4.83	5.79	6.76	7.72	8.69	9.65
Guatemala 50 Centavos	1859	25.00	0.903	0.726		0.73	1.45	2.18	2.90	7.26	10.89	14.52	18.15	21.78	25.41	29.04	32.67	36.30
Guatemala 50 Centavos	1962, 1963	12.00	0.720	0.278		0.28	0.56	0.83	1.11	2.78	4.17	5.56	6.95	8.34	9.73	11.12	12.51	13.90
Guatemala 1 Peso	1870	12.50	0.835	0.336		0.34	0.67	1.01	1.34	3.36	5.04	6.72	8.40	10.08	11.76	13.44	15.12	16.80

Country & Denomination	Years Minted	Grams Weight	Fine-ness	Troy (ASW)	Code	$ Value 1	$ Value 2	$ Value 3	$ Value 4	$ Value 10	$ Value 15	$ Value 20	$ Value 25	$ Value 30	$ Value 35	$ Value 40	$ Value 45	$ Value 50
Guatemala 1 Peso	1862-1869	27.00	0.903	0.784		0.78	1.57	2.35	3.14	7.84	11.76	15.68	19.60	23.52	27.44	31.36	35.28	39.20
Guatemala 1 Peso	1869-1897	25.00	0.900	0.723		0.72	1.45	2.17	2.89	7.23	10.85	14.46	18.08	21.69	25.31	28.92	32.54	36.15
Guatemala 1/2 Quetzal	1925	16.67	0.720	0.386		0.39	0.77	1.16	1.54	3.86	5.79	7.72	9.65	11.58	13.51	15.44	17.37	19.30
Guatemala 1 Quetzal	1925	33.33	0.720	0.772		0.77	1.54	2.32	3.09	7.72	11.58	15.44	19.30	23.16	27.02	30.88	34.74	38.60
Guatemala 1 Quetzal	1992-2000	27.00	0.925	0.803	S	0.80	1.61	2.41	3.21	8.03	12.05	16.06	20.08	24.09	28.11	32.12	36.14	40.15
Guernsey 25 pence	1972-1981	28.28	0.925	0.841	N, S	0.84	1.68	2.52	3.36	8.41	12.62	16.82	21.03	25.23	29.44	33.64	37.85	42.05
Guernsey 50 pence	2000	8.10	0.925	0.241	N	0.24	0.48	0.72	0.96	2.41	3.62	4.82	6.03	7.23	8.44	9.64	10.85	12.05
Guernsey 1 Pound	1995-2000	9.50	0.925	0.283	N	0.28	0.57	0.85	1.13	2.83	4.25	5.66	7.08	8.49	9.91	11.32	12.74	14.15
Guernsey 2 Pounds	1985-1997	28.28	0.925	0.841	N, S	0.84	1.68	2.52	3.36	8.41	12.62	16.82	21.03	25.23	29.44	33.64	37.85	42.05
Guernsey 5 Pounds	1995-2000	28.28	0.925	0.841	N, S	0.84	1.68	2.52	3.36	8.41	12.62	16.82	21.03	25.23	29.44	33.64	37.85	42.05
Guernsey 10 Pounds	2000	141.75	0.999	4.553	N	4.55	9.11	13.66	18.21	45.53	68.30	91.06	113.83	136.59	159.36	182.12	204.89	227.65
Guinea 100 Francs	1969-1970	5.65	0.999	0.182		0.18	0.36	0.55	0.73	1.82	2.73	3.64	4.55	5.46	6.37	7.28	8.19	9.10
Guinea 100 Francs	1988	16.00	0.999	0.514		0.51	1.03	1.54	2.06	5.14	7.71	10.28	12.85	15.42	17.99	20.56	23.13	25.70
Guinea 200 Francs	1969-1970	11.70	0.999	0.376		0.38	0.75	1.13	1.50	3.76	5.64	7.52	9.40	11.28	13.16	15.04	16.92	18.80
Guinea 200 Francs	1988	16.00	0.999	0.514		0.51	1.03	1.54	2.06	5.14	7.71	10.28	12.85	15.42	17.99	20.56	23.13	25.70
Guinea 250 Francs	1969-1970	14.53	0.999	0.467		0.47	0.93	1.40	1.87	4.67	7.01	9.34	11.68	14.01	16.35	18.68	21.02	23.35
Guinea 300 Francs	1988	16.00	0.999	0.514		0.51	1.03	1.54	2.06	5.14	7.71	10.28	12.85	15.42	17.99	20.56	23.13	25.70
Guinea 500 Francs	1969-1970	29.08	0.999	0.935		0.94	1.87	2.81	3.74	9.35	14.03	18.70	23.38	28.05	32.73	37.40	42.08	46.75
Guinea 1000 Francs	1990	25.00	0.999	0.804		0.80	1.61	2.41	3.22	8.04	12.06	16.08	20.10	24.12	28.14	32.16	36.18	40.20
Guinea 2000 Francs	1995	31.47	0.925	0.936		0.94	1.87	2.81	3.74	9.36	14.04	18.72	23.40	28.08	32.76	37.44	42.12	46.80
Guinea 500 Syli	1977	40.00	0.925	1.190		1.19	2.38	3.57	4.76	11.90	17.85	23.80	29.75	35.70	41.65	47.60	53.55	59.50
Guinea-Bissau 10 Escudos	1952	5.00	0.720	0.116		0.12	0.23	0.35	0.46	1.16	1.74	2.32	2.90	3.48	4.06	4.64	5.22	5.80
Guinea-Bissau 20 Escudos	1952	10.00	0.720	0.232		0.23	0.46	0.70	0.93	2.32	3.48	4.64	5.80	6.96	8.12	9.28	10.44	11.60
Guinea-Bissau 10,000 Pesos	1991	16.00	0.999	0.514		0.51	1.03	1.54	2.06	5.14	7.72	10.29	12.86	15.43	18.00	20.58	23.15	25.72
Guinea-Bissau 10,000 Pesos	1991	11.97	0.999	0.385		0.39	0.77	1.16	1.54	3.85	5.78	7.70	9.63	11.55	13.48	15.40	17.33	19.25
Guinea-Bissau 10,000 Pesos	1992	20.00	0.999	0.640		0.64	1.28	1.92	2.56	6.40	9.60	12.80	16.00	19.20	22.40	25.60	28.80	32.00
Guinea-Bissau 10,000 Pesos	1993	15.00	0.999	0.482		0.48	0.96	1.45	1.93	4.82	7.23	9.64	12.05	14.46	16.87	19.28	21.69	24.10
Guinea-Bissau 10,000 Pesos	1994	16.10	0.999	0.518		0.52	1.04	1.55	2.07	5.18	7.77	10.36	12.95	15.54	18.13	20.72	23.31	25.90
Guinea-Bissau 20,000 Pesos	1990	25.00	0.999	0.804		0.80	1.61	2.41	3.22	8.04	12.06	16.08	20.10	24.12	28.14	32.16	36.18	40.20
Guinea-Bissau 20,000 Pesos	1993	20.00	0.999	0.643		0.64	1.29	1.93	2.57	6.43	9.65	12.86	16.08	19.29	22.51	25.72	28.94	32.15
Guinea-Bissau 50,000 Pesos	1996	31.47	0.999	0.936		0.94	1.87	2.81	3.74	9.36	14.04	18.72	23.40	28.08	32.76	37.44	42.12	46.80
Guyana (Brit. Guiana) 1/8 Guilder	1836	0.97	0.816	0.026		0.03	0.05	0.08	0.10	0.26	0.39	0.52	0.65	0.78	0.91	1.04	1.17	1.30
Guyana (Brit. Guiana) ¼ Guilder	1836	1.94	0.816	0.051		0.05	0.10	0.15	0.20	0.51	0.77	1.02	1.28	1.53	1.79	2.04	2.30	2.55
Guyana (Brit. Guiana) ½ Guilder	1836	3.88	0.816	0.102		0.10	0.20	0.31	0.41	1.02	1.53	2.04	2.55	3.06	3.57	4.08	4.59	5.10
Guyana (Brit. Guiana) 1 Guilder	1836	7.77	0.816	0.204		0.20	0.41	0.61	0.82	2.04	3.06	4.08	5.10	6.12	7.14	8.16	9.18	10.20
Guyana (Brit. Guiana) 4 Pence	1901-1943	1.89	0.925	0.056	S	0.06	0.11	0.17	0.22	0.56	0.84	1.12	1.40	1.68	1.96	2.24	2.52	2.80
Guyana (Brit. Guiana) 4 Pence	1944-1945	1.89	0.500	0.030		0.03	0.06	0.09	0.12	0.30	0.45	0.60	0.75	0.90	1.05	1.20	1.35	1.50
Guyana 5 Dollars	1976-1980	37.30	0.500	0.600	N	0.60	1.20	1.80	2.40	6.00	8.99	11.99	14.99	17.99	20.99	23.98	26.98	29.98
Guyana 10 Dollars	1976-1980	43.23	0.925	1.286	N	1.29	2.57	3.86	5.14	12.86	19.29	25.72	32.15	38.58	45.01	51.44	57.87	64.30
Guyana 50 Dollars	1976	48.30	0.925	1.437		1.44	2.87	4.31	5.75	14.37	21.56	28.74	35.93	43.11	50.30	57.48	64.67	71.85
Guyana 50 Dollars	1994	28.28	0.925	0.841		0.84	1.68	2.52	3.36	8.41	12.62	16.82	21.03	25.23	29.44	33.64	37.85	42.06

Country & Denomination	Years Minted	Grams Weight	Fineness	Troy (ASW)	Code	$ Value 1	$ Value 2	$ Value 3	$ Value 4	$ Value 10	$ Value 15	$ Value 20	$ Value 25	$ Value 30	$ Value 35	$ Value 40	$ Value 45	$ Value 50
H																		
Haiti 10 Centimes*	1881-1894	2.50	0.835	0.067	S	0.07	0.13	0.20	0.27	0.67	1.01	1.34	1.68	2.01	2.35	2.68	3.02	3.35
Haiti 20 Centimes	1881-1895	5.00	0.835	0.134	S	0.13	0.27	0.40	0.54	1.34	2.01	2.68	3.35	4.02	4.69	5.36	6.03	6.70
Haiti 50 Centimes	1881-1895	25.00	0.900	0.723	S	0.72	1.45	2.17	2.89	7.23	10.85	14.46	18.08	21.69	25.31	28.92	32.54	36.15
Haiti 50 Centimes	1882-1895	12.50	0.835	0.336	S	0.34	0.67	1.01	1.34	3.36	5.04	6.72	8.40	10.08	11.76	13.44	15.12	16.80
Haiti 5 Gourdes	1969-1971	23.52	0.999	0.756		0.76	1.51	2.27	3.02	7.56	11.33	15.11	18.89	22.67	26.44	30.22	34.00	37.78
Haiti 10 Gourdes	1969-1971	47.05	0.999	1.511		1.51	3.02	4.53	6.04	15.11	22.67	30.22	37.78	45.33	52.89	60.44	68.00	75.55
Haiti 25 Gourdes	1967-1971	117.60	0.999	3.781		3.78	7.56	11.34	15.12	37.81	56.72	75.62	94.53	113.43	132.34	151.24	170.15	189.05
Haiti 25 Gourdes	1973, 1974	10.00	0.925	0.297		0.30	0.59	0.89	1.19	2.97	4.46	5.94	7.43	8.91	10.40	11.88	13.37	14.85
Haiti 25 Gourdes	1974-1976	8.38	0.925	0.249		0.25	0.50	0.75	1.00	2.49	3.74	4.98	6.23	7.47	8.72	9.96	11.21	12.45
Haiti 50 Gourdes	1973-1983	20.00	0.925	0.595	S	0.60	1.19	1.79	2.38	5.95	8.93	11.90	14.88	17.85	20.83	23.80	26.78	29.75
Haiti 50 Gourdes	1973-1976	16.75	0.925	0.498		0.50	1.00	1.49	1.99	4.98	7.47	9.96	12.45	14.94	17.43	19.92	22.41	24.90
Haiti 50 Gourdes	1977	21.30	0.925	0.633		0.63	1.27	1.90	2.53	6.33	9.50	12.66	15.83	18.99	22.16	25.32	28.49	31.65
Haiti 100 Gourdes	1977	43.00	0.925	1.279		1.28	2.56	3.84	5.12	12.79	19.19	25.58	31.98	38.37	44.77	51.16	57.56	63.95
Haiti 100 Gourdes	1981	40.00	0.925	1.190		1.19	2.38	3.57	4.76	11.90	17.85	23.80	29.75	35.70	41.65	47.60	53.55	59.50
Haiti 500 Gourdes	1999	28.23	0.925	0.840		0.84	1.68	2.52	3.36	8.40	12.60	16.80	21.00	25.20	29.40	33.60	37.80	42.00
Hejaz 5 Piastres	1909	6.10	0.917	0.180	A	0.18	0.36	0.54	0.72	1.80	2.70	3.60	4.50	5.39	6.29	7.19	8.09	8.99
Hejaz 10 Piastres	1909	12.05	0.917	0.355	A	0.36	0.71	1.07	1.42	3.55	5.33	7.10	8.88	10.65	12.43	14.20	15.98	17.75
Hejaz 20 Piastres / 1 Riyal	1915-1919	24.10	0.917	0.711	A	0.71	1.42	2.13	2.84	7.11	10.67	14.22	17.78	21.33	24.89	28.44	32.00	35.55
Honduras 5 Centavos*	1871-1902	1.25	0.835	0.034	S	0.03	0.07	0.10	0.14	0.34	0.51	0.68	0.85	1.02	1.19	1.36	1.53	1.70
Honduras 10 Centavos	1871-1900	2.50	0.835	0.067	S	0.07	0.13	0.20	0.27	0.67	1.01	1.34	1.68	2.01	2.35	2.68	3.02	3.35
Honduras 20 Centavos	1931-1958	2.50	0.900	0.072	S	0.07	0.14	0.22	0.29	0.72	1.08	1.44	1.80	2.16	2.52	2.88	3.24	3.60
Honduras 25 Centavos	1871-1899	6.25	0.900	0.181	S	0.18	0.36	0.54	0.72	1.81	2.72	3.62	4.53	5.43	6.34	7.24	8.15	9.05
Honduras 25 Centavos	1899-1913	6.25	0.835	0.168	S	0.17	0.34	0.50	0.67	1.68	2.52	3.36	4.20	5.04	5.88	6.72	7.56	8.40
Honduras 50 Centavos	1871-1910	12.50	0.900	0.362	S	0.36	0.72	1.09	1.45	3.62	5.43	7.24	9.05	10.86	12.67	14.48	16.29	18.10
Honduras 50 Centavos	1931-1951	6.25	0.900	0.181	S	0.18	0.36	0.54	0.72	1.81	2.72	3.62	4.53	5.43	6.34	7.24	8.15	9.05
Honduras 1 Peso	1881-1914	25.00	0.900	0.723	S	0.72	1.45	2.17	2.89	7.23	10.85	14.46	18.08	21.69	25.31	28.92	32.54	36.15
Honduras 1 Lempira	1931-1937	12.50	0.900	0.362	S	0.36	0.72	1.09	1.45	3.62	5.43	7.24	9.05	10.86	12.67	14.48	16.29	18.10
Honduras 1 Lempira	2000	33.63	0.925	1.000	V	1.00	2.00	3.00	4.00	10.00	15.00	20.00	25.00	30.00	35.00	40.00	45.00	50.00
Honduras 100 Lempiras	1992	27.00	0.925	0.803	V	0.80	1.61	2.41	3.21	8.03	12.05	16.06	20.08	24.09	28.11	32.12	36.14	40.15
Hong Kong 5 Cents	1866-1933	1.36	0.800	0.035	S	0.04	0.07	0.11	0.14	0.35	0.53	0.70	0.88	1.05	1.23	1.40	1.58	1.75
Hong Kong 10 Cents	1863-1905	2.72	0.800	0.070	S	0.07	0.14	0.21	0.28	0.70	1.05	1.40	1.75	2.10	2.45	2.80	3.15	3.50
Hong Kong 20 Cents	1863-1905	5.43	0.800	0.140	S	0.14	0.28	0.42	0.56	1.40	2.10	2.80	3.50	4.20	4.90	5.60	6.30	7.00
Hong Kong 1/2 Dollar	1866-1868	13.54	0.900	0.400	V	0.40	0.80	1.20	1.60	4.00	6.00	8.00	10.00	12.00	14.00	16.00	18.00	20.00
Hong Kong 50 Cents	1890-1905	13.58	0.800	0.349	S	0.35	0.70	1.05	1.40	3.49	5.24	6.98	8.73	10.47	12.22	13.96	15.71	17.45
Hong Kong 1 Dollar	1866-1868	28.00	0.900	0.800	V	0.80	1.60	2.40	3.20	8.00	12.00	16.00	20.00	24.00	28.00	32.00	36.00	40.00
Hungary 10 Krajczar*	1837-1848	3.89	0.500	0.063		0.06	0.13	0.19	0.25	0.63	0.95	1.26	1.58	1.89	2.21	2.52	2.84	3.15
Hungary 10 Krajczar	1867-1868	2.00	0.500	0.032		0.03	0.06	0.10	0.13	0.32	0.48	0.64	0.80	0.96	1.12	1.28	1.44	1.60
Hungary 10 Krajczar	1868-1889	1.66	0.400	0.021	S	0.02	0.04	0.06	0.08	0.21	0.32	0.42	0.53	0.63	0.74	0.84	0.95	1.05
Hungary 20 Krajczar	1837-1848	6.68	0.583	0.125		0.13	0.25	0.38	0.50	1.25	1.88	2.50	3.13	3.75	4.38	5.00	5.63	6.25
Hungary 20 Krajczar	1868-1872	2.66	0.500	0.043		0.04	0.09	0.13	0.17	0.43	0.65	0.86	1.08	1.29	1.51	1.72	1.94	2.15

Country & Denomination	Years Minted	Grams Weight	Fineness	Troy (ASW)	Code	$ Value 1	$ Value 2	$ Value 3	$ Value 4	$ Value 10	$ Value 15	$ Value 20	$ Value 25	$ Value 30	$ Value 35	$ Value 40	$ Value 45	$ Value 50
Hungary 1 Forint	1868-1892	12.35	0.900	0.357		0.36	0.71	1.07	1.43	3.57	5.36	7.14	8.93	10.71	12.50	14.28	16.07	17.85
Hungary 1/2 Thaler	1830-1839	14.00	0.833	0.378	s	0.38	0.76	1.13	1.51	3.78	5.67	7.56	9.45	11.34	13.23	15.12	17.01	18.90
Hungary 1 Thaler	1830-1839	28.00	0.833	0.760	s	0.76	1.52	2.28	3.04	7.60	11.40	15.20	19.00	22.80	26.60	30.40	34.20	38.00
Hungary 1 Korona	1892-1916	5.00	0.835	0.134	s	0.13	0.27	0.40	0.54	1.34	2.01	2.68	3.35	4.02	4.69	5.36	6.03	6.70
Hungary 2 Korona	1912-1914	10.00	0.835	0.269	s	0.27	0.54	0.81	1.08	2.69	4.04	5.38	6.73	8.07	9.42	10.76	12.11	13.45
Hungary 5 Korona	1906-1909	24.00	0.900	0.694		0.69	1.39	2.08	2.78	6.94	10.41	13.88	17.35	20.82	24.29	27.76	31.23	34.70
Hungary 1 Pengo	1926-1939	5.00	0.640	0.103	s	0.10	0.21	0.31	0.41	1.03	1.55	2.06	2.58	3.09	3.61	4.12	4.64	5.15
Hungary 2 Pengo	1929-1939	10.00	0.640	0.206	s	0.21	0.41	0.62	0.82	2.06	3.09	4.12	5.15	6.18	7.21	8.24	9.27	10.30
Hungary 5 Pengo	1930	25.33	0.640	0.515		0.52	1.03	1.55	2.06	5.15	7.73	10.30	12.88	15.45	18.03	20.60	23.18	25.75
Hungary 5 Pengo	1930-1939	25.00	0.640	0.521	s	0.52	1.04	1.56	2.08	5.21	7.82	10.42	13.03	15.63	18.24	20.84	23.45	26.05
Hungary 5 Forint	1946	20.00	0.835	0.537		0.54	1.07	1.61	2.15	5.37	8.06	10.74	13.43	16.11	18.80	21.48	24.17	26.85
Hungary 5 Forint	1947-1948	12.00	0.500	0.193		0.19	0.39	0.58	0.77	1.93	2.90	3.86	4.83	5.79	6.76	7.72	8.69	9.65
Hungary 10 Forint	1948	20.00	0.500	0.322		0.32	0.64	0.97	1.29	3.22	4.83	6.44	8.05	9.66	11.27	12.88	14.49	16.10
Hungary 10 Forint	1956	12.50	0.800	0.322		0.32	0.64	0.97	1.29	3.22	4.83	6.44	8.05	9.66	11.27	12.88	14.49	16.10
Hungary 20 Forint	1948	28.00	0.500	0.450		0.45	0.90	1.35	1.80	4.50	6.75	9.00	11.25	13.50	15.75	18.00	20.25	22.50
Hungary 20 Forint	1956	17.50	0.800	0.450		0.45	0.90	1.35	1.80	4.50	6.75	9.00	11.25	13.50	15.75	18.00	20.25	22.50
Hungary 25 Forint	1956	20.00	0.800	0.514		0.51	1.03	1.54	2.06	5.14	7.71	10.28	12.85	15.42	17.99	20.56	23.13	25.70
Hungary 25 Forint	1961-1967	17.50	0.750	0.422	s	0.42	0.84	1.27	1.69	4.22	6.33	8.44	10.55	12.66	14.77	16.88	18.99	21.10
Hungary 25 Forint	1966	12.00	0.640	0.247		0.25	0.49	0.74	0.99	2.47	3.71	4.94	6.18	7.41	8.65	9.88	11.12	12.35
Hungary 50 Forint	1961	20.00	0.750	0.492		0.49	0.98	1.48	1.97	4.92	7.38	9.84	12.30	14.76	17.22	19.68	22.14	24.60
Hungary 50 Forint	1966, 1968	20.00	0.640	0.412		0.41	0.82	1.24	1.65	4.12	6.18	8.24	10.30	12.36	14.42	16.48	18.54	20.60
Hungary 50 Forint	1966-1974	16.00	0.640	0.329		0.33	0.66	0.99	1.32	3.29	4.94	6.58	8.23	9.87	11.52	13.16	14.81	16.45
Hungary 100 Forint	1967	28.00	0.750	0.675		0.68	1.35	2.03	2.70	6.75	10.13	13.50	16.88	20.25	23.63	27.00	30.38	33.75
Hungary 100 Forint	1968	28.00	0.640	0.576		0.58	1.15	1.73	2.30	5.76	8.64	11.52	14.40	17.28	20.16	23.04	25.92	28.80
Hungary 100 Forint	1969-1974	22.00	0.640	0.453	s	0.45	0.91	1.36	1.81	4.53	6.80	9.06	11.33	13.59	15.86	18.12	20.39	22.65
Hungary 200 Forint	1975-1979	28.00	0.640	0.576	s	0.58	1.15	1.73	2.30	5.76	8.64	11.52	14.40	17.28	20.16	23.04	25.92	28.80
Hungary 200 Forint	1980-1985	16.00	0.640	0.329		0.33	0.66	0.99	1.32	3.29	4.94	6.58	8.23	9.87	11.52	13.16	14.81	16.45
Hungary 200 Forint	1992	10.00	0.500	0.161		0.16	0.32	0.48	0.64	1.61	2.42	3.22	4.03	4.83	5.64	6.44	7.25	8.05
Hungary 200 Forint	1992-1998	12.00	0.500	0.193		0.19	0.39	0.58	0.77	1.93	2.90	3.86	4.83	5.79	6.76	7.72	8.69	9.65
Hungary 500 Forint	1980	39.00	0.640	0.803		0.80	1.61	2.41	3.21	8.03	12.05	16.06	20.08	24.09	28.11	32.12	36.14	40.15
Hungary 500 Forint	1981	25.00	0.640	0.514		0.51	1.03	1.54	2.06	5.14	7.71	10.28	12.85	15.42	17.99	20.56	23.13	25.70
Hungary 500 Forint	1981-1986	28.00	0.640	0.576	s	0.58	1.15	1.73	2.30	5.76	8.64	11.52	14.40	17.28	20.16	23.04	25.92	28.80
Hungary 500 Forint	1986-1992	28.00	0.900	0.810		0.81	1.62	2.43	3.24	8.10	12.15	16.20	20.25	24.30	28.35	32.40	36.45	40.50
Hungary 500 Forint	1992-1994	31.46	0.925	0.936		0.94	1.87	2.81	3.74	9.36	14.04	18.72	23.40	28.08	32.76	37.44	42.12	46.80
Hungary 750 Forint	1997, 1998	10.00	0.500	0.161		0.16	0.32	0.48	0.64	1.61	2.42	3.22	4.03	4.83	5.64	6.44	7.25	8.05
Hungary 1000 Forint	1993-1995	31.46	0.925	0.936		0.94	1.87	2.81	3.74	9.36	14.04	18.72	23.40	28.08	32.76	37.44	42.12	46.80
Hungary 2000 Forint	1996-1998	31.46	0.925	0.936		0.94	1.87	2.81	3.74	9.36	14.04	18.72	23.40	28.08	32.76	37.44	42.12	46.80
Hungary 2000 Forint	1999	20.00	0.925	0.595		0.60	1.19	1.79	2.38	5.95	8.93	11.90	14.88	17.85	20.83	23.80	26.78	29.75
Hungary 2000 Forint	2000	15.72	0.925	0.468		0.47	0.94	1.40	1.87	4.68	7.02	9.36	11.70	14.04	16.38	18.72	21.06	23.40
Hungary 3000 Forint	1999-2000	31.46	0.925	0.936		0.94	1.87	2.81	3.74	9.36	14.04	18.72	23.40	28.08	32.76	37.44	42.12	46.80
Iceland 500 Kronur	1974, 1986	20.00	0.925	0.597		0.60	1.19	1.79	2.39	5.97	8.96	11.94	14.93	17.91	20.90	23.88	26.87	29.85
Iceland 500 Kronur	1986	20.00	0.500	0.322		0.32	0.64	0.97	1.29	3.22	4.83	6.44	8.05	9.66	11.27	12.88	14.49	16.10
Iceland 1000 Kronur	1974, 1994	30.00	0.925	0.892		0.89	1.78	2.68	3.57	8.92	13.38	17.84	22.30	26.76	31.22	35.68	40.14	44.60
Iceland 1000 Kronur	2000	27.73	0.900	0.772		0.77	1.54	2.32	3.09	7.72	11.58	15.44	19.30	23.16	27.02	30.88	34.74	38.60

Country & Denomination	Years Minted	Grams Weight	Fineness	Troy (ASW)	Code	$ Value 1	$ Value 2	$ Value 3	$ Value 4	$ Value 10	$ Value 15	$ Value 20	$ Value 25	$ Value 30	$ Value 35	$ Value 40	$ Value 45	$ Value 50
India 2 Annas*	1841-1917	1.46	0.917	0.043	S	0.04	0.09	0.13	0.17	0.43	0.65	0.86	1.08	1.29	1.51	1.72	1.94	2.15
India 1/4 Rupee	1835-1939	2.92	0.917	0.086	S	0.09	0.17	0.26	0.34	0.86	1.29	1.72	2.15	2.58	3.01	3.44	3.87	4.30
India 1/4 Rupee	1940-1945	2.92	0.500	0.047		0.05	0.09	0.14	0.19	0.47	0.71	0.94	1.18	1.41	1.65	1.88	2.12	2.35
India 1/2 Rupee	1835-1939	5.83	0.917	0.172	S	0.17	0.34	0.52	0.69	1.72	2.58	3.44	4.30	5.16	6.02	6.88	7.74	8.60
India 1/2 Rupee	1940-1945	5.83	0.500	0.094		0.09	0.19	0.28	0.38	0.94	1.41	1.88	2.35	2.82	3.29	3.76	4.23	4.70
India 1/2 Rupia	1936	6.00	0.835	0.161		0.16	0.32	0.48	0.64	1.61	2.42	3.22	4.03	4.83	5.64	6.44	7.25	8.05
India 1 Rupee	1835-1939	11.66	0.917	0.344	S	0.34	0.69	1.03	1.38	3.44	5.16	6.88	8.60	10.32	12.04	13.76	15.48	17.20
India 1 Rupee	1939-1945	11.66	0.500	0.187		0.19	0.37	0.56	0.75	1.87	2.81	3.74	4.68	5.61	6.55	7.48	8.42	9.35
India 1 Rupia	1912	11.66	0.917	0.344		0.34	0.69	1.03	1.38	3.44	5.16	6.88	8.60	10.32	12.04	13.76	15.48	17.20
India 1 Rupia	1935	12.00	0.917	0.354		0.35	0.71	1.06	1.42	3.54	5.31	7.08	8.85	10.62	12.39	14.16	15.93	17.70
India 10 Rupees	1969-1971	15.00	0.800	0.386		0.39	0.77	1.16	1.54	3.86	5.79	7.72	9.65	11.58	13.51	15.44	17.37	19.30
India 10 Rupees	1972	22.50	0.500	0.362	N	0.36	0.72	1.09	1.45	3.62	5.43	7.24	9.05	10.86	12.67	14.48	16.29	18.10
India 10 Rupees	1973	22.30	0.500	0.358		0.36	0.72	1.07	1.43	3.58	5.37	7.16	8.95	10.74	12.53	14.32	16.11	17.90
India 20 Rupees	1973	30.00	0.500	0.482		0.48	0.96	1.45	1.93	4.82	7.23	9.64	12.05	14.46	16.87	19.28	21.69	24.10
India 50 Rupees	1974-1979	35.00	0.500	0.558		0.56	1.12	1.67	2.23	5.58	8.37	11.16	13.95	16.74	19.53	22.32	25.11	27.90
India 50 Rupees	1997, 1998	22.50	0.500	0.362		0.36	0.72	1.09	1.45	3.62	5.43	7.24	9.05	10.86	12.67	14.48	16.29	18.10
India 100 Rupees	1980-1999	35.00	0.500	0.573		0.57	1.15	1.72	2.29	5.73	8.60	11.46	14.33	17.19	20.06	22.92	25.79	28.65
India 100 Rupees	1981	29.16	0.925	0.867		0.87	1.73	2.60	3.47	8.67	13.01	17.34	21.68	26.01	30.35	34.68	39.02	43.35
Indonesia 200 Rupiah	1970	8.00	0.999	0.257		0.26	0.51	0.77	1.03	2.57	3.86	5.14	6.43	7.71	9.00	10.28	11.57	12.85
Indonesia 250 Rupiah	1970	10.00	0.999	0.321		0.32	0.64	0.96	1.28	3.21	4.82	6.42	8.03	9.63	11.24	12.84	14.45	16.05
Indonesia 500 Rupiah	1970	20.00	0.999	0.642		0.64	1.28	1.93	2.57	6.42	9.63	12.84	16.05	19.26	22.47	25.68	28.89	32.10
Indonesia 750 Rupiah	1970	30.00	0.999	0.964		0.96	1.93	2.89	3.86	9.64	14.46	19.28	24.10	28.92	33.74	38.56	43.38	48.20
Indonesia 1000 Rupiah	1970	40.00	0.999	1.285		1.29	2.57	3.86	5.14	12.85	19.28	25.70	32.13	38.55	44.98	51.40	57.83	64.25
Indonesia 2000 Rupiah	1974	25.65	0.500	0.412		0.41	0.82	1.24	1.65	4.12	6.18	8.24	10.30	12.36	14.42	16.48	18.54	20.60
Indonesia 2000 Rupiah	1974	28.28	0.925	0.841		0.84	1.68	2.52	3.36	8.41	12.62	16.82	21.03	25.23	29.44	33.64	37.85	42.05
Indonesia 5000 Rupiah	1974	32.00	0.500	0.514		0.51	1.03	1.54	2.06	5.14	7.71	10.28	12.85	15.42	17.99	20.56	23.13	25.70
Indonesia 5000 Rupiah	1974	35.00	0.925	1.041		1.04	2.08	3.12	4.16	10.41	15.62	20.82	26.03	31.23	36.44	41.64	46.85	52.05
Indonesia 10,000 Rupiah	1987, 1990	19.44	0.925	0.578		0.58	1.16	1.73	2.31	5.78	8.67	11.56	14.45	17.34	20.23	23.12	26.01	28.90
Indonesia 10,000 Rupiah	1999	28.28	0.925	0.841		0.84	1.68	2.52	3.36	8.41	12.62	16.82	21.03	25.23	29.44	33.64	37.85	42.05
Iran 1 Shahi Sefid*	1895-1923	0.69	0.900	0.020	A, S	0.02	0.04	0.06	0.08	0.20	0.30	0.40	0.50	0.60	0.70	0.80	0.90	1.00
Iran 3 Shahis	1879-1923	0.80	0.900	0.700	A	0.70	1.40	2.10	2.80	7.00	10.50	14.00	17.50	21.00	24.50	28.00	31.50	35.00
Iran 5 Shahis / ¼ Kran	1878-1924	1.15	0.900	0.133	A, S	0.13	0.27	0.40	0.53	1.33	2.00	2.66	3.33	3.99	4.66	5.32	5.99	6.65
Iran 5 Shahis / ¼ Kran	1925	1.15	0.900	0.133	H	0.13	0.27	0.40	0.53	1.33	2.00	2.66	3.33	3.99	4.66	5.32	5.99	6.65
Iran 500 Dinars / ½ Kran	1879-1924	2.30	0.900	0.067	A, S	0.07	0.13	0.20	0.27	0.67	1.00	1.33	1.67	2.00	2.33	2.66	3.00	3.33
Iran 1000 Dinars / 1 Kran	1877-1925	4.60	0.900	0.133	A, S	0.13	0.27	0.40	0.53	1.33	2.00	2.66	3.33	3.99	4.66	5.32	5.99	6.65
Iran 2000 Dinars	1879-1896	9.21	0.900	0.267	A, S	0.27	0.53	0.80	1.07	2.67	4.01	5.34	6.68	8.01	9.35	10.68	12.02	13.35
Iran 2000 Dinars / 2 Kran	1907-1925	9.21	0.900	0.267	A, S	0.27	0.53	0.80	1.07	2.67	4.01	5.34	6.68	8.01	9.35	10.68	12.02	13.35
Iran 5000 Dinars / 5 Kran	1902-1925	23.03	0.900	0.666	A, S	0.67	1.33	2.00	2.66	6.66	9.99	13.32	16.65	19.98	23.31	26.64	29.97	33.30
Iran 500 Dinars / ½ Kran	1926-1929	2.30	0.900	0.067	A	0.07	0.13	0.20	0.27	0.67	1.00	1.33	1.67	2.00	2.33	2.66	3.00	3.33
Iran 1000 Dinars / 1 Kran	1925-1929	4.60	0.900	0.133	A	0.13	0.27	0.40	0.53	1.33	2.00	2.66	3.33	3.99	4.66	5.32	5.99	6.65
Iran 2000 Dinars / 2 Kran	1925-1929	9.21	0.900	0.267	A	0.27	0.53	0.80	1.07	2.67	4.01	5.34	6.68	8.01	9.35	10.68	12.02	13.35
Iran 5000 Dinars	1876-1893	23.03	0.900	0.666	A	0.67	1.33	2.00	2.66	6.66	9.99	13.32	16.65	19.98	23.31	26.64	29.97	33.30
Iran 5000 Dinars / 5 Kran	1925-1929	23.03	0.900	0.666	A	0.67	1.33	2.00	2.66	6.66	9.99	13.32	16.65	19.98	23.31	26.64	29.97	33.30
Iran 1 Toman	1876-1895	46.05	0.900	1.333	A	1.33	2.67	4.00	5.33	13.33	20.00	26.66	33.33	39.99	46.66	53.32	59.99	66.65

Country & Denomination	Years Minted	Grams Weight	Fineness	Troy (ASW)	Code	$ Value 1	$ Value 2	$ Value 3	$ Value 4	$ Value 10	$ Value 15	$ Value 20	$ Value 25	$ Value 30	$ Value 35	$ Value 40	$ Value 45	$ Value 50
Iran 1/2 Rial	1931-1934	2.50	0.828	0.070	H	0.07	0.14	0.21	0.28	0.70	1.05	1.40	1.75	2.10	2.45	2.80	3.15	3.50
Iran 1 Rial	1931-1934	5.00	0.828	0.133	H	0.13	0.27	0.40	0.53	1.33	2.00	2.66	3.33	3.99	4.66	5.32	5.99	6.65
Iran 1 Rial	1943-1951	1.60	0.600	0.031	H	0.03	0.06	0.09	0.12	0.31	0.47	0.62	0.78	0.93	1.09	1.24	1.40	1.55
Iran 2 Rials	1931-1934	10.00	0.828	0.670	H	0.67	1.34	2.01	2.68	6.70	10.05	13.40	16.75	20.10	23.45	26.80	30.15	33.50
Iran 2 Rials	1943-1951	3.20	0.600	0.062	H	0.06	0.12	0.19	0.25	0.62	0.93	1.24	1.55	1.86	2.17	2.48	2.79	3.10
Iran 5 Rials	1931-1934	25.00	0.828	0.666	H	0.67	1.33	2.00	2.66	6.66	9.99	13.32	16.65	19.98	23.31	26.64	29.97	33.30
Iran 5 Rials	1943-1950	8.00	0.600	0.154	H	0.15	0.31	0.46	0.62	1.54	2.31	3.08	3.85	4.62	5.39	6.16	6.93	7.70
Iran 10 Rials	1944-1947	16.00	0.600	0.309	H	0.31	0.62	0.93	1.24	3.09	4.64	6.18	7.73	9.27	10.82	12.36	13.91	15.45
Iran 25 Rials	1971	7.50	0.999	0.241	H	0.24	0.48	0.72	0.96	2.41	3.62	4.82	6.03	7.23	8.44	9.64	10.85	12.05
Iran 50 Rials	1971	15.00	0.999	0.482	H	0.48	0.96	1.45	1.93	4.82	7.23	9.64	12.05	14.46	16.87	19.28	21.69	24.10
Iran 75 Rials	1971	22.50	0.999	0.723	H	0.72	1.45	2.17	2.89	7.23	10.85	14.46	18.08	21.69	25.31	28.92	32.54	36.15
Iran 100 Rials	1971	30.00	0.999	0.964	H	0.96	1.93	2.89	3.86	9.64	14.46	19.28	24.10	28.92	33.74	38.56	43.38	48.20
Iran 200 Rials	1971	60.00	0.999	1.927	H	1.93	3.85	5.78	7.71	19.27	28.91	38.54	48.18	57.81	67.45	77.08	86.72	96.35
Iraq 20 Fils*	1931-1938	3.60	0.500	0.058		0.06	0.12	0.17	0.23	0.58	0.87	1.16	1.45	1.74	2.03	2.32	2.61	2.90
Iraq 25 Fils	1959	2.50	0.500	0.040		0.04	0.08	0.12	0.16	0.40	0.60	0.80	1.00	1.20	1.40	1.60	1.80	2.00
Iraq 50 Fils	1931-1938	9.00	0.500	0.145		0.15	0.29	0.44	0.58	1.45	2.18	2.90	3.63	4.35	5.08	5.80	6.53	7.25
Iraq 50 Fils	1955	5.00	0.500	0.113		0.11	0.23	0.34	0.45	1.13	1.70	2.26	2.83	3.39	3.96	4.52	5.09	5.65
Iraq 50 Fils	1959	5.00	0.500	0.080		0.08	0.16	0.24	0.32	0.80	1.20	1.60	2.00	2.40	2.80	3.20	3.60	4.00
Iraq 100 Fils	1953	10.00	0.900	0.289		0.29	0.58	0.87	1.16	2.89	4.34	5.78	7.23	8.67	10.12	11.56	13.01	14.45
Iraq 100 Fils	1955, 1959	10.00	0.500	0.161		0.16	0.32	0.48	0.64	1.61	2.42	3.22	4.03	4.83	5.64	6.44	7.25	8.05
Iraq 200 Fils	1932	20.00	0.500	0.322		0.32	0.64	0.97	1.29	3.22	4.83	6.44	8.05	9.66	11.27	12.88	14.49	16.10
Iraq 500 Fils	1959	37.50	0.500	0.600		0.60	1.20	1.80	2.40	6.00	9.00	12.00	15.00	18.00	21.00	24.00	27.00	30.00
Iraq 1 Dinar	1971-1979	31.00	0.900	0.498		0.50	1.00	1.49	1.99	4.98	7.47	9.96	12.45	14.94	17.43	19.92	22.41	24.90
Iraq 1 Dinar	1980	30.53	0.900	0.884		0.88	1.77	2.65	3.54	8.84	13.26	17.68	22.10	26.52	30.94	35.36	39.78	44.20
Ireland 1 Shilling	1928-1942	5.66	0.750	0.136	S	0.14	0.27	0.41	0.54	1.36	2.04	2.72	3.40	4.08	4.76	5.44	6.12	6.80
Ireland 1 Florin	1928-1943	11.31	0.750	0.273	S	0.27	0.55	0.82	1.09	2.73	4.10	5.46	6.83	8.19	9.56	10.92	12.29	13.65
Ireland 1/2 Crown	1928-1943	14.14	0.750	0.341	S	0.34	0.68	1.02	1.36	3.41	5.12	6.82	8.53	10.23	11.94	13.64	15.35	17.05
Ireland 10 Shillings	1966	18.14	0.833	0.486		0.49	0.97	1.46	1.94	4.86	7.29	9.72	12.15	14.58	17.01	19.44	21.87	24.30
Ireland Punt	1995	28.28	0.925	0.841	N	0.84	1.68	2.52	3.36	8.41	12.62	16.82	21.03	25.23	29.44	33.64	37.85	42.05
Isle of Man 1/2 Penny	1975-1984	2.10	0.925	0.062	N, S	0.06	0.12	0.19	0.25	0.62	0.93	1.24	1.55	1.86	2.17	2.48	2.79	3.10
Isle of Man 1/2 Penny	1980	2.10	0.500	0.034	N	0.03	0.07	0.10	0.14	0.34	0.51	0.68	0.85	1.02	1.19	1.36	1.53	1.70
Isle of Man 1 Penny	1975-1996	4.20	0.925	0.124	N, S	0.12	0.25	0.37	0.50	1.24	1.86	2.48	3.10	3.72	4.34	4.96	5.58	6.20
Isle of Man 1 Penny	1980	4.20	0.500	0.068	N	0.07	0.14	0.20	0.27	0.68	1.02	1.36	1.70	2.04	2.38	2.72	3.06	3.40
Isle of Man 2 Pence	1975-1985	8.40	0.925	0.250	N, S	0.25	0.50	0.75	1.00	2.50	3.75	5.00	6.25	7.50	8.75	10.00	11.25	12.50
Isle of Man 2 Pence	1980	8.40	0.500	0.135	N	0.14	0.27	0.41	0.54	1.35	2.03	2.70	3.38	4.05	4.73	5.40	6.08	6.75
Isle of Man 5 Pence	1975-1985	6.50	0.925	0.193	N, S	0.19	0.39	0.58	0.77	1.93	2.90	3.86	4.83	5.79	6.76	7.72	8.69	9.65
Isle of Man 5 Pence	1994, 1996	3.25	0.925	0.097	N	0.10	0.19	0.29	0.39	0.97	1.46	1.94	2.43	2.91	3.40	3.88	4.37	4.85
Isle of Man 5 Pence	1980	3.25	0.500	0.105	N	0.11	0.21	0.32	0.42	1.05	1.58	2.10	2.63	3.15	3.68	4.20	4.73	5.25
Isle of Man 10 Pence	1975-1985	13.00	0.925	0.387	N, S	0.39	0.77	1.16	1.55	3.87	5.81	7.74	9.68	11.61	13.55	15.48	17.42	19.35
Isle of Man 10 Pence	1980	13.00	0.500	0.209	N	0.21	0.42	0.63	0.84	2.09	3.14	4.18	5.23	6.27	7.32	8.36	9.41	10.45
Isle of Man 10 Pence	1992, 1996	8.05	0.925	0.239	N	0.24	0.48	0.72	0.96	2.39	3.59	4.78	5.98	7.17	8.37	9.56	10.76	11.95
Isle of Man 20 Pence	1985	5.00	0.925	0.149	N	0.15	0.30	0.45	0.60	1.49	2.24	2.98	3.73	4.47	5.22	5.96	6.71	7.45

Country & Denomination	Years Minted	Grams Weight	Fineness	Troy (ASW)	Code	$ Value 1	$ Value 2	$ Value 3	$ Value 4	$ Value 10	$ Value 15	$ Value 20	$ Value 25	$ Value 30	$ Value 35	$ Value 40	$ Value 45	$ Value 50
Isle of Man 25 Pence	1972, 1975	28.28	0.925	0.841	N	0.84	1.68	2.52	3.36	8.41	12.62	16.82	21.03	25.23	29.44	33.64	37.85	42.05
Isle of Man 50 Pence	1975-1996	15.50	0.925	0.461	N, S	0.46	0.92	1.38	1.84	4.61	6.92	9.22	11.53	13.83	16.14	18.44	20.75	23.05
Isle of Man 50 Pence	1980, 1982	15.50	0.500	0.249	N	0.25	0.50	0.75	1.00	2.49	3.74	4.98	6.23	7.47	8.72	9.96	11.21	12.45
Isle of Man 50 Pence	1997-2000	8.00	0.925	0.238	N, S	0.24	0.48	0.71	0.95	2.38	3.57	4.76	5.95	7.14	8.33	9.52	10.71	11.90
Isle of Man 1 Pound / Sovereign	1978-1996	4.60	0.925	0.137	N	0.14	0.27	0.41	0.55	1.37	2.06	2.74	3.43	4.11	4.80	5.48	6.17	6.85
Isle of Man 1 Pound / Sovereign	1980	4.60	0.500	0.074	N	0.07	0.15	0.22	0.30	0.74	1.11	1.48	1.85	2.22	2.59	2.96	3.33	3.70
Isle of Man 1 Pound / Sovereign	1996	9.50	0.925	0.283	N	0.28	0.57	0.85	1.13	2.83	4.25	5.66	7.08	8.49	9.91	11.32	12.74	14.15
Isle of Man 5 Pounds	1980	23.84	0.980	0.751	N	0.75	1.50	2.25	3.00	7.51	11.27	15.02	18.78	22.53	26.29	30.04	33.80	37.55
Isle of Man 10 Pounds	1993, 1994	10.00	0.925	0.297	N	0.30	0.59	0.89	1.19	2.97	4.46	5.95	7.44	8.92	10.41	11.90	13.37	14.85
Isle of Man 25 Pounds	1993	28.28	0.925	0.841		0.84	1.68	2.52	3.36	8.41	12.62	16.82	21.03	25.23	29.44	33.64	37.85	42.05
Isle of Man 1 Crown	1970-1987	28.28	0.925	0.841	N	0.84	1.68	2.52	3.36	8.41	12.62	16.82	21.03	25.23	29.44	33.64	37.85	42.05
Isle of Man 1 Crown	1988-2000	31.10	0.999	1.000	N, S	1.00	2.00	3.00	4.00	10.00	15.00	20.00	25.00	30.00	35.00	40.00	45.00	50.00
Isle of Man 1 Crown	1989-2000	28.28	0.925	0.841	N	0.84	1.68	2.52	3.36	8.41	12.62	16.82	21.03	25.23	29.44	33.64	37.85	42.05
Isle of Man 5 Crown	1987-2000	155.55	0.999	5.000		5.00	10.00	15.00	20.00	50.00	75.00	100.00	125.00	150.00	175.00	200.00	225.00	250.00
Isle of Man 10 Crown	1987-1992	311.03	0.999	10.000		10.00	20.00	30.00	40.00	100.00	150.00	200.00	250.00	300.00	350.00	400.00	450.00	500.00
Isle of Man 10 Crown	1997	311.03	0.925	9.249		9.25	18.50	27.75	37.00	92.49	138.74	184.98	231.23	277.47	323.72	369.96	416.21	462.45
Isle of Man 1 Angel	1995	31.10	0.999	1.000		1.00	2.00	3.00	4.00	10.00	15.00	20.00	25.00	30.00	35.00	40.00	45.00	50.00
Isle of Man 15 ECUs	1994-1995	10.00	0.925	0.297		0.30	0.59	0.89	1.19	2.97	4.46	5.95	7.44	8.92	10.41	11.90	13.38	14.87
Isle of Man 25 ECUs	1994-1995	19.20	0.925	0.571		0.57	1.14	1.71	2.28	5.71	8.57	11.42	14.28	17.13	19.99	22.84	25.70	28.55
Isle of Man 10 Euro	1996-1998	10.00	0.925	0.297		0.30	0.59	0.89	1.19	2.97	4.46	5.95	7.44	8.92	10.41	11.90	13.38	14.87
Isle of Man 15 Euro	1996	19.20	0.925	0.571		0.57	1.14	1.71	2.28	5.71	8.57	11.42	14.28	17.13	19.99	22.84	25.70	28.55
Israel 250 Prutot	1949	14.40	0.500	0.232	N	0.23	0.46	0.70	0.93	2.32	3.48	4.64	5.80	6.96	8.12	9.28	10.44	11.60
Israel 500 Prutot	1949	25.50	0.500	0.410		0.41	0.82	1.23	1.64	4.10	6.15	8.20	10.25	12.30	14.35	16.40	18.45	20.50
Israel 5 Lirot	1958-1967	25.00	0.900	0.723		0.72	1.45	2.17	2.89	7.23	10.85	14.46	18.08	21.69	25.31	28.92	32.54	36.15
Israel 5 Lirot	1972	20.00	0.750	0.482		0.48	0.96	1.45	1.93	4.82	7.23	9.64	12.05	14.46	16.87	19.28	21.69	24.10
Israel 5 Lirot	1973	20.00	0.500	0.322		0.32	0.64	0.97	1.29	3.22	4.83	6.44	8.05	9.66	11.27	12.88	14.49	16.10
Israel 10 Lirot	1967	26.00	0.935	0.782		0.78	1.56	2.35	3.13	7.82	11.73	15.64	19.55	23.46	27.37	31.28	35.19	39.10
Israel 10 Lirot	1968-1976	26.00	0.900	0.752		0.75	1.50	2.26	3.01	7.52	11.28	15.04	18.80	22.56	26.32	30.08	33.84	37.60
Israel 10 Lirot	1976	20.00	0.500	0.322		0.32	0.64	0.97	1.29	3.22	4.83	6.44	8.05	9.66	11.27	12.88	14.49	16.10
Israel 25 Lirot	1974	26.00	0.935	0.782		0.78	1.56	2.35	3.13	7.82	11.73	15.64	19.55	23.46	27.37	31.28	35.19	39.10
Israel 25 Lirot	1975-1976	26.00	0.900	0.752		0.75	1.50	2.26	3.01	7.52	11.28	15.04	18.80	22.56	26.32	30.08	33.84	37.60
Israel 25 Lirot	1975-1976	30.00	0.800	0.772		0.77	1.54	2.32	3.09	7.72	11.58	15.44	19.30	23.16	27.02	30.88	34.74	38.60
Israel 25 Lirot	1977	20.00	0.500	0.322		0.32	0.64	0.97	1.29	3.22	4.83	6.44	8.05	9.66	11.27	12.88	14.49	16.10
Israel 25 Lirot	1977, 1978	26.00	0.900	0.753		0.75	1.51	2.26	3.01	7.53	11.30	15.06	18.83	22.59	26.36	30.12	33.89	37.65
Israel 50 Lirot	1978-1979	20.00	0.500	0.322		0.32	0.64	0.97	1.29	3.22	4.83	6.44	8.05	9.66	11.27	12.88	14.49	16.10
Israel 100 Lirot	1979	20.00	0.500	0.322		0.32	0.64	0.97	1.29	3.22	4.83	6.44	8.05	9.66	11.27	12.88	14.49	16.10
Israel 200 Lirot	1980	26.00	0.900	0.753		0.75	1.51	2.26	3.01	7.53	11.30	15.06	18.83	22.59	26.36	30.12	33.89	37.65
Israel 1 Sheqel	1981-1985	14.40	0.850	0.394		0.39	0.79	1.18	1.58	3.94	5.91	7.88	9.85	11.82	13.79	15.76	17.73	19.70
Israel 2 Sheqalim	1981-1985	28.80	0.850	0.787		0.79	1.57	2.36	3.15	7.87	11.81	15.74	19.68	23.61	27.55	31.48	35.42	39.35
Israel 25 Sheqel	1980	26.00	0.900	0.753		0.75	1.51	2.26	3.01	7.53	11.30	15.06	18.83	22.59	26.36	30.12	33.89	37.65
Israel 1/2 New Sheqel	1986-1990	7.20	0.850	0.197	N	0.20	0.39	0.59	0.79	1.97	2.96	3.94	4.93	5.91	6.90	7.88	8.87	9.85
Israel 1 New Sheqel	1986-1990	14.40	0.850	0.394		0.39	0.79	1.18	1.58	3.94	5.91	7.88	9.85	11.82	13.79	15.76	17.73	19.70
Israel 1 New Sheqel	1991-2000	14.40	0.925	0.428		0.43	0.86	1.28	1.71	4.28	6.42	8.56	10.70	12.84	14.98	17.12	19.26	21.40
Israel 2 New Sheqalim	1986-1990	28.80	0.850	0.787		0.79	1.57	2.36	3.15	7.87	11.81	15.74	19.68	23.61	27.55	31.48	35.42	39.35

Country & Denomination	Years Minted	Grams Weight	Fineness	Troy (ASW)	Code	$ Value 1	$ Value 2	$ Value 3	$ Value 4	$ Value 10	$ Value 15	$ Value 20	$ Value 25	$ Value 30	$ Value 35	$ Value 40	$ Value 45	$ Value 50
Israel 2 New Sheqalim	1991-2000	28.80	0.925	0.857		0.86	1.71	2.57	3.43	8.57	12.86	17.14	21.43	25.71	30.00	34.28	38.57	42.85
Israel 30 New Sheqalim	1996	155.52	0.999	5.000		5.00	10.00	15.00	20.00	50.00	75.00	100.00	125.00	150.00	175.00	200.00	225.00	250.00
Italian Somaliland 1/4 Rupia	1910, 1913	2.92	0.917	0.086		0.09	0.17	0.26	0.34	0.86	1.29	1.72	2.15	2.58	3.01	3.44	3.87	4.30
Italian Somaliland 1/2 Rupia	1910-1919	5.83	0.917	0.172	S	0.17	0.34	0.52	0.69	1.72	2.58	3.44	4.30	5.16	6.02	6.88	7.74	8.60
Italian Somaliland 1 Rupia	1910-1921	11.66	0.917	0.344	S	0.34	0.69	1.03	1.38	3.44	5.16	6.88	8.60	10.32	12.04	13.76	15.48	17.20
Italian Somaliland 5 Lire	1925	6.00	0.835	0.161		0.16	0.32	0.48	0.64	1.61	2.42	3.22	4.03	4.83	5.64	6.44	7.25	8.05
Italian Somaliland 10 Lire	1925	12.00	0.835	0.322		0.32	0.64	0.97	1.29	3.22	4.83	6.44	8.05	9.66	11.27	12.88	14.49	16.10
Italy 10 Grana (Sicily)*	1818-1859	2.29	0.833	0.061	S	0.06	0.12	0.18	0.24	0.61	0.92	1.22	1.53	1.83	2.14	2.44	2.75	3.05
Italy 20 Grana (Sicily)	1826-1859	4.59	0.833	0.123	S	0.12	0.25	0.37	0.49	1.23	1.85	2.46	3.08	3.69	4.31	4.92	5.54	6.15
Italy 60 Grana (Sicily)	1805-1859	13.75	0.833	0.368	S	0.37	0.74	1.10	1.47	3.68	5.52	7.36	9.20	11.04	12.88	14.72	16.56	18.40
Italy 120 Grana (Sicily)	1802-1859	27.50	0.833	0.737	S	0.74	1.47	2.21	2.95	7.37	11.06	14.74	18.43	22.11	25.80	29.48	33.17	36.85
Italy 12 Tari (Sicily)	1801-1810	27.53	0.833	0.782		0.78	1.56	2.35	3.13	7.82	11.73	15.64	19.55	23.46	27.37	31.28	35.19	39.10
Italy 1 Dodici / 1 Carlini (Sicily)	1809, 1810	27.53	0.833	0.737		0.74	1.47	2.21	2.95	7.37	11.06	14.74	18.43	22.11	25.80	29.48	33.17	36.85
Italy 1/4 DiFiorino (Tuscany)	1827	1.72	0.916	0.051		0.05	0.10	0.15	0.20	0.51	0.77	1.02	1.28	1.53	1.79	2.04	2.30	2.55
Italy 1/2 Fiorino (Tuscany)	1827	3.44	0.916	0.101		0.10	0.20	0.30	0.40	1.01	1.52	2.02	2.53	3.03	3.54	4.04	4.55	5.05
Italy 1 Fiorino (Tuscany)	1826-1858	6.88	0.916	0.203	S	0.20	0.41	0.61	0.81	2.03	3.05	4.06	5.08	6.09	7.11	8.12	9.14	10.15
Italy 4 Fiorini (Tuscany)	1826-1859	27.50	0.916	0.810	S	0.81	1.62	2.43	3.24	8.10	12.15	16.20	20.25	24.30	28.35	32.40	36.45	40.50
Italy 1/2 Paolo (Tuscany)	1832-1859	1.37	0.920	0.041	S	0.04	0.08	0.12	0.16	0.41	0.62	0.82	1.03	1.23	1.44	1.64	1.85	2.05
Italy 1 Paolo (Tuscany)	1831-1858	2.74	0.920	0.081	S	0.08	0.16	0.24	0.32	0.81	1.22	1.62	2.03	2.43	2.84	3.24	3.65	4.05
Italy 5 Paoli (Tuscany)	1819-1834	13.75	0.913	0.404	S	0.40	0.81	1.21	1.62	4.04	6.06	8.08	10.10	12.12	14.14	16.16	18.18	20.20
Italy 10 Paoli (Tuscany)	1801-1824	27.50	0.916	0.810	S, V	0.81	1.62	2.43	3.24	8.10	12.15	16.20	20.25	24.30	28.35	32.40	36.45	40.50
Italy 1 Grosso (Papal)	1815-1817	1.32	0.917	0.039		0.04	0.08	0.12	0.16	0.39	0.59	0.78	0.98	1.17	1.37	1.56	1.76	1.95
Italy 4 Baiocchi (Rome)	1849	1.95	0.200	0.013		0.01	0.03	0.04	0.05	0.13	0.20	0.26	0.33	0.39	0.46	0.52	0.59	0.65
Italy 5 Baiocchi (Papal)	1835-1866	1.34	0.900	0.039	N	0.04	0.08	0.12	0.16	0.39	0.59	0.78	0.98	1.17	1.37	1.56	1.76	1.95
Italy 1 Guilo (Papal)	1817	2.64	0.917	0.078		0.08	0.16	0.23	0.31	0.78	1.17	1.56	1.95	2.34	2.73	3.12	3.51	3.90
Italy 10 Baiocchi (Papal)	1836-1865	2.69	0.900	0.078		0.08	0.16	0.23	0.31	0.78	1.17	1.56	1.95	2.34	2.73	3.12	3.51	3.90
Italy 8 Baiocchi (Rome)	1849	3.90	0.200	0.025		0.03	0.05	0.08	0.10	0.25	0.38	0.50	0.63	0.75	0.88	1.00	1.13	1.25
Italy 1 Doppio / 2 Guilo (Papal)	1816-1823	5.29	0.917	0.156		0.16	0.31	0.47	0.62	1.56	2.34	3.12	3.90	4.68	5.46	6.24	7.02	7.80
Italy 16 Baiocchi (Rome)	1849	7.80	0.200	0.050		0.05	0.10	0.15	0.20	0.50	0.75	1.00	1.25	1.50	1.75	2.00	2.25	2.50
Italy 20 Baiocchi (Papal)	1834-1866	5.37	0.900	0.156		0.16	0.31	0.47	0.62	1.56	2.34	3.12	3.90	4.68	5.46	6.24	7.02	7.80
Italy 1 Testone (Papal)	1802, 1803	7.93	0.917	0.234		0.23	0.47	0.70	0.94	2.34	3.51	4.68	5.85	7.02	8.19	9.36	10.53	11.70
Italy 30 Baiocchi (Papal)	1830, 1834	7.93	0.917	0.234		0.23	0.47	0.70	0.94	2.34	3.51	4.68	5.85	7.02	8.19	9.36	10.53	11.70
Italy 30 Baiocchi (Papal)	1836-1846	8.06	0.900	0.233		0.23	0.47	0.70	0.93	2.33	3.50	4.66	5.83	6.99	8.16	9.32	10.49	11.65
Italy 50 Baiocchi (Papal)	1832, 1834	13.21	0.917	0.390		0.39	0.78	1.17	1.56	3.90	5.85	7.80	9.75	11.70	13.65	15.60	17.55	19.50
Italy 50 Baiocchi (Papal)	1835-1857	13.44	0.900	0.389		0.39	0.78	1.17	1.56	3.89	5.84	7.78	9.73	11.67	13.62	15.56	17.51	19.45
Italy 2 Soldi (Lucca)	1835	1.40	0.200	0.009		0.01	0.02	0.03	0.04	0.09	0.14	0.18	0.23	0.27	0.32	0.36	0.41	0.45
Italy 3 Soldi (Lucca)	1835	1.60	0.200	0.010		0.01	0.02	0.03	0.04	0.10	0.15	0.20	0.25	0.30	0.35	0.40	0.45	0.50
Italy 5 Soldi	1808-1830	1.25	0.900	0.036	S	0.04	0.07	0.11	0.14	0.36	0.54	0.72	0.90	1.08	1.26	1.44	1.62	1.80
Italy 5 Soldi (Lucca)	1833, 1838	3.00	0.200	0.019		0.02	0.04	0.06	0.08	0.19	0.29	0.38	0.48	0.57	0.67	0.76	0.86	0.95
Italy 5 Soldi (Lucca)	1866, 1867	1.25	0.835	0.034		0.03	0.07	0.10	0.14	0.34	0.51	0.68	0.85	1.02	1.19	1.36	1.53	1.70
Italy 10 Soldi	1808-1830	2.50	0.900	0.072	S	0.07	0.14	0.22	0.29	0.72	1.08	1.44	1.80	2.16	2.52	2.88	3.24	3.60
Italy 10 Soldi	1814	2.10	0.889	0.060		0.06	0.12	0.18	0.24	0.60	0.90	1.20	1.50	1.80	2.10	2.40	2.70	3.00
Italy 10 Soldi (Tuscany)	1821, 1823	2.51	0.913	0.074		0.07	0.15	0.22	0.30	0.74	1.11	1.48	1.85	2.22	2.59	2.96	3.33	3.70

Country & Denomination	Years Minted	Grams Weight	Fine-ness	Troy (ASW)	Code	$ Value 1	$ Value 2	$ Value 3	$ Value 4	$ Value 10	$ Value 15	$ Value 20	$ Value 25	$ Value 30	$ Value 35	$ Value 40	$ Value 45	$ Value 50
Italy 10 Soldi (Lucca)	1833, 1838	2.36	0.666	0.051		0.05	0.10	0.15	0.20	0.51	0.77	1.02	1.28	1.53	1.79	2.04	2.30	2.55
Italy 10 Soldi (Papal)	1866-1868	2.50	0.835	0.067		0.07	0.13	0.20	0.27	0.67	1.01	1.34	1.68	2.01	2.35	2.68	3.02	3.35
Italy 15 Soldi	1808-1814	3.75	0.900	0.108	S	0.11	0.22	0.32	0.43	1.08	1.62	2.16	2.70	3.24	3.78	4.32	4.86	5.40
Italy 30 Soldi	1801	7.33	0.684	0.161		0.16	0.32	0.48	0.64	1.61	2.42	3.22	4.03	4.83	5.64	6.44	7.25	8.05
Italy 10 Centesimi	1808-1813	2.00	0.200	0.013		0.01	0.03	0.04	0.05	0.13	0.20	0.26	0.33	0.39	0.46	0.52	0.59	0.65
Italy 15 Centesimi	1848	1.26	0.229	0.009		0.01	0.02	0.03	0.04	0.09	0.14	0.18	0.23	0.27	0.32	0.36	0.41	0.45
Italy 20 Centesimi	1863-1867	1.00	0.835	0.027	S	0.03	0.05	0.08	0.11	0.27	0.41	0.54	0.68	0.81	0.95	1.08	1.22	1.35
Italy 25 Centesimi (Sardinia)	1832-1837	1.25	0.900	0.036	S	0.04	0.07	0.11	0.14	0.36	0.54	0.72	0.90	1.08	1.26	1.44	1.62	1.80
Italy 25 Centesimi	1848	1.25	0.900	0.036		0.04	0.07	0.11	0.14	0.36	0.54	0.72	0.90	1.08	1.26	1.44	1.62	1.80
Italy 1/4 Lira	1822-1844	1.62	0.600	0.031		0.03	0.06	0.09	0.12	0.31	0.47	0.62	0.78	0.93	1.09	1.24	1.40	1.55
Italy 1 Mezza / 1/2 Lira (Venice)	1802	4.50	0.250	0.036	S	0.04	0.07	0.11	0.14	0.36	0.54	0.72	0.90	1.08	1.26	1.44	1.62	1.80
Italy 1 Mezza / 1/2 Lira (Sicily)	1813	2.50	0.900	0.072		0.07	0.14	0.22	0.29	0.72	1.08	1.44	1.80	2.16	2.52	2.88	3.24	3.60
Italy 1/2 Lira	1822-1855	2.17	0.900	0.063		0.06	0.13	0.19	0.25	0.63	0.95	1.26	1.58	1.89	2.21	2.52	2.84	3.15
Italy 50 Centesimi	1859-1862	2.50	0.900	0.072		0.07	0.14	0.22	0.29	0.72	1.08	1.44	1.80	2.16	2.52	2.88	3.24	3.60
Italy 50 Centesimi	1859-1867	2.50	0.835	0.067		0.07	0.13	0.20	0.27	0.67	1.01	1.34	1.68	2.01	2.35	2.68	3.02	3.35
Italy 50 Centesimi (Sar, Tus)	1823-1861	2.50	0.900	0.072	S	0.07	0.14	0.22	0.29	0.72	1.08	1.44	1.80	2.16	2.52	2.88	3.24	3.60
Italy 1 Lira (Venice)	1802	11.36	0.250	0.091		0.09	0.18	0.27	0.36	0.91	1.37	1.82	2.28	2.73	3.19	3.64	4.10	4.55
Italy 1 Lira	1808-1815	5.00	0.900	0.144	S	0.14	0.29	0.43	0.58	1.44	2.16	2.88	3.60	4.32	5.04	5.76	6.48	7.20
Italy 1 Lira	1822-1858	4.33	0.900	0.125		0.13	0.25	0.38	0.50	1.25	1.88	2.50	3.13	3.75	4.38	5.00	5.63	6.25
Italy 1 Lira (Sardinia)	1823-1860	5.00	0.900	0.144	S	0.14	0.29	0.43	0.58	1.44	2.16	2.88	3.60	4.32	5.04	5.76	6.48	7.20
Italy 1 Lira	1861, 1862	5.00	0.900	0.144		0.14	0.29	0.43	0.58	1.44	2.16	2.88	3.60	4.32	5.04	5.76	6.48	7.20
Italy 1 Lira (Lucca)	1834-1838	4.72	0.666	0.101	S	0.10	0.20	0.30	0.40	1.01	1.52	2.02	2.53	3.03	3.54	4.04	4.55	5.05
Italy 1 Lira	1863-1917	5.00	0.835	0.134	S	0.13	0.27	0.40	0.54	1.34	2.01	2.68	3.35	4.02	4.69	5.36	6.03	6.70
Italy 1 Lira	1999-2000	14.60	0.835	0.392		0.39	0.78	1.18	1.57	3.92	5.88	7.84	9.80	11.76	13.72	15.68	17.64	19.60
Italy 1-1/2 Lire (Venice)	1802	8.49	0.250	0.068		0.07	0.14	0.20	0.27	0.68	1.02	1.36	1.70	2.04	2.38	2.72	3.06	3.40
Italy 2 Lire (Venice)	1801	8.50	0.250	0.068	V	0.07	0.14	0.20	0.27	0.68	1.02	1.36	1.70	2.04	2.38	2.72	3.06	3.40
Italy 2 Lire	1807-1862	10.00	0.900	0.289	N, S	0.29	0.58	0.87	1.16	2.89	4.34	5.78	7.23	8.67	10.12	11.56	13.01	14.45
Italy 2 Lire (Sardinia)	1823-1854	10.00	0.900	0.289	S	0.29	0.58	0.87	1.16	2.89	4.34	5.78	7.23	8.67	10.12	11.56	13.01	14.45
Italy 2 Lire (Lucca)	1837	9.43	0.666	0.202		0.20	0.40	0.61	0.81	2.02	3.03	4.04	5.05	6.06	7.07	8.08	9.09	10.10
Italy 2 Lire	1863-1917	10.00	0.835	0.268	S	0.27	0.54	0.80	1.07	2.68	4.02	5.36	6.70	8.04	9.38	10.72	12.06	13.40
Italy 1/2 Scudo (Papal)	1802-1829	13.25	0.917	0.391	S	0.39	0.78	1.17	1.56	3.91	5.87	7.82	9.78	11.73	13.69	15.64	17.60	19.55
Italy 1/2 Scudo	1822-1853	12.35	0.900	0.353	S	0.35	0.71	1.06	1.41	3.53	5.30	7.06	8.83	10.59	12.36	14.12	15.89	17.65
Italy 2-1/2 Lire (Papal)	1867	12.50	0.900	0.362		0.36	0.72	1.09	1.45	3.62	5.43	7.24	9.05	10.86	12.67	14.48	16.29	18.10
Italy 4 Lire	1804	16.64	0.889	0.476		0.48	0.95	1.43	1.90	4.76	7.14	9.52	11.90	14.28	16.66	19.04	21.42	23.80
Italy 5 Francs (Piedmont)	1801	25.00	0.900	0.723		0.72	1.45	2.17	2.89	7.23	10.85	14.46	18.08	21.69	25.31	28.92	32.54	36.15
Italy 5 Lire (Tuscany)	1803-1806	19.72	0.958	0.608		0.61	1.22	1.82	2.43	6.08	9.12	12.16	15.20	18.24	21.28	24.32	27.36	30.40
Italy 5 Lire	1807-1878	25.00	0.900	0.723		0.72	1.45	2.17	2.89	7.23	10.85	14.46	18.08	21.69	25.31	28.92	32.54	36.15
Italy 5 Lire	1926-1941	5.00	0.835	0.134	S	0.13	0.27	0.40	0.54	1.34	2.01	2.68	3.35	4.02	4.69	5.36	6.03	6.70
Italy 6 Lire	1816	26.00	0.900	0.752		0.75	1.50	2.26	3.01	7.52	11.28	15.04	18.80	22.56	26.32	30.08	33.84	37.60
Italy 1 Scudo (Papal)	1802-1834	26.43	0.917	0.780	S	0.78	1.56	2.34	3.12	7.80	11.70	15.60	19.50	23.40	27.30	31.20	35.10	39.00
Italy 1 Scudo (Papal)	1835-1856	26.87	0.900	0.778		0.78	1.56	2.33	3.11	7.78	11.67	15.56	19.45	23.34	27.23	31.12	35.01	38.90
Italy 1 Scudo	1821-1853	26.00	0.900	0.752	S	0.75	1.50	2.26	3.01	7.52	11.28	15.04	18.80	22.56	26.32	30.08	33.84	37.60
Italy 8 Lire	1804	33.27	0.889	0.951		0.95	1.90	2.85	3.80	9.51	14.27	19.02	23.78	28.53	33.29	38.04	42.80	47.55
Italy 10 Lire (Tuscany)	1803-1807	39.45	0.958	1.215		1.22	2.43	3.65	4.86	12.15	18.23	24.30	30.38	36.45	42.53	48.60	54.68	60.75
Italy 10 Lire	1926-1936	10.00	0.835	0.268		0.27	0.54	0.80	1.07	2.68	4.02	5.36	6.70	8.04	9.38	10.72	12.06	13.40

Country & Denomination	Years Minted	Grams Weight	Fineness	Troy (ASW)	Code	$ Value 1	$ Value 2	$ Value 3	$ Value 4	$ Value 10	$ Value 15	$ Value 20	$ Value 25	$ Value 30	$ Value 35	$ Value 40	$ Value 45	$ Value 50
Italy 20 Lire	1927-1934	15.00	0.800	0.386		0.39	0.77	1.16	1.54	3.86	5.79	7.72	9.65	11.58	13.51	15.44	17.37	19.30
Italy 20 Lire	1928	20.00	0.600	0.386		0.39	0.77	1.16	1.54	3.86	5.79	7.72	9.65	11.58	13.51	15.44	17.37	19.30
Italy 20 Lire	1936-1941	20.00	0.800	0.515		0.52	1.03	1.55	2.06	5.15	7.73	10.30	12.88	15.45	18.03	20.60	23.18	25.75
Italy 500 Lire	1958-1993	11.00	0.835	0.295	N, S	0.30	0.59	0.89	1.18	2.95	4.43	5.90	7.38	8.85	10.33	11.80	13.28	14.75
Italy 500 Lire	1991-1993	15.00	0.835	0.403	N	0.40	0.81	1.21	1.61	4.03	6.05	8.06	10.08	12.09	14.11	16.12	18.14	20.15
Italy 1000 Lire	1970-2000	14.60	0.835	0.392	N	0.39	0.78	1.18	1.57	3.92	5.88	7.84	9.80	11.76	13.72	15.68	17.64	19.60
Italy 2000 Lire	1997-1999	16.00	0.835	0.430		0.43	0.86	1.29	1.72	4.30	6.45	8.60	10.75	12.90	15.05	17.20	19.35	21.50
Italy 5000 Lire	1993-1999	18.00	0.835	0.483		0.48	0.97	1.45	1.93	4.83	7.25	9.66	12.08	14.49	16.91	19.32	21.74	24.15
Italy 10,000 Lire	1994-2000	22.00	0.835	0.591		0.59	1.18	1.77	2.36	5.91	8.87	11.82	14.78	17.73	20.69	23.64	26.60	29.55
Ivory Coast 10 Francs	1966	25.00	0.925	0.743		0.74	1.49	2.23	2.97	7.43	11.15	14.86	18.58	22.29	26.01	29.72	33.44	37.15
J																		
Jamaica 5 Dollars	1971	42.15	0.925	1.254		1.25	2.51	3.76	5.02	12.54	18.81	25.08	31.35	37.62	43.89	50.16	56.43	62.70
Jamaica 5 Dollars	1972-1973	41.48	0.925	1.234		1.23	2.47	3.70	4.94	12.34	18.51	24.68	30.85	37.02	43.19	49.36	55.53	61.70
Jamaica 5 Dollars	1974-1979	37.60	0.500	0.604	N	0.60	1.21	1.81	2.42	6.04	9.06	12.08	15.10	18.12	21.14	24.16	27.18	30.20
Jamaica 5 Dollars	1980-1993	18.56	0.500	0.298	N, S	0.30	0.60	0.89	1.19	2.98	4.47	5.96	7.45	8.94	10.43	11.92	13.41	14.90
Jamaica 10 Dollars	1972	49.20	0.925	1.463		1.46	2.93	4.39	5.85	14.63	21.95	29.26	36.58	43.89	51.21	58.52	65.84	73.15
Jamaica 10 Dollars	1974-1979	42.80	0.925	1.270	N	1.27	2.54	3.81	5.08	12.70	19.05	25.40	31.75	38.10	44.45	50.80	57.15	63.50
Jamaica 10 Dollars	1979-1993	22.45	0.925	0.668	S	0.67	1.34	2.00	2.67	6.68	10.02	13.36	16.70	20.04	23.38	26.72	30.06	33.40
Jamaica 10 Dollars	1980	30.28	0.500	0.469	N	0.47	0.94	1.41	1.88	4.69	7.04	9.38	11.73	14.07	16.42	18.76	21.11	23.45
Jamaica 10 Dollars	1986-1996	28.28	0.925	0.841	N	0.84	1.68	2.52	3.36	8.41	12.62	16.82	21.03	25.23	29.44	33.64	37.85	42.05
Jamaica 10 Dollars	1994	20.00	0.900	0.322		0.32	0.64	0.97	1.29	3.22	4.83	6.44	8.05	9.66	11.27	12.88	14.49	16.10
Jamaica 25 Dollars	1978-1986	136.08	0.925	4.047		4.05	8.09	12.14	16.19	40.47	60.71	80.94	101.18	121.41	141.65	161.88	182.12	202.35
Jamaica 25 Dollars	1984	23.44	0.925	0.668		0.67	1.34	2.00	2.67	6.68	10.02	13.35	16.69	20.03	23.37	26.71	30.05	33.39
Jamaica 25 Dollars	1987, 1994	37.78	0.925	1.124		1.12	2.25	3.37	4.50	11.24	16.86	22.48	28.10	33.72	39.34	44.96	50.58	56.20
Jamaica 25 Dollars	1988-1992	23.33	0.925	0.694		0.69	1.39	2.08	2.78	6.94	10.41	13.88	17.35	20.82	24.29	27.76	31.23	34.70
Jamaica 25 Dollars	1994-1995	28.20	0.925	0.936		0.94	1.87	2.81	3.74	9.36	14.04	18.72	23.40	28.08	32.76	37.44	42.12	46.80
Jamaica 50 Dollars	1995-2000	28.28	0.925	0.841	S	0.84	1.68	2.52	3.36	8.41	12.62	16.82	21.03	25.23	29.44	33.64	37.85	42.05
Jamaica 50 Dollars	1995, 1998	28.28	0.925	0.841		0.84	1.68	2.52	3.36	8.41	12.62	16.82	21.03	25.23	29.44	33.64	37.85	42.05
Jamaica 100 Dollars	1986-1990	136.08	0.925	4.047	S	4.05	8.09	12.14	16.19	40.47	60.71	80.94	101.18	121.41	141.65	161.88	182.12	202.35
Jamaica 100 Dollars	1992	137.80	0.925	4.100	S	4.10	8.20	12.30	16.40	41.00	61.50	82.00	102.50	123.00	143.50	164.00	184.50	205.00
Japan 5 Sen*	1870-1892	1.25	0.800	0.032		0.03	0.06	0.10	0.13	0.32	0.48	0.64	0.80	0.96	1.12	1.28	1.44	1.60
Japan 10 Sen	1870-1912	2.70	0.800	0.070	S	0.07	0.14	0.21	0.28	0.70	1.05	1.40	1.75	2.10	2.45	2.80	3.15	3.50
Japan 10 Sen	1912-1917	2.25	0.720	0.052		0.05	0.10	0.16	0.21	0.52	0.78	1.04	1.30	1.56	1.82	2.08	2.34	2.60
Japan 20 Sen	1870, 1871	5.00	0.800	0.129		0.13	0.26	0.39	0.52	1.29	1.94	2.58	3.23	3.87	4.52	5.16	5.81	6.45
Japan 20 Sen	1873-1905	5.39	0.800	0.138	S	0.14	0.28	0.41	0.55	1.38	2.07	2.76	3.45	4.14	4.83	5.52	6.21	6.90
Japan 20 Sen	1906-1911	4.05	0.800	0.104		0.10	0.21	0.31	0.42	1.04	1.56	2.08	2.60	3.12	3.64	4.16	4.68	5.20
Japan 50 Sen	1870, 1871	12.50	0.800	0.322	S	0.32	0.64	0.97	1.29	3.22	4.83	6.44	8.05	9.66	11.27	12.88	14.49	16.10
Japan 50 Sen	1873-1905	13.48	0.800	0.347		0.35	0.69	1.04	1.39	3.47	5.21	6.94	8.68	10.41	12.15	13.88	15.62	17.35
Japan 50 Sen	1906-1917	10.10	0.800	0.260		0.26	0.52	0.78	1.04	2.60	3.90	5.20	6.50	7.80	9.10	10.40	11.70	13.00
Japan 50 Sen	1922-1938	4.95	0.720	0.115		0.11	0.23	0.34	0.46	1.15	1.72	2.30	2.87	3.44	4.02	4.59	5.17	5.74
Japan 1 Yen	1870-1914	27.00	0.900	0.780	S	0.78	1.56	2.34	3.12	7.80	11.70	15.60	19.50	23.40	27.30	31.20	35.10	39.00
Japan 1 Trade Dollar	1875-1877	27.22	0.900	0.788		0.79	1.58	2.36	3.15	7.88	11.82	15.76	19.70	23.64	27.58	31.52	35.46	39.40
Japan 100 Yen	1957-1966	4.80	0.600	0.093		0.09	0.19	0.28	0.37	0.93	1.40	1.86	2.33	2.79	3.26	3.72	4.19	4.65
Japan 1000 Yen	1964	20.00	0.925	0.595		0.60	1.19	1.79	2.38	5.95	8.93	11.90	14.88	17.85	20.83	23.80	26.78	29.75
Japan 5000 Yen	1990-1998	15.00	0.925	0.446	S	0.45	0.89	1.34	1.78	4.46	6.69	8.92	11.15	13.38	15.61	17.84	20.07	22.30

Country & Denomination	Years Minted	Grams Weight	Fine-ness	Troy (ASW)	Code	$ Value 1	$ Value 2	$ Value 3	$ Value 4	$ Value 10	$ Value 15	$ Value 20	$ Value 25	$ Value 30	$ Value 35	$ Value 40	$ Value 45	$ Value 50
Jersey 1 Penny	1983	4.20	0.925	0.125	N	0.13	0.25	0.38	0.50	1.25	1.88	2.50	3.13	3.75	4.38	5.00	5.63	6.25
Jersey 2 Pence	1983	8.40	0.925	0.250	N	0.25	0.50	0.75	1.00	2.50	3.75	5.00	6.25	7.50	8.75	10.00	11.25	12.50
Jersey 5 Pence	1983	6.60	0.925	0.196	N	0.20	0.39	0.59	0.78	1.96	2.94	3.92	4.90	5.88	6.86	7.84	8.82	9.80
Jersey 10 Pence	1983	13.20	0.925	0.393	N	0.39	0.79	1.18	1.57	3.93	5.90	7.86	9.83	11.79	13.76	15.72	17.69	19.65
Jersey 20 Pence	1982, 1998	5.83	0.925	0.173	N	0.17	0.35	0.52	0.69	1.73	2.60	3.46	4.33	5.19	6.06	6.92	7.79	8.65
Jersey 25 Pence	1977	28.28	0.925	0.841	N	0.84	1.68	2.52	3.36	8.41	12.62	16.82	21.03	25.23	29.44	33.64	37.85	42.05
Jersey 50 Pence	1972	5.40	0.925	0.160		0.16	0.32	0.48	0.64	1.60	2.40	3.20	4.00	4.80	5.60	6.40	7.20	8.00
Jersey 50 Pence	1983	15.50	0.925	0.461	N	0.46	0.92	1.38	1.84	4.61	6.92	9.22	11.53	13.83	16.14	18.44	20.75	23.05
Jersey 1 Pound	1972	10.84	0.925	0.322		0.32	0.64	0.97	1.29	3.22	4.83	6.44	8.05	9.66	11.27	12.88	14.49	16.10
Jersey 1 Pound	1981	10.45	0.925	0.311	N	0.31	0.62	0.93	1.24	3.11	4.67	6.22	7.78	9.33	10.89	12.44	14.00	15.55
Jersey 1 Pound	1983-1994	11.68	0.925	0.347	N, S	0.35	0.69	1.04	1.39	3.47	5.21	6.94	8.68	10.41	12.15	13.88	15.62	17.35
Jersey 2 Pounds	1972	21.68	0.925	0.651		0.65	1.30	1.95	2.60	6.51	9.77	13.02	16.28	19.53	22.79	26.04	29.30	32.55
Jersey 2 Pounds	1981-1996	28.28	0.925	0.841	N, S	0.84	1.68	2.52	3.36	8.41	12.62	16.82	21.03	25.23	29.44	33.64	37.85	42.05
Jersey 2-1/2 Pounds	1972	27.10	0.925	0.810		0.81	1.62	2.43	3.24	8.10	12.15	16.20	20.25	24.30	28.35	32.40	36.45	40.50
Jersey 5 Pounds	1997-2000	28.28	0.925	0.841	N, S	0.84	1.68	2.52	3.36	8.41	12.62	16.82	21.03	25.23	29.44	33.64	37.85	42.05
						0.00												
Jordan 1/2 Dinar	1969	20.00	0.999	0.642		0.64	1.28	1.93	2.57	6.42	9.63	12.84	16.05	19.26	22.47	25.68	28.89	32.10
Jordan 3/4 Dinar	1969	30.00	0.999	0.964		0.96	1.93	2.89	3.86	9.64	14.46	19.28	24.10	28.92	33.74	38.56	43.38	48.20
Jordan 1 Dinar	1969	40.00	0.999	1.285		1.29	2.57	3.86	5.14	12.85	19.28	25.70	32.13	38.55	44.98	51.40	57.83	64.25
Jordan 1 Dinar	1992	15.00	0.925	0.446		0.45	0.89	1.34	1.78	4.46	6.69	8.92	11.15	13.38	15.61	17.84	20.07	22.30
Jordan 1 Dinar	1996	31.10	0.925	1.000		1.00	2.00	3.00	4.00	10.00	15.00	20.00	25.00	30.00	35.00	40.00	45.00	50.00
Jordan 2-1/2 Dinars	1977	28.28	0.925	0.841		0.84	1.68	2.52	3.36	8.41	12.62	16.82	21.03	25.23	29.44	33.64	37.85	42.05
Jordan 3 Dinars	1977	35.00	0.925	1.040		1.04	2.08	3.12	4.16	10.40	15.60	20.80	26.00	31.20	36.40	41.60	46.80	52.00
Jordan 3 Dinars	1981	23.33	0.925	0.694		0.69	1.39	2.08	2.78	6.94	10.41	13.88	17.35	20.82	24.29	27.76	31.23	34.70
Jordan 5 Dinars	1995, 1999	28.28	0.925	0.841		0.84	1.68	2.52	3.36	8.41	12.62	16.82	21.03	25.23	29.44	33.64	37.85	42.05
Jordan 10 Dinars	1980	30.00	0.925	0.892		0.89	1.78	2.68	3.57	8.92	13.38	17.84	22.30	26.76	31.22	35.68	40.14	44.60
Jordan 10 Dinars	1985	15.20	0.925	0.461		0.46	0.92	1.38	1.84	4.61	6.92	9.22	11.53	13.83	16.14	18.44	20.75	23.05
Jordan 10 Dinars	1999	31.10	0.999	0.999		1.00	2.00	3.00	4.00	9.99	14.99	19.98	24.98	29.97	34.97	39.96	44.96	49.95
Jordan 10 Dinars	2000	31.00	0.999	0.996		1.00	1.99	2.99	3.98	9.96	14.94	19.92	24.90	29.88	34.86	39.84	44.82	49.80
Keeling Cocos 10 Rupees	1977	6.50	0.925	0.193		0.19	0.39	0.58	0.77	1.93	2.90	3.86	4.83	5.79	6.76	7.72	8.69	9.65
Keeling Cocos 25 Rupees	1977	16.25	0.925	0.483		0.48	0.97	1.45	1.93	4.83	7.25	9.66	12.08	14.49	16.91	19.32	21.74	24.15
Kenya 200 Shillings	1978	28.28	0.925	0.841		0.84	1.68	2.52	3.36	8.41	12.62	16.82	21.03	25.23	29.44	33.64	37.85	42.05
Kenya 500 Shillings	1988	28.28	0.925	0.841		0.84	1.68	2.52	3.36	8.41	12.62	16.82	21.03	25.23	29.44	33.64	37.85	42.05
Kenya 500 Shillings	1988	28.33	0.925	0.843		0.84	1.69	2.53	3.37	8.43	12.65	16.86	21.08	25.29	29.51	33.72	37.94	42.15
Kenya 1000 Shillings	1991	28.28	0.925	0.841		0.84	1.68	2.52	3.36	8.41	12.62	16.82	21.03	25.23	29.44	33.64	37.85	42.05
Kiribati 2 Dollars	1998	10.00	0.500	0.161		0.16	0.32	0.48	0.64	1.61	2.42	3.22	4.03	4.83	5.64	6.44	7.25	8.05
Kiribati 5 Dollars	1979	28.16	0.500	0.453		0.45	0.91	1.36	1.81	4.53	6.79	9.05	11.32	13.58	15.84	18.11	20.37	22.64
Kiribati 5 Dollars	1979	28.16	0.925	0.838		0.84	1.68	2.51	3.35	8.38	12.57	16.76	20.95	25.14	29.33	33.52	37.71	41.90
Kiribati 5 Dollars	1981	28.60	0.925	0.851		0.85	1.70	2.55	3.40	8.51	12.77	17.02	21.28	25.53	29.79	34.04	38.30	42.55
Kiribati 5 Dollars	1996-1998	31.47	0.925	0.936	>	0.94	1.87	2.81	3.74	9.36	14.04	18.72	23.40	28.08	32.76	37.44	42.12	46.80
Kiribati 5 Dollars	1997	15.55	0.925	0.463		0.46	0.93	1.39	1.85	4.63	6.95	9.26	11.58	13.89	16.21	18.52	20.84	23.15

K

Country & Denomination	Years Minted	Grams Weight	Fineness	Troy (ASW)	Code	$ Value 1	$ Value 2	$ Value 3	$ Value 4	$ Value 10	$ Value 15	$ Value 20	$ Value 25	$ Value 30	$ Value 35	$ Value 40	$ Value 45	$ Value 50
Kiribati 5 Dollars	2000	31.30	0.999	1.005		1.01	2.01	3.02	4.02	10.05	15.08	20.10	25.13	30.15	35.18	40.20	45.23	50.25
Kiribati 10 Dollars	1984	28.28	0.925	0.841		0.84	1.68	2.52	3.36	8.41	12.62	16.82	21.03	25.23	29.44	33.64	37.85	42.05
Kiribati 10 Dollars	2000	22.22	0.500	0.357		0.36	0.71	1.07	1.43	3.57	5.36	7.14	8.93	10.71	12.50	14.28	16.07	17.85
Kiribati 20 Dollars	1992, 1993	31.47	0.925	0.936		0.94	1.87	2.81	3.74	9.36	14.04	18.72	23.40	28.08	32.76	37.44	42.12	46.80
Kiribati 20 Dollars	2000	21.22	0.999	0.682		0.68	1.36	2.05	2.73	6.82	10.23	13.64	17.05	20.46	23.87	27.28	30.69	34.10
Korea 1 Yang	1892-1898	5.20	0.800	0.134	s	0.13	0.27	0.40	0.54	1.34	2.01	2.68	3.35	4.02	4.69	5.36	6.03	6.70
Korea 5 Yang	1892	26.95	0.900	0.780		0.78	1.56	2.34	3.12	7.80	11.70	15.60	19.50	23.40	27.30	31.20	35.10	39.00
Korea 1 Warn	1888	26.95	0.900	0.780		0.78	1.56	2.34	3.12	7.80	11.70	15.60	19.50	23.40	27.30	31.20	35.10	39.00
Korea 1 Whan	1893	26.95	0.900	0.780		0.78	1.56	2.34	3.12	7.80	11.70	15.60	19.50	23.40	27.30	31.20	35.10	39.00
Korea 1/2 Won	1901	13.50	0.800	0.347		0.35	0.69	1.04	1.39	3.47	5.21	6.94	8.68	10.41	12.15	13.88	15.62	17.35
Korea 1/2 Won	1907-1908	10.13	0.800	0.261		0.26	0.52	0.78	1.04	2.61	3.92	5.22	6.53	7.83	9.14	10.44	11.75	13.05
Korea 10 Chon	1906-1910	2.50	0.800	0.065	s	0.07	0.13	0.20	0.26	0.65	0.98	1.30	1.63	1.95	2.28	2.60	2.93	3.25
Korea 10 Chon	1907	2.25	0.800	0.059		0.06	0.12	0.18	0.24	0.59	0.89	1.18	1.48	1.77	2.07	2.36	2.66	2.95
Korea 20 Chon	1905-1906	5.40	0.800	0.139		0.14	0.28	0.42	0.56	1.39	2.09	2.78	3.48	4.17	4.87	5.56	6.26	6.95
Korea 20 Chon	1905-1910	4.00	0.800	0.104		0.10	0.21	0.31	0.42	1.04	1.56	2.08	2.60	3.12	3.64	4.16	4.68	5.20
Korea (North) 5 Won	1995	12.00	0.999	0.385		0.39	0.77	1.16	1.54	3.85	5.78	7.70	9.63	11.55	13.48	15.40	17.33	19.25
Korea (North) 5 Won	1996-2000	27.00	0.999	0.867	s	0.87	1.73	2.60	3.47	8.67	13.01	17.34	21.68	26.01	30.35	34.68	39.02	43.35
Korea (North) 5 Won	1998	26.80	0.999	0.862		0.86	1.72	2.59	3.45	8.62	12.93	17.24	21.55	25.86	30.17	34.48	38.79	43.10
Korea (North) 5 Won	1999	20.00	0.999	0.642		0.64	1.28	1.93	2.57	6.42	9.63	12.84	16.05	19.26	22.47	25.68	28.89	32.10
Korea (North) 5 Won	2000	15.00	0.999	0.482		0.48	0.96	1.45	1.93	4.82	7.23	9.64	12.05	14.46	16.87	19.28	21.69	24.10
Korea (North) 10 Won	1995	28.00	0.999	0.899		0.90	1.80	2.70	3.60	8.99	13.49	17.98	22.48	26.97	31.47	35.96	40.46	44.95
Korea (North) 10 Won	1995	31.00	0.999	0.995	>	1.00	1.99	2.99	3.98	9.95	14.93	19.90	24.88	29.85	34.83	39.80	44.78	49.75
Korea (North) 10 Won	1995	28.00	0.999	0.899		0.90	1.80	2.70	3.60	8.99	13.49	17.98	22.48	26.97	31.47	35.96	40.46	44.95
Korea (North) 20 Won	1989	14.80	0.999	0.476		0.48	0.95	1.43	1.90	4.76	7.14	9.52	11.90	14.28	16.66	19.04	21.42	23.80
Korea (North) 20 Won	1994, 1995	31.10	0.999	1.000		1.00	2.00	3.00	4.00	10.00	15.00	20.00	25.00	30.00	35.00	40.00	45.00	50.00
Korea (North) 20 Won	1995	50.00	0.999	1.606		1.61	3.21	4.82	6.42	16.06	24.09	32.12	40.15	48.18	56.21	64.24	72.27	80.30
Korea (North) 30 Won	1989	17.00	0.999	0.547		0.55	1.09	1.64	2.19	5.47	8.21	10.94	13.68	16.41	19.15	21.88	24.62	27.35
Korea (North) 50 Won	1992	17.00	0.999	0.547		0.55	1.09	1.64	2.19	5.47	8.21	10.94	13.68	16.41	19.15	21.88	24.62	27.35
Korea (North) 100 Won	1995, 1996	7.00	0.999	0.225		0.23	0.45	0.68	0.90	2.25	3.38	4.50	5.63	6.75	7.88	9.00	10.13	11.25
Korea (North) 200 Won	1991, 1992	15.00	0.999	0.482		0.48	0.96	1.45	1.93	4.82	7.23	9.64	12.05	14.46	16.87	19.28	21.69	24.10
Korea (North) 250 Won	1999	15.00	0.999	0.482		0.48	0.96	1.45	1.93	4.82	7.23	9.64	12.05	14.46	16.87	19.28	21.69	24.10
Korea (North) 500 Won	1987-1996	27.00	0.999	0.867	s	0.87	1.73	2.60	3.47	8.67	13.01	17.34	21.68	26.01	30.35	34.68	39.02	43.35
Korea (North) 500 Won	1990	31.80	0.999	0.868		0.87	1.74	2.60	3.47	8.68	13.02	17.36	21.70	26.04	30.38	34.72	39.06	43.40
Korea (North) 500 Won	1991-1996	31.10	0.999	0.997		1.00	1.99	2.99	3.99	9.97	14.96	19.94	24.93	29.91	34.90	39.88	44.87	49.85
Korea (North) 500 Won	1996	31.52	0.999	1.012		1.01	2.02	3.04	4.05	10.12	15.18	20.24	25.30	30.36	35.42	40.48	45.54	50.60
Korea (North) 2500 Won	1995	155.52	0.999	5.000		5.00	10.00	15.00	20.00	50.00	75.00	100.00	125.00	150.00	175.00	200.00	225.00	250.00
Korea (South) 50 Won	1970, 1971	2.80	0.999	0.090		0.09	0.18	0.27	0.36	0.90	1.35	1.80	2.25	2.70	3.15	3.60	4.05	4.50
Korea (South) 100 Won	1970	5.60	0.999	0.180		0.18	0.36	0.54	0.72	1.80	2.70	3.60	4.50	5.40	6.30	7.20	8.10	9.00
Korea (South) 200 Won	1970	11.20	0.999	0.360		0.36	0.72	1.08	1.44	3.60	5.40	7.20	9.00	10.80	12.60	14.40	16.20	18.00
Korea (South) 250 Won	1970	14.00	0.999	0.450		0.45	0.90	1.35	1.80	4.50	6.75	9.00	11.25	13.50	15.75	18.00	20.25	22.50
Korea (South) 500 Won	1970	28.00	0.999	0.900		0.90	1.80	2.70	3.60	9.00	13.50	18.00	22.50	27.00	31.50	36.00	40.50	45.00
Korea (South) 1000 Won	1970	56.00	0.999	1.800		1.80	3.60	5.40	7.20	18.00	27.00	36.00	45.00	54.00	63.00	72.00	81.00	90.00

Country & Denomination	Years Minted	Grams Weight	Fineness	Troy (ASW)	Code	$ Value 1	$ Value 2	$ Value 3	$ Value 4	$ Value 10	$ Value 15	$ Value 20	$ Value 25	$ Value 30	$ Value 35	$ Value 40	$ Value 45	$ Value 50
Korea (South) 5000 Won	1978	23.00	0.900	0.666		0.67	1.33	2.00	2.66	6.66	9.99	13.32	16.65	19.98	23.31	26.64	29.97	33.30
Korea (South) 5000 Won	1986-	16.81	0.925	0.500	N, S	0.50	1.00	1.50	2.00	5.00	7.50	10.00	12.50	15.00	17.50	20.00	22.50	25.00
Korea (South) 10,000 Won	1982, 1983	15.00	0.900	0.434		0.43	0.87	1.30	1.74	4.34	6.51	8.68	10.85	13.02	15.19	17.36	19.53	21.70
Korea (South) 10,000 Won	1984, 1986	22.30	0.500	0.374		0.37	0.75	1.12	1.50	3.74	5.61	7.48	9.35	11.22	13.09	14.96	16.83	18.70
Korea (South) 10,000 Won	1986-1993	33.62	0.925	1.000		1.00	2.00	3.00	4.00	10.00	15.00	20.00	25.00	30.00	35.00	40.00	45.00	50.00
Korea (South) 10,000 Won	1995	23.00	0.900	0.666	S	0.67	1.33	2.00	2.66	6.66	9.99	13.32	16.65	19.98	23.31	26.64	29.97	33.30
Korea (South) 20,000 Won	1981-1983	23.00	0.900	0.666	V	0.67	1.33	2.00	2.66	6.66	9.99	13.32	16.65	19.98	23.31	26.64	29.97	33.30
Korea (South) 20,000 Won	1986	28.00	0.900	0.800		0.80	1.60	2.40	3.20	8.00	12.00	16.00	20.00	24.00	28.00	32.00	36.00	40.00
Kuwait 5 Fils	1987	3.01	0.925	0.090	N	0.09	0.18	0.27	0.36	0.90	1.35	1.80	2.25	2.70	3.15	3.60	4.05	4.50
Kuwait 10 Fils	1987	4.35	0.925	0.129	N	0.13	0.26	0.39	0.52	1.29	1.94	2.58	3.23	3.87	4.52	5.16	5.81	6.45
Kuwait 20 Fils	1987	3.37	0.925	0.100	N	0.10	0.20	0.30	0.40	1.00	1.50	2.00	2.50	3.00	3.50	4.00	4.50	5.00
Kuwait 50 Fils	1987	5.07	0.925	0.151	N	0.15	0.30	0.45	0.60	1.51	2.27	3.02	3.78	4.53	5.29	6.04	6.80	7.55
Kuwait 100 Fils	1987	7.34	0.925	0.218	N	0.22	0.44	0.65	0.87	2.18	3.27	4.36	5.45	6.54	7.63	8.72	9.81	10.90
Kuwait 2 Dinars	1976	28.28	0.500	0.455		0.46	0.91	1.37	1.82	4.55	6.83	9.10	11.38	13.65	15.93	18.20	20.48	22.75
Kuwait 2 Dinars	1976, 1995	28.28	0.925	0.841		0.84	1.68	2.52	3.36	8.41	12.62	16.82	21.03	25.23	29.44	33.64	37.85	42.05
Kuwait 5 Dinars	1981	28.28	0.925	0.841		0.84	1.68	2.52	3.36	8.41	12.62	16.82	21.03	25.23	29.44	33.64	37.85	42.05
Kuwait 5 Dinars	1986	33.63	0.925	1.000		1.00	2.00	3.00	4.00	10.00	15.00	20.00	25.00	30.00	35.00	40.00	45.00	50.00
Kyrgyzstan 10 Som	1995	28.28	0.925	0.841		0.84	1.68	2.52	3.36	8.41	12.62	16.82	21.03	25.23	29.44	33.64	37.85	42.05

L

Country & Denomination	Years Minted	Grams Weight	Fineness	Troy (ASW)	Code	$ Value 1	$ Value 2	$ Value 3	$ Value 4	$ Value 10	$ Value 15	$ Value 20	$ Value 25	$ Value 30	$ Value 35	$ Value 40	$ Value 45	$ Value 50
Laos 50 Kip	1985	38.20	0.900	1.105	N	1.11	2.21	3.32	4.42	11.05	16.58	22.10	27.63	33.15	38.68	44.20	49.73	55.25
Laos 50 Kip	1988-1994	16.00	0.999	0.514	S, V	0.51	1.03	1.54	2.06	5.14	7.71	10.28	12.85	15.42	17.99	20.56	23.13	25.70
Laos 50 Kip	1988, 1991	12.00	0.999	0.386		0.39	0.77	1.16	1.54	3.86	5.79	7.72	9.65	11.58	13.51	15.44	17.37	19.30
Laos 50 Kip	1991-1996	20.00	0.999	0.642	S	0.64	1.28	1.93	2.57	6.42	9.63	12.84	16.05	19.26	22.47	25.68	28.89	32.10
Laos 50 Kip	1996	15.00	0.999	0.642		0.64	1.28	1.93	2.57	6.42	9.63	12.84	16.05	19.26	22.47	25.68	28.89	32.10
Laos 500 Kip	1998	20.00	0.925	0.595		0.59	1.19	1.78	2.38	5.95	8.92	11.89	14.87	17.84	20.81	23.79	26.76	29.74
Laos 1000 Kip	1971	10.00	0.925	0.297		0.30	0.59	0.89	1.19	2.97	4.46	5.94	7.43	8.91	10.40	11.88	13.37	14.85
Laos 1000 Kip	1996, 1997	31.47	0.925	0.936		0.94	1.87	2.81	3.74	9.36	14.04	18.72	23.40	28.08	32.76	37.44	42.12	46.80
Laos 2500 Kip	1971	20.00	0.925	0.595		0.59	1.19	1.78	2.38	5.95	8.92	11.89	14.87	17.84	20.81	23.79	26.76	29.74
Laos 3000 Kip	1999	20.00	0.925	0.595		0.59	1.19	1.78	2.38	5.95	8.92	11.89	14.87	17.84	20.81	23.79	26.76	29.74
Laos 5000 Kip	1971, 1975	11.70	0.925	0.348		0.35	0.70	1.04	1.39	3.48	5.22	6.96	8.70	10.44	12.18	13.92	15.66	17.40
Laos 5000 Kip	1998	15.00	0.999	0.482		0.48	0.96	1.45	1.93	4.82	7.23	9.64	12.05	14.46	16.87	19.28	21.69	24.10
Laos 5000 Kip	1999	20.05	0.999	0.658		0.66	1.32	1.97	2.63	6.58	9.87	13.16	16.45	19.74	23.03	26.32	29.61	32.90
Laos 10,000 Kip	1971, 1975	23.50	0.925	0.699		0.70	1.40	2.10	2.80	6.99	10.49	13.98	17.48	20.97	24.47	27.96	31.46	34.95
Latvia 1 Lats	1923, 1924	5.00	0.835	0.134		0.13	0.27	0.40	0.54	1.34	2.01	2.68	3.35	4.02	4.69	5.36	6.03	6.70
Latvia 1 Lats	1995	28.28	0.925	0.841		0.84	1.68	2.52	3.36	8.41	12.62	16.82	21.03	25.23	29.44	33.64	37.85	42.05
Latvia 1 Lats	1999	20.00	0.925	0.595		0.59	1.19	1.78	2.38	5.95	8.92	11.89	14.87	17.84	20.81	23.79	26.76	29.74
Latvia 1 Lats	1999, 2000	31.47	0.925	0.936		0.94	1.87	2.81	3.74	9.36	14.04	18.72	23.40	28.08	32.76	37.44	42.12	46.80
Latvia 1 Lats	1999, 2000	15.20	0.925	0.452		0.45	0.90	1.36	1.81	4.52	6.78	9.04	11.30	13.56	15.82	18.08	20.34	22.60
Latvia 2 Lati	1925, 1926	10.00	0.835	0.268		0.27	0.54	0.80	1.07	2.68	4.02	5.36	6.70	8.04	9.38	10.72	12.06	13.40
Latvia 5 Lati	1929-1932	25.00	0.835	0.671	S	0.67	1.34	2.01	2.68	6.71	10.07	13.42	16.78	20.13	23.49	26.84	30.20	33.55
Latvia 10 Latu	1993	25.18	0.925	0.748		0.75	1.50	2.24	2.99	7.48	11.22	14.96	18.70	22.44	26.18	29.92	33.66	37.40
Latvia 10 Latu	1994-1997	31.47	0.925	0.936	V	0.94	1.87	2.81	3.74	9.36	14.04	18.72	23.40	28.08	32.76	37.44	42.12	46.80

Country & Denomination	Years Minted	Grams Weight	Fineness	Troy (ASW)	Code	$ Value 1	$ Value 2	$ Value 3	$ Value 4	$ Value 10	$ Value 15	$ Value 20	$ Value 25	$ Value 30	$ Value 35	$ Value 40	$ Value 45	$ Value 50
Lebanon 10 Piastres	1929	2.00	0.680	0.044		0.04	0.09	0.13	0.18	0.44	0.66	0.88	1.10	1.32	1.54	1.76	1.98	2.20
Lebanon 25 Piastres	1929-1936	5.00	0.680	0.109	s	0.11	0.22	0.33	0.44	1.09	1.64	2.18	2.73	3.27	3.82	4.36	4.91	5.45
Lebanon 50 Piastres	1929-1936	10.00	0.680	0.219	s	0.22	0.44	0.66	0.88	2.19	3.29	4.38	5.48	6.57	7.67	8.76	9.86	10.95
Lebanon 50 Piastres	1952	4.97	0.600	0.096		0.10	0.19	0.29	0.38	0.96	1.44	1.92	2.40	2.88	3.36	3.84	4.32	4.80
Lebanon 10 Livres	1980	19.00	0.500	0.305		0.31	0.61	0.92	1.22	3.05	4.58	6.10	7.63	9.15	10.68	12.20	13.73	15.25
Lesotho 5 Licente	1966	2.89	0.900	0.084		0.08	0.17	0.25	0.34	0.84	1.26	1.68	2.10	2.52	2.94	3.36	3.78	4.20
Lesotho 10 Licente	1966	5.68	0.900	0.164		0.16	0.33	0.49	0.66	1.64	2.46	3.28	4.10	4.92	5.74	6.56	7.38	8.20
Lesotho 20 Licente	1966	11.28	0.900	0.326		0.33	0.65	0.98	1.30	3.26	4.89	6.52	8.15	9.78	11.41	13.04	14.67	16.30
Lesotho 50 Licente	1966	28.10	0.900	0.813		0.81	1.63	2.44	3.25	8.13	12.20	16.26	20.33	24.39	28.46	32.52	36.59	40.65
Lesotho 1 Loti	1985	11.31	0.925	0.336	N	0.34	0.67	1.01	1.34	3.36	5.04	6.72	8.40	10.08	11.76	13.44	15.12	16.80
Lesotho 10 Maloti	1976	25.08	0.925	0.746		0.75	1.49	2.24	2.98	7.46	11.19	14.92	18.65	22.38	26.11	29.84	33.57	37.30
Lesotho 10 Maloti	1979, 1988	28.28	0.925	0.841		0.84	1.68	2.52	3.36	8.41	12.62	16.82	21.03	25.23	29.44	33.64	37.85	42.05
Lesotho 10 Maloti	1980	12.00	0.500	0.193		0.19	0.39	0.58	0.77	1.93	2.90	3.86	4.83	5.79	6.76	7.72	8.69	9.65
Lesotho 10 Maloti	1982, 1985	23.33	0.925	0.694		0.69	1.39	2.08	2.78	6.94	10.41	13.88	17.35	20.82	24.29	27.76	31.23	34.70
Lesotho 10 Maloti	1982	31.10	0.500	0.500		0.50	1.00	1.50	2.00	5.00	7.50	10.00	12.50	15.00	17.50	20.00	22.50	25.00
Lesotho 15 Maloti	1979	33.40	0.925	0.993		0.99	1.99	2.98	3.97	9.93	14.90	19.86	24.83	29.79	34.76	39.72	44.69	49.65
Lesotho 15 Maloti	1981	12.00	0.500	0.193		0.19	0.39	0.58	0.77	1.93	2.90	3.86	4.83	5.79	6.76	7.72	8.69	9.65
Lesotho 25 Maloti	1981	16.82	0.925	0.500		0.50	1.00	1.50	2.00	5.00	7.50	10.00	12.50	15.00	17.50	20.00	22.50	25.00
Lesotho 25 Maloti	1983	28.28	0.925	0.841		0.84	1.68	2.52	3.36	8.41	12.62	16.82	21.03	25.23	29.44	33.64	37.85	42.05
Lesotho 50 Maloti	1980, 1981	33.62	0.925	0.999		1.00	2.00	3.00	4.00	9.99	14.99	19.98	24.98	29.97	34.97	39.96	44.96	49.95
Liberia 10 Cents	1896-1906	2.32	0.925	0.069	s	0.07	0.14	0.21	0.28	0.69	1.04	1.38	1.73	2.07	2.42	2.76	3.11	3.45
Liberia 10 Cents	1960, 1961	2.07	0.900	0.060		0.06	0.12	0.18	0.24	0.60	0.90	1.20	1.50	1.80	2.10	2.40	2.70	3.00
Liberia 25 Cents	1896-1906	5.80	0.925	0.173	s	0.17	0.35	0.52	0.69	1.73	2.60	3.46	4.33	5.19	6.06	6.92	7.79	8.65
Liberia 25 Cents	1960, 1961	5.18	0.900	0.150		0.15	0.30	0.45	0.60	1.50	2.25	3.00	3.75	4.50	5.25	6.00	6.75	7.50
Liberia 50 Cents	1896-1906	11.60	0.925	0.345	s	0.35	0.69	1.04	1.38	3.45	5.18	6.90	8.63	10.35	12.08	13.80	15.53	17.25
Liberia 50 Cents	1960, 1961	10.37	0.900	0.300		0.30	0.60	0.90	1.20	3.00	4.50	6.00	7.50	9.00	10.50	12.00	13.50	15.00
Liberia 1 Dollar	1961, 1962	20.74	0.900	0.600		0.60	1.20	1.80	2.40	6.00	9.00	12.00	15.00	18.00	21.00	24.00	27.00	30.00
Liberia 2 Dollars	1983	28.28	0.925	0.841	N	0.84	1.68	2.52	3.36	8.41	12.62	16.82	21.03	25.23	29.44	33.64	37.85	42.05
Liberia 5 Dollars	1973-1978	34.10	0.900	0.987		0.99	1.97	2.96	3.95	9.87	14.81	19.74	24.68	29.61	34.55	39.48	44.42	49.35
Liberia 5 Dollars	1992-1996	15.55	0.999	0.500	s	0.50	1.00	1.50	2.00	5.00	7.50	10.00	12.50	15.00	17.50	20.00	22.50	25.00
Liberia 5 Dollars	1999	24.97	0.925	0.743		0.74	1.49	2.23	2.97	7.43	11.15	14.86	18.58	22.29	26.01	29.72	33.44	37.15
Liberia 10 Dollars	1985	23.33	0.925	0.694		0.69	1.39	2.08	2.78	6.94	10.41	13.88	17.35	20.82	24.29	27.76	31.23	34.70
Liberia 10 Dollars	1988-2000	31.10	0.999	1.000	>	1.00	2.00	3.00	4.00	10.00	15.00	20.00	25.00	30.00	35.00	40.00	45.00	50.00
Liberia 10 Dollars	1999	15.55	0.999	0.500		0.50	1.00	1.50	2.00	5.00	7.50	10.00	12.50	15.00	17.50	20.00	22.50	25.00
Liberia 10 Dollars	1999, 2000	25.00	0.925	0.744	>	0.74	1.49	2.23	2.98	7.44	11.16	14.88	18.60	22.32	26.04	29.76	33.48	37.20
Liberia 10 Dollars	2000	8.55	0.999	0.275		0.28	0.55	0.83	1.10	2.75	4.13	5.50	6.88	8.25	9.63	11.00	12.38	13.75
Liberia 10 Dollars	2000	8.45	0.999	0.271		0.27	0.54	0.81	1.08	2.71	4.07	5.42	6.78	8.13	9.49	10.84	12.20	13.55
Liberia 10 Dollars	2000	20.15	0.999	0.647	N	0.65	1.29	1.94	2.59	6.47	9.71	12.94	16.18	19.41	22.65	25.88	29.12	32.35
Liberia 10 Dollars	2000	20.50	0.925	0.610	N	0.61	1.22	1.83	2.44	6.10	9.15	12.20	15.25	18.30	21.35	24.40	27.45	30.50
Liberia 20 Dollars	1983	28.28	0.925	0.841	N	0.84	1.68	2.52	3.36	8.41	12.62	16.82	21.03	25.23	29.44	33.64	37.85	42.05
Liberia 20 Dollars	1998	24.94	0.999	0.740		0.74	1.48	2.22	2.96	7.40	11.10	14.80	18.50	22.20	25.90	29.60	33.30	37.00
Liberia 20 Dollars	1997	31.22	0.999	1.003	>	1.00	2.01	3.01	4.01	10.03	15.05	20.06	25.08	30.09	35.11	40.12	45.14	50.15

Country & Denomination	Years Minted	Grams Weight	Fine-ness	Troy (ASW)	Code	$ Value 1	$ Value 2	$ Value 3	$ Value 4	$ Value 10	$ Value 15	$ Value 20	$ Value 25	$ Value 30	$ Value 35	$ Value 40	$ Value 45	$ Value 50
Liberia 20 Dollars	1997	31.35	0.999	1.007		1.01	2.01	3.02	4.03	10.07	15.11	20.14	25.18	30.21	35.25	40.28	45.32	50.35
Liberia 20 Dollars	1997	31.40	0.999	1.009		1.01	2.02	3.03	4.04	10.09	15.14	20.18	25.23	30.27	35.32	40.36	45.41	50.45
Liberia 20 Dollars	2000	20.00	0.999	0.638	>	0.64	1.28	1.91	2.55	6.38	9.57	12.76	15.95	19.14	22.33	25.52	28.71	31.90
Liberia 20 Dollars	1997	77.76	0.999	2.500		2.50	5.00	7.50	10.00	25.00	37.50	50.00	62.50	75.00	87.50	100.00	112.50	125.00
Liberia 50 Dollars	1993	155.52	0.999	5.000		5.00	10.00	15.00	20.00	50.00	75.00	100.00	125.00	150.00	175.00	200.00	225.00	250.00
Liberia 150 Dollars	1993	500.00	0.999	16.076		16.08	32.15	48.23	64.30	160.76	241.14	321.52	401.90	482.28	562.66	643.04	723.42	803.80
Liberia 250 Dollars	1993	500.00	0.999	16.076		16.08	32.15	48.23	64.30	160.76	241.14	321.52	401.90	482.28	562.66	643.04	723.42	803.80
Liberia 300 Dollars	1993, 1998	1000.00	0.999	32.151		32.15	64.30	96.45	128.60	321.51	482.27	643.02	803.78	964.53	1125.29	1286.04	1446.80	1607.55
Libya 5 Dinars*	1981	28.28	0.925	0.841		0.84	1.68	2.52	3.36	8.41	12.62	16.82	21.03	25.23	29.44	33.64	37.85	42.05
Lichtenstein 1 Thaler	1862	18.52	0.900	0.536	s	0.54	1.07	1.61	2.14	5.36	8.04	10.72	13.40	16.08	18.76	21.44	24.12	26.80
Lichtenstein 1 Krone	1900-1915	5.00	0.835	0.134	s	0.13	0.27	0.40	0.54	1.34	2.01	2.68	3.35	4.02	4.69	5.36	6.03	6.70
Lichtenstein 2 Kronen	1912-1915	10.00	0.835	0.268	s	0.27	0.54	0.80	1.07	2.68	4.02	5.36	6.70	8.04	9.38	10.72	12.06	13.40
Lichtenstein 5 Kronen	1900-1915	24.00	0.835	0.694	s	0.69	1.39	2.08	2.78	6.94	10.41	13.88	17.35	20.82	24.29	27.76	31.23	34.70
Lichtenstein 1/2 Frank	1924	2.50	0.835	0.067		0.07	0.13	0.20	0.27	0.67	1.01	1.34	1.68	2.01	2.35	2.68	3.02	3.35
Lichtenstein 1 Frank	1924	5.00	0.835	0.134		0.13	0.27	0.40	0.54	1.34	2.01	2.68	3.35	4.02	4.69	5.36	6.03	6.70
Lichtenstein 2 Franken	1924	10.00	0.835	0.268		0.27	0.54	0.80	1.07	2.68	4.02	5.36	6.70	8.04	9.38	10.72	12.06	13.40
Lichtenstein 5 Franken	1924	25.00	0.835	0.723		0.72	1.45	2.17	2.89	7.23	10.85	14.46	18.08	21.69	25.31	28.92	32.54	36.15
Lichtenstein 10 Franken	1990	30.00	0.900	0.868		0.87	1.74	2.60	3.47	8.68	13.02	17.36	21.70	26.04	30.38	34.72	39.06	43.40
Lithuania 1 Litas	1925	2.70	0.500	0.043		0.04	0.09	0.13	0.17	0.43	0.65	0.86	1.08	1.29	1.51	1.72	1.94	2.15
Lithuania 2 Litu	1925	5.40	0.500	0.087		0.09	0.17	0.26	0.35	0.87	1.31	1.74	2.18	2.61	3.05	3.48	3.92	4.35
Lithuania 5 Litai	1925	13.50	0.500	0.217		0.22	0.43	0.65	0.87	2.17	3.26	4.34	5.43	6.51	7.60	8.68	9.77	10.85
Lithuania 5 Litai	1936	9.00	0.750	0.217		0.22	0.43	0.65	0.87	2.17	3.26	4.34	5.43	6.51	7.60	8.68	9.77	10.85
Lithuania 5 Litai	1998	28.28	0.925	0.841		0.84	1.68	2.52	3.36	8.41	12.62	16.82	21.03	25.23	29.44	33.64	37.85	42.05
Lithuania 10 Litu	1936-1938	18.00	0.750	0.434		0.43	0.87	1.30	1.74	4.34	6.51	8.68	10.85	13.02	15.19	17.36	19.53	21.70
Lithuania 50 Litu	1995-2000	23.30	0.925	0.693		0.69	1.39	2.08	2.77	6.93	10.40	13.86	17.33	20.79	24.26	27.72	31.19	34.65
Lithuania 50 Litu	1999, 2000	28.28	0.925	0.841		0.84	1.68	2.52	3.36	8.41	12.62	16.82	21.03	25.23	29.44	33.64	37.85	42.05
Luxembourg 5 Francs	1929	8.00	0.625	0.161		0.16	0.32	0.48	0.64	1.61	2.42	3.22	4.03	4.83	5.64	6.44	7.25	8.05
Luxembourg 5 Francs	1980	6.78	0.925	0.202	>	0.20	0.40	0.61	0.81	2.02	3.03	4.04	5.05	6.06	7.07	8.08	9.09	10.10
Luxembourg 10 Francs	1929	13.10	0.750	0.326		0.33	0.65	0.98	1.30	3.26	4.89	6.52	8.15	9.78	11.41	13.04	14.67	16.30
Luxembourg 10 Francs	1980	13.50	0.925	0.261		0.26	0.52	0.78	1.04	2.61	3.92	5.22	6.53	7.83	9.14	10.44	11.75	13.05
Luxembourg 20 Francs	1946	5.00	0.835	0.140		0.14	0.28	0.42	0.56	1.40	2.10	2.80	3.50	4.20	4.90	5.60	6.30	7.00
Luxembourg 20 Francs	1980	10.21	0.925	0.304		0.30	0.61	0.91	1.22	3.04	4.56	6.08	7.60	9.12	10.64	12.16	13.68	15.20
Luxembourg 50 Francs	1946	12.50	0.835	0.336		0.34	0.67	1.01	1.34	3.36	5.04	6.72	8.40	10.08	11.76	13.44	15.12	16.80
Luxembourg 100 Francs	1946	25.00	0.835	0.671		0.67	1.34	2.01	2.68	6.71	10.07	13.42	16.78	20.13	23.49	26.84	30.20	33.55
Luxembourg 100 Francs	1963-1964	18.00	0.835	0.483		0.48	0.97	1.45	1.93	4.83	7.25	9.66	12.08	14.49	16.91	19.32	21.74	24.15
Luxembourg 100 Francs	1995	16.10	0.925	0.479		0.48	0.96	1.44	1.92	4.79	7.19	9.58	11.98	14.37	16.77	19.16	21.56	23.95
Luxembourg 250 Francs	1963	25.00	0.900	0.720		0.72	1.44	2.16	2.88	7.20	10.80	14.40	18.00	21.60	25.20	28.80	32.40	36.00
Luxembourg 250 Francs	1994	18.75	0.925	0.558		0.56	1.12	1.67	2.23	5.58	8.37	11.16	13.95	16.74	19.53	22.32	25.11	27.90
Luxembourg 500 Francs	1994-2000	22.85	0.925	0.680	s	0.68	1.36	2.04	2.72	6.80	10.20	13.60	17.00	20.40	23.80	27.20	30.60	34.00

M

Country & Denomination	Years Minted	Grams Weight	Fine-ness	Troy (ASW)	Code	$ Value 1	$ Value 2	$ Value 3	$ Value 4	$ Value 10	$ Value 15	$ Value 20	$ Value 25	$ Value 30	$ Value 35	$ Value 40	$ Value 45	$ Value 50
Macao 1 Pataca	1952	2.50	0.720	0.069		0.07	0.14	0.21	0.28	0.69	1.04	1.38	1.73	2.07	2.42	2.76	3.11	3.45

Country & Denomination	Years Minted	Grams Weight	Fine-ness	Troy (ASW)	Code	$ Value 1	$ Value 2	$ Value 3	$ Value 4	$ Value 10	$ Value 15	$ Value 20	$ Value 25	$ Value 30	$ Value 35	$ Value 40	$ Value 45	$ Value 50
Macao 1 Pataca	1982-1985	9.00	0.925	0.268	N	0.27	0.54	0.80	1.07	2.68	4.02	5.36	6.70	8.04	9.38	10.72	12.06	13.40
Macao 1 Pataca	1982	5.70	0.925	0.170	N	0.17	0.34	0.51	0.68	1.70	2.55	3.40	4.25	5.10	5.95	6.80	7.65	8.50
Macao 5 Patacas	1952	15.00	0.720	0.347		0.35	0.69	1.04	1.39	3.47	5.21	6.94	8.68	10.41	12.15	13.88	15.62	17.35
Macao 5 Patacas	1982-1985	10.70	0.925	0.318	N	0.32	0.64	0.95	1.27	3.18	4.77	6.36	7.95	9.54	11.13	12.72	14.31	15.90
Macao 5 Patacas	1971	10.00	0.650	0.209		0.21	0.42	0.63	0.84	2.09	3.14	4.18	5.23	6.27	7.32	8.36	9.41	10.45
Macao 20 Patacas	1974	18.00	0.650	0.376		0.38	0.75	1.13	1.50	3.76	5.64	7.52	9.40	11.28	13.16	15.04	16.92	18.80
Macao 100 Patacas	1978-2000	28.28	0.925	0.841		0.84	1.68	2.52	3.36	8.41	12.62	16.82	21.03	25.23	29.44	33.64	37.85	42.05
Macedonia 1 Denar	2000	7.00	0.925	0.208	N	0.21	0.42	0.62	0.83	2.08	3.12	4.16	5.20	6.24	7.28	8.32	9.36	10.40
Madagascar 20 Ariary	1974	12.00	0.925	0.357	N	0.36	0.71	1.07	1.43	3.57	5.36	7.14	8.93	10.71	12.50	14.28	16.07	17.85
Madagascar 20 Ariary	1988, 1996	19.44	0.925	0.578	N	0.58	1.16	1.73	2.31	5.78	8.67	11.56	14.45	17.34	20.23	23.12	26.01	28.90
Madeira Islands 25 Escudos	1981	11.00	0.925	0.327	N	0.33	0.65	0.98	1.31	3.27	4.91	6.54	8.18	9.81	11.45	13.08	14.72	16.35
Madeira Islands 100 Escudos	1981	16.50	0.925	0.491	N	0.49	0.98	1.47	1.96	4.91	7.37	9.82	12.28	14.73	17.19	19.64	22.10	24.55
Malawi 5 Kwacha	1978, 1995	28.28	0.925	0.841		0.84	1.68	2.52	3.36	8.41	12.62	16.82	21.03	25.23	29.44	33.64	37.85	42.05
Malawi 5 Kwacha	1997	20.30	0.925	0.604		0.60	1.21	1.81	2.42	6.04	9.06	12.08	15.10	18.12	21.14	24.16	27.18	30.20
Malawi 5 Kwacha	1997	28.50	0.925	0.848		0.85	1.70	2.54	3.39	8.48	12.72	16.96	21.20	25.44	29.68	33.92	38.16	42.40
Malawi 10 Kwacha	1974-1992	28.28	0.925	0.841	S	0.84	1.68	2.52	3.36	8.41	12.62	16.82	21.03	25.23	29.44	33.64	37.85	42.05
Malawi 10 Kwacha	1978	35.00	0.925	1.041		1.04	2.08	3.12	4.16	10.41	15.62	20.82	26.03	31.23	36.44	41.64	46.85	52.05
Malawi 10 Kwacha	1999	20.00	0.925	0.595		0.60	1.19	1.79	2.38	5.95	8.93	11.90	14.88	17.85	20.83	23.80	26.78	29.75
Malawi 20 Kwacha	1996-199	31.50	0.925	0.935	V	0.94	1.87	2.81	3.74	9.35	14.03	18.70	23.38	28.05	32.73	37.40	42.08	46.75
Malaya 5 Cents	1939-1941	1.36	0.750	0.033		0.03	0.07	0.10	0.13	0.33	0.50	0.66	0.83	0.99	1.16	1.32	1.49	1.65
Malaya 5 Cents	1943-1945	1.36	0.500	0.022		0.02	0.04	0.07	0.09	0.22	0.33	0.44	0.55	0.66	0.77	0.88	0.99	1.10
Malaya 10 Cents	1939-1941	2.71	0.750	0.066		0.07	0.13	0.20	0.26	0.66	0.99	1.32	1.65	1.98	2.31	2.64	2.97	3.30
Malaya 10 Cents	1943-1945	2.71	0.500	0.044		0.04	0.09	0.13	0.18	0.44	0.66	0.88	1.10	1.32	1.54	1.76	1.98	2.20
Malaya 20 Cents	1939	5.43	0.750	0.131		0.13	0.26	0.39	0.52	1.31	1.97	2.62	3.28	3.93	4.59	5.24	5.90	6.55
Malaya 20 Cents	1943-1945	5.43	0.500	0.087		0.09	0.17	0.26	0.35	0.87	1.31	1.74	2.18	2.61	3.05	3.48	3.92	4.35
Malaysia 1 Ringit	1969, 1979	17.00	0.925	0.506	N	0.51	1.01	1.52	2.02	5.06	7.59	10.12	12.65	15.18	17.71	20.24	22.77	25.30
Malaysia 1 Ringit	1986	16.85	0.500	0.271	N	0.27	0.54	0.81	1.08	2.71	4.07	5.42	6.78	8.13	9.49	10.84	12.20	13.55
Malaysia 5 Ringit	1986	29.03	0.500	0.466		0.47	0.93	1.40	1.86	4.66	6.99	9.32	11.65	13.98	16.31	18.64	20.97	23.30
Malaysia 10 Ringit	1976	10.82	0.917	0.322		0.32	0.64	0.97	1.29	3.22	4.83	6.44	8.05	9.66	11.27	12.88	14.49	16.10
Malaysia 10 Ringit	1987	10.82	0.500	0.174		0.17	0.35	0.52	0.70	1.74	2.61	3.48	4.35	5.22	6.09	6.96	7.83	8.70
Malaysia 15 Ringit	1976	28.28	0.925	0.841		0.84	1.68	2.52	3.36	8.41	12.62	16.82	21.03	25.23	29.44	33.64	37.85	42.05
Malaysia 15 Ringit	1989	16.73	0.925	0.499		0.50	1.00	1.50	2.00	4.99	7.49	9.98	12.48	14.97	17.47	19.96	22.46	24.95
Malaysia 20 Ringit	1981	16.23	0.500	0.261		0.26	0.52	0.78	1.04	2.61	3.92	5.22	6.53	7.83	9.14	10.44	11.75	13.05
Malaysia 25 Ringit	1976-1982	35.00	0.925	1.041	S	1.04	2.08	3.12	4.16	10.41	15.62	20.82	26.03	31.23	36.44	41.64	46.85	52.05
Malaysia 25 Ringit	1984, 1986	35.00	0.500	0.563		0.56	1.13	1.69	2.25	5.63	8.45	11.26	14.08	16.89	19.71	22.52	25.34	28.15
Malaysia 25 Ringit	1985	23.33	0.925	0.694		0.69	1.39	2.08	2.78	6.94	10.41	13.88	17.35	20.82	24.29	27.76	31.23	34.70
Malaysia 25 Ringit	1989-1999	21.90	0.925	0.647	S	0.65	1.29	1.94	2.59	6.47	9.71	12.94	16.18	19.41	22.65	25.88	29.12	32.35
Malaysia 30 Ringit	1989	22.00	0.925	0.658		0.66	1.32	1.97	2.63	6.58	9.87	13.16	16.45	19.74	23.03	26.32	29.61	32.90

Country & Denomination	Years Minted	Grams Weight	Fine-ness	Troy (ASW)	Code	$ Value 1	$ Value 2	$ Value 3	$ Value 4	$ Value 10	$ Value 15	$ Value 20	$ Value 25	$ Value 30	$ Value 35	$ Value 40	$ Value 45	$ Value 50
Maldive Islands 5 Rufiyaa	1978	19.15	0.925	0.570	N	0.57	1.14	1.71	2.28	5.70	8.55	11.40	14.25	17.10	19.95	22.80	25.65	28.50
Maldive Islands 10 Rufiyaa	1979	25.00	0.925	0.744	N	0.74	1.49	2.23	2.98	7.44	11.16	14.88	18.60	22.32	26.04	29.76	33.48	37.20
Maldive Islands 20 Rufiyaa	1977, 1978	28.28	0.925	0.841		0.84	1.68	2.52	3.36	8.41	12.62	16.82	21.03	25.23	29.44	33.64	37.85	42.05
Maldive Islands 20 Rufiyaa	1977	28.28	0.500	0.455		0.46	0.91	1.37	1.82	4.55	6.83	9.10	11.38	13.65	15.93	18.20	20.48	22.75
Maldive Islands 20 Rufiyaa	1985	19.44	0.925	0.578		0.58	1.16	1.73	2.31	5.78	8.67	11.56	14.45	17.34	20.23	23.12	26.01	28.90
Maldive Islands 20 Rufiyaa	2000	31.22	0.999	1.003		1.00	2.01	3.01	4.01	10.03	15.05	20.06	25.08	30.09	35.11	40.12	45.14	50.15
Maldive Islands 25 Rufiyaa	1978	28.20	0.500	0.460		0.46	0.92	1.38	1.84	4.60	6.90	9.20	11.50	13.80	16.10	18.40	20.70	23.00
Maldive Islands 50 Rufiyaa	1996	10.00	0.500	0.161		0.16	0.32	0.48	0.64	1.61	2.42	3.22	4.03	4.83	5.64	6.44	7.25	8.05
Maldive Islands 50 Rufiyaa	1998	31.30	0.925	0.931		0.93	1.86	2.79	3.72	9.31	13.97	18.62	23.28	27.93	32.59	37.24	41.90	46.55
Maldive Islands 100 Rufiyaa	1979-1985	28.28	0.925	0.841		0.84	1.68	2.52	3.36	8.41	12.62	16.82	21.03	25.23	29.44	33.64	37.85	42.05
Maldive Islands 100 Rufiyaa	1979-1980	28.28	0.800	0.727		0.73	1.45	2.18	2.91	7.27	10.91	14.54	18.18	21.81	25.45	29.08	32.72	36.35
Maldive Islands 100 Rufiyaa	1993	10.00	0.500	0.161		0.16	0.32	0.48	0.64	1.61	2.42	3.22	4.03	4.83	5.64	6.44	7.25	8.05
Maldive Islands 100 Rufiyaa	1998	20.00	0.835	0.537		0.54	1.07	1.61	2.15	5.37	8.06	10.74	13.43	16.11	18.80	21.48	24.17	26.85
Maldive Islands 250 Rufiyaa	1990-1994	31.47	0.925	0.936		0.94	1.87	2.81	3.74	9.36	14.04	18.72	23.40	28.08	32.76	37.44	42.12	46.80
Maldive Islands 250 Rufiyaa	1995	31.24	0.925	0.929		0.93	1.86	2.79	3.72	9.29	13.94	18.58	23.23	27.87	32.52	37.16	41.81	46.45
Maldive Islands 250 Rufiyaa	1996	28.50	0.925	0.848		0.85	1.70	2.54	3.39	8.48	12.72	16.96	21.20	25.44	29.68	33.92	38.16	42.40
Maldive Islands 500 Rufiyaa	1990, 1993	28.28	0.925	0.841		0.84	1.68	2.52	3.36	8.41	12.62	16.82	21.03	25.23	29.44	33.64	37.85	42.05
Mali 10 Francs	1960	25.00	0.900	0.723		0.72	1.45	2.17	2.89	7.23	10.85	14.46	18.08	21.69	25.31	28.92	32.54	36.15
Malta 1 Pound	1972-1973	10.00	0.987	0.317		0.32	0.63	0.95	1.27	3.17	4.76	6.34	7.93	9.51	11.10	12.68	14.27	15.85
Malta 1 Pound	1977, 1979	5.66	0.925	0.168		0.17	0.34	0.50	0.67	1.68	2.52	3.36	4.20	5.04	5.88	6.72	7.56	8.40
Malta 2 Pounds	1972-1973	20.00	0.987	0.635		0.64	1.27	1.91	2.54	6.35	9.53	12.70	15.88	19.05	22.23	25.40	28.58	31.75
Malta 2 Pounds	1974-1976	10.00	0.987	0.317		0.32	0.63	0.95	1.27	3.17	4.76	6.34	7.93	9.51	11.10	12.68	14.27	15.85
Malta 2 Pounds	1977, 1981	11.30	0.925	0.336		0.34	0.67	1.01	1.34	3.36	5.04	6.72	8.40	10.08	11.76	13.44	15.12	16.80
Malta 4 Pounds	1974-1976	20.00	0.987	0.635		0.64	1.27	1.91	2.54	6.35	9.53	12.70	15.88	19.05	22.23	25.40	28.58	31.75
Malta 5 Pounds	1977, 1981	28.28	0.925	0.841		0.84	1.68	2.52	3.36	8.41	12.62	16.82	21.03	25.23	29.44	33.64	37.85	42.05
Malta 5 Liri	1989	17.00	0.925	0.506		0.51	1.01	1.52	2.02	5.06	7.59	10.12	12.65	15.18	17.71	20.24	22.77	25.30
Malta 5 Liri	1984-1999	28.28	0.925	0.841	S	0.84	1.68	2.52	3.36	8.41	12.62	16.82	21.03	25.23	29.44	33.64	37.85	42.05
Malta 5 Liri	1984-1986	20.00	0.925	0.595		0.59	1.19	1.78	2.38	5.95	8.92	11.89	14.87	17.84	20.81	23.79	26.76	29.74
Malta 5 Liri	1994, 1996	31.47	0.925	0.936		0.94	1.87	2.81	3.74	9.36	14.04	18.72	23.40	28.08	32.76	37.44	42.12	46.80
Malta 5 Liri	2000	15.00	0.925	0.446		0.45	0.89	1.34	1.78	4.46	6.69	8.92	11.15	13.38	15.61	17.84	20.07	22.30
Malta 5 Liri / 10 ECU	1993	25.00	0.925	0.744		0.74	1.49	2.23	2.98	7.44	11.16	14.88	18.60	22.32	26.04	29.76	33.48	37.20
Malta, Order of, 1 Scudo	1961-1978	11.96	0.986	0.380		0.38	0.76	1.14	1.52	3.80	5.70	7.60	9.50	11.40	13.30	15.20	17.10	19.00
Malta, Order of, 2 Scudi	1961-1978	24.18	0.986	0.767		0.77	1.53	2.30	3.07	7.67	11.51	15.34	19.18	23.01	26.85	30.68	34.52	38.35
Marshall Islands 1/2 Dollar	1986	15.55	0.999	0.500		0.50	1.00	1.50	2.00	5.00	7.50	10.00	12.50	15.00	17.50	20.00	22.50	25.00
Marshall Islands 1 Dollar	1986	31.10	0.999	1.000		1.00	2.00	3.00	4.00	10.00	15.00	20.00	25.00	30.00	35.00	40.00	45.00	50.00
Marshall Islands 20 Dollars	1994, 1995	15.55	0.999	0.500		0.50	1.00	1.50	2.00	5.00	7.50	10.00	12.50	15.00	17.50	20.00	22.50	25.00
Marshall Islands 20 Dollars	1997	10.37	0.999	0.333		0.33	0.67	1.00	1.33	3.33	5.00	6.66	8.33	9.99	11.66	13.32	14.99	16.65
Marshall Islands 25 Dollars	1988	33.96	0.925	1.010		1.01	2.02	3.03	4.04	10.10	15.15	20.20	25.25	30.30	35.35	40.40	45.45	50.50
Marshall Islands 50 Dollars	1989-1998	31.00	0.999	1.000		1.00	2.00	3.00	4.00	10.00	15.00	20.00	25.00	30.00	35.00	40.00	45.00	50.00
Marshall Islands 75 Dollars	1988	155.67	0.999	5.006		5.01	10.01	15.02	20.02	50.06	75.09	100.12	125.15	150.18	175.21	200.24	225.27	250.30

Country & Denomination	Years Minted	Grams Weight	Fineness	Troy (ASW)	Code	$ Value 1	$ Value 2	$ Value 3	$ Value 4	$ Value 10	$ Value 15	$ Value 20	$ Value 25	$ Value 30	$ Value 35	$ Value 40	$ Value 45	$ Value 50
Mauritius 10 Cents	1877-1897	1.17	0.800	0.030	S	0.03	0.06	0.09	0.12	0.30	0.45	0.60	0.75	0.90	1.05	1.20	1.35	1.50
Mauritius 20 Cents	1877-1899	2.33	0.800	0.060	S	0.06	0.12	0.18	0.24	0.60	0.90	1.20	1.50	1.80	2.10	2.40	2.70	3.00
Mauritius 1/4 Rupee	1934-1938	2.92	0.916	0.082		0.08	0.16	0.25	0.33	0.82	1.23	1.64	2.05	2.46	2.87	3.28	3.69	4.10
Mauritius 1/4 Rupee	1946	2.92	0.500	0.047		0.05	0.09	0.14	0.19	0.47	0.71	0.94	1.18	1.41	1.65	1.88	2.12	2.35
Mauritius 1/2 Rupee	1934	5.83	0.916	0.172		0.17	0.34	0.52	0.69	1.72	2.58	3.44	4.30	5.16	6.02	6.88	7.74	8.60
Mauritius 1/2 Rupee	1946	5.83	0.500	0.094		0.09	0.19	0.28	0.38	0.94	1.41	1.88	2.35	2.82	3.29	3.76	4.23	4.70
Mauritius 1 Rupee	1934-1938	11.66	0.916	0.330		0.33	0.66	0.99	1.32	3.30	4.95	6.60	8.25	9.90	11.55	13.20	14.85	16.50
Mauritius 10 Rupees	1981	28.28	0.925	0.841		0.84	1.68	2.52	3.36	8.41	12.62	16.82	21.03	25.23	29.44	33.64	37.85	42.05
Mauritius 25 Rupees	1975-1977	25.50	0.500	0.457		0.46	0.91	1.37	1.83	4.57	6.86	9.14	11.43	13.71	16.00	18.28	20.57	22.85
Mauritius 25 Rupees	1975-1982	28.28	0.925	0.841	S	0.84	1.68	2.52	3.36	8.41	12.62	16.82	21.03	25.23	29.44	33.64	37.85	42.05
Mauritius 50 Rupees	1975	32.15	0.500	0.517		0.52	1.03	1.55	2.07	5.17	7.76	10.34	12.93	15.51	18.10	20.68	23.27	25.85
Mauritius 50 Rupees	1975	35.00	0.925	1.041		1.04	2.08	3.12	4.16	10.41	15.62	20.82	26.03	31.23	36.44	41.64	46.85	52.05
Mexico 1/2 Real	1801-1869	1.69	0.903	0.049		0.05	0.10	0.15	0.20	0.49	0.74	0.98	1.23	1.47	1.72	1.96	2.21	2.45
Mexico 1 Real	1801-1869	3.38	0.903	0.098		0.10	0.20	0.29	0.39	0.98	1.47	1.96	2.45	2.94	3.43	3.92	4.41	4.90
Mexico 2 Reales	1801-1870	6.77	0.903	0.195		0.20	0.39	0.59	0.78	1.95	2.93	3.90	4.88	5.85	6.83	7.80	8.78	9.75
Mexico 4 Reales	1801-1870	13.54	0.903	0.393		0.39	0.79	1.18	1.57	3.93	5.90	7.86	9.83	11.79	13.76	15.72	17.69	19.65
Mexico 8 Reales	1801-1897	27.07	0.903	0.786		0.79	1.57	2.36	3.14	7.86	11.79	15.72	19.65	23.58	27.51	31.44	35.37	39.30
Mexico 5 Centavos	1868-1904	1.35	0.903	0.039		0.04	0.08	0.12	0.16	0.39	0.59	0.78	0.98	1.17	1.37	1.56	1.76	1.95
Mexico 10 Centavos	1863-1904	2.71	0.903	0.079		0.08	0.16	0.24	0.32	0.79	1.19	1.58	1.98	2.37	2.77	3.16	3.56	3.95
Mexico 10 Centavos	1905-1914	2.50	0.800	0.064		0.06	0.13	0.19	0.26	0.64	0.96	1.28	1.60	1.92	2.24	2.56	2.88	3.20
Mexico 10 Centavos	1919	1.81	0.800	0.047		0.05	0.09	0.14	0.19	0.47	0.71	0.94	1.18	1.41	1.65	1.88	2.12	2.35
Mexico 10 Centavos	1925-1935	1.66	0.720	0.038		0.04	0.08	0.11	0.15	0.38	0.57	0.76	0.95	1.14	1.33	1.52	1.71	1.90
Mexico 20 Centavos	1898-1905	5.42	0.903	0.157		0.16	0.31	0.47	0.63	1.57	2.36	3.14	3.93	4.71	5.50	6.28	7.07	7.85
Mexico 20 Centavos	1905-1914	5.00	0.800	0.129		0.13	0.26	0.39	0.52	1.29	1.94	2.58	3.23	3.87	4.52	5.16	5.81	6.45
Mexico 20 Centavos	1919	3.63	0.800	0.093		0.09	0.19	0.28	0.37	0.93	1.40	1.86	2.33	2.79	3.26	3.72	4.19	4.65
Mexico 20 Centavos	1920-1943	3.33	0.720	0.077		0.08	0.15	0.23	0.31	0.77	1.16	1.54	1.93	2.31	2.70	3.08	3.47	3.85
Mexico 25 Centavos	1869-1892	6.77	0.903	0.197		0.20	0.39	0.59	0.79	1.97	2.96	3.94	4.93	5.91	6.90	7.88	8.87	9.85
Mexico 25 Centavos	1950-1953	3.33	0.300	0.032		0.03	0.06	0.10	0.13	0.32	0.48	0.64	0.80	0.96	1.12	1.28	1.44	1.60
Mexico 50 Centavos	1871-1895	13.54	0.903	0.393		0.39	0.79	1.18	1.57	3.93	5.90	7.86	9.83	11.79	13.76	15.72	17.69	19.65
Mexico 50 Centavos	1905-1918	12.50	0.800	0.322		0.32	0.64	0.97	1.29	3.22	4.83	6.44	8.05	9.66	11.27	12.88	14.49	16.10
Mexico 50 Centavos	1918-1919	9.06	0.800	0.233		0.23	0.47	0.70	0.93	2.33	3.50	4.66	5.83	6.99	8.16	9.32	10.49	11.65
Mexico 50 Centavos	1919-1945	8.33	0.720	0.193		0.19	0.39	0.58	0.77	1.93	2.90	3.86	4.83	5.79	6.76	7.72	8.69	9.65
Mexico 50 Centavos	1935	7.97	0.420	0.108		0.11	0.22	0.32	0.43	1.08	1.62	2.16	2.70	3.24	3.78	4.32	4.86	5.40
Mexico 50 Centavos	1950-1951	6.66	0.300	0.064		0.06	0.13	0.19	0.26	0.64	0.96	1.28	1.60	1.92	2.24	2.56	2.88	3.20
Mexico 1 Peso	1870-1914	27.07	0.903	0.786		0.79	1.57	2.36	3.14	7.86	11.79	15.72	19.65	23.58	27.51	31.44	35.37	39.30
Mexico 1 Peso	1918-1919	18.10	0.800	0.466		0.47	0.93	1.40	1.86	4.66	6.99	9.32	11.65	13.98	16.31	18.64	20.97	23.30
Mexico 1 Peso	1920-1945	16.66	0.720	0.386		0.39	0.77	1.16	1.54	3.86	5.79	7.72	9.65	11.58	13.51	15.44	17.37	19.30
Mexico 1 Peso	1947-1949	14.00	0.500	0.225		0.23	0.45	0.68	0.90	2.25	3.38	4.50	5.63	6.75	7.88	9.00	10.13	11.25
Mexico 1 Peso	1950	13.33	0.300	0.129		0.13	0.26	0.39	0.52	1.29	1.94	2.58	3.23	3.87	4.52	5.16	5.81	6.45
Mexico 1 Peso	1957-1967	16.00	0.100	0.051		0.05	0.10	0.15	0.20	0.51	0.77	1.02	1.28	1.53	1.79	2.04	2.30	2.55
Mexico 2 Pesos	1921	26.67	0.900	0.772		0.77	1.54	2.32	3.09	7.72	11.58	15.44	19.30	23.16	27.02	30.88	34.74	38.60
Mexico 5 Pesos	1947-1948	30.00	0.900	0.868		0.87	1.74	2.60	3.47	8.68	13.02	17.36	21.70	26.04	30.38	34.72	39.06	43.40
Mexico 5 Pesos	1950-1954	27.78	0.720	0.643		0.64	1.29	1.93	2.57	6.43	9.65	12.86	16.08	19.29	22.51	25.72	28.94	32.15
Mexico 5 Pesos	1955-1959	18.05	0.720	0.417		0.42	0.83	1.25	1.67	4.17	6.26	8.34	10.43	12.51	14.60	16.68	18.77	20.85

Country & Denomination	Years Minted	Grams Weight	Fineness	Troy (ASW)	Code	$ Value 1	$ Value 2	$ Value 3	$ Value 4	$ Value 10	$ Value 15	$ Value 20	$ Value 25	$ Value 30	$ Value 35	$ Value 40	$ Value 45	$ Value 50
Mexico 10 Pesos	1955-1960	28.88	0.900	0.836		0.84	1.67	2.51	3.34	8.36	12.54	16.72	20.90	25.08	29.26	33.44	37.62	41.80
Mexico 25 Pesos	1968, 1972	22.50	0.720	0.521		0.52	1.04	1.56	2.08	5.21	7.82	10.42	13.03	15.63	18.24	20.84	23.45	26.05
Mexico 25 Pesos	1985	7.78	0.720	0.180		0.18	0.36	0.54	0.72	1.80	2.70	3.60	4.50	5.40	6.30	7.20	8.10	9.00
Mexico 25 Pesos	1985, 1986	8.41	0.925	0.245		0.25	0.49	0.74	0.98	2.45	3.68	4.90	6.13	7.35	8.58	9.80	11.03	12.25
Mexico 25 Pesos	1992	7.78	0.999	0.250		0.25	0.50	0.75	1.00	2.50	3.75	5.00	6.25	7.50	8.75	10.00	11.25	12.50
Mexico 50 Pesos	1985	15.55	0.720	0.360		0.36	0.72	1.08	1.44	3.60	5.40	7.20	9.00	10.80	12.60	14.40	16.20	18.00
Mexico 50 Pesos	1985, 1986	16.83	0.925	0.500		0.50	1.00	1.50	2.00	5.00	7.50	10.00	12.50	15.00	17.50	20.00	22.50	25.00
Mexico 50 Pesos	1988, 1992	15.55	0.999	0.500		0.50	1.00	1.50	2.00	5.00	7.50	10.00	12.50	15.00	17.50	20.00	22.50	25.00
Mexico 100 Pesos	1977-1979	27.77	0.720	0.643		0.64	1.29	1.93	2.57	6.43	9.65	12.86	16.08	19.29	22.51	25.72	28.94	32.15
Mexico 100 Pesos	1985	31.10	0.720	0.720		0.72	1.44	2.16	2.88	7.20	10.80	14.40	18.00	21.60	25.20	28.80	32.40	36.00
Mexico 100 Pesos	1985-1987	32.63	0.925	1.000	N	1.00	2.00	3.00	4.00	10.00	15.00	20.00	25.00	30.00	35.00	40.00	45.00	50.00
Mexico 100 Pesos	1988, 1992	31.10	0.999	1.000	N	1.00	2.00	3.00	4.00	10.00	15.00	20.00	25.00	30.00	35.00	40.00	45.00	50.00
Mexico 100 Pesos	1991	32.63	0.925	1.000	N	1.00	2.00	3.00	4.00	10.00	15.00	20.00	25.00	30.00	35.00	40.00	45.00	50.00
Mexico 100 Pesos	1991	27.00	0.925	0.803	N	0.80	1.61	2.41	3.21	8.03	12.05	16.06	20.08	24.09	28.11	32.12	36.14	40.15
Mexico 200 Pesos	1986	62.21	0.999	2.000	N	2.00	4.00	6.00	8.00	20.00	30.00	40.00	50.00	60.00	70.00	80.00	90.00	100.00
Mexico 500 Pesos	1985	33.45	0.925	1.000	N	1.00	2.00	3.00	4.00	10.00	15.00	20.00	25.00	30.00	35.00	40.00	45.00	50.00
Mexico 1000 Pesos	1992	155.52	0.999	5.000	N	5.00	10.00	15.00	20.00	50.00	75.00	100.00	125.00	150.00	175.00	200.00	225.00	250.00
Mexico Nuevo Peso	1993-1998	7.77	0.999	0.250	N, V	0.25	0.50	0.75	1.00	2.50	3.75	5.00	6.25	7.50	8.75	10.00	11.25	12.50
Mexico 2 Nuevo Pesos	1993-1998	15.55	0.999	0.500	N, V	0.50	1.00	1.50	2.00	5.00	7.50	10.00	12.50	15.00	17.50	20.00	22.50	25.00
Mexico 5 Nuevo Pesos	1993	31.00	0.999	0.996	N	1.00	1.99	2.99	3.98	9.96	14.94	19.92	24.90	29.88	34.86	39.84	44.82	49.80
Mexico 5 Nuevo Pesos	1994-2000	27.00	0.925	0.803	N, S	0.80	1.61	2.41	3.21	8.03	12.05	16.06	20.08	24.09	28.11	32.12	36.14	40.15
Mexico 5 Nuevo Pesos	1993-2000	31.10	0.999	0.999	N, V	1.00	2.00	3.00	4.00	9.99	14.99	19.98	24.98	29.97	34.97	39.96	44.96	49.95
Mexico 5 Pesos	1996-2000	31.12	0.999	1.000	V	1.00	2.00	3.00	4.00	10.00	15.00	20.00	25.00	30.00	35.00	40.00	45.00	50.00
Mexico 5 Pesos	1999	19.60	0.925	0.641	N	0.64	1.28	1.92	2.56	6.41	9.62	12.82	16.03	19.23	22.44	25.64	28.85	32.05
Mexico 10 Nuevo Pesos	1992-1998	155.31	0.999	4.988	N, V	4.99	9.98	14.96	19.95	49.88	74.82	99.76	124.70	149.64	174.58	199.52	224.46	249.40
Mexico 10 Pesos	1999-2000	62.03	0.999	1.992		1.99	3.98	5.98	7.97	19.92	29.88	39.84	49.80	59.76	69.72	79.68	89.64	99.60
Mexico 50 Nuevo Pesos	1993-1996	15.55	0.925	0.500	N	0.50	1.00	1.50	2.00	5.00	7.50	10.00	12.50	15.00	17.50	20.00	22.50	25.00
Mexico 1/20 Onza	1991-2000	1.56	0.999	0.050		0.05	0.10	0.15	0.20	0.50	0.75	1.00	1.25	1.50	1.75	2.00	2.25	2.50
Mexico 1/10 Onza	1991-2000	3.11	0.999	0.100		0.10	0.20	0.30	0.40	1.00	1.50	2.00	2.50	3.00	3.50	4.00	4.50	5.00
Mexico 1/4 Onza	1991-2000	7.78	0.999	0.250		0.25	0.50	0.75	1.00	2.50	3.75	5.00	6.25	7.50	8.75	10.00	11.25	12.50
Mexico 1/2 Onza	1991-2000	15.55	0.999	0.500		0.50	1.00	1.50	2.00	5.00	7.50	10.00	12.50	15.00	17.50	20.00	22.50	25.00
Mexico 1 Onza	1949-1980	33.63	0.925	1.000	S	1.00	2.00	3.00	4.00	10.00	15.00	20.00	25.00	30.00	35.00	40.00	45.00	50.00
Mexico 1 Onza	1991-2000	31.10	0.999	1.000		1.00	2.00	3.00	4.00	10.00	15.00	20.00	25.00	30.00	35.00	40.00	45.00	50.00
Mexico 2 Onzas	1996-2000	62.21	0.999	2.000		2.00	4.00	6.00	8.00	20.00	30.00	40.00	50.00	60.00	70.00	80.00	90.00	100.00
Mexico 5 Onzas	1996-2000	155.52	0.999	2.000		2.00	4.00	6.00	8.00	20.00	30.00	40.00	50.00	60.00	70.00	80.00	90.00	100.00
Moldava 50 Lei	2000	13.50	0.985	0.527		0.53	1.05	1.58	2.11	5.27	7.91	10.54	13.18	15.81	18.45	21.08	23.72	26.35
Moldava 100 Lei	1996, 1998	28.28	0.925	0.841		0.84	1.68	2.52	3.36	8.41	12.62	16.82	21.03	25.23	29.44	33.64	37.85	42.05
Moldava 100 Lei	2000	31.10	0.925	0.925		0.93	1.85	2.78	3.70	9.25	13.88	18.50	23.13	27.75	32.38	37.00	41.63	46.25
Mombasa 2 Annas	1890	1.46	0.917	0.043		0.04	0.09	0.13	0.17	0.43	0.65	0.86	1.08	1.29	1.51	1.72	1.94	2.15
Mombasa 1/2 Rupee	1890	2.92	0.917	0.086		0.09	0.17	0.26	0.34	0.86	1.29	1.72	2.15	2.58	3.01	3.44	3.87	4.30
Mombasa 1/4 Rupee	1890	5.83	0.917	0.172		0.17	0.34	0.52	0.69	1.72	2.58	3.44	4.30	5.16	6.02	6.88	7.74	8.60
Mombasa 1 Rupee	1888	11.66	0.917	0.344		0.34	0.69	1.03	1.38	3.44	5.16	6.88	8.60	10.32	12.04	13.76	15.48	17.20
Monaco 5 Francs	1837	25.00	0.900	0.723		0.72	1.45	2.17	2.89	7.23	10.85	14.46	18.08	21.69	25.31	28.92	32.54	36.15

Country & Denomination	Years Minted	Grams Weight	Fineness	Troy (ASW)	Code	$ Value 1	$ Value 2	$ Value 3	$ Value 4	$ Value 10	$ Value 15	$ Value 20	$ Value 25	$ Value 30	$ Value 35	$ Value 40	$ Value 45	$ Value 50
Monaco 5 Francs	1960, 1966	12.00	0.835	0.322		0.32	0.64	0.97	1.29	3.22	4.83	6.44	8.05	9.66	11.27	12.88	14.49	16.10
Monaco 10 Francs	1966	25.00	0.900	0.723		0.72	1.45	2.17	2.89	7.23	10.85	14.46	18.08	21.69	25.31	28.92	32.54	36.15
Monaco 50 Francs	1974-1976	30.00	0.900	0.868		0.87	1.74	2.60	3.47	8.68	13.02	17.36	21.70	26.04	30.38	34.72	39.06	43.40
Monaco 100 Francs	1982-1999	15.00	0.900	0.434	s	0.43	0.87	1.30	1.74	4.34	6.51	8.68	10.85	13.02	15.19	17.36	19.53	21.70
Mongolia 10 Mongo	1925	1.80	0.500	0.029		0.03	0.06	0.09	0.12	0.29	0.44	0.58	0.73	0.87	1.02	1.16	1.31	1.45
Mongolia 15 Mongo	1925	2.70	0.500	0.043		0.04	0.09	0.13	0.17	0.43	0.65	0.86	1.08	1.29	1.51	1.72	1.94	2.15
Mongolia 20 Mongo	1925	3.60	0.500	0.058		0.06	0.12	0.17	0.23	0.58	0.87	1.16	1.45	1.74	2.03	2.32	2.61	2.90
Mongolia 50 Mongo	1925	10.00	0.900	0.289		0.29	0.58	0.87	1.16	2.89	4.34	5.78	7.23	8.67	10.12	11.56	13.01	14.45
Mongolia 1 Tugrik	1925	20.00	0.900	0.579		0.58	1.16	1.74	2.32	5.79	8.69	11.58	14.48	17.37	20.27	23.16	26.06	28.95
Mongolia 25 Tugrik	1976-1989	28.28	0.925	0.841	s	0.84	1.68	2.52	3.36	8.41	12.62	16.82	21.03	25.23	29.44	33.64	37.85	42.05
Mongolia 25 Tugrik	1980-1987	19.44	0.925	0.578	s	0.58	1.16	1.73	2.31	5.78	8.67	11.56	14.45	17.34	20.23	23.12	26.01	28.90
Mongolia 50 Tugrik	1976	35.00	0.925	1.040		1.04	2.08	3.12	4.16	10.40	15.60	20.80	26.00	31.20	36.40	41.60	46.80	52.00
Mongolia 50 Tugrik	1992, 1993	31.10	0.999	1.000		1.00	2.00	3.00	4.00	10.00	15.00	20.00	25.00	30.00	35.00	40.00	45.00	50.00
Mongolia 100 Tugrik	1989, 1990	28.00	0.900	0.810		0.81	1.62	2.43	3.24	8.10	12.15	16.20	20.25	24.30	28.35	32.40	36.45	40.50
Mongolia 250 Tugrik	1992, 1993	31.47	0.925	0.936		0.94	1.87	2.81	3.74	9.36	14.04	18.72	23.40	28.08	32.76	37.44	42.12	46.80
Mongolia 500 Tugrik	1995-1997	31.10	0.999	1.000		1.00	2.00	3.00	4.00	10.00	15.00	20.00	25.00	30.00	35.00	40.00	45.00	50.00
Mongolia 500 Tugrik	1996-1999	25.00	0.925	0.744	s, v	0.74	1.49	2.23	2.98	7.44	11.16	14.88	18.60	22.32	26.04	29.76	33.48	37.20
Mongolia 500 Tugrik	1997	15.00	0.925	0.446		0.45	0.89	1.34	1.78	4.46	6.69	8.92	11.15	13.38	15.61	17.84	20.07	22.30
Mongolia 500 Tugrik	1998, 1999	20.00	0.500	0.322	v	0.32	0.64	0.97	1.29	3.22	4.83	6.44	8.05	9.66	11.27	12.88	14.49	16.10
Mongolia 500 Tugrik	1998, 1999	31.46	0.999	1.000	v	1.00	2.00	3.00	4.00	10.00	15.00	20.00	25.00	30.00	35.00	40.00	45.00	50.00
Mongolia 1000 Tugrik	1996	156.61	0.999	5.000		5.00	10.00	15.00	20.00	50.00	75.00	100.00	125.00	150.00	175.00	200.00	225.00	250.00
Mongolia 1200 Tugrik	1996, 1997	7.70	0.999	0.250		0.25	0.50	0.75	1.00	2.50	3.75	5.00	6.25	7.50	8.75	10.00	11.25	12.50
Mongolia 2500 Tugrik	1995-1999	155.50	0.999	5.000	>	5.00	10.00	15.00	20.00	50.00	75.00	100.00	125.00	150.00	175.00	200.00	225.00	250.00
Mongolia 5000 Tugrik	1997	155.50	0.999	5.000		5.00	10.00	15.00	20.00	50.00	75.00	100.00	125.00	150.00	175.00	200.00	225.00	250.00
Mongolia 5000 Tugrik	1996, 1997	31.00	0.999	1.000	>	1.00	2.00	3.00	4.00	10.00	15.00	20.00	25.00	30.00	35.00	40.00	45.00	50.00
Mongolia 10,000 Tugrik	1996	1000.10	0.999	32.158		32.16	64.32	96.47	128.63	321.58	482.37	643.16	803.95	964.74	1125.53	1286.32	1447.11	1607.90
Montenegro 1 Perper	1909-1914	5.00	0.835	0.134	s	0.13	0.27	0.40	0.54	1.34	2.01	2.68	3.35	4.02	4.69	5.36	6.03	6.70
Montenegro 2 Perper	1909-1914	10.00	0.835	0.269	s	0.27	0.54	0.81	1.08	2.69	4.04	5.38	6.73	8.07	9.42	10.76	12.11	13.45
Montenegro 5 Perper	1909-1914	24.00	0.835	0.694	s	0.69	1.39	2.08	2.78	6.94	10.41	13.88	17.35	20.82	24.29	27.76	31.23	34.70
Morocco 1/2 Dirham	1881-1901	1.46	0.835	0.039	A, s	0.04	0.08	0.12	0.16	0.39	0.59	0.78	0.98	1.17	1.37	1.56	1.76	1.95
Morocco 1/20 Rial	1902, 1903	1.25	0.835	0.034	A	0.03	0.07	0.10	0.13	0.34	0.51	0.67	0.84	1.01	1.18	1.35	1.52	1.69
Morocco 1 Dirham	1881-1896	2.91	0.835	0.078	A, s	0.08	0.16	0.23	0.31	0.78	1.17	1.56	1.95	2.34	2.73	3.12	3.51	3.90
Morocco 1 Dirham / 1/10 Rial	1902-1912	2.50	0.835	0.067	A, s	0.07	0.13	0.20	0.27	0.67	1.01	1.34	1.68	2.01	2.35	2.68	3.02	3.35
Morocco 2-1/2 Dirhams	1895-1900	7.28	0.835	0.195	A	0.20	0.39	0.59	0.78	1.95	2.93	3.90	4.88	5.85	6.83	7.80	8.78	9.75
Morocco 2-1/2 Dirhams / ¼ Rial	1902-1912	6.25	0.835	0.168	A, s	0.17	0.34	0.50	0.67	1.68	2.52	3.36	4.20	5.04	5.88	6.72	7.56	8.40
Morocco 5 Dirhams	1895-1900	14.56	0.835	0.391	A, s	0.39	0.78	1.17	1.56	3.91	5.87	7.82	9.78	11.73	13.69	15.64	17.60	19.55
Morocco 5 Dirhams / ½ Rial	1902-1913	12.50	0.835	0.336	A, s	0.34	0.67	1.01	1.34	3.36	5.04	6.72	8.40	10.08	11.76	13.44	15.12	16.80
Morocco 10 Dirhams	1895	25.00	0.900	0.843	A	0.84	1.69	2.53	3.37	8.43	12.65	16.86	21.08	25.29	29.51	33.72	37.94	42.15
Morocco 10 Dirhams / 1 Rial	1902-1918	25.00	0.900	0.843	A, s	0.84	1.69	2.53	3.37	8.43	12.65	16.86	21.08	25.29	29.51	33.72	37.94	42.15
Morocco 5 Francs	1928-1933	5.00	0.680	0.109	A, s	0.11	0.22	0.33	0.44	1.09	1.64	2.18	2.73	3.27	3.82	4.36	4.91	5.45
Morocco 10 Francs	1928-1933	10.00	0.680	0.219	A, s	0.22	0.44	0.66	0.88	2.19	3.29	4.38	5.48	6.57	7.67	8.76	9.86	10.95
Morocco 20 Francs	1928-1933	20.00	0.680	0.437	A, s	0.44	0.87	1.31	1.75	4.37	6.56	8.74	10.93	13.11	15.30	17.48	19.67	21.85

Country & Denomination	Years Minted	Grams Weight	Fineness	Troy (ASW)	Code	$ Value 1	$ Value 2	$ Value 3	$ Value 4	$ Value 10	$ Value 15	$ Value 20	$ Value 25	$ Value 30	$ Value 35	$ Value 40	$ Value 45	$ Value 50
Morocco 100 Francs	1952	4.00	0.720	0.093	A	0.09	0.19	0.28	0.37	0.93	1.40	1.86	2.33	2.79	3.26	3.72	4.19	4.65
Morocco 200 Francs	1952	8.00	0.720	0.185	A	0.19	0.37	0.56	0.74	1.85	2.78	3.70	4.63	5.55	6.48	7.40	8.33	9.25
Morocco 500 Francs	1956	22.50	0.900	0.651	A	0.65	1.30	1.95	2.60	6.51	9.77	13.02	16.28	19.53	22.79	26.04	29.30	32.55
Morocco 1 Dirham	1960	6.00	0.600	0.116	A	0.12	0.23	0.35	0.46	1.16	1.74	2.32	2.90	3.48	4.06	4.64	5.22	5.80
Morocco 5 Dirham	1965	11.75	0.720	0.272	A	0.27	0.54	0.82	1.09	2.72	4.08	5.44	6.80	8.16	9.52	10.88	12.24	13.60
Morocco 50 Dirham	1975-1980	35.00	0.925	1.041	A	1.04	2.08	3.12	4.16	10.41	15.62	20.82	26.03	31.23	36.44	41.64	46.85	52.05
Morocco 100 Dirham	1983	25.00	0.925	0.743	A	0.74	1.49	2.23	2.97	7.43	11.15	14.86	18.58	22.29	26.01	29.72	33.44	37.15
Morocco 100 Dirhams	1985-1987	15.00	0.925	0.446	A	0.45	0.89	1.34	1.78	4.46	6.69	8.92	11.15	13.38	15.61	17.84	20.07	22.30
Morocco 150 Dirham	1980, 1981	35.00	0.925	1.041	A	1.04	2.08	3.12	4.16	10.41	15.62	20.82	26.03	31.23	36.44	41.64	46.85	52.05
Morocco 200 Dirhams	1987-1998	15.00	0.925	0.446	S	0.45	0.89	1.34	1.78	4.46	6.69	8.92	11.15	13.38	15.61	17.84	20.07	22.30
Morocco 250 Dirhams	2000	25.00	0.925	0.743		0.74	1.49	2.23	2.97	7.43	11.15	14.86	18.58	22.29	26.01	29.72	33.44	37.15
Mozambique 2-1/2 Escudos	1935-1951	3.50	0.650	0.073	S	0.07	0.15	0.22	0.29	0.73	1.10	1.46	1.83	2.19	2.56	2.92	3.29	3.65
Mozambique 5 Escudos	1935-1949	7.00	0.650	0.146	S	0.15	0.29	0.44	0.58	1.46	2.19	2.92	3.65	4.38	5.11	5.84	6.57	7.30
Mozambique 5 Escudos	1960	4.00	0.650	0.084		0.08	0.17	0.25	0.34	0.84	1.26	1.68	2.10	2.52	2.94	3.36	3.78	4.20
Mozambique 10 Escudos	1936-1938	12.50	0.835	0.336		0.34	0.67	1.01	1.34	3.36	5.04	6.72	8.40	10.08	11.76	13.44	15.12	16.80
Mozambique 10 Escudos	1952-1960	5.00	0.720	0.116	S	0.12	0.23	0.35	0.46	1.16	1.74	2.32	2.90	3.48	4.06	4.64	5.22	5.80
Mozambique 10 Escudos	1966	5.00	0.680	0.110		0.11	0.22	0.33	0.44	1.10	1.65	2.20	2.75	3.30	3.85	4.40	4.95	5.50
Mozambique 20 Escudos	1952-1960	10.00	0.720	0.232	S	0.23	0.46	0.70	0.93	2.32	3.48	4.64	5.80	6.96	8.12	9.28	10.44	11.60
Mozambique 20 Escudos	1966	10.00	0.680	0.219		0.22	0.44	0.66	0.88	2.19	3.29	4.38	5.48	6.57	7.67	8.76	9.86	10.95
Mozambique 250 Meticais	1985	28.28	0.925	0.841		0.84	1.68	2.52	3.36	8.41	12.62	16.82	21.03	25.23	29.44	33.64	37.85	42.05
Mozambique 500 Meticais	1980	19.40	0.800	0.499		0.50	1.00	1.50	2.00	4.99	7.49	9.98	12.48	14.97	17.47	19.96	22.46	24.95
Mozambique 500 Meticais	1989-1990	16.00	0.999	0.515		0.52	1.03	1.55	2.06	5.15	7.73	10.30	12.88	15.45	18.03	20.60	23.18	25.75
Mozambique 1000 Meticais	1988	28.28	0.925	0.841	N	0.84	1.68	2.52	3.36	8.41	12.62	16.82	21.03	25.23	29.44	33.64	37.85	42.05
Mozambique 1000 Meticais	1998	24.62	0.925	0.732		0.73	1.46	2.20	2.93	7.32	10.98	14.64	18.30	21.96	25.62	29.28	32.94	36.60
Mozambique 5000 Meticais	1997	411.42	0.999	13.214		13.21	26.43	39.64	52.86	132.14	198.21	264.28	330.35	396.42	462.49	528.56	594.63	660.70
Mozambique 10,000 Meticais	1994	20.00	0.999	0.643		0.64	1.29	1.93	2.57	6.43	9.65	12.86	16.08	19.29	22.51	25.72	28.94	32.15
Mozambique 10,000 Meticais	1994	21.06	0.999	0.676		0.68	1.35	2.03	2.70	6.76	10.14	13.52	16.90	20.28	23.66	27.04	30.42	33.80
Mozambique 10,000 Meticais	1997, 1998	822.85	0.999	26.429		26.43	52.86	79.29	105.72	264.29	396.44	528.58	660.73	792.87	925.02	1057.16	1189.31	1321.45
Muscat & Oman ½ Dhofari Rial	1947	14.03	0.500	0.226	A	0.23	0.45	0.68	0.90	2.26	3.39	4.52	5.65	6.78	7.91	9.04	10.17	11.30
Muscat & Oman ½ Saidi Rial	1960	14.03	0.500	0.226	A	0.23	0.45	0.68	0.90	2.26	3.39	4.52	5.65	6.78	7.91	9.04	10.17	11.30
Muscat & Oman Saidi Rial	1958	28.07	0.500	0.451	A	0.45	0.90	1.35	1.80	4.51	6.77	9.02	11.28	13.53	15.79	18.04	20.30	22.55
Muscat & Oman Saidi Rial	1958	28.07	0.833	0.752	A	0.75	1.50	2.26	3.01	7.52	11.28	15.04	18.80	22.56	26.32	30.08	33.84	37.60
Myanmar (Burma) 1 Pe*	1852	0.73	0.917	0.022		0.02	0.04	0.07	0.09	0.22	0.33	0.44	0.55	0.66	0.77	0.88	0.99	1.10
Myanmar (Burma) 1 Mu	1852	1.46	0.917	0.043		0.04	0.09	0.13	0.17	0.43	0.65	0.86	1.08	1.29	1.51	1.72	1.94	2.15
Myanmar (Burma) 5 Mu	1852	5.83	0.917	0.172		0.17	0.34	0.52	0.69	1.72	2.58	3.44	4.30	5.16	6.02	6.88	7.74	8.60
Myanmar (Burma) 1 Mat	1852	2.92	0.917	0.086		0.09	0.17	0.26	0.34	0.86	1.29	1.72	2.15	2.58	3.01	3.44	3.87	4.30
Myanmar (Burma) 1 Kyat	1852	11.66	0.917	0.344	V	0.34	0.69	1.03	1.38	3.44	5.16	6.88	8.60	10.32	12.04	13.76	15.48	17.20
Myanmar 500 Kyat	1998	20.00	0.925	0.595		0.59	1.19	1.78	2.38	5.95	8.92	11.89	14.87	17.84	20.81	23.79	26.76	29.74
N																		
Nagorno-Karab. 25,000 Drams*	1998	31.22	0.999	1.003		1.00	2.01	3.01	4.01	10.03	15.05	20.06	25.08	30.09	35.11	40.12	45.14	50.15
Nagorno-Karab. 25,000 Drams	1998	30.80	0.999	0.989		0.99	1.98	2.97	3.96	9.89	14.84	19.78	24.73	29.67	34.62	39.56	44.51	49.45
Nagorno-Karab. 50,000 Drams	1998	155.52	0.999	5.000		5.00	10.00	15.00	20.00	50.00	75.00	100.00	125.00	150.00	175.00	200.00	225.00	250.00

Country & Denomination	Years Minted	Grams Weight	Fine-ness	Troy (ASW)	Code	$ Value 1	$ Value 2	$ Value 3	$ Value 4	$ Value 10	$ Value 15	$ Value 20	$ Value 25	$ Value 30	$ Value 35	$ Value 40	$ Value 45	$ Value 50
Namibia 10 Dollars	1995	28.28	0.925	0.841		0.84	1.68	2.52	3.36	8.41	12.62	16.82	21.03	25.23	29.44	33.64	37.85	42.05
Namibia 10 Dollars	1995-2000	25.00	0.925	0.744	s	0.74	1.49	2.23	2.98	7.44	11.16	14.88	18.60	22.32	26.04	29.76	33.48	37.20
Namibia 20 Dollars	1998	155.52	0.999	5.000		5.00	10.00	15.00	20.00	50.00	75.00	100.00	125.00	150.00	175.00	200.00	225.00	250.00
Nauru Island 10 Dollars	1993-1995	31.47	0.925	0.936		0.94	1.87	2.81	3.74	9.36	14.04	18.72	23.40	28.08	32.76	37.44	42.12	46.80
Nauru Island 10 Dollars	1993	38.70	0.925	1.151		1.15	2.30	3.45	4.60	11.51	17.27	23.02	28.78	34.53	40.29	46.04	51.80	57.55
Nepal 20 Paisa*	1932-1953	2.22	0.333	0.024	s	0.02	0.05	0.07	0.10	0.24	0.36	0.48	0.60	0.72	0.84	0.96	1.08	1.20
Nepal 50 Paisa	1932-1953	5.54	0.333	0.059	s	0.06	0.12	0.18	0.24	0.59	0.89	1.18	1.48	1.77	2.07	2.36	2.66	2.95
Nepal 1 Rupee	1932-1952	11.08	0.800	0.285	s	0.29	0.57	0.86	1.14	2.85	4.28	5.70	7.13	8.55	9.98	11.40	12.83	14.25
Nepal 1 Rupee	1950	11.08	0.333	0.119		0.12	0.24	0.36	0.48	1.19	1.79	2.38	2.98	3.57	4.17	4.76	5.36	5.95
Nepal 10 Rupees	1968	15.60	0.600	0.301		0.30	0.60	0.90	1.20	3.01	4.52	6.02	7.53	9.03	10.54	12.04	13.55	15.05
Nepal 10 Rupees	1974	8.00	0.250	0.064		0.06	0.13	0.19	0.26	0.64	0.96	1.28	1.60	1.92	2.24	2.56	2.88	3.20
Nepal 20 Rupees	1975, 1979	15.00	0.500	0.239		0.24	0.48	0.72	0.96	2.39	3.59	4.78	5.98	7.17	8.37	9.56	10.76	11.95
Nepal 20 Rupees	1979	15.00	0.925	0.446		0.45	0.89	1.34	1.78	4.46	6.69	8.92	11.15	13.38	15.61	17.84	20.07	22.30
Nepal 25 Rupees	1974	25.60	0.500	0.412		0.41	0.82	1.24	1.65	4.12	6.18	8.24	10.30	12.36	14.42	16.48	18.54	20.60
Nepal 25 Rupees	1974-1975	28.28	0.925	0.841		0.84	1.68	2.52	3.36	8.41	12.62	16.82	21.03	25.23	29.44	33.64	37.85	42.05
Nepal 25 Rupees	1985	12.00	0.250	0.097		0.10	0.19	0.29	0.39	0.97	1.46	1.94	2.43	2.91	3.40	3.88	4.37	4.85
Nepal 50 Rupees	1974	31.80	0.500	0.511		0.51	1.02	1.53	2.04	5.11	7.67	10.22	12.78	15.33	17.89	20.44	23.00	25.55
Nepal 50 Rupees	1974	35.00	0.925	1.041		1.04	2.08	3.12	4.16	10.41	15.62	20.82	26.03	31.23	36.44	41.64	46.85	52.05
Nepal 50 Rupees	1974	25.00	0.925	0.744		0.74	1.49	2.23	2.98	7.44	11.16	14.88	18.60	22.32	26.04	29.76	33.48	37.20
Nepal 50 Rupees	1974	25.00	0.500	0.402		0.40	0.80	1.21	1.61	4.02	6.03	8.04	10.05	12.06	14.07	16.08	18.09	20.10
Nepal 50 Rupees	1981, 1982	15.00	0.500	0.239		0.24	0.48	0.72	0.96	2.39	3.59	4.78	5.98	7.17	8.37	9.56	10.76	11.95
Nepal 50 Rupees	1981	15.00	0.400	0.193		0.19	0.39	0.58	0.77	1.93	2.90	3.86	4.83	5.79	6.76	7.72	8.69	9.65
Nepal 100 Rupees	1974	25.00	0.500	0.402		0.40	0.80	1.21	1.61	4.02	6.03	8.04	10.05	12.06	14.07	16.08	18.09	20.10
Nepal 100 Rupees	1974	19.44	0.500	0.313		0.31	0.63	0.94	1.25	3.13	4.70	6.26	7.83	9.39	10.96	12.52	14.09	15.65
Nepal 100 Rupees	1981	25.50	0.500	0.405		0.41	0.81	1.22	1.62	4.05	6.08	8.10	10.13	12.15	14.18	16.20	18.23	20.25
Nepal 100 Rupees	1981	25.50	0.925	0.758		0.76	1.52	2.27	3.03	7.58	11.37	15.16	18.95	22.74	26.53	30.32	34.11	37.90
Nepal 100 Rupees	1983	31.10	0.925	0.925		0.93	1.85	2.78	3.70	9.25	13.88	18.50	23.13	27.75	32.38	37.00	41.63	46.25
Nepal 100 Rupees	1985	15.00	0.500	0.239		0.24	0.48	0.72	0.96	2.39	3.59	4.78	5.98	7.17	8.37	9.56	10.76	11.95
Nepal 100 Rupees	1995	12.00	0.600	0.232		0.23	0.46	0.70	0.93	2.32	3.48	4.65	5.81	6.97	8.13	9.29	10.45	11.62
Nepal 100 Rupees	1999	12.50	0.500	0.200		0.20	0.40	0.60	0.80	2.00	3.00	4.00	5.00	6.00	7.00	8.00	9.00	10.00
Nepal 200 Rupees	1987	15.00	0.600	0.289		0.29	0.58	0.87	1.16	2.89	4.34	5.78	7.23	8.67	10.12	11.56	13.01	14.45
Nepal 250 Rupees	1981, 1982	28.28	0.925	0.841		0.84	1.68	2.52	3.36	8.41	12.62	16.82	21.03	25.23	29.44	33.64	37.85	42.05
Nepal 250 Rupees	1986-1995	19.44	0.925	0.578		0.58	1.16	1.73	2.31	5.78	8.67	11.56	14.45	17.34	20.23	23.12	26.01	28.90
Nepal 300 Rupees	1986	25.30	0.500	0.407		0.41	0.81	1.22	1.63	4.07	6.11	8.14	10.18	12.21	14.25	16.28	18.32	20.35
Nepal 300 Rupees	1987	25.00	0.925	0.744		0.74	1.49	2.23	2.98	7.44	11.16	14.88	18.60	22.32	26.04	29.76	33.48	37.20
Nepal 300 Rupees	1990-1994	18.00	0.925	0.540	s, v	0.54	1.08	1.62	2.16	5.40	8.10	10.80	13.50	16.20	18.90	21.60	24.30	27.00
Nepal 350 Rupees	1987	23.30	0.500	0.375		0.38	0.75	1.13	1.50	3.75	5.63	7.50	9.38	11.25	13.13	15.00	16.88	18.75
Nepal 500 Rupee	1987	35.00	0.500	0.563		0.56	1.13	1.69	2.25	5.63	8.45	11.26	14.08	16.89	19.71	22.52	25.34	28.15
Nepal 500 Rupee	1989	31.10	0.999	0.999		1.00	2.00	3.00	4.00	9.99	14.99	19.98	24.98	29.97	34.97	39.96	44.96	49.95
Nepal 500 Rupee	1992, 1993	31.47	0.925	0.936		0.94	1.87	2.81	3.74	9.36	14.04	18.72	23.40	28.08	32.76	37.44	42.12	46.80
Nepal 500 Rupee	1992	31.83	0.925	0.947		0.95	1.89	2.84	3.79	9.47	14.21	18.94	23.68	28.41	33.15	37.88	42.62	47.35
Nepal 500 Rupee	1993	28.28	0.925	0.841		0.84	1.68	2.52	3.36	8.41	12.62	16.82	21.03	25.23	29.44	33.64	37.85	42.05
Nepal 500 Rupee	1994	35.20	0.900	1.000		1.00	2.00	3.00	4.00	10.00	15.00	20.00	25.00	30.00	35.00	40.00	45.00	50.00
Nepal 500 Rupee	1995	31.10	0.925	0.925		0.93	1.85	2.78	3.70	9.25	13.88	18.50	23.13	27.75	32.38	37.00	41.63	46.25
Nepal 500 Rupee	1995	31.35	0.999	1.007		1.01	2.01	3.02	4.03	10.07	15.11	20.14	25.18	30.21	35.25	40.28	45.32	50.35

Country & Denomination	Years Minted	Grams Weight	Fineness	Troy (ASW)	Code	$ Value 1	$ Value 2	$ Value 3	$ Value 4	$ Value 10	$ Value 15	$ Value 20	$ Value 25	$ Value 30	$ Value 35	$ Value 40	$ Value 45	$ Value 50
Nepal 500 Rupees	1997	19.44	0.925	0.578		0.58	1.16	1.73	2.31	5.78	8.67	11.56	14.45	17.34	20.23	23.12	26.01	28.90
Nepal 500 Rupee	1998	25.20	0.925	0.749		0.75	1.50	2.25	3.00	7.49	11.24	14.98	18.73	22.47	26.22	29.96	33.71	37.45
Nepal 600 Rupee	1988	31.10	0.999	0.999		1.00	2.00	3.00	4.00	9.99	14.99	19.98	24.98	29.97	34.97	39.96	44.96	49.95
Nepal 1000 Rupee	1988	155.52	0.999	5.000		5.00	10.00	15.00	20.00	50.00	75.00	100.00	125.00	150.00	175.00	200.00	225.00	250.00
Nepal 1500 Rupee	1997	31.10	0.925	0.925		0.93	1.85	2.78	3.70	9.25	13.88	18.50	23.13	27.75	32.38	37.00	41.63	46.25
Nepal 1500 Rupee	1998, 2000	20.00	0.925	0.595		0.60	1.19	1.79	2.38	5.95	8.93	11.90	14.88	17.85	20.83	23.80	26.78	29.75
Nepal 2000 Rupee	1996, 1998	31.24	0.999	1.003	>	1.00	2.01	3.01	4.01	10.03	15.05	20.06	25.08	30.09	35.11	40.12	45.14	50.15
Nepal 2000 Rupee	1998	20.00	0.925	0.595		0.60	1.19	1.79	2.38	5.95	8.93	11.90	14.88	17.85	20.83	23.80	26.78	29.75
Nepal 2000 Rupee	1988	31.17	0.999	1.011		1.01	2.02	3.03	4.04	10.11	15.17	20.22	25.28	30.33	35.39	40.44	45.50	50.55
Nepal 2500 Rupee	1993-1997	155.52	0.999	5.000	>	5.00	10.00	15.00	20.00	50.00	75.00	100.00	125.00	150.00	175.00	200.00	225.00	250.00
Netherlands 1 Rijksdaalder	1801-1816	28.08	0.868	0.784	S, V	0.78	1.57	2.35	3.14	7.84	11.76	15.68	19.60	23.52	27.44	31.36	35.28	39.20
Netherlands 5 Cents	1818-1828	0.08	0.569	0.015	S	0.02	0.03	0.05	0.06	0.15	0.23	0.30	0.38	0.45	0.53	0.60	0.68	0.75
Netherlands 5 Cents	1848-1887	0.69	0.640	0.014	S	0.01	0.03	0.04	0.06	0.14	0.21	0.28	0.35	0.42	0.49	0.56	0.63	0.70
Netherlands 10 Cents	1818-1828	1.69	0.569	0.031	S	0.03	0.06	0.09	0.12	0.31	0.47	0.62	0.78	0.93	1.09	1.24	1.40	1.55
Netherlands 10 Cents	1848-1945	1.40	0.640	0.029	S	0.03	0.06	0.09	0.12	0.29	0.44	0.58	0.73	0.87	1.02	1.16	1.31	1.45
Netherlands 25 Cents	1817-1830	4.23	0.569	0.077	S	0.08	0.15	0.23	0.31	0.77	1.16	1.54	1.93	2.31	2.70	3.08	3.47	3.85
Netherlands 25 Cents	1848-1945	3.58	0.640	0.074	S	0.07	0.15	0.22	0.30	0.74	1.11	1.48	1.85	2.22	2.59	2.96	3.33	3.70
Netherlands 1/2 Gulden	1818-1830	5.38	0.893	0.154	S	0.15	0.31	0.46	0.62	1.54	2.31	3.08	3.85	4.62	5.39	6.16	6.93	7.70
Netherlands 1/2 Gulden	1904-1919	5.00	0.945	0.152	S	0.15	0.30	0.46	0.61	1.52	2.28	3.04	3.80	4.56	5.32	6.08	6.84	7.60
Netherlands 1/2 Gulden	1921-1930	5.00	0.720	0.116	S	0.12	0.23	0.35	0.46	1.16	1.74	2.32	2.90	3.48	4.06	4.64	5.22	5.80
Netherlands 1 Florin	1807	10.53	0.912	0.310		0.31	0.62	0.93	1.24	3.10	4.65	6.20	7.75	9.30	10.85	12.40	13.95	15.50
Netherlands 1 Gulden	1808-1810	10.53	0.912	0.310		0.31	0.62	0.93	1.24	3.10	4.65	6.20	7.75	9.30	10.85	12.40	13.95	15.50
Netherlands 1 Gulden	1818-1837	10.77	0.893	0.309		0.31	0.62	0.93	1.24	3.09	4.64	6.18	7.73	9.27	10.82	12.36	13.91	15.45
Netherlands 1 Gulden	1840-1917	10.00	0.945	0.304		0.30	0.61	0.91	1.22	3.04	4.56	6.08	7.60	9.12	10.64	12.16	13.68	15.20
Netherlands 1 Gulden	1922-1945	10.00	0.720	0.232		0.23	0.46	0.70	0.93	2.32	3.48	4.64	5.80	6.96	8.12	9.28	10.44	11.60
Netherlands 1 Gulden	1954-1967	6.50	0.720	0.150	S	0.15	0.30	0.45	0.60	1.50	2.25	3.00	3.75	4.50	5.25	6.00	6.75	7.50
Netherlands 1 Gulden	1980	6.50	0.720	0.150	N	0.15	0.30	0.45	0.60	1.50	2.25	3.00	3.75	4.50	5.25	6.00	6.75	7.50
Netherlands 2-1/2 Gulden	1808	28.35	0.912	0.800		0.80	1.60	2.40	3.20	8.00	12.00	16.00	20.00	24.00	28.00	32.00	36.00	40.00
Netherlands 2-1/2 Gulden	1840-1874	25.00	0.945	0.759	S	0.76	1.52	2.28	3.04	7.59	11.39	15.18	18.98	22.77	26.57	30.36	34.16	37.95
Netherlands 2-1/2 Gulden	1929-1940	25.00	0.720	0.579	S	0.58	1.16	1.74	2.32	5.79	8.69	11.58	14.48	17.37	20.27	23.16	26.06	28.95
Netherlands 2-1/2 Gulden	1959-1966	15.00	0.720	0.347		0.35	0.69	1.04	1.39	3.47	5.21	6.94	8.68	10.41	12.15	13.88	15.62	17.35
Netherlands 3 Gulden	1817-1832	39.29	0.893	0.927		0.93	1.85	2.78	3.71	9.27	13.91	18.54	23.18	27.81	32.45	37.08	41.72	46.35
Netherlands 10 Gulden	1970-1973	25.00	0.720	0.579	S	0.58	1.16	1.74	2.32	5.79	8.69	11.58	14.48	17.37	20.27	23.16	26.06	28.95
Netherlands 10 Gulden	1994	15.00	0.720	0.347		0.35	0.69	1.04	1.39	3.47	5.21	6.94	8.68	10.41	12.15	13.88	15.62	17.35
Netherlands 10 Gulden	1995-1999	15.00	0.800	0.389	S	0.39	0.78	1.17	1.56	3.89	5.84	7.78	9.73	11.67	13.62	15.56	17.51	19.45
Netherlands 50 Gulden	1982-1998	25.00	0.925	0.744	S	0.74	1.49	2.23	2.98	7.44	11.16	14.88	18.60	22.32	26.04	29.76	33.48	37.20
Neth. Antilles 1/10 Gulden	1954-1970	1.40	0.640	0.029	S	0.03	0.06	0.09	0.12	0.29	0.44	0.58	0.73	0.87	1.02	1.16	1.31	1.45
Neth. Antilles 1/4 Gulden	1954-1970	3.58	0.640	0.074	S	0.07	0.15	0.22	0.30	0.74	1.11	1.48	1.85	2.22	2.59	2.96	3.33	3.70
Netherlands Antilles 1 Gulden	1952-1970	10.00	0.720	0.232	S	0.23	0.46	0.70	0.93	2.32	3.48	4.64	5.80	6.96	8.12	9.28	10.44	11.60
Neth. Antilles 2-1/2 Gulden	1964	25.00	0.720	0.579		0.58	1.16	1.74	2.32	5.79	8.69	11.58	14.48	17.37	20.27	23.16	26.06	28.95
Netherlands Antilles 10 Gulden	1978	25.00	0.720	0.580		0.58	1.16	1.74	2.32	5.80	8.70	11.60	14.50	17.40	20.30	23.20	26.10	29.00
Netherlands Antilles 25 Gulden	1973-1977	45.00	0.925	1.240		1.24	2.48	3.72	4.96	12.40	18.60	24.80	31.00	37.20	43.40	49.60	55.80	62.00
Netherlands Antilles 25 Gulden	1979	27.22	0.925	0.810		0.81	1.62	2.43	3.24	8.10	12.15	16.20	20.25	24.30	28.35	32.40	36.45	40.50

Country & Denomination	Years Minted	Grams Weight	Fine-ness	Troy (ASW)	Code	$ Value 1	$ Value 2	$ Value 3	$ Value 4	$ Value 10	$ Value 15	$ Value 20	$ Value 25	$ Value 30	$ Value 35	$ Value 40	$ Value 45	$ Value 50
Netherlands Antilles 25 Gulden	1990-2000	25.00	0.925	0.744		0.74	1.49	2.23	2.98	7.44	11.16	14.88	18.60	22.32	26.04	29.76	33.48	37.20
Netherlands Antilles 50 Gulden	1980	24.00	0.500	0.386		0.39	0.77	1.16	1.54	3.86	5.79	7.72	9.65	11.58	13.51	15.44	17.37	19.30
Netherlands Antilles 50 Gulden	1982	25.00	0.925	0.744		0.74	1.49	2.23	2.98	7.44	11.16	14.88	18.60	22.32	26.04	29.76	33.48	37.20
Neth. East Indies 1/10 Gulden	1854-1945	1.40	0.720	0.029		0.03	0.06	0.09	0.12	0.29	0.44	0.58	0.73	0.87	1.02	1.16	1.31	1.45
Neth. East Indies 1/4 Gulden	1854-1945	3.60	0.720	0.074		0.07	0.15	0.22	0.30	0.74	1.11	1.48	1.85	2.22	2.59	2.96	3.33	3.70
Neth. East Indies 1 Gulden	1943	10.00	0.720	0.232		0.23	0.46	0.70	0.93	2.32	3.48	4.64	5.80	6.96	8.12	9.28	10.44	11.60
Neth. East Indies 2-1/2 Gulden	1943	25.00	0.720	0.579		0.58	1.16	1.74	2.32	5.79	8.69	11.58	14.48	17.37	20.27	23.16	26.06	28.95
New Brunswick (Can.) 5 Cents	1862, 1864	1.16	0.925	0.035		0.04	0.07	0.12	0.16	0.35	0.60	0.80	0.88	1.05	1.23	1.40	1.58	1.75
New Brunswick (Can.) 10 Cents	1862, 1864	2.32	0.925	0.069		0.07	0.14	0.21	0.28	0.69	1.05	1.40	1.73	2.07	2.42	2.76	3.11	3.45
New Brunswick (Can.) 20 Cents	1862, 1864	4.65	0.925	0.138		0.14	0.28	0.42	0.56	1.38	2.10	2.80	3.45	4.14	4.83	5.52	6.21	6.90
New Hebrides 100 Francs	1966	25.00	0.835	0.671		0.67	1.34	2.01	2.68	6.71	10.07	13.42	16.78	20.13	23.49	26.84	30.20	33.55
New Zealand 3 Pence	1933-1946	1.40	0.500	0.023		0.02	0.05	0.07	0.09	0.23	0.35	0.46	0.58	0.69	0.81	0.92	1.04	1.15
New Zealand 6 Pence	1933-1946	2.83	0.500	0.045		0.05	0.09	0.14	0.18	0.45	0.68	0.90	1.13	1.35	1.58	1.80	2.03	2.25
New Zealand 1 Shilling	1933-1946	5.65	0.500	0.091		0.09	0.18	0.27	0.36	0.91	1.37	1.82	2.28	2.73	3.19	3.64	4.10	4.55
New Zealand 1 Florin	1933-1946	11.31	0.500	0.182		0.18	0.36	0.55	0.73	1.82	2.73	3.64	4.55	5.46	6.37	7.28	8.19	9.10
New Zealand 1/2 Crown	1933-1946	14.14	0.500	0.227		0.23	0.45	0.68	0.91	2.27	3.41	4.54	5.68	6.81	7.95	9.08	10.22	11.35
New Zealand 1 Crown	1935, 1949	28.28	0.500	0.455		0.46	0.91	1.37	1.82	4.55	6.83	9.10	11.38	13.65	15.93	18.20	20.48	22.75
New Zealand 5 Cents	1990	3.27	0.925	0.097	N	0.10	0.19	0.29	0.39	0.97	1.46	1.94	2.43	2.91	3.40	3.88	4.37	4.85
New Zealand 10 Cents	1990	6.53	0.925	0.194	N	0.19	0.39	0.58	0.78	1.94	2.91	3.88	4.85	5.82	6.79	7.76	8.73	9.70
New Zealand 20 Cents	1990	13.07	0.925	0.389	N	0.39	0.78	1.17	1.56	3.89	5.84	7.78	9.73	11.67	13.62	15.56	17.51	19.45
New Zealand 50 Cents	1990	15.74	0.925	0.468	N	0.47	0.94	1.40	1.87	4.68	7.02	9.36	11.70	14.04	16.38	18.72	21.06	23.40
New Zealand 1 Dollar	1974-1990	27.22	0.925	0.809	N, S	0.81	1.62	2.43	3.24	8.09	12.14	16.18	20.23	24.27	28.32	32.36	36.41	40.45
New Zealand 1 Dollar	1990	8.00	0.925	0.238	N	0.24	0.48	0.71	0.95	2.38	3.57	4.76	5.95	7.14	8.33	9.52	10.71	11.90
New Zealand 2 Dollars	1990, 1993	10.00	0.925	0.297	N	0.30	0.59	0.89	1.19	2.97	4.46	5.94	7.43	8.91	10.40	11.88	13.37	14.85
New Zealand 5 Dollars	1991	27.60	0.925	0.821	N	0.82	1.64	2.46	3.28	8.21	12.32	16.42	20.53	24.63	28.74	32.84	36.95	41.05
New Zealand 5 Dollars	1992-1996	27.22	0.925	0.809	N	0.81	1.62	2.43	3.24	8.09	12.14	16.18	20.23	24.27	28.32	32.36	36.41	40.45
New Zealand 5 Dollars	1993	31.47	0.925	0.936	N	0.94	1.87	2.81	3.74	9.36	14.04	18.72	23.40	28.08	32.76	37.44	42.12	46.80
New Zealand 5 Dollars	1995-1999	28.28	0.925	0.841	N	0.84	1.68	2.52	3.36	8.41	12.62	16.82	21.03	25.23	29.44	33.64	37.85	42.05
New Zealand 5 Dollars	1998	29.20	0.925	0.868	N	0.87	1.74	2.60	3.47	8.68	13.02	17.36	21.70	26.04	30.38	34.72	39.06	43.40
New Zealand 5 Dollars	1998	6.00	0.999	0.193	N	0.19	0.39	0.58	0.77	1.93	2.90	3.86	4.83	5.79	6.76	7.72	8.69	9.65
New Zealand 5 Dollars	1999	31.05	0.925	0.923	N	0.92	1.85	2.77	3.69	9.23	13.85	18.46	23.08	27.69	32.31	36.92	41.54	46.15
New Zealand 5 Dollars	2000	31.13	0.999	0.999	N	1.00	2.00	3.00	4.00	9.99	14.99	19.98	24.98	29.97	34.97	39.96	44.96	49.95
New Zealand 10 Dollars	1998	15.45	0.999	0.496	N	0.50	0.99	1.49	1.98	4.96	7.44	9.92	12.40	14.88	17.36	19.84	22.32	24.80
New Zealand 10 Dollars	2000	28.37	0.925	0.844		0.84	1.69	2.53	3.38	8.44	12.66	16.88	21.10	25.32	29.54	33.76	37.98	42.20
New Zealand 20 Dollars	1995	31.10	0.925	0.925		0.93	1.85	2.78	3.70	9.25	13.88	18.50	23.13	27.75	32.38	37.00	41.63	46.25
New Zealand 20 Dollars	1997	28.28	0.925	0.841		0.84	1.68	2.52	3.36	8.41	12.62	16.82	21.03	25.23	29.44	33.64	37.85	42.05
Newfoundland (Can.) 5 Cents	1865-1943	1.17	0.925	0.035	S	0.04	0.07	0.11	0.14	0.35	0.53	0.70	0.88	1.05	1.23	1.40	1.58	1.75
Newfoundland (Can.) 5 Cents	1944-1947	1.17	0.800	0.030		0.03	0.06	0.09	0.12	0.30	0.45	0.60	0.75	0.90	1.05	1.20	1.35	1.50
Newfoundland (Can.) 10 Cents	1865-1944	2.33	0.925	0.070	S	0.07	0.14	0.21	0.28	0.70	1.05	1.40	1.75	2.10	2.45	2.80	3.15	3.50
Newfoundland (Can.) 10 Cents	1945-1947	2.33	0.800	0.060		0.06	0.12	0.18	0.24	0.60	0.90	1.20	1.50	1.80	2.10	2.40	2.70	3.00

Country & Denomination	Years Minted	Grams Weight	Fine-ness	Troy (ASW)	Code	$ Value 1	$ Value 2	$ Value 3	$ Value 4	$ Value 10	$ Value 15	$ Value 20	$ Value 25	$ Value 30	$ Value 35	$ Value 40	$ Value 45	$ Value 50
Newfoundland (Can.) 20 Cents	1865-1912	4.71	0.925	0.140	s	0.14	0.28	0.42	0.56	1.40	2.10	2.80	3.50	4.20	4.90	5.60	6.30	7.00
Newfoundland (Can.) 25 Cents	1917, 1919	5.83	0.925	0.173		0.17	0.35	0.52	0.69	1.73	2.60	3.46	4.33	5.19	6.06	6.92	7.79	8.65
Newfoundland (Can.) 50 Cents	1870-1919	11.78	0.925	0.350	s	0.35	0.70	1.05	1.40	3.50	5.25	7.00	8.75	10.50	12.25	14.00	15.75	17.50
Nicaragua 5 Centavos	1880, 1887	1.25	0.800	0.032		0.03	0.06	0.10	0.13	0.32	0.48	0.64	0.80	0.96	1.12	1.28	1.44	1.60
Nicaragua 10 Centavos	1880-1936	2.50	0.800	0.064	s	0.06	0.13	0.19	0.26	0.64	0.96	1.28	1.60	1.92	2.24	2.56	2.88	3.20
Nicaragua 25 Centavos	1880	5.00	0.800	0.129		0.13	0.26	0.39	0.52	1.29	1.94	2.58	3.23	3.87	4.52	5.16	5.81	6.45
Nicaragua 25 Centavos	1912-1936	6.30	0.800	0.161	s	0.16	0.32	0.48	0.64	1.61	2.42	3.22	4.03	4.83	5.64	6.44	7.25	8.05
Nicaragua 50 Centavos	1912-1929	12.50	0.800	0.322	s	0.32	0.64	0.97	1.29	3.22	4.83	6.44	8.05	9.66	11.27	12.88	14.49	16.10
Nicaragua 1 Cordoba	1912	25.00	0.900	0.723		0.72	1.45	2.17	2.89	7.23	10.85	14.46	18.08	21.69	25.31	28.92	32.54	36.15
Nicaragua 1 Cordoba	1991	27.00	0.925	0.803		0.80	1.61	2.41	3.21	8.03	12.05	16.06	20.08	24.09	28.11	32.12	36.14	40.15
Nicaragua 1 Cordoba	1994	13.82	0.925	0.411		0.41	0.82	1.23	1.64	4.11	6.17	8.22	10.28	12.33	14.39	16.44	18.50	20.55
Nicaragua 1 Cordoba	1995	14.17	0.925	0.421		0.42	0.84	1.26	1.68	4.21	6.32	8.42	10.53	12.63	14.74	16.84	18.95	21.05
Nicaragua 1 Cordoba	1995	13.96	0.925	0.370		0.37	0.74	1.11	1.48	3.70	5.55	7.40	9.25	11.10	12.95	14.80	16.65	18.50
Nicaragua 5 Cordobas	1994, 1997	27.00	0.925	0.803		0.80	1.61	2.41	3.21	8.03	12.05	16.06	20.08	24.09	28.11	32.12	36.14	40.15
Nicaragua 10 Cordobas	1991	25.70	0.999	0.826		0.83	1.65	2.48	3.30	8.26	12.39	16.52	20.65	24.78	28.91	33.04	37.17	41.30
Nicaragua 10 Cordobas	1991	19.95	0.999	0.641		0.64	1.28	1.92	2.56	6.41	9.62	12.82	16.03	19.23	22.44	25.64	28.85	32.05
Nicaragua 10 Cordobas	1999	27.20	0.925	0.803		0.80	1.61	2.41	3.21	8.03	12.05	16.06	20.08	24.09	28.11	32.12	36.14	40.15
Nicaragua 20 Cordobas	1975	5.00	0.925	0.150		0.15	0.30	0.45	0.60	1.50	2.25	3.00	3.75	4.50	5.25	6.00	6.75	7.50
Nicaragua 50 Cordobas	1975	12.57	0.925	0.374		0.37	0.75	1.12	1.50	3.74	5.61	7.48	9.35	11.22	13.09	14.96	16.83	18.70
Nicaragua 50 Cordobas	1988	16.60	0.825	0.440		0.44	0.88	1.32	1.76	4.40	6.60	8.80	11.00	13.20	15.40	17.60	19.80	22.00
Nicaragua 50 Cordobas	2000	27.00	0.925	0.803		0.80	1.61	2.41	3.21	8.03	12.05	16.06	20.08	24.09	28.11	32.12	36.14	40.15
Nicaragua 100 Cordobas	1975	25.14	0.925	0.669		0.67	1.34	2.01	2.68	6.69	10.04	13.38	16.73	20.07	23.42	26.76	30.11	33.45
Nicaragua 250 Cordobas	1992	171.07	0.999	5.495		5.50	10.99	16.49	21.98	54.95	82.43	109.90	137.38	164.85	192.33	219.80	247.28	274.75
Nicaragua 500 Cordobas	1980	14.00	0.925	0.416		0.42	0.83	1.25	1.66	4.16	6.24	8.32	10.40	12.48	14.56	16.64	18.72	20.80
Nicaragua 500 Cordobas	1984	14.00	0.999	0.450		0.45	0.90	1.35	1.80	4.50	6.75	9.00	11.25	13.50	15.75	18.00	20.25	22.50
Nicaragua 2000 Cordobas	1988	16.60	0.825	0.440		0.44	0.88	1.32	1.76	4.40	6.60	8.80	11.00	13.20	15.40	17.60	19.80	22.00
Nicaragua 10,000 Cordobas	1989, 1990	20.00	0.999	0.643		0.64	1.29	1.93	2.57	6.43	9.65	12.86	16.08	19.29	22.51	25.72	28.94	32.15
Nicaragua 10,000 Cordobas	1990	26.00	0.999	0.835		0.84	1.67	2.51	3.34	8.35	12.53	16.70	20.88	25.05	29.23	33.40	37.58	41.75
Nicaragua 10,000 Cordobas	1990	26.40	0.999	0.848		0.85	1.70	2.54	3.39	8.48	12.72	16.96	21.20	25.44	29.68	33.92	38.16	42.40
Nicaragua 10,000 Cordobas	1990	20.40	0.999	0.655		0.66	1.31	1.97	2.62	6.55	9.83	13.10	16.38	19.65	22.93	26.20	29.48	32.75
Nicaragua 10,000 Cordobas	1990	25.90	0.999	0.832		0.83	1.66	2.50	3.33	8.32	12.48	16.64	20.80	24.96	29.12	33.28	37.44	41.60
Niger 10 Francs	1968	20.00	0.900	0.585		0.59	1.17	1.76	2.34	5.85	8.78	11.70	14.63	17.55	20.48	23.40	26.33	29.25
Niger 10 Francs	1968	24.54	0.900	0.710		0.71	1.42	2.13	2.84	7.10	10.65	14.20	17.75	21.30	24.85	28.40	31.95	35.50
Niger 500 Francs	1960	10.00	0.900	0.289		0.29	0.58	0.87	1.16	2.89	4.34	5.78	7.23	8.67	10.12	11.56	13.01	14.45
Niger 1000 Francs	1960	20.00	0.900	0.579		0.58	1.16	1.74	2.32	5.79	8.69	11.58	14.48	17.37	20.27	23.16	26.06	28.95
Nigeria 100 Naira	1994	28.28	0.925	0.841		0.84	1.68	2.52	3.36	8.41	12.62	16.82	21.03	25.23	29.44	33.64	37.85	42.05
Niue 1 Dollar	1996	10.00	0.500	0.161		0.16	0.32	0.48	0.64	1.61	2.42	3.22	4.03	4.83	5.64	6.44	7.25	8.05
Niue 5 Dollars	1991-1993	9.93	0.500	0.160		0.16	0.32	0.48	0.64	1.60	2.40	3.20	4.00	4.80	5.60	6.40	7.20	8.00
Niue 5 Dollars	1996	31.50	0.925	0.937		0.94	1.87	2.81	3.75	9.37	14.06	18.74	23.43	28.11	32.80	37.48	42.17	46.85
Niue 5 Dollars	1996	31.84	0.925	0.945		0.95	1.89	2.84	3.78	9.45	14.18	18.90	23.63	28.35	33.08	37.80	42.53	47.25
Niue 5 Dollars	1997-1999	31.30	0.925	0.930	v	0.93	1.86	2.79	3.72	9.30	13.95	18.60	23.25	27.90	32.55	37.20	41.85	46.50

Country & Denomination	Years Minted	Grams Weight	Fineness	Troy (ASW)	Code	$ Value 1	$ Value 2	$ Value 3	$ Value 4	$ Value 10	$ Value 15	$ Value 20	$ Value 25	$ Value 30	$ Value 35	$ Value 40	$ Value 45	$ Value 50
Niue 10 Dollars	1991	10.00	0.925	0.297		0.30	0.59	0.89	1.19	2.97	4.46	5.94	7.43	8.91	10.40	11.88	13.37	14.85
Niue 10 Dollars	1991-1992	31.50	0.999	1.010	>	1.01	2.02	3.03	4.04	10.10	15.15	20.20	25.25	30.30	35.35	40.40	45.45	50.50
Niue 10 Dollars	1992	31.47	0.925	0.936		0.94	1.87	2.81	3.74	9.36	14.04	18.72	23.40	28.08	32.76	37.44	42.12	46.80
Niue 10 Dollars	1997-2000	28.28	0.925	0.841		0.84	1.68	2.52	3.36	8.41	12.62	16.82	21.03	25.23	29.44	33.64	37.85	42.05
Niue 10 Dollars	1993	31.47	0.925	0.936		0.94	1.87	2.81	3.74	9.36	14.04	18.72	23.40	28.08	32.76	37.44	42.12	46.80
Niue 20 Dollars	1993	27.10	0.625	0.545		0.55	1.09	1.64	2.18	5.45	8.18	10.90	13.63	16.35	19.08	21.80	24.53	27.25
Niue 50 Dollars	1987-1988	28.28	0.925	0.841		0.84	1.68	2.52	3.36	8.41	12.62	16.82	21.03	25.23	29.44	33.64	37.85	42.05
Niue 50 Dollars	1988-1989	31.10	0.999	1.000		1.00	2.00	3.00	4.00	10.00	15.00	20.00	25.00	30.00	35.00	40.00	45.00	50.00
Niue 50 Dollars	1989-1990	38.20	0.925	1.136		1.14	2.27	3.41	4.54	11.36	17.04	22.72	28.40	34.08	39.76	45.44	51.12	56.80
Niue 50 Dollars	1990	28.56	0.925	0.898		0.90	1.80	2.69	3.59	8.98	13.47	17.96	22.45	26.94	31.43	35.92	40.41	44.90
Niue 50 Dollars	1993-1994	155.52	0.999	5.000	>	5.00	10.00	15.00	20.00	50.00	75.00	100.00	125.00	150.00	175.00	200.00	225.00	250.00
Niue 100 Dollars	1987-1990	155.52	0.999	5.000	>	5.00	10.00	15.00	20.00	50.00	75.00	100.00	125.00	150.00	175.00	200.00	225.00	250.00
Niue 200 Dollars	1987	311.04	0.999	10.000		10.00	20.00	30.00	40.00	100.00	150.00	200.00	250.00	300.00	350.00	400.00	450.00	500.00

North Korea-see Korea (North)

Country & Denomination	Years Minted	Grams Weight	Fineness	Troy (ASW)	Code	$ Value 1	$ Value 2	$ Value 3	$ Value 4	$ Value 10	$ Value 15	$ Value 20	$ Value 25	$ Value 30	$ Value 35	$ Value 40	$ Value 45	$ Value 50
Norway 2 Skilling	1801-1871	1.50	0.250	0.012	N,S	0.01	0.02	0.04	0.05	0.12	0.18	0.24	0.30	0.36	0.42	0.48	0.54	0.60
Norway 3 Skilling	1868-1873	2.25	0.250	0.018	S	0.02	0.04	0.05	0.07	0.18	0.27	0.36	0.45	0.54	0.63	0.72	0.81	0.90
Norway 4 Skilling	1809	2.05	0.250	0.017		0.02	0.03	0.05	0.07	0.17	0.26	0.34	0.43	0.51	0.60	0.68	0.77	0.85
Norway 4 Skilling	1825-1871	3.00	0.250	0.024	S	0.02	0.05	0.07	0.10	0.24	0.36	0.48	0.60	0.72	0.84	0.96	1.08	1.20
Norway 8 Skilling / ½ Mark	1809	2.73	0.375	0.033		0.03	0.07	0.10	0.13	0.33	0.50	0.66	0.83	0.99	1.16	1.32	1.49	1.65
Norway 8 Skilling / ½ Mark	1817, 1819	3.37	0.500	0.054		0.05	0.11	0.16	0.22	0.54	0.81	1.08	1.35	1.62	1.89	2.16	2.43	2.70
Norway 8 Skilling / ½ Mark	1825, 1827	1.93	0.875	0.054		0.05	0.11	0.16	0.22	0.54	0.81	1.08	1.35	1.62	1.89	2.16	2.43	2.70
Norway 12 Skilling	1845-1873	2.89	0.875	0.081	S	0.08	0.16	0.24	0.32	0.81	1.22	1.62	2.03	2.43	2.84	3.24	3.65	4.05
Norway 24 Skilling	1819	7.31	0.687	0.162		0.16	0.32	0.49	0.65	1.62	2.43	3.24	4.05	4.86	5.67	6.48	7.29	8.10
Norway 24 Skilling	1823-1865	5.78	0.875	0.163	S	0.16	0.33	0.49	0.65	1.63	2.45	3.26	4.08	4.89	5.71	6.52	7.34	8.15
Norway 1/15 Specie Daler	1801, 1802	3.37	0.500	0.054		0.05	0.11	0.16	0.22	0.54	0.81	1.08	1.35	1.62	1.89	2.16	2.43	2.70
Norway 1/5 Specie Daler	1801, 1803	7.31	0.875	0.162	S	0.16	0.32	0.49	0.65	1.62	2.43	3.24	4.05	4.86	5.67	6.48	7.29	8.10
Norway 1/3 Specie Daler	1801-1803	9.63	0.875	0.271		0.27	0.54	0.81	1.08	2.71	4.07	5.42	6.78	8.13	9.49	10.84	12.20	13.55
Norway 1/2 Specie Daler	1819-1873	14.45	0.875	0.407		0.41	0.81	1.22	1.63	4.07	6.11	8.14	10.18	12.21	14.25	16.28	18.32	20.35
Norway 1 Specie Daler	1819-1869	28.89	0.875	0.813	S	0.81	1.63	2.44	3.25	8.13	12.20	16.26	20.33	24.39	28.46	32.52	36.59	40.65
Norway 10 Ore	1874-1919	1.45	0.400	0.019	S	0.02	0.04	0.06	0.08	0.19	0.29	0.38	0.48	0.57	0.67	0.76	0.86	0.95
Norway 25 Ore	1876-1919	2.42	0.600	0.047	S	0.05	0.09	0.14	0.19	0.47	0.71	0.94	1.18	1.41	1.65	1.88	2.12	2.35
Norway 50 Ore	1874-1919	5.00	0.600	0.097	S	0.10	0.19	0.29	0.39	0.97	1.46	1.94	2.43	2.91	3.40	3.88	4.37	4.85
Norway 1 Krone	1875-1917	7.50	0.800	0.193	S	0.19	0.39	0.58	0.77	1.93	2.90	3.86	4.83	5.79	6.76	7.72	8.69	9.65
Norway 2 Kroner	1878-1914	15.00	0.800	0.386	S	0.39	0.77	1.16	1.54	3.86	5.79	7.72	9.65	11.58	13.51	15.44	17.37	19.30
Norway 10 Kroner	1964	20.00	0.900	0.571		0.57	1.14	1.71	2.28	5.71	8.57	11.42	14.28	17.13	19.99	22.84	25.70	28.55
Norway 25 Kroner	1970	29.00	0.900	0.816		0.84	1.63	2.52	3.36	8.16	12.60	16.80	20.40	24.48	28.56	32.64	36.72	40.80
Norway 50 Kroner	1978	27.00	0.925	0.803		0.80	1.61	2.41	3.21	8.03	12.05	16.06	20.08	24.09	28.11	32.12	36.14	40.15
Norway 50 Kroner	1991-1995	16.81	0.925	0.500	S	0.50	1.00	1.50	2.00	5.00	7.50	10.00	12.50	15.00	17.50	20.00	22.50	25.00
Norway 100 Kroner	1982	24.73	0.925	0.736		0.74	1.47	2.21	2.94	7.36	11.04	14.72	18.40	22.08	25.76	29.44	33.12	36.80
Norway 100 Kroner	1991-1993	33.62	0.925	1.000		1.00	2.00	3.00	4.00	10.00	15.00	20.00	25.00	30.00	35.00	40.00	45.00	50.00
Norway 100 Kroner	1999	33.80	0.925	1.005		1.01	2.01	3.02	4.02	10.05	15.08	20.10	25.13	30.15	35.18	40.20	45.23	50.25
Norway 175 Kroner	1989	26.50	0.925	0.788		0.79	1.58	2.36	3.15	7.88	11.82	15.76	19.70	23.64	27.58	31.52	35.46	39.40
Norway 200 Kroner	1980	26.80	0.625	0.539		0.54	1.08	1.62	2.16	5.39	8.09	10.78	13.48	16.17	18.87	21.56	24.26	26.95

Country & Denomination	Years Minted	Grams Weight	Fine-ness	Troy (ASW)	Code	$ Value 1	$ Value 2	$ Value 3	$ Value 4	$ Value 10	$ Value 15	$ Value 20	$ Value 25	$ Value 30	$ Value 35	$ Value 40	$ Value 45	$ Value 50
O																		
Oman 15 Baisa	1985	20.00	0.925	0.595	A	0.60	1.19	1.79	2.38	5.95	8.93	11.90	14.88	17.85	20.83	23.80	26.78	29.75
Oman 1/2 Rial	1988-1994	28.28	0.925	0.841	A, S	0.84	1.68	2.52	3.36	8.41	12.62	16.82	21.03	25.23	29.44	33.64	37.85	42.05
Oman 1/2 Rial	1992	15.00	0.925	0.446	A	0.45	0.89	1.34	1.78	4.46	6.69	8.92	11.15	13.38	15.61	17.84	20.07	22.30
Oman 1 Rial	1978	15.00	0.500	0.241	A	0.24	0.48	0.72	0.96	2.41	3.62	4.82	6.03	7.23	8.44	9.64	10.85	12.05
Oman 1 Rial	1982	15.00	0.925	0.441	A	0.44	0.88	1.32	1.76	4.41	6.62	8.82	11.03	13.23	15.44	17.64	19.85	22.05
Oman 1 Rial	1995	10.00	0.925	0.297	A	0.30	0.59	0.89	1.19	2.97	4.46	5.94	7.43	8.91	10.40	11.88	13.37	14.85
Oman 1 Rial	1995-1999	28.28	0.925	0.841	A	0.84	1.68	2.52	3.36	8.41	12.62	16.82	21.03	25.23	29.44	33.64	37.85	42.05
Oman 1 Rial	2000	27.87	0.925	0.829	A	0.83	1.66	2.49	3.32	8.29	12.44	16.58	20.73	24.87	29.02	33.16	37.31	41.45
Oman 2 Rials	1990	20.00	0.925	0.595	A	0.60	1.19	1.79	2.38	5.95	8.93	11.90	14.88	17.85	20.83	23.80	26.78	29.75
Oman 2-1/2 Rial	1976-1991	28.28	0.925	0.841	A, S	0.84	1.68	2.52	3.36	8.41	12.62	16.82	21.03	25.23	29.44	33.64	37.85	42.05
Oman 5 Rial	1976	35.00	0.925	1.041	A	1.04	2.08	3.12	4.16	10.41	15.62	20.82	26.03	31.23	36.44	41.64	46.85	52.05
Oman 5 Rial	1995	18.80	0.925	0.559	A	0.56	1.12	1.68	2.24	5.59	8.39	11.18	13.98	16.77	19.57	22.36	25.16	27.95
Oman 10 Rials	1995	23.20	0.925	0.690	A	0.69	1.38	2.07	2.76	6.90	10.35	13.80	17.25	20.70	24.15	27.60	31.05	34.50
Oman 20 Rials	1995	27.40	0.925	0.815	A	0.82	1.63	2.45	3.26	8.15	12.23	16.30	20.38	24.45	28.53	32.60	36.68	40.75
Oman 25 Rials	1995	31.70	0.925	0.943	A	0.94	1.89	2.83	3.77	9.43	14.15	18.86	23.58	28.29	33.01	37.72	42.44	47.15
P																		
Pakistan 100 Rupees	1976	28.28	0.925	0.841		0.84	1.68	2.52	3.36	8.41	12.62	16.82	21.03	25.23	29.44	33.64	37.85	42.05
Pakistan 100 Rupees	1977	20.44	0.925	0.608		0.61	1.22	1.82	2.43	6.08	9.12	12.16	15.20	18.24	21.28	24.32	27.36	30.40
Pakistan 150 Rupees	1976	35.00	0.925	1.041		1.04	2.08	3.12	4.16	10.41	15.62	20.82	26.03	31.23	36.44	41.64	46.85	52.05
Palau 5 Dollars	1992-2000	25.00	0.900	0.723	S	0.72	1.45	2.17	2.89	7.23	10.85	14.46	18.08	21.69	25.31	28.92	32.54	36.15
Palau 5 Dollars	1998-2000	24.64	0.900	0.713	S	0.71	1.43	2.14	2.85	7.13	10.70	14.26	17.83	21.39	24.96	28.52	32.09	35.65
Palau 5 Dollars	1999-2000	25.00	0.925	0.744		0.74	1.49	2.23	2.98	7.44	11.16	14.88	18.60	22.32	26.04	29.76	33.48	37.20
Palau 20 Dollars	1994-2000	155.00	0.999	4.999	V	5.00	10.00	15.00	20.00	49.99	74.99	99.98	124.98	149.97	174.97	199.96	224.96	249.95
Panama 2-1/2 Centesimos	1904	1.25	0.900	0.036		0.04	0.07	0.11	0.14	0.36	0.54	0.72	0.90	1.08	1.26	1.44	1.62	1.80
Panama 5 Centesimos	1904	2.50	0.900	0.072		0.07	0.14	0.22	0.29	0.72	1.08	1.44	1.80	2.16	2.52	2.88	3.24	3.60
Panama 10 Centesimos	1904	5.00	0.900	0.145		0.15	0.29	0.44	0.58	1.45	2.18	2.90	3.63	4.35	5.08	5.80	6.53	7.25
Panama 25 Centesimos	1904	12.50	0.900	0.362		0.36	0.72	1.09	1.45	3.62	5.43	7.24	9.05	10.86	12.67	14.48	16.29	18.10
Panama 50 Centesimos	1904	25.00	0.900	0.723		0.72	1.45	2.17	2.89	7.23	10.85	14.46	18.08	21.69	25.31	28.92	32.54	36.15
Panama 1/10 Balboa	1930-1961	2.50	0.900	0.072		0.07	0.14	0.22	0.29	0.72	1.08	1.44	1.80	2.16	2.52	2.88	3.24	3.60
Panama 1/4 Balboa	1930-1961	6.30	0.900	0.181		0.18	0.36	0.54	0.72	1.81	2.72	3.62	4.53	5.43	6.34	7.24	8.15	9.05
Panama 1/2 Balboa	1930-1961	12.50	0.900	0.362		0.36	0.72	1.09	1.45	3.62	5.43	7.24	9.05	10.86	12.67	14.48	16.29	18.10
Panama 1/2 Balboa	1966-1993	12.50	0.400	0.161	N, S	0.16	0.32	0.48	0.64	1.61	2.42	3.22	4.03	4.83	5.64	6.44	7.25	8.05
Panama 1 Balboa	1931-1974	26.73	0.900	0.774		0.77	1.55	2.32	3.10	7.74	11.61	15.48	19.35	23.22	27.09	30.96	34.83	38.70
Panama 1 Balboa	1975-1979	26.73	0.925	0.795		0.80	1.59	2.39	3.18	7.95	11.93	15.90	19.88	23.85	27.83	31.80	35.78	39.75
Panama 1 Balboa	1980-1985	20.74	0.500	0.333		0.33	0.67	1.00	1.33	3.33	5.00	6.66	8.33	9.99	11.66	13.32	14.99	16.65
Panama 5 Balboas	1970	35.70	0.925	1.062		1.06	2.12	3.19	4.25	10.62	15.93	21.24	26.55	31.86	37.17	42.48	47.79	53.10
Panama 5 Balboas	1972	35.00	0.900	1.013		1.01	2.03	3.04	4.05	10.13	15.20	20.26	25.33	30.39	35.46	40.52	45.59	50.65
Panama 5 Balboas	1975-1979	35.12	0.925	1.045	N	1.05	2.09	3.14	4.18	10.45	15.68	20.90	26.13	31.35	36.58	41.80	47.03	52.25
Panama 5 Balboas	1980-1985	23.33	0.500	0.375	N, V	0.38	0.75	1.13	1.50	3.75	5.63	7.50	9.38	11.25	13.13	15.00	16.88	18.75
Panama 5 Balboas	1982	24.16	0.925	0.719	N	0.72	1.44	2.16	2.88	7.19	10.79	14.38	17.98	21.57	25.17	28.76	32.36	35.95
Panama 10 Balboas	1978-1979	42.48	0.925	1.264	N	1.26	2.53	3.79	5.06	12.64	18.96	25.28	31.60	37.92	44.24	50.56	56.88	63.20
Panama 10 Balboas	1980, 1982	26.50	0.500	0.426		0.43	0.85	1.28	1.70	4.26	6.39	8.52	10.65	12.78	14.91	17.04	19.17	21.30

Country & Denomination	Years Minted	Grams Weight	Fine-ness	Troy (ASW)	Code	$ Value 1	$ Value 2	$ Value 3	$ Value 4	$ Value 10	$ Value 15	$ Value 20	$ Value 25	$ Value 30	$ Value 35	$ Value 40	$ Value 45	$ Value 50
Panama 10 Balboas	1999	31.00	0.925	0.922		0.92	1.84	2.77	3.69	9.22	13.83	18.44	23.05	27.66	32.27	36.88	41.49	46.10
Panama 20 Balboas	1971-1979	129.59	0.925	3.854		3.85	7.71	11.56	15.42	38.54	57.81	77.08	96.35	115.62	134.89	154.16	173.43	192.70
Panama 20 Balboas	1980-1985	119.88	0.500	1.927	S	1.93	3.85	5.78	7.71	19.27	28.91	38.54	48.18	57.81	67.45	77.08	86.72	96.35
Panama 20 Balboas	1981, 1983	118.57	0.500	1.906		1.91	3.81	5.72	7.62	19.06	28.59	38.12	47.65	57.18	66.71	76.24	85.77	95.30
Papua New Guinea 1 Shilling	1935-1945	5.60	0.925	0.170		0.17	0.34	0.51	0.68	1.70	2.55	3.40	4.25	5.10	5.95	6.80	7.65	8.50
Papua New Guinea 5 Kina	1975-1980	27.60	0.500	0.444	N	0.44	0.89	1.33	1.78	4.44	6.66	8.88	11.10	13.32	15.54	17.76	19.98	22.20
Papua New Guinea 5 Kina	1981-1984	28.28	0.925	0.841		0.84	1.68	2.52	3.36	8.41	12.62	16.82	21.03	25.23	29.44	33.64	37.85	42.05
Papua New Guinea 5 Kina	1992	23.33	0.925	0.694		0.69	1.39	2.08	2.78	6.94	10.41	13.88	17.35	20.82	24.29	27.76	31.23	34.70
Papua New Guinea 5 Kina	1994-1998	31.45	0.925	0.935	V	0.94	1.87	2.81	3.74	9.35	14.03	18.70	23.38	28.05	32.73	37.40	42.08	46.75
Papua New Guinea 5 Kina	1994	27.78	0.900	0.804		0.80	1.61	2.41	3.22	8.04	12.06	16.08	20.10	24.12	28.14	32.16	36.18	40.20
Papua New Guinea 5 Kina	1997	20.00	0.900	0.579		0.58	1.16	1.74	2.32	5.79	8.69	11.58	14.48	17.37	20.27	23.16	26.06	28.95
Papua New Guinea 10 Kina	1975-1983	41.60	0.925	1.237	N	1.24	2.47	3.71	4.95	12.37	18.56	24.74	30.93	37.11	43.30	49.48	55.67	61.85
Papua New Guinea 10 Kina	1977-1982	40.50	0.925	1.205	N, S, V	1.21	2.41	3.62	4.82	12.05	18.08	24.10	30.13	36.15	42.18	48.20	54.23	60.25
Papua New Guinea 10 Kina	1975-1983	41.60	0.925	1.237	N	1.24	2.47	3.71	4.95	12.37	18.56	24.74	30.93	37.11	43.30	49.48	55.67	61.85
Papua New Guinea 10 Kina	1982	35.60	0.925	1.059		1.06	2.12	3.18	4.24	10.59	15.89	21.18	26.48	31.77	37.07	42.36	47.66	52.95
Papua New Guinea 10 Kina	1991	42.12	0.925	1.253	N	1.25	2.51	3.76	5.01	12.53	18.80	25.06	31.33	37.59	43.86	50.12	56.39	62.65
Papua New Guinea 10 Kina	1998	155.50	0.999	4.994		4.99	9.99	14.98	19.98	49.94	74.91	99.88	124.85	149.82	174.79	199.76	224.73	249.70
Papua New Guinea 25 Kina	1994	136.00	0.925	4.045		4.05	8.09	12.14	16.18	40.45	60.68	80.90	101.13	121.35	141.58	161.80	182.03	202.25
Paraguay 1 Peso	1889	25.00	0.900	0.723		0.72	1.45	2.17	2.89	7.23	10.85	14.46	18.08	21.69	25.31	28.92	32.54	36.15
Paraguay 1 Guarani	1997, 2000	27.00	0.925	0.804	V	0.80	1.61	2.41	3.22	8.04	12.06	16.08	20.10	24.12	28.14	32.16	36.18	40.20
Paraguay 150 Guaranies	1972-1975	25.00	0.999	0.803		0.80	1.61	2.41	3.21	8.03	12.05	16.06	20.08	24.09	28.11	32.12	36.14	40.15
Paraguay 300 Guaranies	1968	26.60	0.925	0.616		0.62	1.23	1.85	2.46	6.16	9.24	12.32	15.40	18.48	21.56	24.64	27.72	30.80
Paraguay 1000 Guaranies	1987-1988	28.70	0.999	0.922		0.92	1.84	2.77	3.69	9.22	13.83	18.44	23.05	27.66	32.27	36.88	41.49	46.10
						0.00												
Peru 1/4 Real	1800-1822	0.85	0.896	0.024	S	0.02	0.05	0.07	0.10	0.24	0.37	0.49	0.61	0.73	0.85	0.98	1.10	1.22
Peru 1/4 Real	1826-1856	0.84	0.903	0.024	S	0.02	0.05	0.07	0.10	0.24	0.37	0.49	0.61	0.73	0.85	0.98	1.10	1.22
Peru 1/2 Real	1800-1821	1.69	0.896	0.049		0.05	0.10	0.15	0.19	0.49	0.73	0.97	1.22	1.46	1.70	1.95	2.19	2.44
Peru 1/2 Real	1826-1856	1.69	0.903	0.048		0.05	0.10	0.14	0.19	0.48	0.72	0.96	1.20	1.44	1.68	1.92	2.16	2.40
Peru 1/2 Real	1858-1882	1.25	0.900	0.036	S	0.04	0.07	0.11	0.14	0.36	0.54	0.72	0.90	1.08	1.26	1.44	1.62	1.80
Peru 1 Real	1800-1823	3.38	0.896	0.098		0.10	0.20	0.29	0.39	0.98	1.46	1.95	2.44	2.93	3.41	3.90	4.39	4.88
Peru 1 Real	1826-1856	3.38	0.903	0.098	S	0.10	0.20	0.29	0.39	0.98	1.47	1.96	2.45	2.94	3.43	3.92	4.41	4.90
Peru 1 Real	1859-1861	2.50	0.900	0.072		0.07	0.14	0.22	0.29	0.72	1.08	1.44	1.80	2.16	2.52	2.88	3.24	3.60
Peru 2 Reales	1800-1823	6.77	0.896	0.195	S	0.20	0.39	0.59	0.78	1.95	2.93	3.90	4.88	5.85	6.83	7.80	8.78	9.75
Peru 2 Reales	1825-1856	6.77	0.903	0.197	S	0.20	0.39	0.59	0.79	1.97	2.96	3.94	4.93	5.91	6.90	7.88	8.87	9.85
Peru 4 Reales	1800-1821	13.53	0.896	0.377		0.38	0.75	1.13	1.51	3.77	5.66	7.54	9.43	11.31	13.20	15.08	16.97	18.85
Peru 4 Reales	1835-1840	13.00	0.667	0.279		0.28	0.56	0.84	1.12	2.79	4.19	5.58	6.98	8.37	9.77	11.16	12.56	13.95
Peru 4 Reales	1842-1857	13.54	0.903	0.393		0.39	0.79	1.18	1.57	3.93	5.90	7.86	9.83	11.79	13.76	15.72	17.69	19.65
Peru 8 Reales	1800-1824	27.07	0.896	0.780	S	0.78	1.56	2.34	3.12	7.80	11.70	15.60	19.50	23.40	27.30	31.20	35.10	39.00
Peru 8 Reales	1825-1857	27.07	0.903	0.786	S	0.79	1.57	2.36	3.14	7.86	11.79	15.72	19.65	23.58	27.51	31.44	35.37	39.30
Peru 25 Centavos	1859	6.25	0.900	0.181		0.18	0.36	0.54	0.72	1.81	2.72	3.62	4.53	5.43	6.34	7.24	8.15	9.05
Peru 50 Centavos	1858, 1859	12.00	0.900	0.350		0.35	0.70	1.05	1.40	3.50	5.25	7.00	8.75	10.50	12.25	14.00	15.75	17.50
Peru 50 Centimos	1858	12.00	0.900	0.350		0.35	0.70	1.05	1.40	3.50	5.25	7.00	8.75	10.50	12.25	14.00	15.75	17.50
Peru 1/2 Dinero	1863-1917	1.25	0.900	0.036		0.04	0.07	0.11	0.14	0.36	0.54	0.72	0.90	1.08	1.26	1.44	1.62	1.80

Country & Denomination	Years Minted	Grams Weight	Fineness	Troy (ASW)	Code	$ Value 1	$ Value 2	$ Value 3	$ Value 4	$ Value 10	$ Value 15	$ Value 20	$ Value 25	$ Value 30	$ Value 35	$ Value 40	$ Value 45	$ Value 50
Peru 1 Dinero	1863-1916	2.50	0.900	0.072		0.07	0.14	0.22	0.29	0.72	1.08	1.44	1.80	2.16	2.52	2.88	3.24	3.60
Peru 1/5 Sol	1863-1917	5.00	0.900	0.145		0.15	0.29	0.44	0.58	1.45	2.18	2.90	3.63	4.35	5.08	5.80	6.53	7.25
Peru 1/2 Sol	1864-1917	12.50	0.900	0.362		0.36	0.72	1.09	1.45	3.62	5.43	7.24	9.05	10.86	12.67	14.48	16.29	18.10
Peru 1/2 Sol	1922-1935	12.50	0.500	0.201	S	0.20	0.40	0.60	0.80	2.01	3.02	4.02	5.03	6.03	7.04	8.04	9.05	10.05
Peru 1/2 Sol	1976	9.35	0.900	0.271		0.27	0.54	0.81	1.08	2.71	4.07	5.42	6.78	8.13	9.49	10.84	12.20	13.55
Peru 1 Sol	1864-1916	25.00	0.900	0.723	S	0.72	1.45	2.17	2.89	7.23	10.85	14.46	18.08	21.69	25.31	28.92	32.54	36.15
Peru 1 Sol	1922-1935	25.00	0.500	0.402	S	0.40	0.80	1.21	1.61	4.02	6.03	8.04	10.05	12.06	14.07	16.08	18.09	20.10
Peru 1 Peseta	1880	5.00	0.900	0.145		0.15	0.29	0.44	0.58	1.45	2.18	2.90	3.63	4.35	5.08	5.80	6.53	7.25
Peru 5 Pesetas	1880-1882	25.00	0.900	0.723		0.72	1.45	2.17	2.89	7.23	10.85	14.46	18.08	21.69	25.31	28.92	32.54	36.15
Peru 20 Soles	1965, 1966	8.00	0.900	0.231	>	0.23	0.46	0.69	0.92	2.31	3.47	4.62	5.78	6.93	8.09	9.24	10.40	11.55
Peru 50 Soles	1971	21.45	0.800	0.552		0.55	1.10	1.66	2.21	5.52	8.28	11.04	13.80	16.56	19.32	22.08	24.84	27.60
Peru 100 Soles	1973	22.45	0.800	0.577		0.58	1.15	1.73	2.31	5.77	8.66	11.54	14.43	17.31	20.20	23.08	25.97	28.85
Peru 200 Soles	1974-1977	22.00	0.800	0.570		0.57	1.14	1.71	2.28	5.70	8.55	11.40	14.25	17.10	19.95	22.80	25.65	28.50
Peru 400 Soles	1976	28.10	0.900	0.813		0.81	1.63	2.44	3.25	8.13	12.20	16.26	20.33	24.39	28.46	32.52	36.59	40.65
Peru 1000 Soles	1979	15.55	0.500	0.250		0.25	0.50	0.75	1.00	2.50	3.75	5.00	6.25	7.50	8.75	10.00	11.25	12.50
Peru 5000 Soles	1979	31.11	0.925	0.925		0.93	1.85	2.78	3.70	9.25	13.88	18.50	23.13	27.75	32.38	37.00	41.63	46.25
Peru 5000 Soles	1982	23.37	0.925	0.695		0.70	1.39	2.09	2.78	6.95	10.43	13.90	17.38	20.85	24.33	27.80	31.28	34.75
Peru 10000 Soles	1982	16.80	0.925	0.500		0.50	1.00	1.50	2.00	5.00	7.50	10.00	12.50	15.00	17.50	20.00	22.50	25.00
Peru 1/2 Inti	1989	16.80	0.925	0.500		0.50	1.00	1.50	2.00	5.00	7.50	10.00	12.50	15.00	17.50	20.00	22.50	25.00
Peru 100 Intis	1986	11.11	0.925	0.327		0.33	0.65	0.98	1.31	3.27	4.91	6.54	8.18	9.81	11.45	13.08	14.72	16.35
Peru 200 Intis	1986	22.04	0.925	0.654		0.65	1.31	1.96	2.62	6.54	9.81	13.08	16.35	19.62	22.89	26.16	29.43	32.70
Peru 1 Nuevo Sol	1991, 2000	27.00	0.925	0.803		0.80	1.61	2.41	3.21	8.03	12.05	16.06	20.08	24.09	28.11	32.12	36.14	40.15
Peru 1 Nuevo Sol	1994-1999	33.63	0.925	1.000		1.00	2.00	3.00	4.00	10.00	15.00	20.00	25.00	30.00	35.00	40.00	45.00	50.00
Peru 1 Nuevo Sol	1994	20.00	0.999	0.643		0.64	1.29	1.93	2.57	6.43	9.65	12.86	16.08	19.29	22.51	25.72	28.94	32.15
Peru 20 Nuevo Soles	1992	33.63	0.925	1.000	S	1.00	2.00	3.00	4.00	10.00	15.00	20.00	25.00	30.00	35.00	40.00	45.00	50.00
Peru 50 Nuevo Soles	1993	33.63	0.925	1.000	N	1.00	2.00	3.00	4.00	10.00	15.00	20.00	25.00	30.00	35.00	40.00	45.00	50.00
Philippines 10 Centimos*	1864-1868	2.60	0.900	0.075		0.08	0.15	0.23	0.30	0.75	1.13	1.50	1.88	2.25	2.63	3.00	3.38	3.75
Philippines 10 Centimos	1880-1885	2.60	0.835	0.070		0.07	0.14	0.21	0.28	0.70	1.05	1.40	1.75	2.10	2.45	2.80	3.15	3.50
Philippines 10 Centavos	1903-1906	2.69	0.900	0.078		0.08	0.16	0.23	0.31	0.78	1.17	1.56	1.95	2.34	2.73	3.12	3.51	3.90
Philippines 10 Centavos	1907-1945	2.00	0.750	0.048	S	0.05	0.10	0.14	0.19	0.48	0.72	0.96	1.20	1.44	1.68	1.92	2.16	2.40
Philippines 20 Centavos	1903-1906	5.38	0.900	0.156		0.16	0.31	0.47	0.62	1.56	2.34	3.12	3.90	4.68	5.46	6.24	7.02	7.80
Philippines 20 Centavos	1907-1945	4.00	0.750	0.097	S	0.10	0.19	0.29	0.39	0.97	1.46	1.94	2.43	2.91	3.40	3.88	4.37	4.85
Philippines 50 Centavos	1903-1905	13.48	0.900	0.390		0.39	0.78	1.17	1.56	3.90	5.85	7.80	9.75	11.70	13.65	15.60	17.55	19.50
Philippines 50 Centavos	1907-1947	10.00	0.750	0.241	S	0.24	0.48	0.72	0.96	2.41	3.62	4.82	6.03	7.23	8.44	9.64	10.85	12.05
Philippines 1/2 Peso	1961	12.50	0.900	0.362		0.36	0.72	1.09	1.45	3.62	5.43	7.24	9.05	10.86	12.67	14.48	16.29	18.10
Philippines 1 Peso	1897	25.00	0.900	0.723		0.72	1.45	2.17	2.89	7.23	10.85	14.46	18.08	21.69	25.31	28.92	32.54	36.15
Philippines 1 Peso	1903-1905	26.96	0.900	0.780		0.78	1.56	2.34	3.12	7.80	11.70	15.60	19.50	23.40	27.30	31.20	35.10	39.00
Philippines 1 Peso	1907-1912	20.00	0.800	0.514		0.51	1.03	1.54	2.06	5.14	7.71	10.28	12.85	15.42	17.99	20.56	23.13	25.70
Philippines 1 Peso	1947	20.00	0.900	0.579		0.58	1.16	1.74	2.32	5.79	8.69	11.58	14.48	17.37	20.27	23.16	26.06	28.95
Philippines 1 Piso	1961-1967	26.00	0.900	0.752	S	0.75	1.50	2.26	3.01	7.52	11.28	15.04	18.80	22.56	26.32	30.08	33.84	37.60
Philippines 1 Piso	1969, 1970	26.45	0.900	0.765		0.77	1.53	2.30	3.06	7.65	11.48	15.30	19.13	22.95	26.78	30.60	34.43	38.25
Philippines 25 Pisos	1974	26.40	0.900	0.764		0.76	1.53	2.29	3.06	7.64	11.46	15.28	19.10	22.92	26.74	30.56	34.38	38.20
Philippines 25 Pisos	1975-1982	25.00	0.500	0.402		0.40	0.80	1.21	1.61	4.02	6.03	8.04	10.05	12.06	14.07	16.08	18.09	20.10
Philippines 25 Pisos	1986	18.41	0.925	0.548		0.55	1.10	1.64	2.19	5.48	8.22	10.96	13.70	16.44	19.18	21.92	24.66	27.40

Country & Denomination	Years Minted	Grams Weight	Fine-ness	Troy (ASW)	Code	$ Value 1	$ Value 2	$ Value 3	$ Value 4	$ Value 10	$ Value 15	$ Value 20	$ Value 25	$ Value 30	$ Value 35	$ Value 40	$ Value 45	$ Value 50
Philippines 50 Pisos	1975-1982	27.40	0.925	0.815	S	0.82	1.63	2.45	3.26	8.15	12.23	16.30	20.38	24.45	28.53	32.60	36.68	40.75
Philippines 100 Pisos	1983	25.00	0.500	0.402		0.40	0.80	1.21	1.61	4.02	6.03	8.04	10.05	12.06	14.07	16.08	18.09	20.10
Philippines 100 Pisos	1994	10.00	0.925	0.297		0.30	0.59	0.89	1.19	2.97	4.46	5.94	7.43	8.91	10.40	11.88	13.37	14.85
Philippines 100 Pisos	1994	16.73	0.800	0.430		0.43	0.86	1.29	1.72	4.30	6.45	8.60	10.75	12.90	15.05	17.20	19.35	21.50
Philippines 150 Pisos	1991	16.82	0.925	0.500		0.50	1.00	1.50	2.00	5.00	7.50	10.00	12.50	15.00	17.50	20.00	22.50	25.00
Philippines 200 Pisos	1987,1990	25.00	0.925	0.744		0.74	1.49	2.23	2.98	7.44	11.16	14.88	18.60	22.32	26.04	29.76	33.48	37.20
Philippines 200 Pisos	1994	15.56	0.999	0.500		0.50	1.00	1.50	2.00	5.00	7.50	10.00	12.50	15.00	17.50	20.00	22.50	25.00
Philippines 500 Pisos	1988	28.00	0.925	0.744		0.74	1.49	2.23	2.98	7.44	11.16	14.88	18.60	22.32	26.04	29.76	33.48	37.20
Philippines 500 Pisos	1994	23.10	0.925	0.687		0.69	1.37	2.06	2.75	6.87	10.31	13.74	17.18	20.61	24.05	27.48	30.92	34.35
Philippines 500 Pisos	1997-1999	28.28	0.925	0.841		0.84	1.68	2.52	3.36	8.41	12.62	16.82	21.03	25.23	29.44	33.64	37.85	42.05
Philippines 1000 Pisos	1994	31.10	0.999	0.999		1.00	2.00	3.00	4.00	9.99	14.99	19.98	24.98	29.97	34.97	39.96	44.96	49.95
Pitcairn Islands 1 Dollar	1988-1990	28.28	0.925	0.841	N	0.84	1.68	2.52	3.36	8.41	12.62	16.82	21.03	25.23	29.44	33.64	37.85	42.05
Pitcairn Islands 5 Dollars	1997	31.56	0.925	0.939		0.94	1.88	2.82	3.76	9.39	14.09	18.78	23.48	28.17	32.87	37.56	42.26	46.95
Pitcairn Islands 50 Dollars	1988-1990	155.60	0.999	5.000		5.00	10.00	15.00	20.00	50.00	75.00	100.00	125.00	150.00	175.00	200.00	225.00	250.00
Poland 5 Groszy	1811, 1812	2.20	0.210	0.015		0.02	0.03	0.05	0.06	0.15	0.23	0.30	0.38	0.45	0.53	0.60	0.68	0.75
Poland 5 Groszy	1816-1832	1.45	0.192	0.009		0.01	0.02	0.03	0.04	0.09	0.14	0.18	0.23	0.27	0.32	0.36	0.41	0.45
Poland 10 Groszy	1810-1813	2.99	0.245	0.024	S	0.02	0.05	0.07	0.10	0.24	0.36	0.48	0.60	0.72	0.84	0.96	1.08	1.20
Poland 10 Groszy	1816-1840	2.90	0.192	0.018	S	0.02	0.04	0.05	0.07	0.18	0.27	0.36	0.45	0.54	0.63	0.72	0.81	0.90
Poland 10 Groszy	1831	2.80	0.192	0.017		0.02	0.03	0.05	0.07	0.17	0.26	0.34	0.43	0.51	0.60	0.68	0.77	0.85
Poland 40 Groszy	1842-1850	4.10	0.868	0.114	S	0.11	0.23	0.34	0.46	1.14	1.71	2.28	2.85	3.42	3.99	4.56	5.13	5.70
Poland 50 Groszy	1842-1850	5.18	0.868	0.145	S	0.15	0.29	0.44	0.58	1.45	2.18	2.90	3.63	4.35	5.08	5.80	6.53	7.25
Poland 1/6 Talara	1811-1814	4.98	0.535	0.086		0.09	0.17	0.26	0.34	0.86	1.29	1.72	2.15	2.58	3.01	3.44	3.87	4.30
Poland 1/3 Talara	1810-1814	8.66	0.625	0.174		0.17	0.35	0.52	0.70	1.74	2.61	3.48	4.35	5.22	6.09	6.96	7.83	8.70
Poland 1 Talar	1811-1814	22.92	0.720	0.531	S	0.53	1.06	1.59	2.12	5.31	7.97	10.62	13.28	15.93	18.59	21.24	23.90	26.55
Poland 1 Zloty	1818-1834	4.55	0.593	0.087		0.09	0.17	0.26	0.35	0.87	1.31	1.74	2.18	2.61	3.05	3.48	3.92	4.35
Poland 1 Zloty	1832-1841	3.07	0.868	0.086		0.09	0.17	0.26	0.34	0.86	1.29	1.72	2.15	2.58	3.01	3.44	3.87	4.30
Poland 1 Zloty	1924-1925	5.00	0.750	0.121		0.12	0.24	0.36	0.48	1.21	1.82	2.42	3.03	3.63	4.24	4.84	5.45	6.05
Poland 2 Zlote	1816-1830	9.09	0.593	0.173	S	0.17	0.35	0.52	0.69	1.73	2.60	3.46	4.33	5.19	6.06	6.92	7.79	8.65
Poland 2 Zlote	1831	8.98	0.593	0.171		0.17	0.34	0.51	0.68	1.71	2.57	3.42	4.28	5.13	5.99	6.84	7.70	8.55
Poland 2 Zlote	1834-1841	6.21	0.868	0.173		0.17	0.35	0.52	0.69	1.73	2.60	3.46	4.33	5.19	6.06	6.92	7.79	8.65
Poland 2 Zlote	1924-1925	10.00	0.750	0.240	S	0.24	0.48	0.72	0.96	2.40	3.60	4.80	6.00	7.20	8.40	9.60	10.80	12.00
Poland 2 Zlote	1932-1936	4.40	0.750	0.106	S	0.11	0.21	0.32	0.42	1.06	1.59	2.12	2.65	3.18	3.71	4.24	4.77	5.30
Poland 5 Zlotych	1816-1833	15.59	0.868	0.435	S	0.44	0.87	1.31	1.74	4.35	6.53	8.70	10.88	13.05	15.23	17.40	19.58	21.75
Poland 5 Zlotych	1833-1841	15.54	0.868	0.434		0.43	0.87	1.30	1.74	4.34	6.51	8.68	10.85	13.02	15.19	17.36	19.53	21.70
Poland 5 Zlotych	1831	15.49	0.868	0.432		0.43	0.86	1.30	1.73	4.32	6.48	8.64	10.80	12.96	15.12	17.28	19.44	21.60
Poland 5 Zlotych	1925	25.00	0.900	0.723	N	0.72	1.45	2.17	2.89	7.23	10.85	14.46	18.08	21.69	25.31	28.92	32.54	36.15
Poland 5 Zlotych	1928-1932	18.00	0.750	0.424	S	0.42	0.85	1.27	1.70	4.24	6.36	8.48	10.60	12.72	14.84	16.96	19.08	21.20
Poland 5 Zlotych	1932-1936	11.00	0.750	0.265	S	0.27	0.53	0.80	1.06	2.65	3.98	5.30	6.63	7.95	9.28	10.60	11.93	13.25
Poland 10 Zlotych	1820-1841	31.10	0.868	0.868	S	0.87	1.74	2.60	3.47	8.68	13.02	17.36	21.70	26.04	30.38	34.72	39.06	43.40
Poland 10 Zlotych	1932-1939	22.00	0.750	0.531		0.53	1.06	1.59	2.12	5.31	7.97	10.62	13.28	15.93	18.59	21.24	23.90	26.55
Poland 100 Zlotych	1966	20.10	0.900	0.579		0.58	1.16	1.74	2.32	5.79	8.69	11.58	14.48	17.37	20.27	23.16	26.06	28.95
Poland 100 Zlotych	1973-1983	16.50	0.625	0.332		0.33	0.66	1.00	1.33	3.32	4.98	6.64	8.30	9.96	11.62	13.28	14.94	16.60
Poland 100 Zlotych	1982-1986	14.15	0.750	0.341	S	0.34	0.68	1.02	1.36	3.41	5.12	6.82	8.53	10.23	11.94	13.64	15.35	17.05

Country & Denomination	Years Minted	Grams Weight	Fineness	Troy (ASW)	Code	$ Value 1	$ Value 2	$ Value 3	$ Value 4	$ Value 10	$ Value 15	$ Value 20	$ Value 25	$ Value 30	$ Value 35	$ Value 40	$ Value 45	$ Value 50
Poland 200 Zlotych	1974-1976	14.47	0.625	0.291		0.29	0.58	0.87	1.16	2.91	4.37	5.82	7.28	8.73	10.19	11.64	13.10	14.55
Poland 200 Zlotych	1979-1984	17.60	0.750	0.424		0.42	0.85	1.27	1.70	4.24	6.36	8.48	10.60	12.72	14.84	16.96	19.08	21.20
Poland 200 Zlotych	1982-1986	28.30	0.750	0.683	S	0.68	1.37	2.05	2.73	6.83	10.25	13.66	17.08	20.49	23.91	27.32	30.74	34.15
Poland 500 Zlotych	1984	16.50	0.625	0.328		0.33	0.66	0.98	1.31	3.28	4.92	6.56	8.20	9.84	11.48	13.12	14.76	16.40
Poland 500 Zlotych	1985-1988	16.50	0.750	0.398		0.40	0.80	1.19	1.59	3.98	5.97	7.96	9.95	11.94	13.93	15.92	17.91	19.90
Poland 1000 Zlotych	1982-1983	14.50	0.750	0.350		0.35	0.70	1.05	1.40	3.50	5.25	7.00	8.75	10.50	12.25	14.00	15.75	17.50
Poland 5000 Zlotych	1989	16.50	0.750	0.398		0.40	0.80	1.19	1.59	3.98	5.97	7.96	9.95	11.94	13.93	15.92	17.91	19.90
Poland 10,000 Zlotych	1986	28.31	0.900	0.819		0.82	1.64	2.46	3.28	8.19	12.29	16.38	20.48	24.57	28.67	32.76	36.86	40.95
Poland 10,000 Zlotych	1987	19.06	0.750	0.458		0.46	0.92	1.37	1.83	4.58	6.87	9.16	11.45	13.74	16.03	18.32	20.61	22.90
Poland 10,000 Zlotych	1988-1989	31.10	0.999	1.000		1.00	2.00	3.00	4.00	10.00	15.00	20.00	25.00	30.00	35.00	40.00	45.00	50.00
Poland 20,000 Zlotych	1989	19.00	0.750	0.456		0.46	0.91	1.37	1.82	4.56	6.84	9.12	11.40	13.68	15.96	18.24	20.52	22.80
Poland 50,000 Zlotych	1988	19.30	0.750	0.465		0.47	0.93	1.40	1.86	4.65	6.98	9.30	11.63	13.95	16.28	18.60	20.93	23.25
Poland 100,000 Zlotych	1990	31.10	0.999	1.000		1.00	2.00	3.00	4.00	10.00	15.00	20.00	25.00	30.00	35.00	40.00	45.00	50.00
Poland 100,000 Zlotych	1991-1994	16.50	0.750	0.398	S	0.40	0.80	1.19	1.59	3.98	5.97	7.96	9.95	11.94	13.93	15.92	17.91	19.90
Poland 200,000 Zlotych	1990	155.50	0.999	5.000		5.00	10.00	15.00	20.00	50.00	75.00	100.00	125.00	150.00	175.00	200.00	225.00	250.00
Poland 200,000 Zlotych	1990	19.27	0.999	0.619		0.62	1.24	1.86	2.48	6.19	9.29	12.38	15.48	18.57	21.67	24.76	27.86	30.95
Poland 200,000 Zlotych	1991	38.90	0.999	1.250		1.25	2.50	3.75	5.00	12.50	18.75	25.00	31.25	37.50	43.75	50.00	56.25	62.50
Poland 200,000 Zlotych	1991	30.10	0.925	0.925		0.93	1.85	2.78	3.70	9.25	13.88	18.50	23.13	27.75	32.38	37.00	41.63	46.25
Poland 200,000 Zlotych	1991-1994	19.33	0.750	0.466		0.47	0.93	1.40	1.86	4.66	6.99	9.32	11.65	13.98	16.31	18.64	20.97	23.30
Poland 200,000 Zlotych	1992	31.10	0.999	1.000		1.00	2.00	3.00	4.00	10.00	15.00	20.00	25.00	30.00	35.00	40.00	45.00	50.00
Poland 300,000 Zlotych	1993, 1994	31.10	0.999	1.000		1.00	2.00	3.00	4.00	10.00	15.00	20.00	25.00	30.00	35.00	40.00	45.00	50.00
Poland 300,000 Zlotych	1993, 1994	31.10	0.925	0.927		0.93	1.85	2.78	3.71	9.27	13.91	18.54	23.18	27.81	32.45	37.08	41.72	46.35
Poland 10 Zlotych	1995-1996	16.50	0.925	0.491		0.49	0.98	1.47	1.96	4.91	7.37	9.82	12.28	14.73	17.19	19.64	22.10	24.55
Poland 10 Zlotych	1997-2000	14.14	0.925	0.421		0.42	0.84	1.26	1.68	4.21	6.32	8.42	10.53	12.63	14.74	16.84	18.95	21.05
Poland 20 Zlotych	1995	31.10	0.999	1.000		1.00	2.00	3.00	4.00	10.00	15.00	20.00	25.00	30.00	35.00	40.00	45.00	50.00
Poland 20 Zlotych	1995, 1996	31.10	0.925	0.924	>	0.92	1.85	2.77	3.70	9.24	13.86	18.48	23.10	27.72	32.34	36.96	41.58	46.20
Poland 20 Zlotych	1997, 1998	28.50	0.925	0.848	>	0.85	1.70	2.54	3.39	8.48	12.72	16.96	21.20	25.44	29.68	33.92	38.16	42.40
Poland 20 Zlotych	1998-2000	28.20	0.925	0.841	>	0.84	1.68	2.52	3.36	8.41	12.62	16.82	21.03	25.23	29.44	33.64	37.85	42.05
Portugal 50 Reis*	1855-1893	1.25	0.917	0.037	S	0.04	0.07	0.11	0.15	0.37	0.56	0.74	0.93	1.11	1.30	1.48	1.67	1.85
Portugal 100 Reis	1836-1853	2.96	0.917	0.087	S	0.09	0.17	0.26	0.35	0.87	1.31	1.74	2.18	2.61	3.05	3.48	3.92	4.35
Portugal 100 Reis	1854-1898	2.50	0.907	0.074	S	0.07	0.15	0.22	0.29	0.74	1.11	1.47	1.84	2.21	2.58	2.95	3.32	3.69
Portugal 100 Reis	1909, 1910	2.50	0.835	0.067		0.07	0.13	0.20	0.27	0.67	1.01	1.34	1.68	2.01	2.35	2.68	3.02	3.35
Portugal 200 Reis	1836-1843	5.92	0.917	0.175	S	0.18	0.35	0.53	0.70	1.75	2.63	3.50	4.38	5.25	6.13	7.00	7.88	8.75
Portugal 200 Reis	1854-1898	5.00	0.917	0.147	S	0.15	0.29	0.44	0.59	1.47	2.21	2.94	3.68	4.41	5.15	5.88	6.62	7.35
Portugal 200 Reis	1909	5.00	0.835	0.134		0.13	0.27	0.40	0.54	1.34	2.01	2.68	3.36	4.03	4.70	5.37	6.04	6.71
Portugal 500 Reis	1837-1853	14.80	0.917	0.436	S	0.44	0.87	1.31	1.74	4.36	6.54	8.72	10.90	13.08	15.26	17.44	19.62	21.80
Portugal 500 Reis	1854-1910	12.50	0.917	0.368	S	0.37	0.74	1.10	1.47	3.68	5.52	7.36	9.20	11.04	12.88	14.72	16.56	18.40
Portugal 1000 Reis	1837-1845	29.60	0.917	0.873	S	0.87	1.75	2.62	3.49	8.73	13.10	17.46	21.83	26.19	30.56	34.92	39.29	43.65
Portugal 1000 Reis	1898-1910	25.00	0.917	0.737		0.74	1.47	2.21	2.95	7.37	11.06	14.74	18.43	22.11	25.80	29.48	33.17	36.85
Portugal 10 Centavos	1915	2.50	0.835	0.067		0.07	0.13	0.20	0.27	0.67	1.01	1.34	1.68	2.01	2.35	2.68	3.02	3.35
Portugal 20 Centavos	1913, 1916	5.00	0.835	0.134		0.13	0.27	0.40	0.54	1.34	2.01	2.68	3.35	4.02	4.69	5.36	6.03	6.70
Portugal 50 Centavos	1912-1916	12.50	0.835	0.336	S	0.34	0.67	1.01	1.34	3.36	5.04	6.72	8.40	10.08	11.76	13.44	15.12	16.80
Portugal 1 Escudo	1910-1916	25.00	0.835	0.671	S	0.67	1.34	2.01	2.68	6.71	10.07	13.42	16.78	20.13	23.49	26.84	30.20	33.55
Portugal 2-1/2 Escudos	1932-1951	3.50	0.650	0.073	S	0.07	0.15	0.22	0.29	0.73	1.10	1.46	1.83	2.19	2.56	2.92	3.29	3.65

Country & Denomination	Years Minted	Grams Weight	Fineness	Troy (ASW)	Code	$ Value 1	$ Value 2	$ Value 3	$ Value 4	$ Value 10	$ Value 15	$ Value 20	$ Value 25	$ Value 30	$ Value 35	$ Value 40	$ Value 45	$ Value 50
Portugal 5 Escudos	1932-1960	7.00	0.650	0.146	S	0.15	0.29	0.44	0.58	1.46	2.19	2.92	3.65	4.38	5.11	5.84	6.57	7.30
Portugal 10 Escudos	1928-1955	12.50	0.835	0.336	S	0.34	0.67	1.01	1.34	3.36	5.04	6.72	8.40	10.08	11.76	13.44	15.12	16.80
Portugal 10 Escudos	1960	12.50	0.680	0.273		0.27	0.55	0.82	1.09	2.73	4.10	5.46	6.83	8.19	9.56	10.92	12.29	13.65
Portugal 20 Escudos	1953, 1960	21.00	0.800	0.540		0.54	1.08	1.62	2.16	5.40	8.10	10.80	13.50	16.20	18.90	21.60	24.30	27.00
Portugal 20 Escudos	1966	10.00	0.650	0.209		0.21	0.42	0.63	0.84	2.09	3.14	4.18	5.23	6.27	7.32	8.36	9.41	10.45
Portugal 25 Escudos	1985, 1986	11.00	0.925	0.327		0.33	0.65	0.98	1.31	3.27	4.91	6.54	8.18	9.81	11.45	13.08	14.72	16.35
Portugal 50 Escudos	1968-1972	18.00	0.650	0.376	S	0.38	0.75	1.13	1.50	3.76	5.64	7.52	9.40	11.28	13.16	15.04	16.92	18.80
Portugal 100 Escudos	1976	18.00	0.650	0.376		0.38	0.75	1.13	1.50	3.76	5.64	7.52	9.40	11.28	13.16	15.04	16.92	18.80
Portugal 100 Escudos	1985-1988	16.50	0.925	0.491	N	0.49	0.98	1.47	1.96	4.91	7.37	9.82	12.28	14.73	17.19	19.64	22.10	24.55
Portugal 100 Escudos	1987-1990	21.00	0.925	0.625	N	0.63	1.25	1.88	2.50	6.25	9.38	12.50	15.63	18.75	21.88	25.00	28.13	31.25
Portugal 100 Escudos	1990-1995	18.50	0.925	0.550	N	0.55	1.10	1.65	2.20	5.50	8.25	11.00	13.75	16.50	19.25	22.00	24.75	27.50
Portugal 200 Escudos	1991-2000	26.50	0.925	0.788	N	0.79	1.58	2.36	3.15	7.88	11.82	15.76	19.70	23.64	27.58	31.52	35.46	39.40
Portugal 250 Escudos	1976	25.00	0.650	0.547	N	0.55	1.09	1.64	2.19	5.47	8.21	10.94	13.68	16.41	19.15	21.88	24.62	27.35
Portugal 250 Escudos	1984	23.00	0.925	0.684	N	0.68	1.37	2.05	2.74	6.84	10.26	13.68	17.10	20.52	23.94	27.36	30.78	34.20
Portugal 250 Escudos	1988-1989	28.00	0.925	0.833	N	0.83	1.67	2.50	3.33	8.33	12.50	16.66	20.83	24.99	29.16	33.32	37.49	41.65
Portugal 500 Escudos	1983	7.00	0.835	0.188	N	0.19	0.38	0.56	0.75	1.88	2.82	3.76	4.70	5.64	6.58	7.52	8.46	9.40
Portugal 500 Escudos	1995-2000	14.00	0.500	0.225	N	0.23	0.45	0.68	0.90	2.25	3.38	4.50	5.63	6.75	7.88	9.00	10.13	11.25
Portugal 750 Escudos	1983	12.50	0.835	0.336		0.34	0.67	1.01	1.34	3.36	5.04	6.72	8.40	10.08	11.76	13.44	15.12	16.80
Portugal 1000 Escudos	1983	17.00	0.925	0.506		0.51	1.01	1.52	2.02	5.06	7.59	10.12	12.65	15.18	17.71	20.24	22.77	25.30
Portugal 1000 Escudos	1983	21.00	0.835	0.564		0.56	1.13	1.69	2.26	5.64	8.46	11.28	14.10	16.92	19.74	22.56	25.38	28.20
Portugal 1000 Escudos	1994-1997	28.00	0.925	0.833		0.83	1.67	2.50	3.33	8.33	12.50	16.66	20.83	24.99	29.16	33.32	37.49	41.65
Portugal 1000 Escudos	1997-2000	27.00	0.925	0.803		0.80	1.61	2.41	3.21	8.03	12.05	16.06	20.08	24.09	28.11	32.12	36.14	40.15
Portugal 1000 Escudos	1994-1997	28.00	0.500	0.450		0.45	0.90	1.35	1.80	4.50	6.75	9.00	11.25	13.50	15.75	18.00	20.25	22.50
Portugal 1000 Escudos	1997-2000	27.00	0.500	0.434		0.43	0.87	1.30	1.74	4.34	6.51	8.68	10.85	13.02	15.19	17.36	19.53	21.70
Q																		
Port. India (Goa) 1/8 Tanga	1881	1.46	0.917	0.043		0.04	0.09	0.13	0.17	0.43	0.65	0.86	1.08	1.29	1.51	1.72	1.94	2.15
Port. India (Goa) 1/4 Rupia	1881	2.92	0.917	0.086		0.09	0.17	0.26	0.34	0.86	1.29	1.72	2.15	2.58	3.01	3.44	3.87	4.30
Port. India (Goa) 1/2 Rupia	1881-1885	5.83	0.917	0.172	S	0.17	0.34	0.52	0.69	1.72	2.58	3.44	4.30	5.16	6.02	6.88	7.74	8.60
Port. India (Goa) 1 Rupia	1881-1935	11.66	0.917	0.344	S	0.34	0.69	1.03	1.38	3.44	5.16	6.88	8.60	10.32	12.04	13.76	15.48	17.20
Qatar 100 Riyals	1998	22.30	0.660	0.660	A	0.66	1.32	1.98	2.64	6.60	9.90	13.20	16.50	19.80	23.10	26.40	29.70	33.00
Qatar 200 Riyals	1998	22.30	0.925	0.660	A	0.66	1.32	1.98	2.64	6.60	9.90	13.20	16.50	19.80	23.10	26.40	29.70	33.00
R																		
Quaiti Hadhramaut 4 Khumsi*	1925	0.65	0.900	0.019	A	0.02	0.04	0.06	0.08	0.19	0.29	0.38	0.48	0.57	0.67	0.76	0.86	0.95
Quaiti Hadhramaut 8 Khumsi	1925	1.10	0.900	0.032	A	0.03	0.06	0.10	0.13	0.32	0.48	0.64	0.80	0.96	1.12	1.28	1.44	1.60
Quaiti Hadhramaut 15 Khumsi	1925	2.00	0.900	0.058	A	0.06	0.12	0.17	0.23	0.58	0.87	1.16	1.45	1.74	2.03	2.32	2.61	2.90
Quaiti Hadhramaut 30 Khumsi	1925	3.95	0.900	0.114	A	0.11	0.23	0.34	0.46	1.14	1.71	2.28	2.85	3.42	3.99	4.56	5.13	5.70
Quaiti Hadhramaut 45 Khumsi	1925	5.90	0.900	0.171	A	0.17	0.34	0.51	0.68	1.71	2.57	3.42	4.28	5.13	5.99	6.84	7.70	8.55
Quaiti Hadhramaut 60 Khumsi	1925	7.80	0.900	0.226	A	0.23	0.45	0.68	0.90	2.26	3.39	4.52	5.65	6.78	7.91	9.04	10.17	11.30
Ras Al Khaima 1 Riyal	1969	3.95	0.640	0.081	A	0.08	0.16	0.24	0.32	0.81	1.22	1.62	2.03	2.43	2.84	3.24	3.65	4.05
Ras Al Khaima 2 Riyals	1969	6.45	0.835	0.173	A	0.17	0.35	0.52	0.69	1.73	2.60	3.46	4.33	5.19	6.06	6.92	7.79	8.65
Ras Al Khaima 2-1/2 Riyals	1970	7.50	0.925	0.223	A	0.22	0.45	0.67	0.89	2.23	3.35	4.46	5.58	6.69	7.81	8.92	10.04	11.15
Ras Al Khaima 5 Riyals	1970	15.00	0.835	0.403	A	0.40	0.81	1.21	1.61	4.03	6.05	8.06	10.08	12.09	14.11	16.12	18.14	20.15
Ras Al Khaima 7-1/2 Riyals	1970	22.50	0.925	0.669	A	0.67	1.34	2.01	2.68	6.69	10.04	13.38	16.73	20.07	23.42	26.76	30.11	33.45

Country & Denomination	Years Minted	Grams Weight	Fineness	Troy (ASW)	Code	$ Value 1	$ Value 2	$ Value 3	$ Value 4	$ Value 10	$ Value 15	$ Value 20	$ Value 25	$ Value 30	$ Value 35	$ Value 40	$ Value 45	$ Value 50
Ras Al Khaima 10 Riyals	1970	30.00	0.925	0.892	A	0.89	1.78	2.68	3.57	8.92	13.38	17.84	22.30	26.76	31.22	35.68	40.14	44.60
Ras Al Khaima 15 Riyals	1970	44.90	0.925	1.338	A	1.34	2.68	4.01	5.35	13.38	20.07	26.76	33.45	40.14	46.83	53.52	60.21	66.90
Rhodesia & Nyasaland 3 Pence	1955	1.41	0.500	0.023		0.02	0.05	0.07	0.09	0.23	0.35	0.46	0.58	0.69	0.81	0.92	1.04	1.15
Rhodesia & Nyasaland 6 Pence	1955	2.83	0.500	0.046		0.05	0.09	0.14	0.18	0.46	0.69	0.92	1.15	1.38	1.61	1.84	2.07	2.30
Rhodesia & Nyasaland Shilling	1955	5.66	0.500	0.091		0.09	0.18	0.27	0.36	0.91	1.37	1.82	2.28	2.73	3.19	3.64	4.10	4.55
Rhodesia & Nyasa. 2 Shillings	1955	11.31	0.500	0.182		0.18	0.36	0.55	0.73	1.82	2.73	3.64	4.55	5.46	6.37	7.28	8.19	9.10
Rhodesia & Nyasa. 1/2 Crown	1955	14.14	0.500	0.227		0.23	0.45	0.68	0.91	2.27	3.41	4.54	5.68	6.81	7.95	9.08	10.22	11.35
Romania 50 Bani	1873-1914	2.50	0.835	0.067	S	0.07	0.13	0.20	0.27	0.67	1.01	1.34	1.68	2.01	2.35	2.68	3.02	3.35
Romania 1 Leu	1870-1914	5.00	0.835	0.134	S	0.13	0.27	0.40	0.54	1.34	2.01	2.68	3.35	4.02	4.69	5.36	6.03	6.70
Romania 2 Lei	1872-1914	10.00	0.835	0.268	S	0.27	0.54	0.80	1.07	2.68	4.02	5.36	6.70	8.04	9.38	10.72	12.06	13.40
Romania 5 Lei	1880-1906	25.00	0.900	0.723	S	0.72	1.45	2.17	2.89	7.23	10.85	14.46	18.08	21.69	25.31	28.92	32.54	36.15
Romania 100 Lei	1932	12.00	0.500	0.163		0.16	0.33	0.49	0.65	1.63	2.45	3.26	4.08	4.89	5.71	6.52	7.34	8.15
Romania 200 Lei	1942	6.00	0.835	0.161		0.16	0.32	0.48	0.64	1.61	2.42	3.22	4.03	4.83	5.64	6.44	7.25	8.05
Romania 250 Lei	1935	13.50	0.750	0.326		0.33	0.65	0.98	1.30	3.26	4.89	6.52	8.15	9.78	11.41	13.04	14.67	16.30
Romania 250 Lei	1939-1941	12.00	0.835	0.322		0.32	0.64	0.97	1.29	3.22	4.83	6.44	8.05	9.66	11.27	12.88	14.49	16.10
Romania 500 Lei	1941	24.90	0.835	0.671		0.67	1.34	2.01	2.68	6.71	10.07	13.42	16.78	20.13	23.49	26.84	30.20	33.55
Romania 500 Lei	1944	12.00	0.700	0.270		0.27	0.54	0.81	1.08	2.70	4.05	5.40	6.75	8.10	9.45	10.80	12.15	13.50
Romania 25,000 Lei	1946	12.50	0.700	0.281		0.28	0.56	0.84	1.12	2.81	4.22	5.62	7.03	8.43	9.84	11.24	12.65	14.05
Romania 100,000 Lei	1946	25.00	0.700	0.563		0.56	1.13	1.69	2.25	5.63	8.45	11.26	14.08	16.89	19.71	22.52	25.34	28.15
Romania 50 Lei	1983	13.88	0.925	0.413		0.41	0.83	1.24	1.65	4.13	6.20	8.26	10.33	12.39	14.46	16.52	18.59	20.65
Romania 100 Lei	1982, 1983	27.75	0.925	0.825		0.83	1.65	2.48	3.30	8.25	12.38	16.50	20.63	24.75	28.88	33.00	37.13	41.25
Romania 100 Lei	1995	27.50	0.925	0.818		0.82	1.64	2.45	3.27	8.18	12.27	16.36	20.45	24.54	28.63	32.72	36.81	40.90
Romania 100 Lei	1996-1999	27.00	0.925	0.803	S	0.80	1.61	2.41	3.21	8.03	12.05	16.06	20.08	24.09	28.11	32.12	36.14	40.15
Romania 500 Lei	2000	27.00	0.925	0.803	N	0.80	1.61	2.41	3.21	8.03	12.05	16.06	20.08	24.09	28.11	32.12	36.14	40.15
Russia 5 Kopeks	1810-1858	1.04	0.868	0.029		0.03	0.06	0.09	0.12	0.29	0.44	0.58	0.73	0.87	1.02	1.16	1.31	1.45
Russia 5 Kopeks	1859-1866	1.04	0.750	0.025		0.03	0.05	0.08	0.10	0.25	0.38	0.50	0.63	0.75	0.88	1.00	1.13	1.25
Russia 5 Kopeks	1867-1915	0.90	0.500	0.014	N	0.01	0.03	0.04	0.06	0.14	0.21	0.28	0.35	0.42	0.49	0.56	0.63	0.70
Russia 10 Kopeks	1801-1866	2.07	0.868	0.058	N	0.06	0.12	0.17	0.23	0.58	0.87	1.16	1.45	1.74	2.03	2.32	2.61	2.90
Russia 10 Kopeks	1874-1931	1.80	0.500	0.029	S	0.03	0.06	0.09	0.12	0.29	0.44	0.58	0.73	0.87	1.02	1.16	1.31	1.45
Russia 15 Kopeks	1860-1866	3.11	0.750	0.075		0.08	0.15	0.23	0.30	0.75	1.13	1.50	1.88	2.25	2.63	3.00	3.38	3.75
Russia 15 Kopeks	1867-1931	2.70	0.500	0.043		0.04	0.09	0.13	0.17	0.43	0.65	0.86	1.08	1.29	1.51	1.72	1.94	2.15
Russia 20 Kopeks	1810-1858	4.15	0.868	0.116	S	0.12	0.23	0.35	0.46	1.16	1.74	2.32	2.90	3.48	4.06	4.64	5.22	5.80
Russia 20 Kopeks	1859-1866	4.15	0.750	0.099		0.10	0.20	0.30	0.40	0.99	1.49	1.98	2.48	2.97	3.47	3.96	4.46	4.95
Russia 20 Kopeks	1867-1931	3.59	0.500	0.058	S	0.06	0.12	0.17	0.23	0.58	0.87	1.16	1.45	1.74	2.03	2.32	2.61	2.90
Russia 1/4 Rouble	1802-1810	4.14	0.868	0.116		0.12	0.23	0.35	0.46	1.16	1.74	2.32	2.90	3.48	4.06	4.64	5.22	5.80
Russia 25 Kopeks	1832-1885	5.18	0.868	0.145		0.15	0.29	0.44	0.58	1.45	2.18	2.90	3.63	4.35	5.08	5.80	6.53	7.25
Russia 25 Kopeks	1886-1901	5.00	0.900	0.145		0.15	0.29	0.44	0.58	1.45	2.18	2.90	3.63	4.35	5.08	5.80	6.53	7.25
Russia 1/2 Rouble / 1 Poltina	1801-1885	10.36	0.868	0.289		0.29	0.58	0.87	1.16	2.89	4.34	5.78	7.23	8.67	10.12	11.56	13.01	14.45
Russia 50 Kopeks	1886-1927	10.00	0.900	0.289	S	0.29	0.58	0.87	1.16	2.89	4.34	5.78	7.23	8.67	10.12	11.56	13.01	14.45
Russia 1 Rouble	1801-1883	20.73	0.868	0.579		0.58	1.16	1.74	2.32	5.79	8.69	11.58	14.48	17.37	20.27	23.16	26.06	28.95
Russia 1 Rouble	1886-1924	20.00	0.900	0.579	S	0.58	1.16	1.74	2.32	5.79	8.69	11.58	14.48	17.37	20.27	23.16	26.06	28.95
Russia 1 Rouble	1993	15.55	0.900	0.450	N	0.45	0.90	1.35	1.80	4.50	6.75	9.00	11.25	13.50	15.75	18.00	20.25	22.50

Country & Denomination	Years Minted	Grams Weight	Fine- ness	Troy (ASW)	Code	$ Value 1	$ Value 2	$ Value 3	$ Value 4	$ Value 10	$ Value 15	$ Value 20	$ Value 25	$ Value 30	$ Value 35	$ Value 40	$ Value 45	$ Value 50
Russia 1 Rouble	1997	8.42	0.925	0.250	N	0.25	0.50	0.75	1.00	2.50	3.75	5.00	6.25	7.50	8.75	10.00	11.25	12.50
Russia 1 Rouble	1995-2000	17.46	0.900	0.505	N	0.51	1.01	1.52	2.02	5.05	7.58	10.10	12.63	15.15	17.68	20.20	22.73	25.25
Russia 1 Rouble	1998	17.55	0.900	0.508	N	0.51	1.02	1.52	2.03	5.08	7.62	10.16	12.70	15.24	17.78	20.32	22.86	25.40
Russia 1-1/2 Rouble / 10 Zlotych	1835-1839	31.10	0.868	0.868		0.87	1.74	2.60	3.47	8.68	13.02	17.36	21.70	26.04	30.38	34.72	39.06	43.40
Russia 2 Roubles	1994-1997	15.87	0.500	0.255	N	0.26	0.51	0.77	1.02	2.55	3.83	5.10	6.38	7.65	8.93	10.20	11.48	12.75
Russia 2 Roubles	1998	16.81	0.925	0.499	N	0.50	1.00	1.50	2.00	4.99	7.49	9.98	12.48	14.97	17.47	19.96	22.46	24.95
Russia 2 Roubles	1998-2000	17.00	0.925	0.506	N	0.51	1.01	1.52	2.02	5.06	7.59	10.12	12.65	15.18	17.71	20.24	22.77	25.30
Russia 3 Roubles	1988-1998	34.56	0.900	1.000	N	1.00	2.00	3.00	4.00	10.00	15.00	20.00	25.00	30.00	35.00	40.00	45.00	50.00
Russia 3 Roubles	1998-2000	34.88	0.900	1.005	N	1.01	2.01	3.02	4.02	10.05	15.08	20.10	25.13	30.15	35.18	40.20	45.23	50.25
Russia 5 Roubles	1977-1980	16.67	0.900	0.482		0.48	0.96	1.45	1.93	4.82	7.23	9.64	12.05	14.46	16.87	19.28	21.69	24.10
Russia 10 Roubles	1977-1980	33.30	0.900	0.964		0.96	1.93	2.89	3.86	9.64	14.46	19.28	24.10	28.92	33.74	38.56	43.38	48.20
Russia 25 Roubles	1993	156.04	0.999	5.011		5.01	10.02	15.03	20.04	50.11	75.17	100.22	125.28	150.33	175.39	200.44	225.50	250.55
Russia 25 Roubles	1994	172.83	0.999	5.000		5.00	10.00	15.00	20.00	50.00	75.00	100.00	125.00	150.00	175.00	200.00	225.00	250.00
Russia 25 Roubles	1995	155.50	0.900	4.499		4.50	9.00	13.50	18.00	44.99	67.49	89.98	112.48	134.97	157.47	179.96	202.46	224.95
Russia 25 Roubles	1996	155.50	0.999	5.000	V	5.00	10.00	15.00	20.00	50.00	75.00	100.00	125.00	150.00	175.00	200.00	225.00	250.00
Russia 25 Roubles	1996-1997	172.83	0.900	5.000		5.00	10.00	15.00	20.00	50.00	75.00	100.00	125.00	150.00	175.00	200.00	225.00	250.00
Russia 25 Roubles	1999, 2000	173.29	0.900	5.014	V	5.01	10.03	15.04	20.06	50.14	75.21	100.28	125.35	150.42	175.49	200.56	225.63	250.70
Russia 100 Roubles	1995	1000.21	0.900	28.940		28.94	57.88	86.82	115.76	289.40	434.10	578.80	723.50	868.20	1012.90	1157.60	1302.30	1447.00
Russia 100 Roubles	1995-1996	912.37	0.900	26.400		26.40	52.80	79.20	105.60	264.00	396.00	528.00	660.00	792.00	924.00	1056.00	1188.00	1320.00
Russia 100 Roubles	1995-2000	1111.09	0.900	32.150	S	32.15	64.30	96.45	128.60	321.50	482.25	643.00	803.75	964.50	1125.25	1286.00	1446.75	1607.50
Rwanda 100 Francs	1990, 1993	31.23	0.999	1.004	V	1.00	2.01	3.01	4.02	10.04	15.06	20.08	25.10	30.12	35.14	40.16	45.18	50.20
Rwanda 200 Francs	1972	18.00	0.800	0.463		0.46	0.93	1.39	1.85	4.63	6.95	9.26	11.58	13.89	16.21	18.52	20.84	23.15
Rwanda 1000 Francs	1989	31.64	0.999	1.018		1.02	2.04	3.05	4.07	10.18	15.27	20.36	25.45	30.54	35.63	40.72	45.81	50.90
S																		
Saharawi Arab Rep. 500 Pesetas	1991	15.84	0.999	0.509		0.51	1.02	1.53	2.04	5.09	7.64	10.18	12.73	15.27	17.82	20.36	22.91	25.45
Saharawi Arab Rep. 500 Pesetas	1992-1997	20.00	0.999	0.643	N	0.64	1.29	1.93	2.57	6.43	9.65	12.86	16.08	19.29	22.51	25.72	28.94	32.15
Saharawi Arab Rep. 500 Pesetas	1992-1997	16.00	0.999	0.514	N	0.51	1.03	1.54	2.06	5.14	7.71	10.28	12.85	15.42	17.99	20.56	23.13	25.70
Saharawi Arab Rep. 10 ECU	1992	31.00	0.999	0.996		1.00	1.99	2.99	3.98	9.96	14.94	19.92	24.90	29.88	34.86	39.84	44.82	49.80
Saharawi Arab R. 1000 Pesetas	1996-1998	30.50	0.999	0.977		0.98	1.95	2.93	3.91	9.77	14.66	19.54	24.43	29.31	34.20	39.08	43.97	48.85
Saharawi Arab R. 1000 Pesetas	1997	15.00	0.999	0.480	V	0.48	0.96	1.44	1.92	4.80	7.20	9.60	12.00	14.40	16.80	19.20	21.60	24.00
Saharawi Arab R. 5000 Pesetas	1996	33.54	0.920	0.998		1.00	2.00	2.99	3.99	9.98	14.97	19.96	24.95	29.94	34.93	39.92	44.91	49.90
Saint Helena 25 Pence*	1973-1983	28.28	0.925	0.841	N, S	0.84	1.68	2.52	3.36	8.41	12.62	16.82	21.03	25.23	29.44	33.64	37.85	42.05
Saint Helena 50 Pence	1984-2000	28.28	0.925	0.841	N, S	0.84	1.68	2.52	3.36	8.41	12.62	16.82	21.03	25.23	29.44	33.64	37.85	42.05
Saint Helena 50 Pence	1986, 1994	28.28	0.925	0.841	N	0.84	1.68	2.52	3.36	8.41	12.62	16.82	21.03	25.23	29.44	33.64	37.85	42.05
Saint Helena 1 Pound	1984	9.50	0.925	0.283	N	0.28	0.57	0.85	1.13	2.83	4.25	5.66	7.08	8.49	9.91	11.32	12.74	14.15
Saint Helena 2 Pounds	1993	28.28	0.925	0.841		0.84	1.68	2.52	3.36	8.41	12.62	16.82	21.03	25.23	29.44	33.64	37.85	42.05
Saint Helena 5 Pounds	1990	28.28	0.925	0.841		0.84	1.68	2.52	3.36	8.41	12.62	16.82	21.03	25.23	29.44	33.64	37.85	42.05
Saint Helena 25 Pounds	1986	155.00	0.999	0.498		0.50	1.00	1.49	1.99	4.98	7.47	9.96	12.45	14.94	17.43	19.92	22.41	24.90
Saint Helena 25 Pounds	1996	155.52	0.999	5.000		5.00	10.00	15.00	20.00	50.00	75.00	100.00	125.00	150.00	175.00	200.00	225.00	250.00
Saint Kitts 10 Dollars*	1985	28.28	0.925	0.841	N	0.84	1.68	2.52	3.36	8.41	12.62	16.82	21.03	25.23	29.44	33.64	37.85	42.05
Saint Kitts 20 Dollars	1982, 1983	28.28	0.925	0.841	N	0.84	1.68	2.52	3.36	8.41	12.62	16.82	21.03	25.23	29.44	33.64	37.85	42.05
Saint Kitts 100 Dollars	1988	129.59	0.925	3.854		3.85	7.71	11.56	15.42	38.54	57.81	77.08	96.35	115.62	134.89	154.16	173.43	192.70

Country & Denomination	Years Minted	Grams Weight	Fineness	Troy (ASW)	Code	$ Value 1	$ Value 2	$ Value 3	$ Value 4	$ Value 10	$ Value 15	$ Value 20	$ Value 25	$ Value 30	$ Value 35	$ Value 40	$ Value 45	$ Value 50
Saint Lucia 5 Dollars	1986	28.28	0.925	0.841	N	0.84	1.68	2.52	3.36	8.41	12.62	16.82	21.03	25.23	29.44	33.64	37.85	42.05
Saint Lucia 10 Dollars	1982-1986	28.28	0.925	0.841	N, S	0.84	1.68	2.52	3.36	8.41	12.62	16.82	21.03	25.23	29.44	33.64	37.85	42.05
Saint Lucia 100 Dollars	1988	129.59	0.925	3.854		3.85	7.71	11.56	15.42	38.54	57.81	77.08	96.35	115.62	134.89	154.16	173.43	192.70
Saint Vincent 10 Dollars	1985	28.28	0.925	0.841	N	0.84	1.68	2.52	3.36	8.41	12.62	16.82	21.03	25.23	29.44	33.64	37.85	42.05
Saint Vincent 100 Dollars	1988	129.59	0.925	3.850		3.85	7.70	11.55	15.40	38.50	57.75	77.00	96.25	115.50	134.75	154.00	173.25	192.50
Samoa 1 Sene	1974	1.95	0.925	0.058	N	0.06	0.12	0.17	0.23	0.58	0.87	1.16	1.45	1.74	2.03	2.32	2.61	2.90
Samoa 2 Sene	1974	3.80	0.925	0.113	N	0.11	0.23	0.34	0.45	1.13	1.70	2.26	2.83	3.39	3.96	4.52	5.09	5.65
Samoa 5 Sene	1974	3.25	0.925	0.097	N	0.10	0.19	0.29	0.39	0.97	1.46	1.94	2.43	2.91	3.40	3.88	4.37	4.85
Samoa 10 Sene	1974	6.37	0.925	0.189	N	0.19	0.38	0.57	0.76	1.89	2.84	3.78	4.73	5.67	6.62	7.56	8.51	9.45
Samoa 20 Sene	1974	12.70	0.925	0.378	N	0.38	0.76	1.13	1.51	3.78	5.67	7.56	9.45	11.34	13.23	15.12	17.01	18.90
Samoa 50 Sene	1974	15.40	0.925	0.458	N	0.46	0.92	1.37	1.83	4.58	6.87	9.16	11.45	13.74	16.03	18.32	20.61	22.90
Samoa 1 Tala	1974	27.70	0.925	0.824	N	0.82	1.65	2.47	3.30	8.24	12.36	16.48	20.60	24.72	28.84	32.96	37.08	41.20
Samoa 1 Tala	1974	31.15	0.925	0.926	N	0.93	1.85	2.78	3.70	9.26	13.89	18.52	23.15	27.78	32.41	37.04	41.67	46.30
Samoa 1 Tala	1976-1978	30.40	0.925	0.904	N	0.90	1.81	2.71	3.62	9.04	13.56	18.08	22.60	27.12	31.64	36.16	40.68	45.20
Samoa 1 Tala	1996	10.00	0.500	0.161		0.16	0.32	0.48	0.64	1.61	2.42	3.22	4.03	4.83	5.64	6.44	7.25	8.05
Samoa 2 Tala	1998	42.41	0.925	1.364		1.36	2.73	4.09	5.46	13.64	20.46	27.28	34.10	40.92	47.74	54.56	61.38	68.20
Samoa 5 Tala	1997	15.55	0.925	0.463		0.46	0.93	1.39	1.85	4.63	6.95	9.26	11.58	13.89	16.21	18.52	20.84	23.15
Samoa 10 Tala	1979, 1980	31.33	0.500	0.504		0.50	1.01	1.51	2.02	5.04	7.56	10.08	12.60	15.12	17.64	20.16	22.68	25.20
Samoa 10 Tala	1979, 1980	31.33	0.500	0.504		0.50	1.01	1.51	2.02	5.04	7.56	10.08	12.60	15.12	17.64	20.16	22.68	25.20
Samoa 10 Tala	1979-2000	31.40	0.925	0.936	S, V	0.94	1.87	2.81	3.74	9.36	14.04	18.72	23.40	28.08	32.76	37.44	42.12	46.80
Samoa 10 Tala	1987, 1988	31.10	0.999	1.000		1.00	2.00	3.00	4.00	10.00	15.00	20.00	25.00	30.00	35.00	40.00	45.00	50.00
Samoa 10 Tala	1992-1996	31.86	0.925	0.948	S, V	0.95	1.90	2.84	3.79	9.48	14.22	18.96	23.70	28.44	33.18	37.92	42.66	47.40
Samoa 25 Tala	1986, 1987	155.50	0.999	5.000		5.00	10.00	15.00	20.00	50.00	75.00	100.00	125.00	150.00	175.00	200.00	225.00	250.00
San Marino 50 Centesimi	1898	2.50	0.835	0.067	S	0.07	0.13	0.20	0.27	0.67	1.01	1.34	1.68	2.01	2.35	2.68	3.02	3.35
San Marino 1 Lira	1898, 1906	5.00	0.835	0.134	S	0.13	0.27	0.40	0.54	1.34	2.01	2.68	3.35	4.02	4.69	5.36	6.03	6.70
San Marino 2 Lire	1898, 1906	10.00	0.835	0.268		0.27	0.54	0.80	1.07	2.68	4.02	5.36	6.70	8.04	9.38	10.72	12.06	13.40
San Marino 5 Lire	1898	25.00	0.900	0.723		0.72	1.45	2.17	2.89	7.23	10.85	14.46	18.08	21.69	25.31	28.92	32.54	36.15
San Marino 5 Lire	1931-1938	5.00	0.835	0.134		0.13	0.27	0.40	0.54	1.34	2.01	2.68	3.35	4.02	4.69	5.36	6.03	6.70
San Marino 10 Lire	1931-1938	10.00	0.835	0.268		0.27	0.54	0.80	1.07	2.68	4.02	5.36	6.70	8.04	9.38	10.72	12.06	13.40
San Marino 500 Lire	1972-1994	11.00	0.835	0.295		0.30	0.59	0.89	1.18	2.95	4.43	5.90	7.38	8.85	10.33	11.80	13.28	14.75
San Marino 1000 Lire	1977-1997	14.60	0.835	0.392		0.39	0.78	1.18	1.57	3.92	5.88	7.84	9.80	11.76	13.72	15.68	17.64	19.60
San Marino 5000 Lire	1995-2000	18.00	0.835	0.483		0.48	0.97	1.45	1.93	4.83	7.25	9.66	12.08	14.49	16.91	19.32	21.74	24.15
San Marino 10,000 Lire	1995-2000	22.00	0.835	0.591		0.59	1.18	1.77	2.36	5.91	8.87	11.82	14.78	17.73	20.69	23.64	26.60	29.55
São Tomé 2-1/2 Escudos*	1939-1951	3.50	0.650	0.073		0.07	0.15	0.22	0.29	0.73	1.10	1.46	1.83	2.19	2.56	2.92	3.29	3.65
São Tomé 5 Escudos	1939-1952	7.00	0.650	0.146		0.15	0.29	0.44	0.58	1.46	2.19	2.92	3.65	4.38	5.11	5.84	6.57	7.30
São Tomé 10 Escudos	1939	12.50	0.835	0.336		0.34	0.67	1.01	1.34	3.36	5.04	6.72	8.40	10.08	11.76	13.44	15.12	16.80
São Tomé 10 Escudos	1951	12.50	0.720	0.273		0.27	0.55	0.82	1.09	2.73	4.10	5.46	6.83	8.19	9.56	10.92	12.29	13.65
São Tomé 50 Escudos	1970	18.00	0.650	0.376		0.38	0.75	1.13	1.50	3.76	5.64	7.52	9.40	11.28	13.16	15.04	16.92	18.80
São Tomé 100 Dobras	1984, 1985	28.28	0.925	0.841	N	0.84	1.68	2.52	3.36	8.41	12.62	16.82	21.03	25.23	29.44	33.64	37.85	42.05
São Tomé 1000 Dobras	1990	23.74	0.925	0.706	N	0.71	1.41	2.12	2.82	7.06	10.59	14.12	17.65	21.18	24.71	28.24	31.77	35.30

Country & Denomination	Years Minted	Grams Weight	Fine-ness	Troy (ASW)	Code	$ Value 1	$ Value 2	$ Value 3	$ Value 4	$ Value 10	$ Value 15	$ Value 20	$ Value 25	$ Value 30	$ Value 35	$ Value 40	$ Value 45	$ Value 50
São Tomé 1000 Dobras	1993-1998	25.00	0.925	0.744	S, V	0.74	1.49	2.23	2.98	7.44	11.16	14.88	18.60	22.32	26.04	29.76	33.48	37.20
São Tomé 5 ECU	1993-1998	25.00	0.925	0.744		0.74	1.49	2.23	2.98	7.44	11.16	14.88	18.60	22.32	26.04	29.76	33.48	37.20
São Tomé 1000 Dobras	1997, 1998	31.10	0.999	1.000	N	1.00	2.00	3.00	4.00	10.00	15.00	20.00	25.00	30.00	35.00	40.00	45.00	50.00
São Tomé 1 Euro	1999	31.10	0.925	0.925		0.93	1.85	2.78	3.70	9.25	13.88	18.50	23.13	27.75	32.38	37.00	41.63	46.25
São Tomé 7-1/2 Euros	1997	25.00	0.925	0.804		0.80	1.61	2.41	3.22	8.04	12.06	16.08	20.10	24.12	28.14	32.16	36.18	40.20
Sarawak 5 Cents	1900-1915	1.35	0.800	0.035	S	0.04	0.07	0.11	0.14	0.35	0.53	0.70	0.88	1.05	1.23	1.40	1.58	1.75
Sarawak 5 Cents	1920	1.35	0.400	0.017		0.02	0.03	0.05	0.07	0.17	0.26	0.34	0.43	0.51	0.60	0.68	0.77	0.85
Sarawak 10 Cents	1900-1915	2.71	0.800	0.070	S	0.07	0.14	0.21	0.28	0.70	1.05	1.40	1.75	2.10	2.45	2.80	3.15	3.50
Sarawak 10 Cents	1920	2.71	0.400	0.035		0.04	0.07	0.11	0.14	0.35	0.53	0.70	0.88	1.05	1.23	1.40	1.58	1.75
Sarawak 20 Cents	1900-1915	5.43	0.800	0.140	S	0.14	0.28	0.42	0.56	1.40	2.10	2.80	3.50	4.20	4.90	5.60	6.30	7.00
Sarawak 20 Cents	1927	5.08	0.400	0.065		0.07	0.13	0.20	0.26	0.65	0.98	1.30	1.63	1.95	2.28	2.60	2.93	3.25
Sarawak 50 Cents	1900-1906	13.57	0.800	0.349	S	0.35	0.70	1.05	1.40	3.49	5.24	6.98	8.73	10.47	12.22	13.96	15.71	17.45
Sarawak 50 Cents	1927	10.30	0.500	0.166		0.17	0.33	0.50	0.66	1.66	2.49	3.32	4.15	4.98	5.81	6.64	7.47	8.30
Saudi Arabia 1/4 Riyal	1881	2.92	0.917	0.086	A	0.09	0.17	0.26	0.34	0.86	1.29	1.72	2.15	2.58	3.01	3.44	3.87	4.30
Saudi Arabia 1/4 Riyal	1935	3.10	0.917	0.091	A	0.09	0.18	0.27	0.36	0.91	1.37	1.82	2.28	2.73	3.19	3.64	4.10	4.55
Saudi Arabia 1/4 Riyal	1954	2.95	0.917	0.087	A	0.09	0.17	0.26	0.35	0.87	1.31	1.74	2.18	2.61	3.05	3.48	3.92	4.35
Saudi Arabia 1/2 Riyal	1881-1935	5.83	0.917	0.172	A, S	0.17	0.34	0.52	0.69	1.72	2.58	3.44	4.30	5.16	6.02	6.88	7.74	8.60
Saudi Arabia 1/2 Riyal	1954	5.85	0.917	0.175	A	0.18	0.35	0.53	0.70	1.75	2.63	3.50	4.38	5.25	6.13	7.00	7.88	8.75
Saudi Arabia 1 Riyal	1881-1935	11.66	0.917	0.344	A, S	0.34	0.69	1.03	1.38	3.44	5.16	6.88	8.60	10.32	12.04	13.76	15.48	17.20
Senegal 50 Francs	1975	28.28	0.925	0.841		0.84	1.68	2.52	3.36	8.41	12.62	16.82	21.03	25.23	29.44	33.64	37.85	42.05
Senegal 150 Francs	1975	79.97	0.925	2.378		2.38	4.76	7.13	9.51	23.78	35.67	47.56	59.45	71.34	83.23	95.12	107.01	118.90
Serbia 50 Para	1875-1915	2.50	0.835	0.067	S	0.07	0.13	0.20	0.27	0.67	1.01	1.34	1.68	2.01	2.35	2.68	3.02	3.35
Serbia 1 Dinar	1875-1915	5.00	0.835	0.134	S	0.13	0.27	0.40	0.54	1.34	2.01	2.68	3.35	4.02	4.69	5.36	6.03	6.70
Serbia 2 Dinara	1875-1915	10.00	0.835	0.268	S	0.27	0.54	0.80	1.07	2.68	4.02	5.36	6.70	8.04	9.38	10.72	12.06	13.40
Serbia 5 Dinara	1879-1904	25.00	0.900	0.723	S	0.72	1.45	2.17	2.89	7.23	10.85	14.46	18.08	21.69	25.31	28.92	32.54	36.15
Seychelles 25 Cents	1939-1944	2.92	0.500	0.047	S	0.05	0.09	0.14	0.19	0.47	0.71	0.94	1.18	1.41	1.65	1.88	2.12	2.35
Seychelles 1/2 Rupee	1939	5.83	0.500	0.094		0.09	0.19	0.28	0.38	0.94	1.41	1.88	2.35	2.82	3.29	3.76	4.23	4.70
Seychelles 1 Rupee	1939	11.66	0.500	0.187		0.19	0.37	0.56	0.75	1.87	2.81	3.74	4.68	5.61	6.55	7.48	8.42	9.35
Seychelles 5 Rupees	1972, 1974	15.50	0.925	0.461	N	0.46	0.92	1.38	1.84	4.61	6.92	9.22	11.53	13.83	16.14	18.44	20.75	23.05
Seychelles 10 Rupees	1974, 1976	28.28	0.925	0.841	N	0.84	1.68	2.52	3.36	8.41	12.62	16.82	21.03	25.23	29.44	33.64	37.85	42.05
Seychelles 10 Rupees	1993	10.00	0.925	0.297		0.30	0.59	0.89	1.19	2.97	4.46	5.94	7.43	8.91	10.40	11.88	13.37	14.85
Seychelles 10 Rupees	1996	10.00	0.500	0.161		0.16	0.32	0.48	0.64	1.61	2.42	3.22	4.03	4.83	5.64	6.44	7.25	8.05
Seychelles 20 Rupees	1983	19.44	0.925	0.578	N	0.58	1.16	1.73	2.31	5.78	8.67	11.56	14.45	17.34	20.23	23.12	26.01	28.90
Seychelles 25 Rupees	1977	28.28	0.500	0.455		0.46	0.91	1.37	1.82	4.55	6.83	9.10	11.38	13.65	15.93	18.20	20.48	22.75
Seychelles 25 Rupees	1977-1999	28.28	0.925	0.841	N, S	0.84	1.68	2.52	3.36	8.41	12.62	16.82	21.03	25.23	29.44	33.64	37.85	42.05
Seychelles 25 Rupees	1993-1996	31.46	0.925	0.936	N	0.94	1.87	2.81	3.74	9.36	14.04	18.72	23.40	28.08	32.76	37.44	42.12	46.80
Seychelles 25 Rupees	1993-1997	19.44	0.925	0.578	N, S	0.58	1.16	1.73	2.31	5.78	8.67	11.56	14.45	17.34	20.23	23.12	26.01	28.90
Seychelles 50 Rupees	1978	28.28	0.925	0.841		0.84	1.68	2.52	3.36	8.41	12.62	16.82	21.03	25.23	29.44	33.64	37.85	42.05
Seychelles 50 Rupees	1980, 1985	19.44	0.925	0.578		0.58	1.16	1.73	2.31	5.78	8.67	11.56	14.45	17.34	20.23	23.12	26.01	28.90
Seychelles 100 Rupees	1978, 1981	31.65	0.925	0.941		0.94	1.88	2.82	3.76	9.41	14.12	18.82	23.53	28.23	32.94	37.64	42.35	47.05

Country & Denomination	Years Minted	Grams Weight	Fine-ness	Troy (ASW)	Code	$ Value 1	$ Value 2	$ Value 3	$ Value 4	$ Value 10	$ Value 15	$ Value 20	$ Value 25	$ Value 30	$ Value 35	$ Value 40	$ Value 45	$ Value 50
Seychelles 100 Rupees	1981	35.00	0.500	0.563		0.56	1.13	1.69	2.25	5.63	8.45	11.26	14.08	16.89	19.71	22.52	25.34	28.15
Seychelles 100 Rupees	1986-1988	19.44	0.925	0.578	N	0.58	1.16	1.73	2.31	5.78	8.67	11.56	14.45	17.34	20.23	23.12	26.01	28.90
Sharjah 5 Rupees	1964	25.00	0.720	0.579	A	0.58	1.16	1.74	2.32	5.79	8.69	11.58	14.48	17.37	20.27	23.16	26.06	28.95
Sharjah 1 Riyal	1969	3.00	0.990	0.096	A	0.10	0.19	0.29	0.38	0.96	1.44	1.92	2.40	2.88	3.36	3.84	4.32	4.80
Sharjah 2 Riyals	1969	6.00	0.999	0.193	A	0.19	0.39	0.58	0.77	1.93	2.90	3.87	4.83	5.80	6.77	7.73	8.70	9.67
Sharjah 5 Riyals	1969	15.00	0.999	0.482	A	0.48	0.96	1.45	1.93	4.82	7.23	9.64	12.05	14.46	16.87	19.28	21.69	24.10
Sharjah 10 Riyals	1969	30.00	0.999	0.965	A	0.97	1.93	2.90	3.86	9.65	14.48	19.30	24.13	28.95	33.78	38.60	43.43	48.25
Sierra Leone 1 Leone	1964	22.62	0.500	0.674	N	0.67	1.35	2.02	2.70	6.74	10.11	13.48	16.85	20.22	23.59	26.96	30.33	33.70
Sierra Leone 1 Leone	1974, 1980	28.28	0.925	0.841	N	0.84	1.68	2.52	3.36	8.41	12.62	16.82	21.03	25.23	29.44	33.64	37.85	42.05
Sierra Leone 1 Leone	1987	9.50	0.925	0.283	N	0.28	0.57	0.85	1.13	2.83	4.25	5.66	7.08	8.49	9.91	11.32	12.74	14.15
Sierra Leone 10 Leones	1983, 1987	28.28	0.925	0.841	S	0.84	1.68	2.52	3.36	8.41	12.62	16.82	21.03	25.23	29.44	33.64	37.85	42.05
Sierra Leone 5 Dollars	1997, 1998	15.55	0.999	0.500		0.50	1.00	1.50	2.00	5.00	7.50	10.00	12.50	15.00	17.50	20.00	22.50	25.00
Sierra Leone 10 Dollars	1997-2000	28.28	0.925	0.841		0.84	1.68	2.52	3.36	8.41	12.62	16.82	21.03	25.23	29.44	33.64	37.85	42.05
Singapore 1 Cent	1981	2.92	0.925	0.087	N	0.09	0.17	0.26	0.35	0.87	1.31	1.74	2.18	2.61	3.05	3.48	3.92	4.35
Singapore 1 Cent	1985-2000	1.18	0.925	0.054	N	0.05	0.11	0.16	0.22	0.54	0.81	1.08	1.35	1.62	1.89	2.16	2.43	2.70
Singapore 5 Cents	1981	1.65	0.925	0.049	N	0.05	0.10	0.15	0.20	0.49	0.74	0.98	1.23	1.47	1.72	1.96	2.21	2.45
Singapore 5 Cents	1985-2000	2.00	0.925	0.060	N	0.06	0.12	0.18	0.24	0.60	0.90	1.20	1.50	1.80	2.10	2.40	2.70	3.00
Singapore 10 Cents	1981	3.35	0.925	0.100	N	0.10	0.20	0.30	0.40	1.00	1.50	2.00	2.50	3.00	3.50	4.00	4.50	5.00
Singapore 10 Cents	1985-2000	3.05	0.925	0.091	N	0.09	0.18	0.27	0.36	0.91	1.37	1.82	2.28	2.73	3.19	3.64	4.10	4.55
Singapore 20 Cents	1981	6.51	0.925	0.194	N	0.19	0.39	0.58	0.78	1.94	2.91	3.88	4.85	5.82	6.79	7.76	8.73	9.70
Singapore 20 Cents	1985-2000	5.24	0.925	0.156	N	0.16	0.31	0.47	0.62	1.56	2.34	3.12	3.90	4.68	5.46	6.24	7.02	7.80
Singapore 50 Cents	1981	10.82	0.925	0.322	N	0.32	0.64	0.97	1.29	3.22	4.83	6.44	8.05	9.66	11.27	12.88	14.49	16.10
Singapore 50 Cents	1985-2000	8.56	0.925	0.255	N	0.26	0.51	0.77	1.02	2.55	3.83	5.10	6.38	7.65	8.93	10.20	11.48	12.75
Singapore 1 Dollar	1975-1984	18.05	0.925	0.727	N	0.73	1.45	2.18	2.91	7.27	10.91	14.54	18.18	21.81	25.45	29.08	32.72	36.35
Singapore 1 Dollar	1985	9.97	0.925	0.300	N	0.30	0.60	0.90	1.20	3.00	4.50	6.00	7.50	9.00	10.50	12.00	13.50	15.00
Singapore 1 Dollar	1987-2000	8.43	0.925	0.251	N	0.25	0.50	0.75	1.00	2.51	3.77	5.02	6.28	7.53	8.79	10.04	11.30	12.55
Singapore 2 Dollars	1987-2000	20.00	0.925	0.595	N	0.60	1.19	1.79	2.38	5.95	8.93	11.90	14.88	17.85	20.83	23.80	26.78	29.75
Singapore 5 Dollars	1973	25.00	0.500	0.402		0.40	0.80	1.21	1.61	4.02	6.03	8.04	10.05	12.06	14.07	16.08	18.09	20.10
Singapore 5 Dollars	1981	18.05	0.925	0.537		0.54	1.07	1.61	2.15	5.37	8.06	10.74	13.43	16.11	18.80	21.48	24.17	26.85
Singapore 5 Dollars	1987-2000	20.00	0.925	0.595		0.60	1.19	1.79	2.38	5.95	8.93	11.90	14.88	17.85	20.83	23.80	26.78	29.75
Singapore 10 Dollars	1972, 1973	31.10	0.900	0.900		0.90	1.80	2.70	3.60	9.00	13.50	18.00	22.50	27.00	31.50	36.00	40.50	45.00
Singapore 10 Dollars	1974-1988	31.10	0.500	0.500	N	0.50	1.00	1.50	2.00	5.00	7.50	10.00	12.50	15.00	17.50	20.00	22.50	25.00
Singapore 10 Dollars	1990-1992	31.10	0.925	0.925	N	0.93	1.85	2.78	3.70	9.25	13.88	18.50	23.13	27.75	32.38	37.00	41.63	46.25
Singapore 10 Dollars	1993-2000	62.21	0.999	2.000	N	2.00	4.00	6.00	8.00	20.00	30.00	40.00	50.00	60.00	70.00	80.00	90.00	100.00
Singapore 50 Dollars	1980, 1981	31.10	0.500	0.500	N	0.50	1.00	1.50	2.00	5.00	7.50	10.00	12.50	15.00	17.50	20.00	22.50	25.00
Slovakia 10 Korun	1944	7.00	0.500	0.113		0.11	0.23	0.34	0.45	1.13	1.69	2.25	2.81	3.38	3.94	4.50	5.06	5.63
Slovakia 20 Korun	1939, 1941	15.00	0.500	0.241		0.24	0.48	0.72	0.96	2.41	3.62	4.82	6.03	7.23	8.44	9.64	10.85	12.06
Slovakia 50 Korun	1944	16.50	0.700	0.371		0.37	0.74	1.11	1.48	3.71	5.57	7.42	9.28	11.13	12.99	14.84	16.70	18.55
Slovakia 10 Korun	1993	8.50	0.750	0.253		0.25	0.51	0.76	1.01	2.53	3.80	5.06	6.33	7.59	8.86	10.12	11.39	12.65
Slovakia 100 Korun	1993	13.00	0.750	0.314		0.31	0.63	0.94	1.26	3.14	4.71	6.28	7.85	9.42	10.99	12.56	14.13	15.70
Slovakia 200 Korun	1993-2000	20.00	0.750	0.482		0.48	0.96	1.45	1.93	4.82	7.23	9.64	12.05	14.46	16.87	19.28	21.69	24.10

Country & Denomination	Years Minted	Grams Weight	Fine-ness	Troy (ASW)	Code	$ Value 1.00	$ Value 2.00	$ Value 3.00	$ Value 4.00	$ Value 10.00	$ Value 15.00	$ Value 20.00	$ Value 25.00	$ Value 30.00	$ Value 35.00	$ Value 40.00	$ Value 45.00	$ Value 50.00
Slovakia 500 Korun	1994-2000	33.63	0.925	1.000		1.00	2.00	3.00	4.00	10.00	15.00	20.00	25.00	30.00	35.00	40.00	45.00	50.00
Slovenia 500 Tolarjev	1991-1997	15.00	0.925	0.446	s	0.45	0.89	1.34	1.78	4.46	6.69	8.92	11.15	13.38	15.61	17.84	20.07	22.30
Solomon Islands 1 Dollar	1991-1998	28.28	0.925	0.841	N	0.84	1.68	2.52	3.36	8.41	12.62	16.82	21.03	25.23	29.44	33.64	37.85	42.05
Solomon Islands 5 Dollars	1977-1995	28.28	0.925	0.841	N	0.84	1.68	2.52	3.36	8.41	12.62	16.82	21.03	25.23	29.44	33.64	37.85	42.05
Solomon Islands 5 Dollars	1996	28.20	0.925	0.839		0.84	1.68	2.52	3.36	8.39	12.59	16.78	20.98	25.17	29.37	33.56	37.76	41.95
Solomon Islands 5 Dollars	1998	9.94	0.525	0.168		0.17	0.34	0.50	0.67	1.68	2.52	3.36	4.20	5.04	5.88	6.72	7.56	8.40
Solomon Islands 5 Dollars	1999	20.10	0.800	0.517		0.52	1.03	1.55	2.07	5.17	7.76	10.34	12.93	15.51	18.10	20.68	23.27	25.85
Solomon Islands 5 Dollars	2000	24.91	0.925	0.741		0.74	1.48	2.22	2.96	7.41	11.12	14.82	18.53	22.23	25.94	29.64	33.35	37.05
Solomon Islands 10 Dollars	1979-1982	42.27	0.925	1.260	N	1.26	2.52	3.78	5.04	12.60	18.90	25.20	31.50	37.80	44.10	50.40	56.70	63.00
Solomon Islands 10 Dollars	1983	40.50	0.925	1.205	N	1.21	2.41	3.62	4.82	12.05	18.08	24.10	30.13	36.15	42.18	48.20	54.23	60.25
Solomon Islands 10 Dollars	1984	33.44	0.925	0.995		1.00	1.99	2.99	3.98	9.95	14.93	19.90	24.88	29.85	34.83	39.80	44.78	49.75
Solomon Islands 10 Dollars	1991	31.80	0.925	0.946		0.95	1.89	2.84	3.78	9.46	14.19	18.92	23.65	28.38	33.11	37.84	42.57	47.30
Solomon Islands 10 Dollars	1991	31.42	0.925	0.936		0.94	1.87	2.81	3.74	9.36	14.04	18.72	23.40	28.08	32.76	37.44	42.12	46.80
Solomon Islands 10 Dollars	1992-1993	31.47	0.925	0.936	V	0.94	1.87	2.81	3.74	9.36	14.04	18.72	23.40	28.08	32.76	37.44	42.12	46.80
Solomon Islands 10 Dollars	1993-1994	28.28	0.925	0.841		0.84	1.68	2.52	3.36	8.41	12.62	16.82	21.03	25.23	29.44	33.64	37.85	42.05
Solomon Islands 10 Dollars	1995-2000	31.50	0.925	0.938	V	0.94	1.88	2.81	3.75	9.38	14.07	18.76	23.45	28.14	32.83	37.52	42.21	46.90
Solomon Islands 25 Dollars	2000	500.00	0.999	16.059		16.06	32.12	48.18	64.24	160.59	240.89	321.18	401.48	481.77	562.07	642.36	722.66	802.95
Solomon Islands 50 Dollars	1994	155.50	0.999	5.000		5.00	10.00	15.00	20.00	50.00	75.00	100.00	125.00	150.00	175.00	200.00	225.00	250.00
Solomon Islands 50 Dollars	1995	31.47	0.925	0.936	V	0.94	1.87	2.81	3.74	9.36	14.04	18.72	23.40	28.08	32.76	37.44	42.12	46.80
Somalia 50 Centesimi	1950	3.80	0.250	0.031		0.03	0.06	0.09	0.12	0.31	0.47	0.62	0.78	0.93	1.09	1.24	1.40	1.55
Somalia 1 Somalo	1950	7.60	0.250	0.061		0.06	0.12	0.18	0.24	0.61	0.92	1.22	1.53	1.83	2.14	2.44	2.75	3.05
Somalia 10 Shillings	1979	28.28	0.925	0.841	N	0.84	1.68	2.52	3.36	8.41	12.62	16.82	21.03	25.23	29.44	33.64	37.85	42.05
Somalia 25 Shillings	1984	28.28	0.925	0.841	N	0.84	1.68	2.52	3.36	8.41	12.62	16.82	21.03	25.23	29.44	33.64	37.85	42.05
Somalia 150 Shillings	1983	28.28	0.925	0.841	N	0.84	1.68	2.52	3.36	8.41	12.62	16.82	21.03	25.23	29.44	33.64	37.85	42.05
Somalia 150 Shillings	2000	14.90	0.999	0.477	V	0.48	0.95	1.43	1.91	4.77	7.16	9.54	11.93	14.31	16.70	19.08	21.47	23.85
Somalia 250 Shillings	1998	23.60	0.925	0.700	V	0.70	1.40	2.10	2.80	7.00	10.50	14.00	17.50	21.00	24.50	28.00	31.50	35.00
Somalia 250 Shillings	1998-2000	24.83	0.900	0.719		0.72	1.44	2.16	2.88	7.19	10.79	14.38	17.98	21.57	25.17	28.76	32.36	35.95
Somalia 250 Shillings	1999, 2000	23.00	0.925	0.684	V	0.68	1.37	2.05	2.74	6.84	10.26	13.68	17.10	20.52	23.94	27.36	30.78	34.20
Somalia 5000 Shillings	1998	7.06	0.999	0.227		0.23	0.45	0.68	0.91	2.27	3.41	4.54	5.68	6.81	7.95	9.08	10.22	11.35
Somalia 10,000 Shillings	1998	15.00	0.999	0.482		0.48	0.96	1.45	1.93	4.82	7.23	9.64	12.05	14.46	16.87	19.28	21.69	24.10
South Africa 3 Pence	1892-1897	1.41	0.925	0.042		0.04	0.08	0.13	0.17	0.42	0.63	0.84	1.05	1.26	1.47	1.68	1.89	2.10
South Africa 3 Pence	1923-1952	1.41	0.800	0.036		0.04	0.07	0.11	0.14	0.36	0.54	0.72	0.90	1.08	1.26	1.44	1.62	1.80
South Africa 3 Pence	1953-1960	1.41	0.500	0.023		0.02	0.05	0.07	0.09	0.23	0.35	0.46	0.58	0.69	0.81	0.92	1.04	1.15
South Africa 6 Pence	1892-1897	2.83	0.925	0.084		0.08	0.17	0.25	0.34	0.84	1.26	1.68	2.10	2.52	2.94	3.36	3.78	4.20
South Africa 6 Pence	1923-1950	2.83	0.800	0.070		0.07	0.14	0.21	0.28	0.70	1.05	1.40	1.75	2.10	2.45	2.80	3.15	3.50
South Africa 6 Pence	1951-1960	2.83	0.500	0.045		0.05	0.09	0.14	0.18	0.45	0.68	0.90	1.13	1.35	1.58	1.80	2.03	2.25
South Africa Shilling	1892-1897	5.66	0.925	0.168		0.17	0.34	0.50	0.67	1.68	2.52	3.36	4.20	5.04	5.88	6.72	7.56	8.40
South Africa Shilling	1923-1950	5.66	0.800	0.146		0.15	0.29	0.44	0.58	1.46	2.19	2.92	3.65	4.38	5.11	5.84	6.57	7.30
South Africa Shilling	1951-1960	5.66	0.500	0.091		0.09	0.18	0.27	0.36	0.91	1.37	1.82	2.28	2.73	3.19	3.64	4.10	4.55
South Africa 2 Shillings	1892-1897	11.31	0.925	0.336		0.34	0.67	1.01	1.34	3.36	5.04	6.72	8.40	10.08	11.76	13.44	15.12	16.80
South Africa 1 Florin	1923-1930	11.31	0.800	0.291		0.29	0.58	0.87	1.16	2.91	4.37	5.82	7.28	8.73	10.19	11.64	13.10	14.55

Country & Denomination	Years Minted	Grams Weight	Fineness	Troy (ASW)	Code	$ Value 1	$ Value 2	$ Value 3	$ Value 4	$ Value 10	$ Value 15	$ Value 20	$ Value 25	$ Value 30	$ Value 35	$ Value 40	$ Value 45	$ Value 50
South Africa 2 Shillings	1931-1950	11.31	0.800	0.291		0.29	0.58	0.87	1.16	2.91	4.37	5.82	7.28	8.73	10.19	11.64	13.10	14.55
South Africa 2 Shillings	1951-1960	11.31	0.500	0.182		0.18	0.36	0.55	0.73	1.82	2.73	3.64	4.55	5.46	6.37	7.28	8.19	9.10
South Africa 2-1/2 Shillings	1892-1897	14.14	0.925	0.421		0.42	0.84	1.26	1.68	4.21	6.32	8.42	10.53	12.63	14.74	16.84	18.95	21.05
South Africa 2-1/2 Shillings	1923-1950	14.10	0.800	0.364		0.36	0.73	1.09	1.46	3.64	5.46	7.28	9.10	10.92	12.74	14.56	16.38	18.20
South Africa 2-1/2 Shillings	1951-1960	14.10	0.500	0.227		0.23	0.45	0.68	0.91	2.27	3.41	4.54	5.68	6.81	7.95	9.08	10.22	11.35
South Africa 5 Shillings	1892	28.28	0.925	0.841		0.84	1.68	2.52	3.36	8.41	12.62	16.82	21.03	25.23	29.44	33.64	37.85	42.05
South Africa 5 Shillings	1947-1950	28.28	0.800	0.727		0.73	1.45	2.18	2.91	7.27	10.91	14.54	18.18	21.81	25.45	29.08	32.72	36.35
South Africa 5 Shillings	1951-1960	28.28	0.500	0.455		0.46	0.91	1.37	1.82	4.55	6.83	9.10	11.38	13.65	15.93	18.20	20.48	22.75
South Africa 2-1/2 Cents	1961-1964	1.41	0.500	0.023		0.02	0.05	0.07	0.09	0.23	0.35	0.46	0.58	0.69	0.81	0.92	1.04	1.15
South Africa 5 Cents	1961-1964	2.83	0.500	0.045		0.05	0.09	0.14	0.18	0.45	0.68	0.90	1.13	1.35	1.58	1.80	2.03	2.25
South Africa 10 Cents	1961-1964	5.66	0.500	0.091		0.09	0.18	0.27	0.36	0.91	1.37	1.82	2.28	2.73	3.19	3.64	4.10	4.55
South Africa 20 Cents	1961-1964	11.31	0.500	0.182		0.18	0.36	0.55	0.73	1.82	2.73	3.64	4.55	5.46	6.37	7.28	8.19	9.10
South Africa 50 Cents	1961-1964	28.28	0.500	0.455		0.46	0.91	1.37	1.82	4.55	6.83	9.10	11.38	13.65	15.93	18.20	20.48	22.75
South Africa 50 Cents	2000	76.40	0.925	2.272		2.27	4.54	6.82	9.09	22.72	34.08	45.44	56.80	68.16	79.52	90.88	102.24	113.60
South Africa 1 Rand	1965-1990	15.00	0.800	0.386		0.39	0.77	1.16	1.54	3.86	5.79	7.72	9.65	11.58	13.51	15.44	17.37	19.30
South Africa 1 Rand	1991-2000	15.00	0.925	0.446		0.45	0.89	1.34	1.78	4.46	6.69	8.92	11.15	13.38	15.61	17.84	20.07	22.30
South Africa 2 Rand	1992-2000	33.60	0.925	1.000	>	1.00	2.00	3.00	4.00	10.00	15.00	20.00	25.00	30.00	35.00	40.00	45.00	50.00
South Georgia 2 Pounds	2000	28.28	0.925	0.841	N	0.84	1.68	2.52	3.36	8.41	12.62	16.82	21.03	25.23	29.44	33.64	37.85	42.05
South Korea-see Korea (South)																		
Southern Rhodesia 3 Pence	1932-1942	1.41	0.925	0.042		0.04	0.08	0.13	0.17	0.42	0.63	0.84	1.05	1.26	1.47	1.68	1.89	2.10
Southern Rhodesia 3 Pence	1944-1946	1.41	0.500	0.023		0.02	0.05	0.07	0.09	0.23	0.35	0.46	0.58	0.69	0.81	0.92	1.04	1.15
Southern Rhodesia 6 Pence	1932-1942	2.83	0.925	0.084		0.08	0.17	0.25	0.34	0.84	1.26	1.68	2.10	2.52	2.94	3.36	3.78	4.20
Southern Rhodesia 6 Pence	1944, 1946	2.83	0.500	0.045		0.05	0.09	0.14	0.18	0.45	0.68	0.90	1.13	1.35	1.58	1.80	2.03	2.25
Southern Rhodesia 1 Shilling	1932-1942	5.66	0.925	0.168		0.17	0.34	0.50	0.67	1.68	2.52	3.36	4.20	5.04	5.88	6.72	7.56	8.40
Southern Rhodesia 1 Shilling	1944, 1946	5.66	0.500	0.091		0.09	0.18	0.27	0.36	0.91	1.37	1.82	2.28	2.73	3.19	3.64	4.10	4.55
Southern Rhodesia 2 Shillings	1932-1942	11.31	0.925	0.336		0.34	0.67	1.01	1.34	3.36	5.04	6.72	8.40	10.08	11.76	13.44	15.12	16.80
Southern Rhodesia 2 Shillings	1944, 1946	11.31	0.500	0.182		0.18	0.36	0.55	0.73	1.82	2.73	3.64	4.55	5.46	6.37	7.28	8.19	9.10
Southern Rhodesia 1/2 Crown	1932-1942	14.14	0.925	0.421		0.42	0.84	1.26	1.68	4.21	6.32	8.42	10.53	12.63	14.74	16.84	18.95	21.05
Southern Rhodesia 1/2 Crown	1944, 1946	14.14	0.500	0.227		0.23	0.45	0.68	0.91	2.27	3.41	4.54	5.68	6.81	7.95	9.08	10.22	11.35
Southern Rhodesia Crown	1953	28.28	0.500	0.455		0.46	0.91	1.37	1.82	4.55	6.83	9.10	11.38	13.65	15.93	18.20	20.48	22.75
Spain 1/2 Real	1802-1833	1.69	0.812	0.044	s	0.04	0.09	0.13	0.18	0.44	0.66	0.88	1.10	1.32	1.54	1.76	1.98	2.20
Spain 1 Real	1801-1852	3.38	0.812	0.088	s	0.09	0.18	0.26	0.35	0.88	1.32	1.76	2.20	2.64	3.08	3.52	3.96	4.40
Spain 1 Real	1812, 1813	1.35	0.903	0.039		0.04	0.08	0.12	0.16	0.39	0.59	0.78	0.98	1.17	1.37	1.56	1.76	1.95
Spain 1 Real	1852-1864	1.31	0.900	0.038		0.04	0.08	0.11	0.15	0.38	0.57	0.76	0.95	1.14	1.33	1.52	1.71	1.90
Spain 2 Reales	1801-1851	6.77	0.812	0.177		0.18	0.35	0.53	0.71	1.77	2.66	3.54	4.43	5.31	6.20	7.08	7.97	8.85
Spain 2 Reales	1811-1813	2.71	0.903	0.079		0.08	0.16	0.24	0.32	0.79	1.19	1.58	1.98	2.37	2.77	3.16	3.56	3.95
Spain 2 Reales	1852-1864	2.63	0.900	0.076		0.08	0.15	0.23	0.30	0.76	1.14	1.52	1.90	2.28	2.66	3.04	3.42	3.80
Spain 4 Reales	1803-1849	13.54	0.896	0.390	s	0.39	0.78	1.17	1.56	3.90	5.85	7.80	9.75	11.70	13.65	15.60	17.55	19.50
Spain 4 Reales	1808-1823	5.42	0.903	0.157	s	0.16	0.31	0.47	0.63	1.57	2.36	3.14	3.93	4.71	5.50	6.28	7.07	7.85
Spain 4 Reales	1852-1864	5.26	0.900	0.152		0.15	0.30	0.46	0.61	1.52	2.28	3.04	3.80	4.56	5.32	6.08	6.84	7.60
Spain 8 Reales	1802-1830	27.07	0.903	0.786		0.79	1.57	2.36	3.14	7.86	11.79	15.72	19.65	23.58	27.51	31.44	35.37	39.30

Country & Denomination	Years Minted	Grams Weight	Fine-ness	Troy (ASW)	Code	$ Value 1	$ Value 2	$ Value 3	$ Value 4	$ Value 10	$ Value 15	$ Value 20	$ Value 25	$ Value 30	$ Value 35	$ Value 40	$ Value 45	$ Value 50
Spain 10 Reales	1809-1843	13.54	0.903	0.393	s	0.39	0.79	1.18	1.57	3.93	5.90	7.86	9.83	11.79	13.76	15.72	17.69	19.65
Spain 10 Reales	1851-1864	13.15	0.900	0.380		0.38	0.76	1.14	1.52	3.80	5.70	7.60	9.50	11.40	13.30	15.20	17.10	19.00
Spain 20 Reales	1809-1850	27.08	0.903	0.786	s	0.79	1.57	2.36	3.14	7.86	11.79	15.72	19.65	23.58	27.51	31.44	35.37	39.30
Spain 20 Reales	1850-1864	26.29	0.900	0.761		0.76	1.52	2.28	3.04	7.61	11.42	15.22	19.03	22.83	26.64	30.44	34.25	38.05
Spain 10 Centimos	1864-1868	1.30	0.810	0.034		0.03	0.07	0.10	0.14	0.34	0.51	0.68	0.85	1.02	1.19	1.36	1.53	1.70
Spain 20 Centimos	1864-1868	2.60	0.810	0.068		0.07	0.14	0.20	0.27	0.68	1.02	1.36	1.70	2.04	2.38	2.72	3.06	3.40
Spain 20 Centimos	1869-1926	1.00	0.835	0.027	s	0.03	0.05	0.08	0.11	0.27	0.41	0.54	0.68	0.81	0.95	1.08	1.22	1.35
Spain 40 Centimos	1864-1868	5.19	0.810	0.135		0.14	0.27	0.41	0.54	1.35	2.03	2.70	3.38	4.05	4.73	5.40	6.08	6.75
Spain 50 Centimos	1869-1926	2.50	0.835	0.067	s	0.07	0.13	0.20	0.27	0.67	1.01	1.34	1.68	2.01	2.35	2.68	3.02	3.35
Spain 1 Escudo	1865-1868	12.98	0.900	0.376		0.38	0.75	1.13	1.50	3.76	5.64	7.52	9.40	11.28	13.16	15.04	16.92	18.80
Spain 2 Escudos	1865-1868	25.96	0.900	0.751		0.75	1.50	2.25	3.00	7.51	11.27	15.02	18.78	22.53	26.29	30.04	33.80	37.55
Spain 1 Peseta	1869-1933	5.00	0.835	0.134	s	0.13	0.27	0.40	0.54	1.34	2.01	2.68	3.35	4.02	4.69	5.36	6.03	6.70
Spain 2 Pesetas	1869-1905	10.00	0.835	0.269	s	0.27	0.54	0.81	1.08	2.69	4.04	5.38	6.73	8.07	9.42	10.76	12.11	13.45
Spain 5 Pesetas	1869-1899	25.00	0.900	0.723	s	0.72	1.45	2.17	2.89	7.23	10.85	14.46	18.08	21.69	25.31	28.92	32.54	36.15
Spain 100 Pesetas	1966	19.00	0.800	0.489		0.49	0.98	1.47	1.96	4.89	7.34	9.78	12.23	14.67	17.12	19.56	22.01	24.45
Spain 200 Pesetas	1992	3.37	0.925	0.100		0.10	0.20	0.30	0.40	1.00	1.50	2.00	2.50	3.00	3.50	4.00	4.50	5.00
Spain 500 Pesetas	1989-1992	6.75	0.925	0.201		0.20	0.40	0.60	0.80	2.01	3.02	4.02	5.03	6.03	7.04	8.04	9.05	10.05
Spain 1000 Pesetas	1989-1999	13.50	0.925	0.402	s, v	0.40	0.80	1.21	1.61	4.02	6.03	8.04	10.05	12.06	14.07	16.08	18.09	20.10
Spain 1500 Pesetas	1999	19.83	0.925	0.590		0.59	1.18	1.77	2.36	5.90	8.85	11.80	14.75	17.70	20.65	23.60	26.55	29.50
Spain 2000 Pesetas	1989-2000	27.00	0.925	0.803	s, v	0.80	1.61	2.41	3.21	8.03	12.05	16.06	20.08	24.09	28.11	32.12	36.14	40.15
Spain 2000 Pesetas	1994-2000	18.00	0.925	0.535	s	0.54	1.07	1.61	2.14	5.35	8.03	10.70	13.38	16.05	18.73	21.40	24.08	26.75
Spain 5000 Pesetas	1989-1997	54.00	0.925	1.606	s	1.61	3.21	4.82	6.42	16.06	24.09	32.12	40.15	48.18	56.21	64.24	72.27	80.30
Spain 10,000 Pesetas	1989-1997	168.75	0.925	5.019	s	5.02	10.04	15.06	20.08	50.19	75.29	100.38	125.48	150.57	175.67	200.76	225.86	250.95
Sri Lanka 1 Rupee	1992	7.13	0.925	0.212		0.21	0.42	0.64	0.85	2.12	3.18	4.24	5.30	6.36	7.42	8.48	9.54	10.60
Sri Lanka 100 Rupees	1991	10.20	0.925	0.303		0.30	0.61	0.91	1.21	3.03	4.55	6.06	7.58	9.09	10.61	12.12	13.64	15.15
Sri Lanka 500 Rupees	1990, 1993	28.28	0.925	0.841		0.84	1.68	2.52	3.36	8.41	12.62	16.82	21.03	25.23	29.44	33.64	37.85	42.05
Sri Lanka 1000 Rupees	1998-2000	28.28	0.925	0.841		0.84	1.68	2.52	3.36	8.41	12.62	16.82	21.03	25.23	29.44	33.64	37.85	42.05
Straits Settlements 5 Cents	1871-1903	1.36	0.800	0.035		0.04	0.07	0.11	0.14	0.35	0.53	0.70	0.88	1.05	1.23	1.40	1.58	1.75
Straits Settlements 5 Cents	1910	1.36	0.600	0.026		0.03	0.05	0.08	0.10	0.26	0.39	0.52	0.65	0.78	0.91	1.04	1.17	1.30
Straits Settlements 5 Cents	1918-1920	1.36	0.400	0.017		0.02	0.03	0.05	0.07	0.17	0.26	0.34	0.43	0.51	0.60	0.68	0.77	0.85
Straits Settlements 10 Cents	1871-1903	2.71	0.800	0.070		0.07	0.14	0.21	0.28	0.70	1.05	1.40	1.75	2.10	2.45	2.80	3.15	3.50
Straits Settlements 10 Cents	1909-1917	2.71	0.600	0.052	s	0.05	0.10	0.16	0.21	0.52	0.78	1.04	1.30	1.56	1.82	2.08	2.34	2.60
Straits Settlements 10 Cents	1918-1920	2.71	0.400	0.035		0.04	0.07	0.11	0.14	0.35	0.53	0.70	0.88	1.05	1.23	1.40	1.58	1.75
Straits Settlements 10 Cents	1926-1927	2.71	0.600	0.052		0.05	0.10	0.16	0.21	0.52	0.78	1.04	1.30	1.56	1.82	2.08	2.34	2.60
Straits Settlements 20 Cents	1871-1903	5.43	0.800	0.140		0.14	0.28	0.42	0.56	1.40	2.10	2.80	3.50	4.20	4.90	5.60	6.30	7.00
Straits Settlements 20 Cents	1910-1917	5.43	0.600	0.105	s	0.11	0.21	0.32	0.42	1.05	1.58	2.10	2.63	3.15	3.68	4.20	4.73	5.25
Straits Settlements 20 Cents	1919	5.43	0.400	0.070		0.07	0.14	0.21	0.28	0.70	1.05	1.40	1.75	2.10	2.45	2.80	3.15	3.50
Straits Settlements 50 Cents	1926-1935	5.43	0.600	0.105	s	0.11	0.21	0.32	0.42	1.05	1.58	2.10	2.63	3.15	3.68	4.20	4.73	5.25
Straits Settlements 50 Cents	1886-1905	13.58	0.800	0.349		0.35	0.70	1.05	1.40	3.49	5.24	6.98	8.73	10.47	12.22	13.96	15.71	17.45
Straits Settlements 50 Cents	1907-1908	10.10	0.900	0.292		0.29	0.58	0.88	1.17	2.92	4.38	5.84	7.30	8.76	10.22	11.68	13.14	14.60
Straits Settlements 50 Cents	1920-1921	8.42	0.500	0.135		0.14	0.27	0.41	0.54	1.35	2.03	2.70	3.38	4.05	4.73	5.40	6.08	6.75
Straits Settlements 1 Dollar	1903-1904	26.95	0.900	0.780		0.78	1.56	2.34	3.12	7.80	11.70	15.60	19.50	23.40	27.30	31.20	35.10	39.00
Straits Settlements 1 Dollar	1907-1909	20.21	0.900	0.585		0.59	1.17	1.76	2.34	5.85	8.78	11.70	14.63	17.55	20.48	23.40	26.33	29.25

Country & Denomination	Years Minted	Grams Weight	Fineness	Troy (ASW)	Code	$ Value 1	$ Value 2	$ Value 3	$ Value 4	$ Value 10	$ Value 15	$ Value 20	$ Value 25	$ Value 30	$ Value 35	$ Value 40	$ Value 45	$ Value 50
Straits Settlements 1 Dollar	1919-1926	16.85	0.500	0.271	S	0.27	0.54	0.81	1.08	2.71	4.07	5.42	6.78	8.13	9.49	10.84	12.20	13.55
Sudan 2-1/2 Pounds	1976	20.30	0.925	0.841		0.84	1.68	2.52	3.36	8.41	12.62	16.82	21.03	25.23	29.44	33.64	37.85	42.05
Sudan 5 Pounds	1976	35.00	0.925	1.041		1.04	2.08	3.12	4.16	10.41	15.62	20.82	26.03	31.23	36.44	41.64	46.85	52.05
Sudan 5 Pounds	1978	17.50	0.925	0.521		0.52	1.04	1.56	2.08	5.21	7.82	10.42	13.03	15.63	18.24	20.84	23.45	26.05
Sudan 5 Pounds	1981	28.28	0.925	0.841		0.84	1.68	2.52	3.36	8.41	12.62	16.82	21.03	25.23	29.44	33.64	37.85	42.05
Sudan 5 Pounds	1981, 1984	19.44	0.925	0.578		0.58	1.16	1.73	2.31	5.78	8.67	11.56	14.45	17.34	20.23	23.12	26.01	28.90
Sudan 10 Pounds	1978-1981	35.00	0.925	1.041	S	1.04	2.08	3.12	4.16	10.41	15.62	20.82	26.03	31.23	36.44	41.64	46.85	52.05
						0.00												
Suriname 10 Cents	1942	1.40	0.640	0.029		0.03	0.06	0.09	0.12	0.29	0.44	0.58	0.73	0.87	1.02	1.16	1.31	1.45
Suriname 1 Gulden	1962-1966	10.00	0.720	0.232	S	0.23	0.46	0.70	0.93	2.32	3.48	4.64	5.80	6.96	8.12	9.28	10.44	11.60
Suriname 10 Gulden	1976	15.95	0.925	0.474		0.47	0.95	1.42	1.90	4.74	7.11	9.48	11.85	14.22	16.59	18.96	21.33	23.70
Suriname 25 Gulden	1976	26.20	0.925	0.779		0.78	1.56	2.34	3.12	7.79	11.69	15.58	19.48	23.37	27.27	31.16	35.06	38.95
Suriname 25 Guilder	1981	15.50	0.925	0.461		0.46	0.92	1.38	1.84	4.61	6.92	9.22	11.53	13.83	16.14	18.44	20.75	23.05
Suriname 25 Gulden	1985	25.10	0.925	0.744		0.74	1.49	2.23	2.98	7.44	11.16	14.88	18.60	22.32	26.04	29.76	33.48	37.20
Suriname 25 Guilder	1990, 1991	28.28	0.925	0.841		0.84	1.68	2.52	3.36	8.41	12.62	16.82	21.03	25.23	29.44	33.64	37.85	42.05
Suriname 30 Gulden	1987	14.30	0.925	0.425		0.43	0.85	1.28	1.70	4.25	6.38	8.50	10.63	12.75	14.88	17.00	19.13	21.25
Suriname 50 Guilder	1988, 1990	28.28	0.925	0.841		0.84	1.68	2.52	3.36	8.41	12.62	16.82	21.03	25.23	29.44	33.64	37.85	42.05
Suriname 50 Guilder	1990, 1992	26.00	0.925	0.773		0.77	1.55	2.32	3.09	7.73	11.60	15.46	19.33	23.19	27.06	30.92	34.79	38.65
Suriname 100 Gulden	1991-1994	20.00	0.999	0.642	S, V	0.64	1.28	1.93	2.57	6.42	9.63	12.84	16.05	19.26	22.47	25.68	28.89	32.10
Suriname 12,500 Gulden	1999	28.28	0.925	0.841		0.84	1.68	2.52	3.36	8.41	12.62	16.82	21.03	25.23	29.44	33.64	37.85	42.05
Swaziland 5 Cents	1967	2.75	0.800	0.071		0.07	0.14	0.21	0.28	0.71	1.07	1.42	1.78	2.13	2.49	2.84	3.20	3.55
Swaziland 10 Cents	1968	4.38	0.800	0.113		0.11	0.23	0.34	0.45	1.13	1.70	2.26	2.83	3.39	3.96	4.52	5.09	5.65
Swaziland 20 Cents	1968	6.63	0.800	0.171		0.17	0.34	0.51	0.68	1.71	2.57	3.42	4.28	5.13	5.99	6.84	7.70	8.55
Swaziland 50 Cents	1968	10.39	0.800	0.267		0.27	0.53	0.80	1.07	2.67	4.01	5.34	6.68	8.01	9.35	10.68	12.02	13.35
Swaziland 1 Lilangeni	1968	15.00	0.800	0.386	N	0.39	0.77	1.16	1.54	3.86	5.79	7.72	9.65	11.58	13.51	15.44	17.37	19.30
Swaziland 2 Emalangeni	1981	17.00	0.925	0.506	N	0.51	1.01	1.52	2.02	5.06	7.59	10.12	12.65	15.18	17.71	20.24	22.77	25.30
Swaziland 5 Emalangeni	1974	10.30	0.925	0.306		0.31	0.61	0.92	1.22	3.06	4.59	6.12	7.65	9.18	10.71	12.24	13.77	15.30
Swaziland 7-1/2 Emalangeni	1974	16.20	0.925	0.482		0.48	0.96	1.45	1.93	4.82	7.23	9.64	12.05	14.46	16.87	19.28	21.69	24.10
Swaziland 10 Emalangeni	1975	25.50	0.925	0.758		0.76	1.52	2.27	3.03	7.58	11.37	15.16	18.95	22.74	26.53	30.32	34.11	37.90
Swaziland 15 Emalangeni	1974	32.60	0.925	0.970		0.97	1.94	2.91	3.88	9.70	14.55	19.40	24.25	29.10	33.95	38.80	43.65	48.50
Swaziland 25 Emalangeni	1981, 1986	28.28	0.925	0.841	S	0.84	1.68	2.52	3.36	8.41	12.62	16.82	21.03	25.23	29.44	33.64	37.85	42.05
						0.00												
Sweden 1/32 Riksdaler	1851-1853	1.06	0.750	0.026		0.03	0.05	0.08	0.10	0.26	0.39	0.52	0.65	0.78	0.91	1.04	1.17	1.30
Sweden 1/24 Riksdaler	1810-1816	2.77	0.382	0.034		0.03	0.07	0.10	0.14	0.34	0.51	0.68	0.85	1.02	1.19	1.36	1.53	1.70
Sweden 1/16 Riksdaler	1835-1855	2.13	0.750	0.051	S	0.05	0.10	0.15	0.20	0.51	0.77	1.02	1.28	1.53	1.79	2.04	2.30	2.55
Sweden 1/12 Riksdaler	1831-1833	2.83	0.750	0.068		0.07	0.14	0.20	0.27	0.68	1.02	1.36	1.70	2.04	2.38	2.72	3.06	3.40
Sweden 1/8 Riksdaler	1830-1837	4.25	0.750	0.102	S	0.10	0.20	0.31	0.41	1.02	1.53	2.04	2.55	3.06	3.57	4.08	4.59	5.10
Sweden 1/6 Riksdaler	1800-1852	6.20	0.691	0.138		0.14	0.28	0.41	0.55	1.38	2.07	2.76	3.45	4.14	4.83	5.52	6.21	6.90
Sweden 1/4 Riksdaler	1830-1852	8.50	0.750	0.205	S	0.21	0.41	0.62	0.82	2.05	3.08	4.10	5.13	6.15	7.18	8.20	9.23	10.25
Sweden 1/3 Riksdaler	1813-1829	9.75	0.878	0.275	S	0.28	0.55	0.83	1.10	2.75	4.13	5.50	6.88	8.25	9.63	11.00	12.38	13.75
Sweden 1/2 Riksdaler	1819-1873	14.45	0.875	0.407	S	0.41	0.81	1.22	1.63	4.07	6.11	8.14	10.18	12.21	14.25	16.28	18.32	20.35
Sweden 1/2 Riksdaler	1831-1852	17.00	0.750	0.410	S	0.41	0.82	1.23	1.64	4.10	6.15	8.20	10.25	12.30	14.35	16.40	18.45	20.50
Sweden 1 Riksdaler	1801-1818	29.36	0.878	0.829	S	0.83	1.66	2.49	3.32	8.29	12.44	16.58	20.73	24.87	29.02	33.16	37.31	41.45

Country & Denomination	Years Minted	Grams Weight	Fineness	Troy (ASW)	Code	$ Value 1	$ Value 2	$ Value 3	$ Value 4	$ Value 10	$ Value 15	$ Value 20	$ Value 25	$ Value 30	$ Value 35	$ Value 40	$ Value 45	$ Value 50
Sweden 1 Riksdaler	1818-1829	29.25	0.878	0.826	s	0.83	1.65	2.48	3.30	8.26	12.39	16.52	20.65	24.78	28.91	33.04	37.17	41.30
Sweden 1 Riksdaler	1831-1855	34.00	0.750	0.820	s	0.82	1.64	2.46	3.28	8.20	12.30	16.40	20.50	24.60	28.70	32.80	36.90	41.00
Sweden 1 Riksdaler Riksmynt	1857-1873	8.50	0.750	0.205	s	0.21	0.41	0.62	0.82	2.05	3.08	4.10	5.13	6.15	7.18	8.20	9.23	10.25
Sweden 2 Riksdaler Riksmynt	1857-1871	17.00	0.750	0.410	s	0.41	0.82	1.23	1.64	4.10	6.15	8.20	10.25	12.30	14.35	16.40	18.45	20.50
Sweden 1 Riksdaler Specie	1856-1871	34.00	0.750	0.820	s	0.82	1.64	2.46	3.28	8.20	12.30	16.40	20.50	24.60	28.70	32.80	36.90	41.00
Sweden 10 Ore	1874-1962	1.45	0.400	0.019	N,S	0.02	0.04	0.06	0.08	0.19	0.29	0.38	0.48	0.57	0.67	0.76	0.86	0.95
Sweden 25 Ore	1876-1941	2.42	0.600	0.047	N,S	0.05	0.09	0.14	0.19	0.47	0.71	0.94	1.18	1.41	1.65	1.88	2.12	2.35
Sweden 25 Ore	1943-1961	2.32	0.400	0.030	N,S	0.03	0.06	0.09	0.12	0.30	0.45	0.60	0.75	0.90	1.05	1.20	1.35	1.50
Sweden 50 Ore	1875-1939	5.00	0.600	0.097	N,S	0.10	0.19	0.29	0.39	0.97	1.46	1.94	2.43	2.91	3.40	3.88	4.37	4.85
Sweden 50 Ore	1943-1961	4.80	0.400	0.062	N,S	0.06	0.12	0.19	0.25	0.62	0.93	1.24	1.55	1.86	2.17	2.48	2.79	3.10
Sweden 1 Krona	1875-1942	7.50	0.800	0.193	s	0.19	0.39	0.58	0.77	1.93	2.90	3.86	4.83	5.79	6.76	7.72	8.69	9.65
Sweden 1 Krona	1942-1968	7.00	0.400	0.090	s	0.09	0.18	0.27	0.36	0.90	1.35	1.80	2.25	2.70	3.15	3.60	4.05	4.50
Sweden 2 Kronor	1876-1940	15.00	0.800	0.386	s	0.39	0.77	1.16	1.54	3.86	5.79	7.72	9.65	11.58	13.51	15.44	17.37	19.30
Sweden 2 Kronor	1942-1966	14.00	0.400	0.180	s	0.18	0.36	0.54	0.72	1.80	2.70	3.60	4.50	5.40	6.30	7.20	8.10	9.00
Sweden 5 Kronor	1935	25.00	0.900	0.723		0.72	1.45	2.17	2.89	7.23	10.85	14.46	18.08	21.69	25.31	28.92	32.54	36.15
Sweden 5 Kronor	1952	22.70	0.400	0.292		0.29	0.58	0.88	1.17	2.92	4.38	5.84	7.30	8.76	10.22	11.68	13.14	14.60
Sweden 5 Kronor	1954-1971	18.00	0.400	0.232	s	0.23	0.46	0.70	0.93	2.32	3.48	4.64	5.80	6.96	8.12	9.28	10.44	11.60
Sweden 10 Kronor	1972	18.00	0.830	0.480		0.48	0.96	1.44	1.92	4.80	7.20	9.60	12.00	14.40	16.80	19.20	21.60	24.00
Sweden 50 Kronor	1975-1976	27.00	0.925	0.803		0.80	1.61	2.41	3.21	8.03	12.05	16.06	20.08	24.09	28.11	32.12	36.14	40.15
Sweden 100 Kronor	1983-1988	16.00	0.925	0.476	s	0.48	0.95	1.43	1.90	4.76	7.14	9.52	11.90	14.28	16.66	19.04	21.42	23.80
Sweden 200 Kronor	1980-1998	27.00	0.925	0.803	s	0.80	1.61	2.41	3.21	8.03	12.05	16.06	20.08	24.09	28.11	32.12	36.14	40.15
Sweden 200 Kronor	1999	27.03	0.925	0.804	s	0.80	1.61	2.41	3.22	8.04	12.06	16.08	20.10	24.12	28.14	32.16	36.18	40.20
Switzerland 1/2 Franc*	1850, 1851	2.50	0.900	0.072		0.07	0.14	0.22	0.29	0.72	1.08	1.44	1.80	2.16	2.52	2.88	3.24	3.60
Switzerland 1/2 Franc	1875-1967	2.50	0.835	0.067	s	0.07	0.13	0.20	0.27	0.67	1.01	1.34	1.68	2.01	2.35	2.68	3.02	3.35
Switzerland 1 Franc	1850-1857	5.00	0.900	0.145	s	0.15	0.29	0.44	0.58	1.45	2.18	2.90	3.63	4.35	5.08	5.80	6.53	7.25
Switzerland 1 Franc	1860, 1861	5.00	0.800	0.129		0.13	0.26	0.39	0.52	1.29	1.94	2.58	3.23	3.87	4.52	5.16	5.81	6.45
Switzerland 1 Franc	1875-1967	5.00	0.835	0.134	s	0.13	0.27	0.40	0.54	1.34	2.01	2.68	3.35	4.02	4.69	5.36	6.03	6.70
Switzerland 2 Francs	1850, 1857	10.00	0.900	0.289		0.29	0.58	0.87	1.16	2.89	4.34	5.78	7.23	8.67	10.12	11.56	13.01	14.45
Switzerland 2 Francs	1860-1863	10.00	0.800	0.257	s	0.26	0.51	0.77	1.03	2.57	3.86	5.14	6.43	7.71	9.00	10.28	11.57	12.85
Switzerland 2 Francs	1874-1967	10.00	0.835	0.268	s	0.27	0.54	0.80	1.07	2.68	4.02	5.36	6.70	8.04	9.38	10.72	12.06	13.40
Switzerland 5 Francs	1850-1928	25.00	0.900	0.723	s	0.72	1.45	2.17	2.89	7.23	10.85	14.46	18.08	21.69	25.31	28.92	32.54	36.15
Switzerland 5 Francs	1931-1963	15.00	0.835	0.403	s	0.40	0.81	1.21	1.61	4.03	6.05	8.06	10.08	12.09	14.11	16.12	18.14	20.15
Switzerland 20 Francs	1991-2000	20.00	0.835	0.537		0.54	1.07	1.61	2.15	5.37	8.06	10.74	13.43	16.11	18.80	21.48	24.17	26.85
Switzerland 20 Francs	1998	20.00	0.999	0.803		0.80	1.61	2.41	3.21	8.03	12.05	16.06	20.08	24.09	28.11	32.12	36.14	40.15
Switzerland 50 Francs	1984-2000	25.00	0.900	0.724		0.72	1.45	2.17	2.90	7.24	10.86	14.48	18.10	21.72	25.34	28.96	32.58	36.20
Syria 10 Piastres	1929	2.00	0.680	0.044		0.04	0.09	0.13	0.18	0.44	0.66	0.88	1.10	1.32	1.54	1.76	1.98	2.20
Syria 25 Piastres	1929-1937	5.00	0.680	0.110	s	0.11	0.22	0.33	0.44	1.10	1.65	2.20	2.75	3.30	3.85	4.40	4.95	5.50
Syria 25 Piastres	1947	2.50	0.600	0.048		0.05	0.10	0.14	0.19	0.48	0.72	0.96	1.20	1.44	1.68	1.92	2.16	2.40
Syria 50 Piastres	1929-1937	10.00	0.680	0.219	s	0.22	0.44	0.66	0.88	2.19	3.29	4.38	5.48	6.57	7.67	8.76	9.86	10.95
Syria 50 Piastres	1947	5.00	0.600	0.096		0.10	0.19	0.29	0.38	0.96	1.44	1.92	2.40	2.88	3.36	3.84	4.32	4.80

T

Taiwan--see China, Rep.

Country & Denomination	Years Minted	Grams Weight	Fine-ness	Troy (ASW)	Code	$ Value 1	$ Value 2	$ Value 3	$ Value 4	$ Value 10	$ Value 15	$ Value 20	$ Value 25	$ Value 30	$ Value 35	$ Value 40	$ Value 45	$ Value 50
Tajikistan 20 Roubles	1999	20.00	0.925	0.595		0.60	1.19	1.79	2.38	5.95	8.93	11.90	14.88	17.85	20.83	23.80	26.78	29.75
Tanzania 20 Schillingi	1981, 1986	16.00	0.925	0.476		0.48	0.95	1.43	1.90	4.76	7.14	9.52	11.90	14.28	16.66	19.04	21.42	23.80
Tanzania 25 Schillingi	1974	25.40	0.500	0.408		0.41	0.82	1.22	1.63	4.08	6.12	8.16	10.20	12.24	14.28	16.32	18.36	20.40
Tanzania 25 Schillingi	1974	28.28	0.925	0.841		0.84	1.68	2.52	3.36	8.41	12.62	16.82	21.03	25.23	29.44	33.64	37.85	42.05
Tanzania 25 Schillingi	1991	13.04	0.925	0.388		0.39	0.78	1.16	1.55	3.88	5.82	7.76	9.70	11.64	13.58	15.52	17.46	19.40
Tanzania 50 Schillingi	1974	31.85	0.500	0.512		0.51	1.02	1.54	2.05	5.12	7.68	10.24	12.80	15.36	17.92	20.48	23.04	25.60
Tanzania 50 Schillingi	1974	35.00	0.925	1.041		1.04	2.08	3.12	4.16	10.41	15.62	20.82	26.03	31.23	36.44	41.64	46.85	52.05
Tanzania 100 Schillingi	1984	23.33	0.925	0.694		0.69	1.39	2.08	2.78	6.94	10.41	13.88	17.35	20.82	24.29	27.76	31.23	34.70
Tanzania 100 Schillingi	1986, 1990	19.44	0.925	0.578		0.58	1.16	1.73	2.31	5.78	8.67	11.56	14.45	17.34	20.23	23.12	26.01	28.90
Tanzania 200 Schillingi	1981	28.28	0.925	0.841		0.84	1.68	2.52	3.36	8.41	12.62	16.82	21.03	25.23	29.44	33.64	37.85	42.05
Tanzania 200 Schillingi	1997	20.00	0.500	0.321		0.32	0.64	0.96	1.28	3.21	4.82	6.42	8.03	9.63	11.24	12.84	14.45	16.05
Tanzania 200 Schillingi	1999	15.40	0.925	0.458		0.46	0.92	1.37	1.83	4.58	6.87	9.16	11.45	13.74	16.03	18.32	20.61	22.90
Tanzania 250 Schillingi	1985	28.16	0.925	0.837		0.84	1.67	2.51	3.35	8.37	12.56	16.74	20.93	25.11	29.30	33.48	37.67	41.85
Tanzania 500 Schillingi	1992	20.00	0.999	0.578		0.58	1.16	1.73	2.31	5.78	8.67	11.56	14.45	17.34	20.23	23.12	26.01	28.90
Tanzania 500 Schillingi	1998	33.63	0.925	1.000		1.00	2.00	3.00	4.00	10.00	15.00	20.00	25.00	30.00	35.00	40.00	45.00	50.00
Tanzania 2500 Schillingi	1998	155.36	0.999	5.000		5.00	10.00	15.00	20.00	50.00	75.00	100.00	125.00	150.00	175.00	200.00	225.00	250.00
Tanzania 500 Schillings	1997	31.22	0.925	0.926		0.93	1.85	2.78	3.70	9.26	13.89	18.52	23.15	27.78	32.41	37.04	41.67	46.30
Thailand 1 Salung / ¼ Baht*	1915	3.75	0.800	0.097		0.10	0.19	0.29	0.39	0.97	1.45	1.93	2.41	2.90	3.38	3.86	4.34	4.83
Thailand 1 Salung / ¼ Baht	1917-1925	3.75	0.650	0.078	s	0.08	0.16	0.23	0.31	0.78	1.17	1.56	1.95	2.34	2.73	3.12	3.51	3.90
Thailand 1 Salung / ¼ Baht	1919	3.75	0.500	0.060		0.06	0.12	0.18	0.24	0.60	0.90	1.20	1.50	1.80	2.10	2.40	2.70	3.00
Thailand 2 Salung / ½ Baht	1915	7.50	0.800	0.193		0.19	0.39	0.58	0.77	1.93	2.90	3.86	4.83	5.79	6.76	7.72	8.69	9.65
Thailand 2 Salung / ½ Baht	1919	7.50	0.500	0.121		0.12	0.24	0.36	0.48	1.21	1.82	2.42	3.03	3.63	4.24	4.84	5.45	6.05
Thailand 2 Salung / ½ Baht	1919-1921	7.50	0.650	0.157		0.16	0.31	0.47	0.63	1.57	2.36	3.14	3.93	4.71	5.50	6.28	7.07	7.85
Thailand 25 Satang / ¼ Baht	1929	3.75	0.650	0.078	s	0.08	0.16	0.23	0.31	0.78	1.17	1.56	1.95	2.34	2.73	3.12	3.51	3.90
Thailand 50 Satang / ½ Baht	1929	7.50	0.650	0.157		0.16	0.31	0.47	0.63	1.57	2.36	3.14	3.93	4.71	5.50	6.28	7.07	7.85
Thailand 1 Baht	1857-1860	15.45	0.900	0.447	s	0.45	0.89	1.34	1.79	4.47	6.71	8.94	11.18	13.41	15.65	17.88	20.12	22.35
Thailand 1 Baht	1869-1907	15.20	0.800	0.434		0.43	0.87	1.30	1.74	4.34	6.51	8.68	10.85	13.02	15.19	17.36	19.53	21.70
Thailand 1 Baht	1908-1918	15.00	0.900	0.434	s	0.43	0.87	1.30	1.74	4.34	6.51	8.68	10.85	13.02	15.19	17.36	19.53	21.70
Thailand 2 Baht	1863	30.20	0.900	0.874		0.87	1.75	2.62	3.50	8.74	13.11	17.48	21.85	26.22	30.59	34.96	39.33	43.70
Thailand 4 Baht (Tamlung)	1864	60.4	0.900	1.748		1.75	3.50	5.24	6.99	17.48	26.22	34.96	43.70	52.44	61.18	69.92	78.66	87.40
Thailand 20 Baht	1963	19.60	0.750	0.473		0.47	0.95	1.42	1.89	4.73	7.10	9.46	11.83	14.19	16.56	18.92	21.29	23.65
Thailand 50 Baht	1971	24.70	0.900	0.715		0.72	1.43	2.15	2.86	7.15	10.73	14.30	17.88	21.45	25.03	28.60	32.18	35.75
Thailand 50 Baht	1974	24.85	0.400	0.320		0.32	0.64	0.96	1.28	3.20	4.80	6.40	8.00	9.60	11.20	12.80	14.40	16.00
Thailand 50 Baht	1974	25.55	0.500	0.417		0.42	0.83	1.25	1.67	4.17	6.26	8.34	10.43	12.51	14.60	16.68	18.77	20.85
Thailand 50 Baht	1974	28.28	0.925	0.841		0.84	1.68	2.52	3.36	8.41	12.62	16.82	21.03	25.23	29.44	33.64	37.85	42.05
Thailand 50 Baht	2000	20.00	0.925	0.595		0.60	1.19	1.79	2.38	5.95	8.93	11.90	14.88	17.85	20.83	23.80	26.78	29.75
Thailand 100 Baht	1974	31.70	0.500	0.510		0.51	1.02	1.53	2.04	5.10	7.65	10.20	12.75	15.30	17.85	20.40	22.95	25.50
Thailand 100 Baht	1975	25.00	0.500	0.400		0.40	0.80	1.20	1.60	4.00	6.00	8.00	10.00	12.00	14.00	16.00	18.00	20.00
Thailand 100 Baht	1997	15.00	0.925	0.446		0.45	0.89	1.34	1.78	4.46	6.69	8.92	11.15	13.38	15.61	17.84	20.07	22.30
Thailand 150 Baht	1975-1978	22.00	0.925	0.660		0.66	1.32	1.98	2.64	6.60	9.90	13.20	16.50	19.80	23.10	26.40	29.70	33.00
Thailand 150 Baht	1987-1996	7.50	0.925	0.223	s	0.22	0.45	0.67	0.89	2.23	3.35	4.46	5.58	6.69	7.81	8.92	10.04	11.15
Thailand 200 Baht	1979	22.00	0.925	0.654		0.65	1.31	1.96	2.62	6.54	9.81	13.08	16.35	19.62	22.89	26.16	29.43	32.70
Thailand 200 Baht	1981-1998	23.30	0.925	0.694	v	0.69	1.39	2.08	2.78	6.94	10.41	13.88	17.35	20.82	24.29	27.76	31.23	34.70

Country & Denomination	Years Minted	Grams Weight	Fine-ness	Troy (ASW)	Code	$ Value 1	$ Value 2	$ Value 3	$ Value 4	$ Value 10	$ Value 15	$ Value 20	$ Value 25	$ Value 30	$ Value 35	$ Value 40	$ Value 45	$ Value 50
Thailand 200 Baht	2000	155.51	0.925	4.625		4.63	9.25	13.88	18.50	46.25	69.38	92.50	115.63	138.75	161.88	185.00	208.13	231.25
Thailand 250 Baht	1983	28.28	0.925	0.841	N	0.84	1.68	2.52	3.36	8.41	12.62	16.82	21.03	25.23	29.44	33.64	37.85	42.05
Thailand 300 Baht	1979	22.00	0.925	0.654		0.65	1.31	1.96	2.62	6.54	9.81	13.08	16.35	19.62	22.89	26.16	29.43	32.70
Thailand 300 Baht	1987-1996	15.00	0.925	0.446	S	0.45	0.89	1.34	1.78	4.46	6.69	8.92	11.15	13.38	15.61	17.84	20.07	22.30
Thailand 600 Baht	1980, 1981	14.90	0.925	0.443		0.44	0.89	1.33	1.77	4.43	6.65	8.86	11.08	13.29	15.51	17.72	19.94	22.15
Thailand 600 Baht	1987-1993	30.00	0.925	0.892		0.89	1.78	2.68	3.57	8.92	13.38	17.84	22.30	26.76	31.22	35.68	40.14	44.60
Thailand 600 Baht	1995-2000	22.15	0.925	0.659	V	0.66	1.32	1.98	2.64	6.59	9.89	13.18	16.48	19.77	23.07	26.36	29.66	32.95
Timor 3 Escudos	1958	3.50	0.650	0.073		0.07	0.15	0.22	0.29	0.73	1.10	1.46	1.83	2.19	2.56	2.92	3.29	3.65
Timor 6 Escudos	1958	7.00	0.650	0.146		0.15	0.29	0.44	0.58	1.46	2.19	2.92	3.65	4.38	5.11	5.84	6.57	7.30
Timor 10 Escudos	1964	7.00	0.650	0.146		0.15	0.29	0.44	0.58	1.46	2.19	2.92	3.65	4.38	5.11	5.84	6.57	7.30
Togo 500 Francs	1999, 2000	7.00	0.999	0.225		0.23	0.45	0.68	0.90	2.25	3.38	4.50	5.63	6.75	7.88	9.00	10.13	11.25
Togo 1000 Francs	1999, 2000	14.97	0.999	0.481		0.48	0.96	1.44	1.92	4.81	7.22	9.62	12.03	14.43	16.84	19.24	21.65	24.05
Togo 5000 Francs	1977	24.36	0.925	0.725		0.73	1.45	2.18	2.90	7.25	10.88	14.50	18.13	21.75	25.38	29.00	32.63	36.25
Togo 10,000 Francs	1977	49.32	0.925	1.467		1.47	2.93	4.40	5.87	14.67	22.01	29.34	36.68	44.01	51.35	58.68	66.02	73.35
Tokelau 1 Tala	1978-1982	27.25	0.925	0.810		0.81	1.62	2.43	3.24	8.10	12.15	16.20	20.25	24.30	28.35	32.40	36.45	40.50
Tokelau 5 Tala	1983	28.28	0.925	0.841		0.84	1.68	2.52	3.36	8.41	12.62	16.82	21.03	25.23	29.44	33.64	37.85	42.05
Tokelau 5 Tala	1984-1989	27.05	0.925	0.805	S	0.81	1.61	2.42	3.22	8.05	12.08	16.10	20.13	24.15	28.18	32.20	36.23	40.25
Tokelau 5 Tala	1989	27.21	0.925	0.809		0.81	1.62	2.43	3.24	8.09	12.14	16.18	20.23	24.27	28.32	32.36	36.41	40.45
Tokelau 5 Tala	1993-1998	31.50	0.925	0.937	S, V	0.94	1.87	2.81	3.75	9.37	14.06	18.74	23.43	28.11	32.80	37.48	42.17	46.85
Tokelau 5 Tala	2000	28.12	0.925	0.836		0.84	1.67	2.51	3.34	8.36	12.54	16.72	20.90	25.08	29.26	33.44	37.62	41.80
Tokelau 50 Tala	1991-1993	31.20	0.999	1.000	V	1.00	2.00	3.00	4.00	10.00	15.00	20.00	25.00	30.00	35.00	40.00	45.00	50.00
Tokelau 100 Tala	1996	32.15	0.999	1.000		1.00	2.00	3.00	4.00	10.00	15.00	20.00	25.00	30.00	35.00	40.00	45.00	50.00
Tonga 50 Seniti	1998	20.00	0.925	0.595		0.60	1.19	1.79	2.38	5.95	8.93	11.90	14.88	17.85	20.83	23.80	26.78	29.75
Tonga 1 Pa'anga	1978-1981	24.50	0.999	0.787	N	0.79	1.57	2.36	3.15	7.87	11.81	15.74	19.68	23.61	27.55	31.48	35.42	39.35
Tonga 1 Pa'anga	1982-1984	15.50	0.925	0.461	N	0.46	0.92	1.38	1.84	4.61	6.92	9.22	11.53	13.83	16.14	18.44	20.75	23.05
Tonga 1 Pa'anga	1985	28.28	0.925	0.841	N	0.84	1.68	2.52	3.36	8.41	12.62	16.82	21.03	25.23	29.44	33.64	37.85	42.05
Tonga 1 Pa'anga	1988-1999	31.73	0.925	0.930	N, V	0.93	1.86	2.79	3.72	9.30	13.95	18.60	23.25	27.90	32.55	37.20	41.85	46.50
Tonga 2 Pa'anga	1978-1981	42.10	0.999	1.352	N	1.35	2.70	4.06	5.41	13.52	20.28	27.04	33.80	40.56	47.32	54.08	60.84	67.60
Tonga 2 Pa'anga	1986	28.28	0.925	0.841		0.84	1.68	2.52	3.36	8.41	12.62	16.82	21.03	25.23	29.44	33.64	37.85	42.05
Tonga 2 Pa'anga	1986	28.28	0.500	0.455		0.46	0.91	1.37	1.82	4.55	6.83	9.10	11.38	13.65	15.93	18.20	20.48	22.75
Tonga 2 Pa'anga	1987, 1988	155.52	0.999	5.000		5.00	10.00	15.00	20.00	50.00	75.00	100.00	125.00	150.00	175.00	200.00	225.00	250.00
Tonga 5 Pa'anga	1975	31.00	0.999	1.000		1.00	2.00	3.00	4.00	10.00	15.00	20.00	25.00	30.00	35.00	40.00	45.00	50.00
Tonga 10 Pa'anga	1975	62.00	0.999	2.000		2.00	4.00	6.00	8.00	20.00	30.00	40.00	50.00	60.00	70.00	80.00	90.00	100.00
Tonga 10 Pa'anga	1982	28.28	0.925	0.841		0.84	1.68	2.52	3.36	8.41	12.62	16.82	21.03	25.23	29.44	33.64	37.85	42.05
Tonga 10 Pa'anga	1987	311.04	0.999	10.000		10.00	20.00	30.00	40.00	100.00	150.00	200.00	250.00	300.00	350.00	400.00	450.00	500.00
Tonga 20 Pa'anga	1975	140.00	0.999	4.500		4.50	9.00	13.50	18.00	45.00	67.50	90.00	112.50	135.00	157.50	180.00	202.50	225.00
Tonga 1/2 Hau	1981	28.28	0.925	0.841		0.84	1.68	2.52	3.36	8.41	12.62	16.82	21.03	25.23	29.44	33.64	37.85	42.05
Trinidad & Tobago 1 Cent	1982-1984	2.00	0.925	0.059	N	0.06	0.12	0.18	0.24	0.59	0.89	1.18	1.48	1.77	2.07	2.36	2.66	2.95
Trinidad & Tobago 5 Cents	1981-1984	3.50	0.925	0.104	N	0.10	0.21	0.31	0.42	1.04	1.56	2.08	2.60	3.12	3.64	4.16	4.68	5.20
Trinidad & Tobago 10 Cents	1981-1984	1.50	0.925	0.045	N	0.05	0.09	0.14	0.18	0.45	0.68	0.90	1.13	1.35	1.58	1.80	2.03	2.25

Country & Denomination	Years Minted	Grams Weight	Fineness	Troy (ASW)	Code	$ Value 1	$ Value 2	$ Value 3	$ Value 4	$ Value 10	$ Value 15	$ Value 20	$ Value 25	$ Value 30	$ Value 35	$ Value 40	$ Value 45	$ Value 50
Trinidad & Tobago 25 Cents	1981-1984	3.60	0.925	0.107	N	0.11	0.21	0.32	0.43	1.07	1.61	2.14	2.68	3.21	3.75	4.28	4.82	5.35
Trinidad & Tobago 50 Cents	1981-1984	7.25	0.925	0.216	N	0.22	0.43	0.65	0.86	2.16	3.24	4.32	5.40	6.48	7.56	8.64	9.72	10.80
Trinidad & Tobago 1 Dollar	1981-1984	18.60	0.925	0.553	N	0.55	1.11	1.66	2.21	5.53	8.30	11.06	13.83	16.59	19.36	22.12	24.89	27.65
Trinidad & Tobago 5 Dollars	1971-1984	29.70	0.925	0.883	N, V	0.88	1.77	2.65	3.53	8.83	13.25	17.66	22.08	26.49	30.91	35.32	39.74	44.15
Trinidad & Tobago 10 Dollars	1972-1984	35.00	0.925	1.041	N	1.04	2.08	3.12	4.16	10.41	15.62	20.82	26.03	31.23	36.44	41.64	46.85	52.05
Trinidad & Tobago 10 Dollars	1984	28.28	0.925	0.841		0.84	1.68	2.52	3.36	8.41	12.62	16.82	21.03	25.23	29.44	33.64	37.85	42.05
Trinidad & Tobago 25 Dollars	1980	30.28	0.500	0.487		0.49	0.97	1.46	1.95	4.87	7.31	9.74	12.18	14.61	17.05	19.48	21.92	24.35
Tristan da Cunha 25 Pence	1977-1983	28.28	0.925	0.841	N, S	0.84	1.68	2.52	3.36	8.41	12.62	16.82	21.03	25.23	29.44	33.64	37.85	42.05
Tristan da Cunha 50 Pence	1987-2000	28.28	0.925	0.841	N, S, V	0.84	1.68	2.52	3.36	8.41	12.62	16.82	21.03	25.23	29.44	33.64	37.85	42.05
Tristan da Cunha Crown	1978	28.28	0.925	0.841	N	0.84	1.68	2.52	3.36	8.41	12.62	16.82	21.03	25.23	29.44	33.64	37.85	42.05
Tunisia 8 Kharub	1864-1869	1.80	0.835	0.048	A	0.05	0.10	0.14	0.19	0.48	0.72	0.96	1.20	1.44	1.68	1.92	2.16	2.40
Tunisia 1 Piastre	1862-1866	3.20	0.900	0.093	A	0.09	0.19	0.28	0.37	0.93	1.40	1.86	2.33	2.79	3.26	3.72	4.19	4.65
Tunisia 1 Piastre	1870-1876	3.20	0.835	0.086	A	0.09	0.17	0.26	0.34	0.86	1.29	1.72	2.15	2.58	3.01	3.44	3.87	4.30
Tunisia 2 Piastres	1847-1856	6.50	0.900	0.188	A, S	0.19	0.38	0.56	0.75	1.88	2.82	3.76	4.70	5.64	6.58	7.52	8.46	9.40
Tunisia 2 Piastres	1870-1880	6.40	0.835	0.172	A	0.17	0.34	0.52	0.69	1.72	2.58	3.44	4.30	5.16	6.02	6.88	7.74	8.60
Tunisia 3 Piastres	1855, 1871	9.60	0.835	0.260	A	0.26	0.52	0.78	1.04	2.60	3.90	5.20	6.50	7.80	9.10	10.40	11.70	13.00
Tunisia 4 Piastres	1855-1880	12.80	0.835	0.344	A, S	0.34	0.69	1.03	1.38	3.44	5.16	6.88	8.60	10.32	12.04	13.76	15.48	17.20
Tunisia 5 Piastres	1847-1859	16.00	0.900	0.463	A	0.46	0.93	1.39	1.85	4.63	6.95	9.26	11.58	13.89	16.21	18.52	20.84	23.15
Tunisia 50 Centimes	1891-1928	2.50	0.835	0.067	A	0.07	0.13	0.20	0.27	0.67	1.01	1.34	1.68	2.01	2.35	2.68	3.02	3.35
Tunisia 1 Franc	1891-1928	5.00	0.835	0.134	A	0.13	0.27	0.40	0.54	1.34	2.01	2.68	3.35	4.02	4.69	5.36	6.03	6.70
Tunisia 1 Franc	1928	5.50	0.835	0.148	A	0.15	0.30	0.44	0.59	1.48	2.22	2.96	3.70	4.44	5.18	5.92	6.66	7.40
Tunisia 2 Francs	1891-1927	10.00	0.835	0.269	A	0.27	0.54	0.81	1.08	2.69	4.04	5.38	6.73	8.07	9.42	10.76	12.11	13.45
Tunisia 2 Francs	1928	8.60	0.835	0.231	A	0.23	0.46	0.69	0.92	2.31	3.47	4.62	5.78	6.93	8.09	9.24	10.40	11.55
Tunisia 5 Francs	1934-1939	5.00	0.680	0.109	A	0.11	0.22	0.33	0.44	1.09	1.64	2.18	2.73	3.27	3.82	4.36	4.91	5.45
Tunisia 10 Francs	1930-1944	10.00	0.680	0.219	A	0.22	0.44	0.66	0.88	2.19	3.29	4.38	5.48	6.57	7.67	8.76	9.86	10.95
Tunisia 20 Francs	1930-1944	20.00	0.680	0.437	A	0.44	0.87	1.31	1.75	4.37	6.56	8.74	10.93	13.11	15.30	17.48	19.67	21.85
Tunisia 1 Dinar	1969	20.00	0.925	0.595	A	0.60	1.19	1.79	2.38	5.95	8.93	11.90	14.88	17.85	20.83	23.80	26.78	29.75
Tunisia 1 Dinar	1970	18.00	0.680	0.394	A	0.39	0.79	1.18	1.58	3.94	5.91	7.88	9.85	11.82	13.79	15.76	17.73	19.70
Tunisia 5 Dinars	1976	24.00	0.680	0.525	A, N	0.53	1.05	1.58	2.10	5.25	7.88	10.50	13.13	15.75	18.38	21.00	23.63	26.25
Tunisia 5 Dinars	1982	27.22	0.925	0.810	A, N	0.81	1.62	2.43	3.24	8.10	12.15	16.20	20.25	24.30	28.35	32.40	36.45	40.50
Tunisia 10 Dinars	1978-1988	38.00	0.900	1.096	A, N, S	1.10	2.19	3.29	4.38	10.96	16.44	21.92	27.40	32.88	38.36	43.84	49.32	54.80
Turkey 5 Para*	1901-1905	1.00	0.100	0.003	A	0.00	0.01	0.01	0.01	0.03	0.05	0.06	0.08	0.09	0.11	0.12	0.14	0.15
Turkey 10 Para	1901-1905	2.00	0.100	0.006	A	0.01	0.01	0.02	0.02	0.06	0.09	0.12	0.15	0.18	0.21	0.24	0.27	0.30
Turkey 20 Para	1839-1862	0.60	0.830	0.016	A	0.02	0.03	0.05	0.06	0.16	0.24	0.32	0.40	0.48	0.56	0.64	0.72	0.80
Turkey 40 Para	1861-1866	1.20	0.830	0.032	A	0.03	0.06	0.10	0.13	0.32	0.48	0.64	0.80	0.96	1.12	1.28	1.44	1.60
Turkey 1 Kurush	1845-1908	1.20	0.830	0.032	A, S	0.03	0.06	0.10	0.13	0.32	0.48	0.64	0.80	0.96	1.12	1.28	1.44	1.60
Turkey 2 Kurush	1846-1911	2.41	0.830	0.064	A, S	0.06	0.13	0.19	0.26	0.64	0.96	1.28	1.60	1.92	2.24	2.56	2.88	3.20
Turkey 5 Kurush	1845-1911	6.00	0.830	0.161	A, S	0.16	0.32	0.48	0.64	1.61	2.42	3.22	4.03	4.83	5.64	6.44	7.25	8.05
Turkey 10 Kurush	1845-1911	12.03	0.830	0.321	A, S	0.32	0.64	0.96	1.28	3.21	4.82	6.42	8.03	9.63	11.24	12.84	14.45	16.05
Turkey 20 Kurush	1845-1918	24.06	0.830	0.642	A, S	0.64	1.28	1.93	2.57	6.42	9.63	12.84	16.05	19.26	22.47	25.68	28.89	32.10
Turkey 25 Kurus	1935-1937	3.00	0.830	0.080		0.08	0.16	0.24	0.32	0.80	1.20	1.60	2.00	2.40	2.80	3.20	3.60	4.00
Turkey 50 Kurus	1935-1937	6.00	0.830	0.160		0.16	0.32	0.48	0.64	1.60	2.40	3.20	4.00	4.80	5.60	6.40	7.20	8.00

Country & Denomination	Years Minted	Grams Weight	Fineness	Troy (ASW)	Code	$ Value 1	$ Value 2	$ Value 3	$ Value 4	$ Value 10	$ Value 15	$ Value 20	$ Value 25	$ Value 30	$ Value 35	$ Value 40	$ Value 45	$ Value 50
Turkey 50 Kurus	1947-1948	3.50	0.600	0.070		0.07	0.14	0.21	0.28	0.70	1.05	1.40	1.75	2.10	2.45	2.80	3.15	3.50
Turkey 100 Kurus	1934-1939	12.00	0.830	0.320		0.32	0.64	0.96	1.28	3.20	4.80	6.40	8.00	9.60	11.20	12.80	14.40	16.00
Turkey 1/2 Lira	1981	7.86	0.925	0.234	N	0.23	0.47	0.70	0.94	2.34	3.51	4.68	5.85	7.02	8.19	9.36	10.53	11.70
Turkey 1 Lira	1937-1941	12.00	0.830	0.320		0.32	0.64	0.96	1.28	3.20	4.80	6.40	8.00	9.60	11.20	12.80	14.40	16.00
Turkey 1 Lira	1947-1948	7.50	0.600	0.145		0.15	0.29	0.44	0.58	1.45	2.18	2.90	3.63	4.35	5.08	5.80	6.53	7.25
Turkey 1 Lira	1981	16.00	0.925	0.470	N	0.47	0.94	1.41	1.88	4.70	7.05	9.40	11.75	14.10	16.45	18.80	21.15	23.50
Turkey 2-1/2 Lira	1965	11.80	0.925	0.351	N	0.35	0.70	1.05	1.40	3.51	5.27	7.02	8.78	10.53	12.29	14.04	15.80	17.55
Turkey 5 Lira	1960, 1975	14.70	0.925	0.437	N	0.44	0.87	1.31	1.75	4.37	6.56	8.74	10.93	13.11	15.30	17.48	19.67	21.85
Turkey 10 Lira	1960	15.00	0.830	0.400		0.40	0.80	1.20	1.60	4.00	6.00	8.00	10.00	12.00	14.00	16.00	18.00	20.00
Turkey 25 Lira	1970	14.60	0.830	0.390		0.39	0.78	1.17	1.56	3.90	5.85	7.80	9.75	11.70	13.65	15.60	17.55	19.50
Turkey 50 Lira	1971	19.00	0.830	0.507		0.51	1.01	1.52	2.03	5.07	7.61	10.14	12.68	15.21	17.75	20.28	22.82	25.35
Turkey 50 Lira	1972	20.10	0.830	0.536		0.54	1.07	1.61	2.14	5.36	8.04	10.72	13.40	16.08	18.76	21.44	24.12	26.80
Turkey 50 Lira	1973	13.00	0.900	0.376		0.38	0.75	1.13	1.50	3.76	5.64	7.52	9.40	11.28	13.16	15.04	16.92	18.80
Turkey 50 Lira	1977	8.85	0.830	0.236		0.24	0.47	0.71	0.94	2.36	3.54	4.72	5.90	7.08	8.26	9.44	10.62	11.80
Turkey 100 Lira	1973	22.00	0.900	0.637		0.64	1.27	1.91	2.55	6.37	9.56	12.74	15.93	19.11	22.30	25.48	28.67	31.85
Turkey 100 Lira	1988	5.10	0.925	0.152	N	0.15	0.30	0.46	0.61	1.52	2.28	3.04	3.80	4.56	5.32	6.08	6.84	7.60
Turkey 150 Lira	1978-1979	9.00	0.800	0.231		0.23	0.46	0.69	0.92	2.31	3.47	4.62	5.78	6.93	8.09	9.24	10.40	11.55
Turkey 200 Lira	1978	9.00	0.830	0.240		0.24	0.48	0.72	0.96	2.40	3.60	4.80	6.00	7.20	8.40	9.60	10.80	12.00
Turkey 500 Lira	1979, 1982	23.33	0.925	0.694	N	0.69	1.39	2.08	2.78	6.94	10.41	13.88	17.35	20.82	24.29	27.76	31.23	34.70
Turkey 500 Lira	1980	9.00	0.900	0.260		0.26	0.52	0.78	1.04	2.60	3.90	5.20	6.50	7.80	9.10	10.40	11.70	13.00
Turkey 500 Lira	1984	28.28	0.925	0.841	N	0.84	1.68	2.52	3.36	8.41	12.62	16.82	21.03	25.23	29.44	33.64	37.85	42.05
Turkey 500 Lira	1989	7.60	0.925	0.226	N	0.23	0.45	0.68	0.90	2.26	3.39	4.52	5.65	6.78	7.91	9.04	10.17	11.30
Turkey 1500 Lira	1981-1983	16.00	0.925	0.476		0.48	0.95	1.43	1.90	4.76	7.14	9.52	11.90	14.28	16.66	19.04	21.42	23.80
Turkey 3000 Lira	1981-1983	28.28	0.925	0.841		0.84	1.68	2.52	3.36	8.41	12.62	16.82	21.03	25.23	29.44	33.64	37.85	42.05
Turkey 3000 Lira	1983	16.00	0.925	0.476		0.48	0.95	1.43	1.90	4.76	7.14	9.52	11.90	14.28	16.66	19.04	21.42	23.80
Turkey 5000 Lira	1984-1988	23.33	0.925	0.694		0.69	1.39	2.08	2.78	6.94	10.41	13.88	17.35	20.82	24.29	27.76	31.23	34.70
Turkey 10,000 Lira	1986-1988	23.33	0.925	0.694	N	0.69	1.39	2.08	2.78	6.94	10.41	13.88	17.35	20.82	24.29	27.76	31.23	34.70
Turkey 20,000 Lira	1988-1990	23.32	0.925	0.694		0.69	1.39	2.08	2.78	6.94	10.41	13.88	17.35	20.82	24.29	27.76	31.23	34.70
Turkey 20,000 Lira	1990	23.42	0.925	0.697	N	0.70	1.39	2.09	2.79	6.97	10.46	13.94	17.43	20.91	24.40	27.88	31.37	34.85
Turkey 50,000 Lira	1990	28.28	0.925	0.841	N	0.84	1.68	2.52	3.36	8.41	12.62	16.82	21.03	25.23	29.44	33.64	37.85	42.05
Turkey 50,000 Lira	1991	22.87	0.925	0.680		0.68	1.36	2.04	2.72	6.80	10.20	13.60	17.00	20.40	23.80	27.20	30.60	34.00
Turkey 50,000 Lira	1992-1995	23.33	0.925	0.694	S	0.69	1.39	2.08	2.78	6.94	10.41	13.88	17.35	20.82	24.29	27.76	31.23	34.70
Turkey 50,000 Lira	1992-1993	23.08	0.925	0.618	V	0.62	1.24	1.85	2.47	6.18	9.27	12.36	15.45	18.54	21.63	24.72	27.81	30.90
Turkey 50,000 Lira	1994	22.84	0.925	0.679		0.68	1.36	2.04	2.72	6.79	10.19	13.58	16.98	20.37	23.77	27.16	30.56	33.95
Turkey 50,000 Lira	1994, 1995	31.47	0.925	0.936	N	0.94	1.87	2.81	3.74	9.36	14.04	18.72	23.40	28.08	32.76	37.44	42.12	46.80
Turkey 75,000 Lira	1996	31.47	0.925	0.936	V	0.94	1.87	2.81	3.74	9.36	14.04	18.72	23.40	28.08	32.76	37.44	42.12	46.80
Turkey 75,000 Lira	1996	23.20	0.925	0.690		0.69	1.38	2.07	2.76	6.90	10.35	13.80	17.25	20.70	24.15	27.60	31.05	34.50
Turkey 75,000 Lira	1996	23.40	0.925	0.695	V	0.70	1.39	2.09	2.78	6.95	10.43	13.90	17.38	20.85	24.33	27.80	31.28	34.75
Turkey 100,000 Lira	1996, 1997	31.47	0.925	0.936	N	0.94	1.87	2.81	3.74	9.36	14.04	18.72	23.40	28.08	32.76	37.44	42.12	46.80
Turkey 100,000 Lira	1996	31.77	0.925	0.945		0.95	1.89	2.84	3.78	9.45	14.18	18.90	23.63	28.35	33.08	37.80	42.53	47.25
Turkey 100,000 Lira	1997	31.57	0.925	0.939	N	0.94	1.88	2.82	3.76	9.39	14.09	18.78	23.48	28.17	32.87	37.56	42.26	46.95
Turkey 150,000 Lira	1997	31.35	0.925	0.933	V	0.93	1.87	2.80	3.73	9.33	14.00	18.66	23.33	27.99	32.66	37.32	41.99	46.65
Turkey 150,000 Lira	1997	31.44	0.925	0.935		0.94	1.87	2.81	3.74	9.35	14.03	18.70	23.38	28.05	32.73	37.40	42.08	46.75
Turkey 250,000 Lira	1998	31.15	0.925	0.926		0.93	1.85	2.78	3.70	9.26	13.89	18.52	23.15	27.78	32.41	37.04	41.67	46.30
Turkey 250,000 Lira	1998	31.58	0.925	0.939		0.94	1.88	2.82	3.76	9.39	14.09	18.78	23.48	28.17	32.87	37.56	42.26	46.95

Country & Denomination	Years Minted	Grams Weight	Fineness	Troy (ASW)	Code	$ Value 1	$ Value 2	$ Value 3	$ Value 4	$ Value 10	$ Value 15	$ Value 20	$ Value 25	$ Value 30	$ Value 35	$ Value 40	$ Value 45	$ Value 50
Turkey 250,000 Lira	1998	31.44	0.925	0.935		0.94	1.87	2.81	3.74	9.35	14.03	18.70	23.38	28.05	32.73	37.40	42.08	46.75
Turkey 250,000 Lira	1998	31.35	0.925	0.933		0.93	1.87	2.80	3.73	9.33	14.00	18.66	23.33	27.99	32.66	37.32	41.99	46.65
Turkey 250,000 Lira	1998	23.33	0.925	0.693		0.69	1.39	2.08	2.77	6.93	10.40	13.86	17.33	20.79	24.26	27.72	31.19	34.65
Turkey 300,000 Lira	1998	31.32	0.925	0.932	>	0.93	1.86	2.80	3.73	9.32	13.98	18.64	23.30	27.96	32.62	37.28	41.94	46.60
Turkey 300,000 Lira	1999	31.44	0.925	0.935		0.94	1.87	2.81	3.74	9.35	14.03	18.70	23.38	28.05	32.73	37.40	42.08	46.75
Turkey 400,000 Lira	1999	31.44	0.925	0.935	>	0.94	1.87	2.81	3.74	9.35	14.03	18.70	23.38	28.05	32.73	37.40	42.08	46.75
Turkey 750,000 Lira	2000	31.40	0.925	0.934	>	0.93	1.87	2.80	3.74	9.34	14.01	18.68	23.35	28.02	32.69	37.36	42.03	46.70
Turkey 750,000 Lira	2000	23.33	0.925	0.694	>	0.69	1.39	2.08	2.78	6.94	10.41	13.88	17.35	20.82	24.29	27.76	31.23	34.70
Turkmenistan 500 Manat	1996-2000	28.28	0.925	0.841	S	0.84	1.68	2.52	3.36	8.41	12.62	16.82	21.03	25.23	29.44	33.64	37.85	42.05
Turks & Caicos 1 Crown	1986-1990	28.28	0.925	0.841	N, S	0.84	1.68	2.52	3.36	8.41	12.62	16.82	21.03	25.23	29.44	33.64	37.85	42.05
Turks & Caicos 1 Crown	1991	31.12	0.999	1.000	N	1.00	2.00	3.00	4.00	10.00	15.00	20.00	25.00	30.00	35.00	40.00	45.00	50.00
Turks & Caicos 5 Crowns	1975-1977	24.24	0.500	0.390		0.39	0.78	1.17	1.56	3.90	5.85	7.80	9.75	11.70	13.65	15.60	17.55	19.50
Turks & Caicos 5 Crowns	1980	14.58	0.500	0.234		0.23	0.47	0.70	0.94	2.34	3.51	4.68	5.85	7.02	8.19	9.36	10.53	11.70
Turks & Caicos 5 Crowns	1992	28.28	0.925	0.840		0.84	1.68	2.52	3.36	8.40	12.60	16.80	21.00	25.20	29.40	33.60	37.80	42.00
Turks & Caicos 5 Crowns	1995	10.00	0.999	0.321	N, V	0.32	0.64	0.96	1.28	3.21	4.82	6.42	8.03	9.63	11.24	12.84	14.45	16.05
Turks & Caicos 10 Crowns	1975-1977	29.98	0.925	0.892		0.89	1.78	2.68	3.57	8.92	13.38	17.84	22.30	26.76	31.22	35.68	40.14	44.60
Turks & Caicos 10 Crowns	1979, 1981	29.70	0.925	0.883		0.88	1.77	2.65	3.53	8.83	13.25	17.66	22.08	26.49	30.91	35.32	39.74	44.15
Turks & Caicos 10 Crowns	1980	23.33	0.500	0.375		0.38	0.75	1.13	1.50	3.75	5.63	7.50	9.38	11.25	13.13	15.00	16.88	18.75
Turks & Caicos 10 Crowns	1982-1985	23.28	0.925	0.692	S	0.69	1.38	2.08	2.77	6.92	10.38	13.84	17.30	20.76	24.22	27.68	31.14	34.60
Turks & Caicos 20 Crowns	1974-1978	38.70	0.925	1.151		1.15	2.30	3.45	4.60	11.51	17.27	23.02	28.78	34.53	40.29	46.04	51.80	57.55
Turks & Caicos 20 Crowns	1989-1991	28.04	0.925	0.834		0.83	1.67	2.50	3.34	8.34	12.51	16.68	20.85	25.02	29.19	33.36	37.53	41.70
Turks & Caicos 20 Crowns	1993-1999	31.23	0.999	1.000		1.00	2.00	3.00	4.00	10.00	15.00	20.00	25.00	30.00	35.00	40.00	45.00	50.00
Turks & Caicos 25 Crowns	1977-1978	43.75	0.925	1.301		1.30	2.60	3.90	5.20	13.01	19.52	26.02	32.53	39.03	45.54	52.04	58.55	65.05
Turks & Caicos 25 Crowns	1995	155.44	0.999	4.993		4.99	9.99	14.98	19.97	49.93	74.90	99.86	124.83	149.79	174.76	199.72	224.69	249.65
Turks & Caicos 50 Crowns	1976	55.18	0.925	1.641		1.64	3.28	4.92	6.56	16.41	24.62	32.82	41.03	49.23	57.44	65.64	73.85	82.05
Turks & Caicos 50 Crowns	1986	136.08	0.925	4.070		4.07	8.14	12.21	16.28	40.70	61.05	81.40	101.75	122.10	142.45	162.80	183.15	203.50
Turks & Caicos 5 Dollars	1996	10.00	0.999	0.321		0.32	0.64	0.96	1.28	3.21	4.82	6.42	8.03	9.63	11.24	12.84	14.45	16.05
Turks & Caicos 20 Dollars	1996	31.23	0.999	1.000		1.00	2.00	3.00	4.00	10.00	15.00	20.00	25.00	30.00	35.00	40.00	45.00	50.00
				0.00		0.00												
Tuvalu 2 Dollars	1996	10.00	0.500	0.161		0.16	0.32	0.48	0.64	1.61	2.42	3.22	4.03	4.83	5.64	6.44	7.25	8.05
Tuvalu 2 Dollars	1997	15.85	0.925	0.471		0.47	0.94	1.41	1.88	4.71	7.07	9.42	11.78	14.13	16.49	18.84	21.20	23.55
Tuvalu 5 Dollars	1976, 1981	28.28	0.925	0.841		0.84	1.68	2.52	3.36	8.41	12.62	16.82	21.03	25.23	29.44	33.64	37.85	42.05
Tuvalu 5 Dollars	1997	31.60	0.925	0.941		0.94	1.88	2.82	3.76	9.41	14.12	18.82	23.53	28.23	32.94	37.64	42.35	47.05
Tuvalu 5 Dollars	1997, 1998	31.52	0.925	0.937	>	0.94	1.87	2.81	3.75	9.37	14.06	18.74	23.43	28.11	32.80	37.48	42.17	46.85
Tuvalu 5 Dollars	1998, 2000	31.20	0.925	0.927	>	0.93	1.85	2.78	3.71	9.27	13.91	18.54	23.18	27.81	32.45	37.08	41.72	46.35
Tuvalu 10 Dollars	1979-1982	35.00	0.925	1.040		1.04	2.08	3.12	4.16	10.40	15.60	20.80	26.00	31.20	36.40	41.60	46.80	52.00
Tuvalu 10 Dollars	1979-1982	35.00	0.500	0.563		0.56	1.13	1.69	2.25	5.63	8.45	11.26	14.08	16.89	19.71	22.52	25.34	28.15
Tuvalu 10 Dollars	1993, 1994	31.47	0.925	0.936		0.94	1.87	2.81	3.74	9.36	14.04	18.72	23.40	28.08	32.76	37.44	42.12	46.80
Tuvalu 10 Dollars	1994	31.70	0.925	0.943		0.94	1.89	2.83	3.77	9.43	14.15	18.86	23.58	28.29	33.01	37.72	42.44	47.15
Tuvalu 20 Dollars	1996	155.50	0.925	4.994		4.99	9.99	14.98	19.98	49.94	74.91	99.88	124.85	149.82	174.79	199.76	224.73	249.70
U																		
Uganda 2 Shillings	1969, 1970	4.00	0.999	0.128		0.13	0.26	0.38	0.51	1.28	1.92	2.56	3.20	3.84	4.48	5.12	5.76	6.40
Uganda 5 Shillings	1969, 1970	10.00	0.999	0.321		0.32	0.64	0.96	1.28	3.21	4.82	6.42	8.03	9.63	11.24	12.84	14.45	16.05

Country & Denomination	Years Minted	Grams Weight	Fine-ness	Troy (ASW)	Code	$ Value 1	$ Value 2	$ Value 3	$ Value 4	$ Value 10	$ Value 15	$ Value 20	$ Value 25	$ Value 30	$ Value 35	$ Value 40	$ Value 45	$ Value 50
Uganda 10 Shillings	1969, 1970	20.00	0.999	0.642		0.64	1.28	1.93	2.57	6.42	9.63	12.84	16.05	19.26	22.47	25.68	28.89	32.10
Uganda 20 Shillings	1969, 1970	40.00	0.999	1.285		1.29	2.57	3.86	5.14	12.85	19.28	25.70	32.13	38.55	44.98	51.40	57.83	64.25
Uganda 25 Shillings	1969, 1970	50.00	0.999	1.606		1.61	3.21	4.82	6.42	16.06	24.09	32.12	40.15	48.18	56.21	64.24	72.27	80.30
Uganda 30 Shillings	1969, 1970	60.00	0.999	1.927		1.93	3.85	5.78	7.71	19.27	28.91	38.54	48.18	57.81	67.45	77.08	86.72	96.35
Uganda 100 Shillings	1981	31.47	0.925	0.936		0.94	1.87	2.81	3.74	9.36	14.04	18.72	23.40	28.08	32.76	37.44	42.12	46.80
Uganda 200 Shillings	1981	31.47	0.925	0.936		0.94	1.87	2.81	3.74	9.36	14.04	18.72	23.40	28.08	32.76	37.44	42.12	46.80
Uganda 500 Shillings	1981	136.00	0.925	4.045		4.05	8.09	12.14	16.18	40.45	60.68	80.90	101.13	121.35	141.58	161.80	182.03	202.25
Uganda 500 Shillings	1981	136.00	0.500	2.186		2.19	4.37	6.56	8.74	21.86	32.79	43.72	54.65	65.58	76.51	87.44	98.37	109.30
Uganda 1000 Shillings	1999	31.56	0.925	0.939	N	0.94	1.88	2.82	3.76	9.39	14.09	18.78	23.48	28.17	32.87	37.56	42.26	46.95
Uganda 1000 Shillings	1999	14.97	0.999	0.481	N	0.48	0.96	1.44	1.92	4.81	7.22	9.62	12.03	14.43	16.84	19.24	21.65	24.05
Uganda 2000 Shillings	1993	19.80	0.999	0.636		0.64	1.27	1.91	2.54	6.36	9.54	12.72	15.90	19.08	22.26	25.44	28.62	31.80
Uganda 2000 Shillings	1993-1996	19.90	0.999	0.639	N, S	0.64	1.28	1.92	2.56	6.39	9.59	12.78	15.98	19.17	22.37	25.56	28.76	31.95
Uganda 2000 Shillings	1993	30.46	0.999	0.978		0.98	1.96	2.93	3.91	9.78	14.67	19.56	24.45	29.34	34.23	39.12	44.01	48.90
Uganda 2000 Shillings	1993, 1996	30.84	0.999	0.990	N	0.99	1.98	2.97	3.96	9.90	14.85	19.80	24.75	29.70	34.65	39.60	44.55	49.50
Uganda 2000 Shillings	1996	7.10	0.999	0.228	N	0.23	0.46	0.68	0.91	2.28	3.42	4.56	5.70	6.84	7.98	9.12	10.26	11.40
Uganda 2000 Shillings	1996	20.26	0.999	0.651	N	0.65	1.30	1.95	2.60	6.51	9.77	13.02	16.28	19.53	22.79	26.04	29.30	32.55
Uganda 2000 Shillings	1997	19.74	0.999	0.635	N	0.64	1.27	1.91	2.54	6.35	9.53	12.70	15.88	19.05	22.23	25.40	28.58	31.75
Uganda 2000 Shillings	1999	31.32	0.999	1.006		1.01	2.01	3.02	4.02	10.06	15.09	20.12	25.15	30.18	35.21	40.24	45.27	50.30
Uganda 2000 Shillings	2000	26.00	0.999	0.835		0.84	1.67	2.51	3.34	8.35	12.53	16.70	20.88	25.05	29.23	33.40	37.58	41.75
Uganda 2000 Shillings	2000	15.75	0.925	0.468		0.47	0.94	1.40	1.87	4.68	7.02	9.36	11.70	14.04	16.38	18.72	21.06	23.40
Uganda 2000 Shillings	2000	25.00	0.925	0.744		0.74	1.49	2.23	2.98	7.44	11.16	14.88	18.60	22.32	26.04	29.76	33.48	37.20
Uganda 5000 Shillings	1992	12.00	0.999	0.386		0.39	0.77	1.16	1.54	3.86	5.79	7.72	9.65	11.58	13.51	15.44	17.37	19.30
Uganda 5000 Shillings	1993	500.00	0.999	16.075		16.08	32.15	48.23	64.30	160.75	241.13	321.50	401.88	482.25	562.63	643.00	723.38	803.75
Uganda 10,000 Shillings	1992, 1993	20.00	0.999	0.643		0.64	1.29	1.93	2.57	6.43	9.65	12.86	16.08	19.29	22.51	25.72	28.94	32.15
Uganda 10,000 Shillings	1993	1000.00	0.999	32.151		32.15	64.30	96.45	128.60	321.51	482.27	643.02	803.78	964.53	1125.29	1286.04	1446.80	1607.55
Uganda 10,000 Shillings	1998	155.50	0.999	4.994		4.99	9.99	14.98	19.98	49.94	74.91	99.88	124.85	149.82	174.79	199.76	224.73	249.70
Ukraine 100,000 Karbovanets	1996	16.81	0.925	0.500		0.50	1.00	1.50	2.00	5.00	7.50	10.00	12.50	15.00	17.50	20.00	22.50	25.00
Ukraine 200,000 Karbovanets	1995, 1996	33.62	0.925	1.000		1.00	2.00	3.00	4.00	10.00	15.00	20.00	25.00	30.00	35.00	40.00	45.00	50.00
Ukraine 10 Hryven	1996	16.81	0.925	0.500		0.50	1.00	1.50	2.00	5.00	7.50	10.00	12.50	15.00	17.50	20.00	22.50	25.00
Ukraine 10 Hryven	1998-2000	33.62	0.925	1.000		1.00	2.00	3.00	4.00	10.00	15.00	20.00	25.00	30.00	35.00	40.00	45.00	50.00
Ukraine 20 Hryven	1996-1998	33.62	0.925	1.000		1.00	2.00	3.00	4.00	10.00	15.00	20.00	25.00	30.00	35.00	40.00	45.00	50.00
Umm al-Quiwain 1 Riyal	1969	3.00	0.990	0.097	A	0.10	0.19	0.29	0.39	0.97	1.46	1.94	2.43	2.91	3.40	3.88	4.37	4.85
Umm al-Quiwain 2 Riyals	1969	6.00	0.999	0.193	A	0.19	0.39	0.58	0.77	1.93	2.90	3.86	4.83	5.79	6.76	7.72	8.69	9.65
Umm al-Quiwain 5 Riyals	1969	15.00	0.999	0.482	A	0.48	0.96	1.45	1.93	4.82	7.23	9.64	12.05	14.46	16.87	19.28	21.69	24.10
Umm al-Quiwain 10 Riyals	1969	30.00	0.999	0.965	A	0.97	1.93	2.90	3.86	9.65	14.48	19.30	24.13	28.95	33.78	38.60	43.43	48.25
U. Arab Emirates 25 Dirhams	1998	20.00	0.925	0.595	A	0.60	1.19	1.79	2.38	5.95	8.93	11.90	14.88	17.85	20.83	23.80	26.78	29.75
U. Arab Emirates 25 Dirhams	2000	20.10	0.925	0.598	A	0.60	1.20	1.79	2.39	5.98	8.97	11.96	14.95	17.94	20.93	23.92	26.91	29.90
U. Arab Emirates 50 Dirhams	1980	27.22	0.925	0.810	A	0.81	1.62	2.43	3.24	8.10	12.15	16.20	20.25	24.30	28.35	32.40	36.45	40.50
U. Arab Emirates 50 Dirhams	1990-2000	40.00	0.925	1.190	A, S	1.19	2.38	3.57	4.76	11.90	17.85	23.80	29.75	35.70	41.65	47.60	53.55	59.50
U. Arab Emirates 50 Dirhams	1999-2000	40.22	0.925	1.200	A	1.20	2.40	3.60	4.80	12.00	18.00	24.00	30.00	36.00	42.00	48.00	54.00	60.00
U. Arab Emirates 50 Dirhams	1998	27.50	0.925	0.818	A	0.82	1.64	2.45	3.27	8.18	12.27	16.36	20.45	24.54	28.63	32.72	36.81	40.90

Country & Denomination	Years Minted	Grams Weight	Fineness	Troy (ASW)	Code	$ Value 1	$ Value 2	$ Value 3	$ Value 4	$ Value 10	$ Value 15	$ Value 20	$ Value 25	$ Value 30	$ Value 35	$ Value 40	$ Value 45	$ Value 50
United States 3 Cents*	1851-1853	0.80	0.750	0.019		0.02	0.04	0.06	0.08	0.19	0.29	0.38	0.48	0.57	0.67	0.76	0.86	0.95
United States 3 Cents	1854-1873	0.75	0.900	0.022		0.02	0.04	0.07	0.09	0.22	0.33	0.44	0.55	0.66	0.77	0.88	0.99	1.10
United States Half Dime	1801-1837	1.35	0.892	0.039		0.04	0.08	0.12	0.16	0.39	0.59	0.78	0.98	1.17	1.37	1.56	1.76	1.95
United States Half Dime	1837-1873	1.24	0.900	0.036		0.04	0.07	0.11	0.14	0.36	0.54	0.72	0.90	1.08	1.26	1.44	1.62	1.80
United States 5 Cents / Nickel	1942-1945	5.00	0.350	0.056		0.06	0.11	0.17	0.22	0.56	0.84	1.12	1.40	1.68	1.96	2.24	2.52	2.80
United States 10 Cents / Dime	1801-1837	2.70	0.892	0.078		0.08	0.16	0.23	0.31	0.78	1.17	1.56	1.95	2.34	2.73	3.12	3.51	3.90
United States 10 Cents / Dime	1837-1853	2.67	0.900	0.077		0.08	0.15	0.23	0.31	0.77	1.16	1.54	1.93	2.31	2.70	3.08	3.47	3.85
United States 10 Cents / Dime	1853-1873	2.49	0.900	0.072		0.07	0.14	0.22	0.29	0.72	1.08	1.44	1.80	2.16	2.52	2.88	3.24	3.60
United States 10 Cents / Dime	1873-1964	2.50	0.900	0.072		0.07	0.14	0.22	0.29	0.72	1.08	1.44	1.80	2.16	2.52	2.88	3.24	3.60
United States 20 Cents	1875-1878	5.00	0.900	0.148		0.15	0.30	0.44	0.59	1.48	2.22	2.96	3.70	4.44	5.18	5.92	6.66	7.40
United States 25 Cents	1804-1838	6.74	0.892	0.194		0.19	0.39	0.58	0.78	1.94	2.91	3.88	4.85	5.82	6.79	7.76	8.73	9.70
United States 25 Cents	1838-1853	6.68	0.900	0.193		0.19	0.39	0.58	0.77	1.93	2.90	3.86	4.83	5.79	6.76	7.72	8.69	9.65
United States 25 Cents	1853-1873	6.22	0.900	0.180		0.18	0.36	0.54	0.72	1.80	2.70	3.60	4.50	5.40	6.30	7.20	8.10	9.00
United States 25 Cents	1854-1855	6.68	0.900	0.193		0.19	0.39	0.58	0.77	1.93	2.90	3.86	4.83	5.79	6.76	7.72	8.69	9.65
United States 25 Cents	1873-1964	6.25	0.900	0.181		0.18	0.36	0.54	0.72	1.81	2.72	3.62	4.53	5.43	6.34	7.24	8.15	9.05
United States Half Dollar	1801-1836	13.48	0.892	0.387		0.39	0.77	1.16	1.55	3.87	5.81	7.74	9.68	11.61	13.55	15.48	17.42	19.35
United States Half Dollar	1836-1853	13.36	0.900	0.387		0.39	0.77	1.16	1.55	3.87	5.81	7.74	9.68	11.61	13.55	15.48	17.42	19.35
United States Half Dollar	1854-1873	12.44	0.900	0.360		0.36	0.72	1.08	1.44	3.60	5.40	7.20	9.00	10.80	12.60	14.40	16.20	18.00
United States 50 Cents	1873-1964	12.50	0.900	0.362		0.36	0.72	1.09	1.45	3.62	5.43	7.24	9.05	10.86	12.67	14.48	16.29	18.10
United States 50 Cents	1965-1970	12.50	0.400	0.148		0.15	0.30	0.44	0.59	1.48	2.22	2.96	3.70	4.44	5.18	5.92	6.66	7.40
United States 1 Dollar	1794-1804	26.96	0.892	0.774		0.77	1.55	2.32	3.10	7.74	11.61	15.48	19.35	23.22	27.09	30.96	34.83	38.70
United States 1 Dollar	1836-1873	26.73	0.900	0.774		0.77	1.55	2.32	3.10	7.74	11.61	15.48	19.35	23.22	27.09	30.96	34.83	38.70
United States 1 Trade Dollar	1873-1885	27.22	0.900	0.788		0.79	1.58	2.36	3.15	7.88	11.82	15.76	19.70	23.64	27.58	31.52	35.46	39.40
United States 1 Dollar	1878-1935	26.73	0.900	0.774		0.77	1.55	2.32	3.10	7.74	11.61	15.48	19.35	23.22	27.09	30.96	34.83	38.70
United States 1 Dollar	1971-1976	24.59	0.400	0.316	S	0.32	0.63	0.95	1.26	3.16	4.74	6.32	7.90	9.48	11.06	12.64	14.22	15.80
Uruguay 1 Centesimo	1979	3.70	0.900	0.107	N	0.11	0.21	0.32	0.43	1.07	1.61	2.14	2.68	3.21	3.75	4.28	4.82	5.35
Uruguay 2 Centesimos	1979	5.20	0.900	0.151	N	0.15	0.30	0.45	0.60	1.51	2.27	3.02	3.78	4.53	5.29	6.04	6.80	7.55
Uruguay 5 Centesimos	1979	7.40	0.900	0.214	N	0.21	0.43	0.64	0.86	2.14	3.21	4.28	5.35	6.42	7.49	8.56	9.63	10.70
Uruguay 10 Centesimos	1877-1893	2.50	0.900	0.072	S	0.07	0.14	0.22	0.29	0.72	1.08	1.44	1.80	2.16	2.52	2.88	3.24	3.60
Uruguay 10 Centesimos	1976, 1977	3.80	0.900	0.110	N	0.11	0.22	0.33	0.44	1.10	1.65	2.20	2.75	3.30	3.85	4.40	4.95	5.50
Uruguay 20 Centesimos	1877-1893	5.00	0.900	0.144	S	0.14	0.29	0.43	0.58	1.44	2.16	2.88	3.60	4.32	5.04	5.76	6.48	7.20
Uruguay 20 Centesimos	1920, 1930	5.00	0.800	0.129		0.13	0.26	0.39	0.52	1.29	1.94	2.58	3.23	3.87	4.52	5.16	5.81	6.45
Uruguay 20 Centesimos	1942, 1954	3.00	0.720	0.069		0.07	0.14	0.21	0.28	0.69	1.04	1.38	1.73	2.07	2.42	2.76	3.11	3.45
Uruguay 20 Centesimos	1976, 1977	6.40	0.900	0.185	N	0.19	0.37	0.56	0.74	1.85	2.78	3.70	4.63	5.55	6.48	7.40	8.33	9.25
Uruguay 50 Centesimos	1877-1894	12.50	0.900	0.362	S	0.36	0.72	1.09	1.45	3.62	5.43	7.24	9.05	10.86	12.67	14.48	16.29	18.10
Uruguay 50 Centesimos	1916, 1917	12.50	0.900	0.362		0.36	0.72	1.09	1.45	3.62	5.43	7.24	9.05	10.86	12.67	14.48	16.29	18.10
Uruguay 50 Centesimos	1943	4.50	0.720	0.103		0.10	0.21	0.31	0.41	1.03	1.55	2.06	2.58	3.09	3.61	4.12	4.64	5.15
Uruguay 50 Centesimos	1976, 1977	9.00	0.900	0.260	N	0.26	0.52	0.78	1.04	2.60	3.90	5.20	6.50	7.80	9.10	10.40	11.70	13.00
Uruguay 1 Peso	1844	27.00	0.875	0.760		0.76	1.52	2.28	3.04	7.60	11.40	15.20	19.00	22.80	26.60	30.40	34.20	38.00
Uruguay 1 Peso	1877	25.50	0.917	0.752		0.75	1.50	2.26	3.01	7.52	11.28	15.04	18.80	22.56	26.32	30.08	33.84	37.60
Uruguay 1 Peso	1878-1895	25.00	0.900	0.724	S	0.72	1.45	2.17	2.90	7.24	10.86	14.48	18.10	21.72	25.34	28.96	32.58	36.20
Uruguay 1 Peso	1917	25.00	0.900	0.724		0.72	1.45	2.17	2.90	7.24	10.86	14.48	18.10	21.72	25.34	28.96	32.58	36.20
Uruguay 1 Peso	1942	9.00	0.720	0.208		0.21	0.42	0.62	0.83	2.08	3.12	4.16	5.20	6.24	7.28	8.32	9.36	10.40
Uruguay 10 Pesos	1961	12.50	0.900	0.362		0.36	0.72	1.09	1.45	3.62	5.43	7.24	9.05	10.86	12.67	14.48	16.29	18.10

Country & Denomination	Years Minted	Grams Weight	Fineness	Troy (ASW)	Code	$ Value 1	$ Value 2	$ Value 3	$ Value 4	$ Value 10	$ Value 15	$ Value 20	$ Value 25	$ Value 30	$ Value 35	$ Value 40	$ Value 45	$ Value 50
Uruguay 50 Pesos	1971	6.02	0.900	0.174		0.17	0.35	0.52	0.70	1.74	2.61	3.48	4.35	5.22	6.09	6.96	7.83	8.70
Uruguay 1000 Pesos	1969	25.00	0.900	0.723		0.72	1.45	2.17	2.89	7.23	10.85	14.46	18.08	21.69	25.31	28.92	32.54	36.15
Uruguay 1 Nuevo Peso	1976	13.50	0.900	0.391	N	0.39	0.78	1.17	1.56	3.91	5.87	7.82	9.78	11.73	13.69	15.64	17.60	19.55
Uruguay 1 Nuevo Peso	1980	7.00	0.900	0.203	N	0.20	0.41	0.61	0.81	2.03	3.05	4.06	5.08	6.09	7.11	8.12	9.14	10.15
Uruguay 1 Nuevo Peso	1981	6.94	0.900	0.201	N	0.20	0.40	0.60	0.80	2.01	3.02	4.02	5.03	6.03	7.04	8.04	9.05	10.05
Uruguay 5 Nuevo Peso	1975	18.43	0.900	0.533	N	0.53	1.07	1.60	2.13	5.33	8.00	10.66	13.33	15.99	18.66	21.32	23.99	26.65
Uruguay 5 Nuevo Pesos	1976, 1980	9.30	0.900	0.269	N	0.27	0.54	0.81	1.08	2.69	4.04	5.38	6.73	8.07	9.42	10.76	12.11	13.45
Uruguay 10 Nuevo Pesos	1981	11.63	0.900	0.337	N	0.34	0.67	1.01	1.35	3.37	5.06	6.74	8.43	10.11	11.80	13.48	15.17	16.85
Uruguay 20 Nuevo Pesos	1984	11.66	0.925	0.347	N	0.35	0.69	1.04	1.39	3.47	5.21	6.94	8.68	10.41	12.15	13.88	15.62	17.35
Uruguay 100 Nuevo Pesos	1981	12.00	0.900	0.347		0.35	0.69	1.04	1.39	3.47	5.21	6.94	8.68	10.41	12.15	13.88	15.62	17.35
Uruguay 500 Nuevo Pesos	1983	12.00	0.900	0.347		0.35	0.69	1.04	1.39	3.47	5.21	6.94	8.68	10.41	12.15	13.88	15.62	17.35
Uruguay 2000 Nuevo Pesos	1983	65.00	0.900	1.881		1.88	3.76	5.64	7.52	18.81	28.22	37.62	47.03	56.43	65.84	75.24	84.65	94.05
Uruguay 2000 Nuevo Pesos	1984	25.00	0.900	0.724		0.72	1.45	2.17	2.90	7.24	10.86	14.48	18.10	21.72	25.34	28.96	32.58	36.20
Uruguay 5000 Nuevo Pesos	1981	12.00	0.900	0.347		0.35	0.69	1.04	1.39	3.47	5.21	6.94	8.68	10.41	12.15	13.88	15.62	17.35
Uruguay 5000 Nuevo Pesos	1987, 1988	25.00	0.900	0.724	N	0.72	1.45	2.17	2.90	7.24	10.86	14.48	18.10	21.72	25.34	28.96	32.58	36.20
Uruguay 25,000 Nuevo Pesos	1992	12.50	0.900	0.362		0.36	0.72	1.09	1.45	3.62	5.43	7.24	9.05	10.86	12.67	14.48	16.29	18.10
Uruguay 50,000 Nuevo Pesos	1991	27.00	0.925	0.803		0.80	1.61	2.41	3.21	8.03	12.05	16.06	20.08	24.09	28.11	32.12	36.14	40.15
Uruguay 50 Pesos Uruguayos	1996	12.50	0.900	0.362		0.36	0.72	1.09	1.45	3.62	5.43	7.24	9.05	10.86	12.67	14.48	16.29	18.10
Uruguay 100 Pesos Uruguayos	1995	25.00	0.999	0.723		0.72	1.45	2.17	2.89	7.23	10.85	14.46	18.08	21.69	25.31	28.92	32.54	36.15
Uruguay 200 Pesos Uruguayos	1994	27.00	0.925	0.803		0.80	1.61	2.41	3.21	8.03	12.05	16.06	20.08	24.09	28.11	32.12	36.14	40.15
Uruguay 200 Pesos Uruguayos	1995	28.28	0.925	0.841		0.84	1.68	2.52	3.36	8.41	12.62	16.82	21.03	25.23	29.44	33.64	37.85	42.05
Uruguay 200 Pesos Uruguayos	1999	25.00	0.900	0.723		0.72	1.45	2.17	2.89	7.23	10.85	14.46	18.08	21.69	25.31	28.92	32.54	36.15
Uruguay 250 Pesos Uruguayos	1997, 2000	27.00	0.925	0.803		0.80	1.61	2.41	3.21	8.03	12.05	16.06	20.08	24.09	28.11	32.12	36.14	40.15
V																		
Vanuatu 10 Vatu	1996	10.00	0.500	0.161		0.16	0.32	0.48	0.64	1.61	2.42	3.22	4.03	4.83	5.64	6.44	7.25	8.05
Vanuatu 20 Vatu	1994	20.00	0.500	0.322		0.32	0.64	0.97	1.29	3.22	4.83	6.44	8.05	9.66	11.27	12.88	14.49	16.10
Vanuatu 20 Vatu	1994	20.00	0.925	0.595		0.60	1.19	1.79	2.38	5.95	8.93	11.90	14.88	17.85	20.83	23.80	26.78	29.75
Vanuatu 50 Vatu	1981	15.00	0.925	0.446	N, S	0.45	0.89	1.34	1.78	4.46	6.69	8.92	11.15	13.38	15.61	17.84	20.07	22.30
Vanuatu 50 Vatu	1988	34.00	0.925	1.011	N, S	1.01	2.02	3.03	4.04	10.11	15.17	20.22	25.28	30.33	35.39	40.44	45.50	50.55
Vanuatu 50 Vatu	1992-1996	31.47	0.925	0.936		0.94	1.87	2.81	3.74	9.36	14.04	18.72	23.40	28.08	32.76	37.44	42.12	46.80
Vanuatu 50 Vatu	1998	30.97	0.925	0.921		0.92	1.84	2.76	3.68	9.21	13.82	18.42	23.03	27.63	32.24	36.84	41.45	46.05
Vatican City 5 Lire	1929-1946	5.00	0.835	0.134		0.13	0.27	0.40	0.54	1.34	2.01	2.68	3.35	4.02	4.69	5.36	6.03	6.70
Vatican City 10 Lire	1929-1946	10.00	0.835	0.268		0.27	0.54	0.80	1.07	2.68	4.02	5.36	6.70	8.04	9.38	10.72	12.06	13.40
Vatican City 500 Lire	1958-1999	11.00	0.835	0.295		0.30	0.59	0.89	1.18	2.95	4.43	5.90	7.38	8.85	10.33	11.80	13.28	14.75
Vatican City 1000 Lire	1978-2000	14.60	0.835	0.392		0.39	0.78	1.18	1.57	3.92	5.88	7.84	9.80	11.76	13.72	15.68	17.64	19.60
Vatican City 2000 Lire	2000	16.00	0.835	0.430		0.43	0.86	1.29	1.72	4.30	6.45	8.60	10.75	12.90	15.05	17.20	19.35	21.50
Vatican City 10,000 Lire	1995-2000	22.00	0.835	0.591		0.59	1.18	1.77	2.36	5.91	8.87	11.82	14.78	17.73	20.69	23.64	26.60	29.55
Venezuela 1/2 Real*	1858	1.15	0.900	0.033		0.03	0.07	0.10	0.13	0.33	0.50	0.66	0.83	0.99	1.16	1.32	1.49	1.65
Venezuela 1 Real	1858	2.30	0.900	0.067		0.07	0.13	0.20	0.27	0.67	1.01	1.34	1.68	2.01	2.35	2.68	3.02	3.35
Venezuela 2 Reales	1858	4.60	0.900	0.133		0.13	0.27	0.40	0.53	1.33	2.00	2.66	3.33	3.99	4.66	5.32	5.99	6.65
Venezuela 5 Reales	1858	11.50	0.900	0.333		0.33	0.67	1.00	1.33	3.33	5.00	6.66	8.33	9.99	11.66	13.32	14.99	16.65
Venezuela 10 Reales	1863	23.00	0.900	0.666		0.67	1.33	2.00	2.66	6.66	9.99	13.32	16.65	19.98	23.31	26.64	29.97	33.30
Venezuela 5 Centavos	1874, 1876	1.25	0.835	0.034		0.03	0.07	0.10	0.14	0.34	0.51	0.68	0.85	1.02	1.19	1.36	1.53	1.70

Country & Denomination	Years Minted	Grams Weight	Fineness	Troy (ASW)	Code	$ Value 1	$ Value 2	$ Value 3	$ Value 4	$ Value 10	$ Value 15	$ Value 20	$ Value 25	$ Value 30	$ Value 35	$ Value 40	$ Value 45	$ Value 50
Venezuela 10 Centavos	1874, 1876	2.50	0.835	0.067		0.07	0.13	0.20	0.27	0.67	1.01	1.34	1.68	2.01	2.35	2.68	3.02	3.35
Venezuela 20 Centavos	1874, 1876	5.00	0.835	0.134		0.13	0.27	0.40	0.54	1.34	2.01	2.68	3.35	4.02	4.69	5.36	6.03	6.70
Venezuela 50 Centavos	1873-1876	12.50	0.835	0.336	S	0.34	0.67	1.01	1.34	3.36	5.04	6.72	8.40	10.08	11.76	13.44	15.12	16.80
Venezuela 1 Venezolano	1876	25.00	0.900	0.723		0.72	1.45	2.17	2.89	7.23	10.85	14.46	18.08	21.69	25.31	28.92	32.54	36.15
Venezuela 1/5 Bolivar	1879	1.00	0.835	0.027		0.03	0.05	0.08	0.11	0.27	0.40	0.54	0.68	0.81	0.95	1.08	1.22	1.35
Venezuela 25 Centimos	1894-1960	1.25	0.835	0.034	S	0.03	0.07	0.10	0.14	0.34	0.51	0.68	0.85	1.02	1.19	1.36	1.53	1.70
Venezuela 50 Centimos	1879-1960	2.50	0.835	0.067	S	0.07	0.13	0.20	0.27	0.67	1.01	1.34	1.68	2.01	2.35	2.68	3.02	3.35
Venezuela 1 Bolivar	1879-1965	5.00	0.835	0.134	S	0.13	0.27	0.40	0.54	1.34	2.01	2.68	3.36	4.03	4.70	5.37	6.04	6.71
Venezuela 2 Bolivars	1879-1965	10.00	0.835	0.269	S	0.27	0.54	0.81	1.08	2.69	4.04	5.38	6.73	8.07	9.42	10.76	12.11	13.45
Venezuela 5 Bolivars	1879-1936	25.00	0.900	0.723	S	0.72	1.45	2.17	2.89	7.23	10.85	14.46	18.08	21.69	25.31	28.92	32.54	36.15
Venezuela 10 Bolivars	1973	30.00	0.900	0.867		0.87	1.73	2.60	3.47	8.67	13.01	17.34	21.68	26.01	30.35	34.68	39.02	43.35
Venezuela 25 Bolivars	1975	28.28	0.925	0.841		0.84	1.68	2.52	3.36	8.41	12.62	16.82	21.03	25.23	29.44	33.64	37.85	42.05
Venezuela 50 Bolivars	1975	35.00	0.925	1.040		1.04	2.08	3.12	4.16	10.40	15.60	20.80	26.00	31.20	36.40	41.60	46.80	52.00
Venezuela 50 Bolivars	1990	31.10	0.900	0.900	N	0.90	1.80	2.70	3.60	9.00	13.50	18.00	22.50	27.00	31.50	36.00	40.50	45.00
Venezuela 75 Bolivars	1980	17.00	0.900	0.492		0.49	0.98	1.48	1.97	4.92	7.38	9.84	12.30	14.76	17.22	19.68	22.14	24.60
Venezuela 100 Bolivars	1980	22.00	0.900	0.637		0.64	1.27	1.91	2.55	6.37	9.56	12.74	15.93	19.11	22.30	25.48	28.67	31.85
Venezuela 100 Bolivars	1981	27.00	0.835	0.725		0.73	1.45	2.18	2.90	7.25	10.88	14.50	18.13	21.75	25.38	29.00	32.63	36.25
Venezuela 100 Bolivars	1983, 1986	31.10	0.900	0.900		0.90	1.80	2.70	3.60	9.00	13.50	18.00	22.50	27.00	31.50	36.00	40.50	45.00
Venezuela 500 Bolivars	1990-1997	31.10	0.900	0.900	S	0.90	1.80	2.70	3.60	9.00	13.50	18.00	22.50	27.00	31.50	36.00	40.50	45.00
Venezuela 1100 Bolivars	1991	27.00	0.925	0.803		0.80	1.61	2.41	3.21	8.03	12.05	16.06	20.08	24.09	28.11	32.12	36.14	40.15
V																		
Vietnam, Soc. Rep. 100 Dong*	1986, 1988	12.00	0.999	0.386	S	0.39	0.77	1.16	1.54	3.86	5.79	7.72	9.65	11.58	13.51	15.44	17.37	19.30
Vietnam, Soc. Rep. 100 Dong	1988	15.99	0.980	0.504		0.50	1.01	1.51	2.02	5.04	7.56	10.08	12.60	15.12	17.64	20.16	22.68	25.20
Vietnam, Soc. Rep. 100 Dong	1989-1997	16.00	0.999	0.514	S	0.51	1.03	1.54	2.06	5.14	7.71	10.28	12.85	15.42	17.99	20.56	23.13	25.70
Vietnam, Soc. Rep. 100 Dong	1995-1996	20.00	0.999	0.642		0.64	1.28	1.93	2.57	6.42	9.63	12.84	16.05	19.26	22.47	25.68	28.89	32.10
Vietnam, Soc. Rep. 1000 Dong	2000	20.00	0.925	0.595		0.60	1.19	1.79	2.38	5.95	8.93	11.90	14.88	17.85	20.83	23.80	26.78	29.75
W																		
West African States 500 Francs	1972	25.00	0.900	0.723		0.72	1.45	2.17	2.89	7.23	10.85	14.46	18.08	21.69	25.31	28.92	32.54	36.15
West African States 5000 Francs	1982	24.95	0.900	0.722	N	0.72	1.44	2.17	2.89	7.22	10.83	14.44	18.05	21.66	25.27	28.88	32.49	36.10
Western Samoa--see Samoa																		
Y																		
Yemen Arab Rep. 2 Buqsha	1963	1.00	0.720	0.020	A, V	0.02	0.04	0.06	0.08	0.20	0.30	0.40	0.50	0.60	0.70	0.80	0.90	1.00
Yemen Arab Rep. 4 Buqsha	1963	1.60	0.720	0.040	A, V	0.04	0.08	0.12	0.16	0.40	0.60	0.80	1.00	1.20	1.40	1.60	1.80	2.00
Yemen Arab Rep. 5 Buqsha	1963	2.40	0.720	0.050	A, V	0.05	0.10	0.15	0.20	0.50	0.75	1.00	1.25	1.50	1.75	2.00	2.25	2.50
Yemen Arab Rep. 8 Buqsha	1963	4.80	0.720	0.100	A, V	0.10	0.20	0.30	0.40	1.00	1.50	2.00	2.50	3.00	3.50	4.00	4.50	5.00
Yemen Arab Rep. 10 Buqsha	1963	5.00	0.720	0.116	A, V	0.12	0.23	0.35	0.46	1.16	1.74	2.32	2.90	3.48	4.06	4.64	5.22	5.80
Yemen Arab Rep. 20 Buqsha	1963	9.85	0.720	0.228	A	0.23	0.46	0.68	0.91	2.28	3.42	4.56	5.70	6.84	7.98	9.12	10.26	11.40
Yemen Arab Rep. 1 Riyal	1963	19.75	0.720	0.457	A	0.46	0.91	1.37	1.83	4.57	6.86	9.14	11.43	13.71	16.00	18.28	20.57	22.85
Yemen Arab Rep. 1 Ryial	1969	12.00	0.925	0.357	A, N	0.36	0.71	1.07	1.43	3.57	5.36	7.14	8.93	10.71	12.50	14.28	16.07	17.85
Yemen Arab Rep. 2 Riyals	1969	25.00	0.925	0.744	A, N	0.74	1.49	2.23	2.98	7.44	11.16	14.88	18.60	22.32	26.04	29.76	33.48	37.20
Yemen Arab Rep. 2-1/2 Riyals	1975	9.00	0.925	0.268	A	0.27	0.54	0.80	1.07	2.68	4.02	5.36	6.70	8.04	9.38	10.72	12.06	13.40
Yemen Arab Rep. 5 Riyals	1975	18.00	0.925	0.535	A	0.54	1.07	1.61	2.14	5.35	8.03	10.70	13.38	16.05	18.73	21.40	24.08	26.75
Yemen Arab Rep. 10 Riyals	1969	12.08	0.925	0.357	A	0.36	0.71	1.07	1.43	3.57	5.36	7.14	8.93	10.71	12.50	14.28	16.07	17.85
Yemen Arab Rep. 10 Riyals	1975	36.00	0.925	1.070	A, V	1.07	2.14	3.21	4.28	10.70	16.05	21.40	26.75	32.10	37.45	42.80	48.15	53.50

Country & Denomination	Years Minted	Grams Weight	Fineness	Troy (ASW)	Code	$ Value 1	$ Value 2	$ Value 3	$ Value 4	$ Value 10	$ Value 15	$ Value 20	$ Value 25	$ Value 30	$ Value 35	$ Value 40	$ Value 45	$ Value 50
Yemen Arab Rep. 15 Riyals	1975	54.00	0.925	1.606	A	1.61	3.21	4.82	6.42	16.06	24.09	32.12	40.15	48.18	56.21	64.24	72.27	80.30
Yemen Arab Rep. 25 Riyals	1981-1985	28.28	0.925	0.841	A, S, V	0.84	1.68	2.52	3.36	8.41	12.62	16.82	21.03	25.23	29.44	33.64	37.85	42.05
Yemen Arab Rep. 50 Riyals	1969	50.00	0.925	1.550	A	1.55	3.10	4.65	6.20	15.50	23.25	31.00	38.75	46.50	54.25	62.00	69.75	77.50
Yemen Dem. Rep. 2 Dinars	1981	28.28	0.925	0.841		0.84	1.68	2.52	3.36	8.41	12.62	16.82	21.03	25.23	29.44	33.64	37.85	42.05
Yemen Dem. Rep. 5 Dinars	1977	12.50	0.925	0.372		0.37	0.74	1.12	1.49	3.72	5.58	7.44	9.30	11.16	13.02	14.88	16.74	18.60
Yugoslavia 10 Dinara	1931	7.00	0.500	0.113		0.11	0.23	0.34	0.45	1.13	1.70	2.26	2.83	3.39	3.96	4.52	5.09	5.65
Yugoslavia 20 Dinara	1931	14.00	0.500	0.225		0.23	0.45	0.68	0.90	2.25	3.38	4.50	5.63	6.75	7.88	9.00	10.13	11.25
Yugoslavia 20 Dinara	1938	9.00	0.750	0.217		0.22	0.43	0.65	0.87	2.17	3.26	4.34	5.43	6.51	7.60	8.68	9.77	10.85
Yugoslavia 20 Dinara	1968	9.00	0.925	0.268		0.27	0.54	0.80	1.07	2.68	4.02	5.36	6.70	8.04	9.38	10.72	12.06	13.40
Yugoslavia 50 Dinara	1932	23.30	0.750	0.563		0.56	1.13	1.69	2.25	5.63	8.45	11.26	14.08	16.89	19.71	22.52	25.34	28.15
Yugoslavia 50 Dinara	1938	15.00	0.750	0.362		0.36	0.72	1.09	1.45	3.62	5.43	7.24	9.05	10.86	12.67	14.48	16.29	18.10
Yugoslavia 50 Dinara	1968	20.00	0.925	0.595		0.60	1.19	1.79	2.38	5.95	8.93	11.90	14.88	17.85	20.83	23.80	26.78	29.75
Yugoslavia 100 Dinara	1978	10.00	0.925	0.297		0.30	0.59	0.89	1.19	2.97	4.46	5.94	7.43	8.91	10.40	11.88	13.37	14.85
Yugoslavia 100 Dinara	1982-1990	13.00	0.925	0.387	S	0.39	0.77	1.16	1.55	3.87	5.81	7.74	9.68	11.61	13.55	15.48	17.42	19.35
Yugoslavia 150 Dinara	1978	12.50	0.925	0.372		0.37	0.74	1.12	1.49	3.72	5.58	7.44	9.30	11.16	13.02	14.88	16.74	18.60
Yugoslavia 150 Dinara	1990	17.00	0.925	0.506		0.51	1.01	1.52	2.02	5.06	7.59	10.12	12.65	15.18	17.71	20.24	22.77	25.30
Yugoslavia 200 Dinara	1977	15.00	0.750	0.362		0.36	0.72	1.09	1.45	3.62	5.43	7.24	9.05	10.86	12.67	14.48	16.29	18.10
Yugoslavia 200 Dinara	1978	15.00	0.925	0.446		0.45	0.89	1.34	1.78	4.46	6.69	8.92	11.15	13.38	15.61	17.84	20.07	22.30
Yugoslavia 250 Dinara	1979	17.50	0.925	0.520		0.52	1.04	1.56	2.08	5.20	7.80	10.40	13.00	15.60	18.20	20.80	23.40	26.00
Yugoslavia 250 Dinara	1982-1984	17.00	0.925	0.506		0.51	1.01	1.52	2.02	5.06	7.59	10.12	12.65	15.18	17.71	20.24	22.77	25.30
Yugoslavia 300 Dinara	1978	20.00	0.925	0.595		0.60	1.19	1.79	2.38	5.95	8.93	11.90	14.88	17.85	20.83	23.80	26.78	29.75
Yugoslavia 350 Dinara	1978	22.50	0.925	0.669		0.67	1.34	2.01	2.68	6.69	10.04	13.38	16.73	20.07	23.42	26.76	30.11	33.45
Yugoslavia 400 Dinara	1978	25.00	0.925	0.744		0.74	1.49	2.23	2.98	7.44	11.16	14.88	18.60	22.32	26.04	29.76	33.48	37.20
Yugoslavia 500 Dinara	1980	8.00	0.925	0.238		0.24	0.48	0.71	0.95	2.38	3.57	4.76	5.95	7.14	8.33	9.52	10.71	11.90
Yugoslavia 500 Dinara	1981	8.00	0.750	0.187		0.19	0.37	0.56	0.75	1.87	2.81	3.74	4.68	5.61	6.55	7.48	8.42	9.35
Yugoslavia 500 Dinara	1982-1984	23.00	0.925	0.684		0.68	1.37	2.05	2.74	6.84	10.26	13.68	17.10	20.52	23.94	27.36	30.78	34.20
Yugoslavia 500 Dinara	1985	13.00	0.925	0.387		0.39	0.77	1.16	1.55	3.87	5.81	7.74	9.68	11.61	13.55	15.48	17.42	19.35
Yugoslavia 1000 Dinara	1980	14.00	0.925	0.416		0.42	0.83	1.25	1.66	4.16	6.24	8.32	10.40	12.48	14.56	16.64	18.72	20.80
Yugoslavia 1000 Dinara	1980	25.90	0.750	0.625		0.63	1.25	1.88	2.50	6.25	9.38	12.50	15.63	18.75	21.88	25.00	28.13	31.25
Yugoslavia 1000 Dinara	1981	14.00	0.750	0.416		0.42	0.83	1.25	1.66	4.16	6.24	8.32	10.40	12.48	14.56	16.64	18.72	20.80
Yugoslavia 1000 Dinara	1981	26.00	0.925	0.773		0.77	1.55	2.32	3.09	7.73	11.60	15.46	19.33	23.19	27.06	30.92	34.79	38.65
Yugoslavia 1000 Dinara	1982	18.00	0.925	0.535		0.54	1.07	1.61	2.14	5.35	8.03	10.70	13.38	16.05	18.73	21.40	24.08	26.75
Yugoslavia 1000 Dinara	1985	23.00	0.925	0.684		0.68	1.37	2.05	2.74	6.84	10.26	13.68	17.10	20.52	23.94	27.36	30.78	34.20
Yugoslavia 1000 Dinara	1985	6.00	0.925	0.178		0.18	0.36	0.53	0.71	1.78	2.67	3.56	4.45	5.34	6.23	7.12	8.01	8.90
Yugoslavia 1500 Dinara	1980, 1982	22.00	0.925	0.654		0.65	1.31	1.96	2.62	6.54	9.81	13.08	16.35	19.62	22.89	26.16	29.43	32.70
Yugoslavia 1500 Dinara	1980	22.00	0.750	0.533		0.53	1.07	1.60	2.13	5.33	8.00	10.66	13.33	15.99	18.66	21.32	23.99	26.65
Yugoslavia 2000 Dinara	1985	14.00	0.925	0.416		0.42	0.83	1.25	1.66	4.16	6.24	8.32	10.40	12.48	14.56	16.64	18.72	20.80
Yugoslavia 3000 Dinara	1985	26.00	0.925	0.773		0.77	1.55	2.32	3.09	7.73	11.60	15.46	19.33	23.19	27.06	30.92	34.79	38.65
Yugoslavia 3000 Dinara	1987	13.00	0.925	0.387		0.39	0.77	1.16	1.55	3.87	5.81	7.74	9.68	11.61	13.55	15.48	17.42	19.35
Yugoslavia 5000 Dinara	1985	17.00	0.925	0.506		0.51	1.01	1.52	2.02	5.06	7.59	10.12	12.65	15.18	17.71	20.24	22.77	25.30
Yugoslavia 5000 Dinara	1989	13.00	0.925	0.387		0.39	0.77	1.16	1.55	3.87	5.81	7.74	9.68	11.61	13.55	15.48	17.42	19.35
Yugoslavia 10,000 Dinara	1989	17.00	0.925	0.506		0.51	1.01	1.52	2.02	5.06	7.59	10.12	12.65	15.18	17.71	20.24	22.77	25.30
Yugoslavia 200 Novih Dinara	1996	13.00	0.925	0.387		0.39	0.77	1.16	1.55	3.87	5.81	7.74	9.68	11.61	13.55	15.48	17.42	19.35

Country & Denomination	Years Minted	Grams Weight	Fine-ness	Troy (ASW)	Code	$ Value 1	$ Value 2	$ Value 3	$ Value 4	$ Value 10	$ Value 15	$ Value 20	$ Value 25	$ Value 30	$ Value 35	$ Value 40	$ Value 45	$ Value 50
Yugoslavia 300 Novih Dinara Z	1996	26.00	0.925	0.773		0.77	1.55	2.32	3.09	7.73	11.60	15.46	19.33	23.19	27.06	30.92	34.79	38.65
Zaire 2-1/2 Zaires	1975	28.28	0.925	0.841		0.84	1.68	2.52	3.36	8.41	12.62	16.82	21.03	25.23	29.44	33.64	37.85	42.05
Zaire 5 Zaires	1971	27.84	0.925	0.828		0.83	1.66	2.48	3.31	8.28	12.42	16.56	20.70	24.84	28.98	33.12	37.26	41.40
Zaire 5 Zaires	1975	35.00	0.925	1.041		1.04	2.08	3.12	4.16	10.41	15.62	20.82	26.03	31.23	36.44	41.64	46.85	52.05
Zaire 500 Nouveaux Zaires	1996	20.00	0.500	0.322		0.32	0.64	0.97	1.29	3.22	4.83	6.44	8.05	9.66	11.27	12.88	14.49	16.10
Zaire 1000 Nouveaux Zaires	1997	29.63	0.925	0.881		0.88	1.76	2.64	3.52	8.81	13.22	17.62	22.03	26.43	30.84	35.24	39.65	44.05
Zaire 1000 Nouveaux Zaires	1997	30.09	0.925	0.895		0.90	1.79	2.69	3.58	8.95	13.43	17.90	22.38	26.85	31.33	35.80	40.28	44.75
Zaire 5000 Nouveaux Zaires	1996	411.42	0.999	13.214		13.21	26.43	39.64	52.86	132.14	198.21	264.28	330.35	396.42	462.49	528.56	594.63	660.70
Zaire 10,000 Nouveaux Zaires	1996	822.85	0.999	26.429		26.43	52.86	79.29	105.72	264.29	396.44	528.58	660.73	792.87	925.02	1057.16	1189.31	1321.45
Zambia 50 Ngwee*	1985	11.66	0.925	0.347	N	0.35	0.69	1.04	1.39	3.47	5.21	6.94	8.68	10.41	12.15	13.88	15.62	17.35
Zambia 5 Kwacha	1979	28.28	0.925	0.841		0.84	1.68	2.52	3.36	8.41	12.62	16.82	21.03	25.23	29.44	33.64	37.85	42.05
Zambia 10 Kwacha	1979	35.00	0.925	1.041		1.04	2.08	3.12	4.16	10.41	15.62	20.82	26.03	31.23	36.44	41.64	46.85	52.05
Zambia 10 Kwacha	1979	31.65	0.925	0.940		0.94	1.88	2.82	3.76	9.40	14.10	18.80	23.50	28.20	32.90	37.60	42.30	47.00
Zambia 10 Kwacha	1980-1989	27.22	0.925	0.809	S	0.81	1.62	2.43	3.24	8.09	12.14	16.18	20.23	24.27	28.32	32.36	36.41	40.45
Zambia 10 Kwacha	1994	20.00	0.999	0.643		0.64	1.29	1.93	2.57	6.43	9.65	12.86	16.08	19.29	22.51	25.72	28.94	32.15
Zambia 20 Kwacha	1994	10.17	0.999	0.327		0.33	0.65	0.98	1.31	3.27	4.91	6.54	8.18	9.81	11.45	13.08	14.72	16.35
Zambia 75 Kwacha	1997	5.00	0.999	0.161		0.16	0.32	0.48	0.64	1.61	2.42	3.22	4.03	4.83	5.64	6.44	7.25	8.05
Zambia 100 Kwacha	1992, 1998	28.28	0.925	0.841	N	0.84	1.68	2.52	3.36	8.41	12.62	16.82	21.03	25.23	29.44	33.64	37.85	42.05
Zambia 250 Kwacha	1993	136.10	0.925	4.047		4.05	8.09	12.14	16.19	40.47	60.71	80.94	101.18	121.41	141.65	161.88	182.12	202.35
Zambia 500 Kwacha	1994	31.77	0.999	1.030		1.03	2.06	3.09	4.12	10.30	15.45	20.60	25.75	30.90	36.05	41.20	46.35	51.50
Zambia 500 Kwacha	1995	223.00	0.999	7.162		7.16	14.32	21.49	28.65	71.62	107.43	143.24	179.05	214.86	250.67	286.48	322.29	358.10
Zambia 500 Kwacha	1997	31.10	0.999	1.000		1.00	2.00	3.00	4.00	10.00	15.00	20.00	25.00	30.00	35.00	40.00	45.00	50.00
Zambia 1000 Kwacha	1999	20.00	0.925	0.595		0.60	1.19	1.79	2.38	5.95	8.93	11.90	14.88	17.85	20.83	23.80	26.78	29.75
Zambia 1000 Kwacha	2000	28.90	0.925	0.860		0.86	1.72	2.58	3.44	8.60	12.90	17.20	21.50	25.80	30.10	34.40	38.70	43.00
Zambia 2000 Kwacha	1994	25.00	0.999	0.803		0.80	1.61	2.41	3.21	8.03	12.05	16.06	20.08	24.09	28.11	32.12	36.14	40.15
Zambia 2000 Kwacha	1997	20.22	0.999	0.650		0.65	1.30	1.95	2.60	6.50	9.75	13.00	16.25	19.50	22.75	26.00	29.25	32.50
Zambia 2000 Kwacha	1998	15.55	0.999	0.500		0.50	1.00	1.50	2.00	5.00	7.50	10.00	12.50	15.00	17.50	20.00	22.50	25.00
Zambia 2500 Kwacha	1997	155.52	0.999	5.000		5.00	10.00	15.00	20.00	50.00	75.00	100.00	125.00	150.00	175.00	200.00	225.00	250.00
Zambia 2500 Kwacha	1998	15.55	0.925	0.463		0.46	0.93	1.39	1.85	4.63	6.95	9.26	11.58	13.89	16.21	18.52	20.84	23.15
Zambia 4000 Kwacha	1997-2000	31.10	0.999	1.000	S, V	1.00	2.00	3.00	4.00	10.00	15.00	20.00	25.00	30.00	35.00	40.00	45.00	50.00
Zambia 4000 Kwacha	1998	30.33	0.999	0.974		0.97	1.95	2.92	3.90	9.74	14.61	19.48	24.35	29.22	34.09	38.96	43.83	48.70
Zambia 4000 Kwacha	2000	25.10	0.925	0.747		0.75	1.49	2.24	2.99	7.47	11.21	14.94	18.68	22.41	26.15	29.88	33.62	37.35
Zambia 4000 Kwacha	2000	20.00	0.925	0.595		0.60	1.19	1.79	2.38	5.95	8.93	11.90	14.88	17.85	20.83	23.80	26.78	29.75
Zambia 5000 Kwacha	1997, 1998	31.20	0.925	0.923	V	0.92	1.85	2.77	3.69	9.23	13.85	18.46	23.08	27.69	32.31	36.92	41.54	46.15
Zambia 5000 Kwacha	1999, 2000	31.20	0.999	1.000	V	1.00	2.00	3.00	4.00	10.00	15.00	20.00	25.00	30.00	35.00	40.00	45.00	50.00
Zambia 5000 Kwacha	2000	31.36	0.925	0.933		0.93	1.87	2.80	3.73	9.33	14.00	18.66	23.33	27.99	32.66	37.32	41.99	46.65
Zambia 10,000 Kwacha	1997	30.20	0.999	0.976	V	0.98	1.95	2.93	3.90	9.76	14.64	19.52	24.40	29.28	34.16	39.04	43.92	48.80
Zambia 20,000 Kwacha	2000	1000.00	0.999	32.119		32.12	64.24	96.36	128.48	321.19	481.79	642.38	802.98	963.57	1124.17	1284.76	1445.36	1605.95
Zimbabwe 10 Dollars	1996	31.10	0.999	1.000		1.00	2.00	3.00	4.00	10.00	15.00	20.00	25.00	30.00	35.00	40.00	45.00	50.00

CPSIA information can be obtained at www.ICGtesting.com
Printed in the USA
LVOW09s1926130115

422667LV00035B/1933/P

9 781466 324275